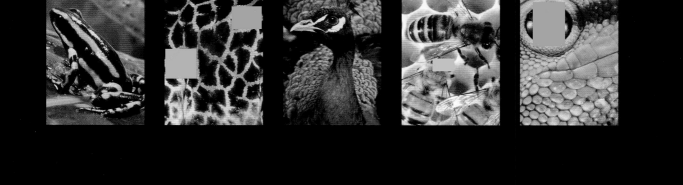

ANIMAL
ENCYCLOPEDIA

Penguin Random House

Senior Editor Sarah Larter

Project Editors Simon Holland, Ben Hoare, Margaret Hynes

Editors Julie Ferris, Jacqueline Fortey, Sue Nicholson

Managing Editor Camilla Hallinan

Special Sales and Custom Publishing Manager Michelle Baxter

Weblink Editors Niki Foreman, John Bennett, Roger Brownlie, Mostyn de Beer, Phil Hunt

Digital Content Manager Fergus Day

DTP Co-ordination Natasha Lu, Pankaj Sharma

DTP Designers Tony Cutting, Sunil Sharma

Publishing Manager Andrew Macintyre

Category Publisher Jonathan Metcalf

Senior Art Editor Smiljka Surla

Project Designers Jacqui Swan, Sheila Collins, Spencer Holbrook

Designers Romi Chakraborty, Kavita Dutta, Nicola Harrison, Adrienne Hutchinson, Yumiko Tahata, Shefali Upadhyay

Managing Art Editor Sophia M Tampakopoulos Turner

Picture Research Marie Ortu, Julia Harris-Voss, Jo Walton

Picture Librarians Sarah Mills, Rose Horridge, Kate Ledwith

Jacket Design Laura Brim

Jacket Copywriter Adam Powley

Jacket Editor Joanna Pocock

Production Shivani Pandey

Art Director Simon Webb

     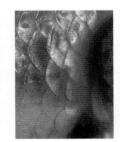

Contributors and Consultants Richard Beatty, David Burnie, Kim Dennis-Bryan, Dr Frances Dipper, Jonathan Elphick, Dr Phil Gates, Daniel Gilpin, Dr Jen Green, Chris Mattison, Dr Katie Parsons, John Woodward

First published in Great Britain as e.encyclopedia animal in 2005
This paperback edition first published in 2015
by Dorling Kindersley Limited, 80 Strand, London WC2R 0RL

Copyright ©2005, 2009, and 2015 Dorling Kindersley Limited
A Penguin Random House Company

2 4 6 8 10 9 7 5 3 1
001–289940–Aug/15

A CIP catalogue for this book is available from the British Library.

ISBN: 978-0-24124-310-7

Printed and bound in Hong Kong

Discover more at
www.dk.com

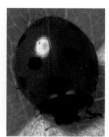

ANIMAL
ENCYCLOPEDIA

CONTENTS

Meerkats live in colonies of 20–40 individuals, sharing a system of burrows. A few members of the group act as sentries. They stand up on their hind legs to look out for any danger, and bark a warning if they spot a predator approaching.

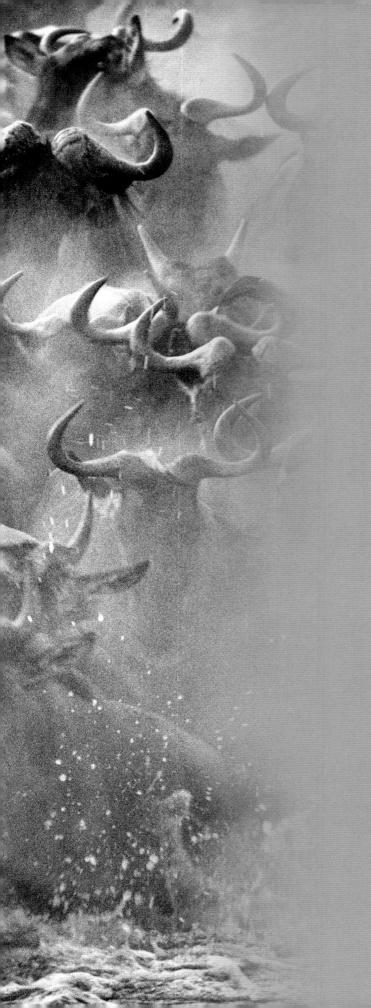

ANIMAL WORLD

◄ BEING ANIMALS
Animals are perhaps the most dominant form
of life on Earth. They are successful because
over time their structure or behaviour has
gradually adapted to help them survive, and
because most of them can move around,
much like this herd of African wildebeest.
This chapter looks at the features that
distinguish animals from other living things
and the scientific method used to define
them. It also examines how animals have
evolved (developed), their complex
relationships with their surroundings,
and the threats many species face.

ANIMAL CHARACTERISTICS

Animals are a diverse group of living things that are found in nearly all parts of the world, including the depths of the oceans, the freezing polar regions, and even on or inside other animals. Animals feed on other organisms, and most can move about freely, although some spend their adult lives in one place. Their bodies are built from many cells, and they have nerves and muscles that enable them to react to the world around them.

CHARACTERISTICS OF LIFE

REPRODUCTION
This newly born lemon shark is just beginning its life. In time, it will become sexually mature, at which point it will find a partner and mate to produce offspring of its own. Reproduction is the key characteristic of all living things, enabling each species to continue, even though its individual members die.

GROWTH
Many living things begin life as a single cell. This cell divides into two cells, which divide into four cells, and so on, and a new organism slowly takes shape. Like most animals, muscovy ducks grow in size and become more complex. When they reproduce, the cycle of growth begins again.

Bones are living body parts formed from cells and minerals

Tentacles are not rigid so they wave about in the water

◀ VERTEBRATE
Horses have the typical features of a vertebrate. All vertebrates have hard, jointed backbones made up of vertebrae, which extend from the neck to the tail. The backbone, skull, ribs, and limbs form the skeleton, which gives the body shape and protects vital organs. Inside the vertebrae is a nerve cord. This carries messages from the brain to other parts of their body.

Notochord strengthens the lancelet's body

LANCELET

CHORDATE ▲
Chordates have a stiff rod called a notochord running along the length of their bodies. Most chordates are back-boned vertebrates, although lancelets and sea squirts have a notochord but no backbone. The notochord supports these simple animals. It is present in vertebrates during their embryonic stage, and is later replaced by the backbone.

◀ INVERTEBRATE
Invertebrates are animals that do not have a backbone. They include about 95 per cent of all the species of animals. Some invertebrates, including this sea anemone, are soft-bodied and live in water. Others, such as molluscs, insects, crabs, and spiders, have a hard outer covering called an exoskeleton, to which their muscles are attached.

NUTRITION
Unlike plants, which make their own food by the process of photosynthesis, animals feed on other organisms. Like this Mormon caterpillar, they use nutrients in their food as a source of energy, and for all the processes involved with the growth, repair, and maintenance of their bodies.

EXCRETION
Animals excrete waste materials that are produced when they digest their food. The main waste products are carbon dioxide and urea. All animals exhale carbon dioxide as they breathe. Birds, such as the blue-footed booby, excrete urea as white uric crystals, while mammals excrete it as urine.

MOVEMENT
Like most animals, this red-footed tortoise moves by using its muscles. These are bundles of cells that are attached to an animal's skeleton. When this tortoise decides to walk, signals flash from its brain through its nerves to its leg muscles, triggering them to contract and relax to move its limbs.

RESPIRATION
Animals, including these hard-working huskies, get their energy through aerobic respiration. This is a process in which oxygen that the animal breathes in from the air combines with food molecules in cells around the body, releasing energy. Water and carbon dioxide are produced as waste products.

SENSING THE WORLD
Animals have sensory systems, which are coordinated by the brain. They allow them to detect what is happening around them and respond appropriately. The two antennae on this moth's head are its organs of smell, which it uses to detect the scent of potential mates.

◄ **SOPHISTICATED ANIMALS**
Like all primates, the douc langurs of southeast Asia have large brains and are capable of learning complicated tasks. Most primates are social animals, living in cooperative family groups. They communicate by using sound, body postures, and facial expressions.

Wide head contains a large brain

◄ **GIANT ANIMAL**
Weighing up to 120 tonnes and reaching 30 m (98 ft) long, the blue whale is the largest living animal on Earth. Animals that grow to a large size must consume vast amounts of food to maintain their bodies, so a blue whale swallows about six tonnes of krill every day. Large animals take many years to reach maturity, reproduce slowly, and often live to a great age. A blue whale can live for up to 80 years.

Skin is usually encrusted with barnacles

Fur covers the bee and keeps it warm

Mite is tiny in relation to the bee

MICROSCOPIC ANIMAL ►
Small animals, such as bees, often have even smaller animals, like this mite, living on them as parasites. Honeybee mites cling to the fur of bees, sucking out their body fluids. Like all parasites, mites weaken their host but do not kill it. This means that they have time to multiply and infect other bees before their host dies.

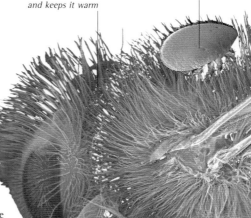

FIND OUT MORE ►► Anatomy **26** • Invertebrates **78–79** • Primates **256** • Reproduction **44–45** • Senses **30–31**

ANIMAL KINGDOM

The animal kingdom is one of five major groups of living things. It is divided into several categories, in which animals are grouped according to their similarities and whether they have recent common ancestors. Animals are given unique scientific names so that people are able to refer to the same creature no matter what language they speak. The first part of the name indicates the genus to which the animal belongs; the second part denotes its species.

CARL LINNAEUS
Swedish, 1789-1854

The botanist Carl Linnaeus devised a simple system for naming and defining living things, on which modern classification is based. In his binomial (two-part) system of classification, every species has its own name. As well as identifying the species, it also shows where it fits into the world of living things.

CLASSIFYING A CAT ▶
This diagram shows the classification hierarchy for the Manx cat, a variety of domestic cat. The animal kingdom is the broadest group, containing all organisms that have animal characteristics. Each successive category – phylum, class, order, family, and genus – contains animals grouped on the basis of more specialized features. The final level contains the species, in this case the domestic cat, whose features are unique.

Jay buries acorns in autumn for later use

▲ VIVID NAME
Scientific names often describe an animal's features. The Latin name for a jay is *Garrulus glandarius*. The first word means "chattering" – jays are well known for being noisy birds, especially when predators are around. The second word means "acorn", which is the jay's favourite food item. Therefore, the Latin name for this species of jay means "chattering acorn-eater".

KINGDOM

This the largest grouping in the classification of living things. It contains organisms with characteristic animal features – they feed, breed, move, and sense their surroundings. There are separate kingdoms for plants, bacteria, protoctists, and fungi.

ANIMAL KINGDOM

PHYLUM

The animal kingdom is divided into 35 smaller groups called phyla (singular, phylum). These groups contain species that share features. For example, cats belong to the Chordata phylum, which includes animals that have a rod called a notochord running along their bodies at some point during their development.

CHORDATE PHYLUM

CLASS

Phyla are divided into smaller groups called classes. Cats belong to the mammal class. They are endothermic (warm-blooded) animals that suckle on milk until they are large enough to feed themselves. Most mammals give birth to live young.

MAMMAL CLASS

ORDER

Within every class there are orders. Cats belong to the Carnivora order, which contains meat-eating animals with specialized teeth. Other mammal orders include insectivores, primates, rodents, and egg-layers (monotremes).

CARNIVORE ORDER

FAMILY

Orders are broken down into families. The cat family, called Felidae, contains large cats, such as lions, and small cats, including domestic cats. They are agile hunters and many have sharp claws that can be retracted.

CAT FAMILY

GENUS

The domestic cat belongs to a group of small species of cat in the genus *Felis*. Large cats, such as lions, tigers, and leopards, belong to genus *Panthera*.

FELIS GENUS

SPECIES

Species and subspecies can interbreed. The domestic cat (*Felis catus*) is descended from the wild cat (*Felis sylvestris*).

DOMESTIC CAT

Gloves prevent the sample from being contaminated

Phial contains the sample of body fluid

IDENTIFYING SPECIES ▶
Scientists identify species and their closest relatives by comparing their genetic code, which is contained in deoxyribonucleic acid (DNA) molecules within their cells. Using a centrifuge to spin special liquids made from body fluids or hair, for example, scientists can extract the DNA to examine it. Closely related species have similar DNA molecules. Studies of DNA help scientists to decide whether an animal belongs to an already identified species, or if it should be given a different name.

NEWLY DISCOVERED SPECIES

▲ VU QUANG OX
New animal species are discovered all the time. The Vu Quang ox was first described as a new species in 1992, based on DNA tests on horns from animals killed in the Vu Quang nature reserve in Vietnam. A living example of this rare and shy animal was not found until 1994.

TREE FROG
The Amazonian rainforest is teeming with life and new species are discovered there regularly. In 1926, the first tree frog in the genus *Allophryne* was discovered. It was thought to be unique up until recently, when this second *Allophryne* species was found in Peru.

MALAYSIAN TIGER
In 1997, DNA studies on the tiger populations in India, China, Indonesia, and Malaysia showed that each population is distinct and should be given a third name to indicate its subspecies. In 2004, the Malaysian tiger was recognized as a subspecies: *Panthera tigris jacksoni*.

FIND OUT MORE ▶▶ Anatomy **26** • Big Cats **268** • Classification **308–309** • Mammals **240–241** • Small Cats **265**

ECOLOGY

The scientific study of the relationship between living organisms and their environment is called ecology. The Earth is divided into a variety of environmental regions, called ecosystems. These ecosystems can vary in size from a small seaside rock pool to an ocean. Each one has its own groups of animal species that interact with other organisms and with their surroundings to keep their ecosystem stable.

POPULATION ▼
Animals of the same species that live in the same area, and interbreed with one another, are called a population. The number of animals in a population depends on how much food is available and how successful they are at reproducing. The term population includes animals that live on their own outside the mating season, animals that form a family group, or a larger group, such as this herd of African elephants.

Starfish eat mussels, creating space for seaweed to grow

Limpets graze on algae, exposing bare rock surfaces to new colonizers

Algae spread over rock surfaces, providing food for grazing herbivores

Velvet crabs scavenge in the pool

▲ ROCK POOL
In a rock pool ecosystem, the seaweed and algae use carbon dioxide and sunlight to produce sugars that they use for their growth. Herbivorous limpets feed on the algae, while carnivorous starfish feed on limpets, mussels, and other shellfish that are attached to the rocks. Crabs at the bottom of the pool are scavengers, feeding on the bodies of dead animals.

Anemone has stinging tentacles to catch small animals

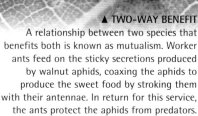

▲ TWO-WAY BENEFIT
A relationship between two species that benefits both is known as mutualism. Worker ants feed on the sticky secretions produced by walnut aphids, coaxing the aphids to produce the sweet food by stroking them with their antennae. In return for this service, the ants protect the aphids from predators.

Individual elephant is a member of the population

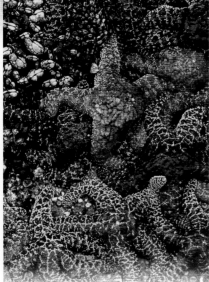

▲ COMPLEX RELATIONSHIPS
Within ecosystems, predators and prey maintain a delicate balance. When predatory ochre sea stars feed on mussels attached to rocks, they create gaps that other species can colonize. If the starfish are removed from the rock, the mussel beds become so dense that no other organism can survive on the rock.

FOOD WEB

Animals eat other living things to obtain energy and nutrients. The flow of energy from one living thing to another is called a food chain. There are many food chains within an ecosystem. Some animals, such as falcons, eat a variety of foods, so chains can be interconnected to form a food web. In a food web, large numbers of different herbivores feed on plants. The plants get their energy from the Sun. Smaller numbers of carnivores eat the herbivores. The top of the food web is dominated by just a few large carnivores. Fungi and bacteria are decomposers. They break down animal bodies when they die, returning nutrients to the soil, where they can be reused for plant growth.

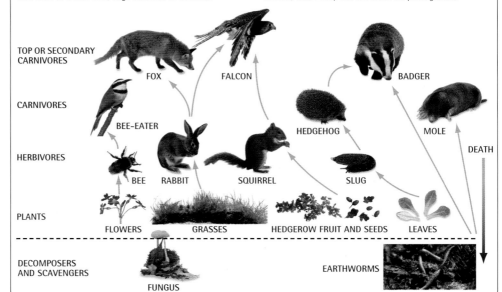

TOP OR SECONDARY CARNIVORES

FOX   FALCON   BADGER

CARNIVORES

BEE-EATER   HEDGEHOG   MOLE

DEATH

HERBIVORES

BEE   RABBIT   SQUIRREL   SLUG

PLANTS

FLOWERS   GRASSES   HEDGEROW FRUIT AND SEEDS   LEAVES

DECOMPOSERS AND SCAVENGERS

FUNGUS   EARTHWORMS

FIND OUT MORE ▶▶ Carnivores 38 • Elephants 288 • Grasslands 56–57 • Herbivores 39

EVOLUTION

CHARLES DARWIN
British, 1809–1882

From 1831–1836, Darwin travelled aboard HMS Beagle on a British scientific expedition around the world. His observations during the journey led him to conceive his theory of evolution. After a further 23 years immersed in scientific study, Darwin published a definition of his theory in a book called The Origin of Species.

The differences between members of the same species are known as variation. Certain variations, such as an ability to run fast, give an individual an advantage over others in its species. It might catch more prey, which means it is more likely to be healthy and to attract a mate. The speedy animal will probably pass on its useful trait to its offspring, and over generations, the species may evolve (change) to become superb hunters. This process, called natural selection, was first described by Charles Darwin in the 19th century.

Feathers are not camouflaged, as the bird has no predators

SPECIALIZED LIMBS

FORELIMB FOR FLIGHT
Bats are well adapted for powered flight, and these adaptations are found in their forelimbs. Unlike birds, in which the wing is supported by the bones of the arm and one finger, a bat's wing membrane, or patagium, is supported by the arm and by four elongated fingers.

FLIPPER FOR SWIMMING
This skeleton clearly shows that, with a shoulder bone, arm, and fingers, a dolphin's arm has the same basic design as all mammalian forelimbs. In life, the sea mammal's fingers are hidden beneath flesh to form a flipper, an adaptation the dolphin has evolved for its life in the water.

HIND LIMB FOR LEAPING
The bones in a frog's hind limbs act like long levers, and are specialized for leaping. The elongated toe bones support the webbing of the feet, providing a broad surface area, which exerts force against the water when the frog swims. The whole structure is light, flexible, and strong.

THE ELEPHANT'S EVOLUTION

Fossil evidence allows scientists to reconstruct the evolutionary history of elephants, which belong to the order Proboscidea. *Moeritherium*, a short-legged, ground-feeder, is the oldest known member of the order. It became extinct 36 million years ago (MYA). Later species evolved to feed on tree foliage, so they grew taller. Their trunks became longer and prehensile, adapted for gripping and wrapping around food.

MOERITHERIUM	PHIOMIA	GOMPHOTHERIUM	DEINOTHERIUM	ASIAN ELEPHANT
50 MYA	35 MYA	20 MYA	2 MYA	PRESENT DAY

NATURAL SELECTION ▶
In the 1880s, pollution caused tree trunks to turn black in the newly industrialized areas of England. Black peppered moths, which were previously rare, began to increase in number, as they were harder for predators to spot than their speckled counterparts. Now, with pollution better controlled, the population of black moths has fallen.

ARTIFICIAL SELECTION

Natural selection favours adaptations that are beneficial to survival, such as the long legs and large ears of this maned wolf. Not all species variety develops by random natural selection. For thousands of years humans have used selective breeding to develop animals with the features they require, such as hunting skills and milk-producing ability. More recently pets, such as this basset hound, have been selected on the basis of mutant genes. Its squat body, short legs, and friendly nature, would be a serious disadvantage to its wild ancestor – the grey wolf.

MANED WOLF

BASSET HOUND

ISLAND ANIMALS ▲
Small populations of animals sometimes reach remote islands by accident, rafting on floating vegetation, for example. When they breed they retain any distinctive characteristics their isolated group may have. Natural selection gradually favours variants that are better suited to their surroundings, and a new and unique species, such as this land iguana, which is found only on the Galapagos Islands, eventually develops.

◀ THE FUTURE?
We can only guess how life might evolve in the future. Over millions of years the environment may change drastically as a result of factors like global warming, and existing top carnivores might become extinct. Alternative predators might evolve, such as the giant terror birds that lived in South America after the dinosaurs became extinct. Maybe the Amazon Basin will be covered by grassland in five million years time, and the descendants of today's caracara might evolve into fearsome birds like the one in this image.

FIND OUT MORE ▶▶ Birds of Prey 206–207 • Ecology 14–15 • Extinction 19

ADAPTATION

Most animals are adapted to survive and reproduce in the habitats in which they live. Their adaptations can be physical, or they may involve the animal's behaviour, or both. There is often competition between species for food and living space in a habitat, so some animals have highly specialized adaptations that allow them to live in their own particular way, avoiding direct competition with neighbouring species.

FLYING DRAGON ▶
The so-called flying dragon of southeast Asia does not actually fly. In fact, this lizard glides from tree to tree in its rainforest habitat, using special flaps of skin between its front and hind limbs. It keeps the flaps folded at the sides of its body when they are not in use, extending them just as it launches itself to escape attack by a predator, or as it travels about in search of insect prey.

▲ LONG FINGERED LEMUR
The aye-aye, a black lemur from Madagascar, is highly adapted for feeding on the insect grubs that tunnel into trees. It uses its acute hearing to detect the grubs as they move. Once it locates its prey, the aye-aye gnaws away some of the wood, then pulls out its meal with its elongated middle finger.

GRIPPING FEET ▶
Rock hyraxes are adapted for climbing in their mountainous habitats in Africa and the Middle East. The soles of their feet have textured pads. These are kept moist by fluid that is secreted by special glands, giving them remarkable grip.

WINTER COAT ▶
As winter approaches in Canada, the snowshoe hare's brown summer coat turns white. This allows the hare to blend in with its snowy surroundings, so it can avoid being detected by predators, such as wolves. The coat also becomes thicker, providing extra warmth for this animal. Bristles on the sides of its feet grow longer, helping to support the hare's weight as it moves on the snow.

Barbels detect scent and electrical impulses from other animals

LAND LEGS ▶
At low tide, mudskipper fish in Africa, southeast Asia, and Australasia walk across mudflats and mangrove swamps using their pectoral fins as legs. They breathe using water that is trapped inside their large gill chambers. To escape predatory fish at high tide, they climb up mangrove roots and out of the water using suckers on their fins.

◀ SHALLOW WATER SPECIALIST
Epaulette sharks live in shallow, inshore reefs in tropical waters. They spend most of their time close to the seabed where they use their strong sense of smell and whisker-like barbels to detect food, such as sea urchins and shellfish. Epaulette sharks can survive in low oxygen conditions by switching off non-essential brain functions. This specialized adaptation allows the species to hunt in tide pools.

FIND OUT MORE ▶▶ Agamids **181** • Evolution **16–17** • Fish **126–127** • Lemurs **257** • Polar Regions **70**

EXTINCTION

Millions of species of animals have become extinct (died out) since life began on Earth. Some of the extinctions were due to the natural process of evolution, but in the past 300 years, humans have boosted this process considerably by destroying natural habitats, polluting the environment, and over-hunting certain species.

DEATH OF THE DINOSAURS ▶
Dinosaurs, including *Tyrannosaurus rex*, became extinct about 65 million years ago. Many scientists have linked their extinction to a massive asteroid strike, which may have caused vast amounts of dust to fill the atmosphere, blocking out the Sun for hundreds of years.

TOO WARM FOR A WOOLLY ▲
A relative of the modern-day Indian elephant, the woolly mammoth was well adapted to live in the tundra of Eurasia and North America during the last Ice Age. Mammoths died out about 3,000 years ago, because they could not cope with the increasing temperatures after the Ice Age ended.

◀ HUNTED TO EXTINCTION
The dodo was a large, pigeon-like bird that once lived on Mauritius in the Indian Ocean. It became extinct in the 17th century because European sailors, who could catch this flightless bird easily, hunted it for food, and cats and rats from the ships preyed on the dodo chicks.

FIND OUT MORE ▶▶ Conservation **22–23** • Evolution **16–17**

AMMONITES

Fossils are the remains of living things that have been preserved. They are usually discovered in rocks, but can also be found in ice or amber. Ammonites are extinct marine molluscs. Fossils such as these provide an important record of how life on Earth evolved (developed).

Class: Cephalopods

Distribution: Live animals dominated the world's oceans. Today, their fossilized remains are found in rocks throughout the world

When ammonites lived: From about 300 million years ago (MYA) until about 65 MYA, when they became extinct at the same time as the dinosaurs

Anatomy: Animals were protected by a hard shell (usually spiral-coiled) that contained a number of air-filled chambers called phragmocones

Diameter: 12 mm–3 m (½ in–10 ft), depending on the species

Maximum weight: 100 kg (220 lb)

Closest living relative: Chambered nautilus, which is a nocturnal animal that lives at depths of up to 600 m (2,000 ft) in the Pacific Ocean

FIND OUT MORE ▸▸ Cephalopods **89** • Extinction **19** • Molluscs **86**

CONSERVATION

The most effective way to conserve an animal species is to protect it in its natural habitat. This can be achieved by controlling hunting, setting up nature reserves, or by reducing pollution or habitat loss. Sometimes the best way to save an animal that is facing extinction is to breed it in captivity, where it can develop and grow in safety. If its numbers increase, the animal can be reintroduced back into the wild.

▲ PERSECUTED CROCODILE
Only 5,000 marsh crocodiles remain in the wild, scattered in small populations in Sri Lanka and India. In the past, it was hunted for its skin, but the hunting of this species is now banned. The marsh crocodile has been bred successfully in captivity; however, many people oppose its release into the wild because they believe this reptile is a danger to them and to their domestic animals.

◄ CRITICALLY ENDANGERED
Mediterranean monk seals are critically endangered as there are fewer than 500 individuals left in the world. Confined to small populations along the coasts of the eastern and southern Mediterranean Sea, they are extremely sensitive to human disturbance and have become reclusive, living in caves with underwater entrances. Their shy behaviour inhibits their breeding, and this, coupled with a low reproductive rate, has affected their numbers. Monk seals are killed deliberately by fishermen who consider the species a pest and a competitor for scarce fish resources.

▲ ISLAND SPECIES
Like many birds that evolved on islands where they have no natural predators, kakapos have lost the power of flight. This has made them vulnerable to the rats and domestic animals that European settlers introduced into New Zealand. There are now fewer than 100 left, but these have been transported to a rat-free island where they are beginning to increase in number.

PROTECTION AND ACTION ▶
The endangered African elephants have been given some protection in national parks, but poaching persists, as traders can get high prices for elephant tusks in the illegal ivory market. In 1989, the authorities in Kenya burned the country's confiscated ivory to show carvers there would be no further supplies of their raw material. Today, Kenya and other African countries control hunting and the sale of ivory, using the profits for wildlife conservation projects.

CONTROLLED HUNTING ▶
Between the late 1960s and early 1980s, many hundreds of thousands of bobcats in North America were killed for their valuable fur, and the numbers of this wild cat were severely reduced. From 1983, the United States and Canada introduced laws restricting the hunting of this species, and today, the bobcat is flourishing.

SANCTUARY FOR WHALES ▶
Most whales, including these pilot whales, have been hunted for their meat and valuable oils. Whale populations were reduced dramatically through overhunting in the 18th, 19th, and 20th centuries. Some species, such as the southern right whale, were hunted almost to extinction. Today, certain countries have agreed not to hunt whales in designated areas of ocean called sanctuaries.

BRED IN CAPTIVITY

GIANT PANDA
This species feeds almost exclusively on bamboo, which means the panda faces starvation if it loses its habitat. Pandas breed poorly in captivity, but in recent years, captive births have increased because more zoos are loaning out their pandas to other zoos for breeding.

ARABIAN ORYX
The Arabian oryx was hunted almost to extinction by the 1960s, when the few remaining animals were taken to the Phoenix Zoo in the United States to be bred in captivity. The oryx was later successfully reintroduced to its natural desert habitat in Oman.

KOMODO DRAGON
These lizards live on a few isolated islands in Indonesia. To guard them against extinction, captive-bred dragons are sent to zoos around the world for breeding. In 1980, the Komodo National Park was created, making this lizard's range a nature reserve.

◀ SAVED FROM EXTINCTION
During the mid-20th century, many farmers in the United States sprayed an insecticide called DDT on their crops. The DDT worked its way up the food chain from insects and small birds to the peregrine falcon. It built up in the fat tissues of the falcons, causing their eggshells to become so thin that they broke when the adults tried to incubate them. The inability to produce young brought this species close to extinction. In 1972, the use of DDT was banned, and the falcon began to reproduce again.

Stripeless rear end is a characteristic feature of the quagga

RESURRECTED SPECIES ▶
The quagga, which is a relative of the plains zebra, was ruthlessly hunted in the 19th century, and the last one died in a zoo in 1883. In 1987, a project began in South Africa to recreate the species, by selectively mating plains zebras that had reduced striping and browner coats like a quagga's. The zoologists compare the genetic material (DNA) of the selectively bred species with that of preserved quagga skins to see how closely the new animals resemble their wild ancestors.

FIND OUT MORE ▶▶ Evolution 16–17 • Extinction 19 • Monitors 184 • Parrots 216–217 • Whales 282–283

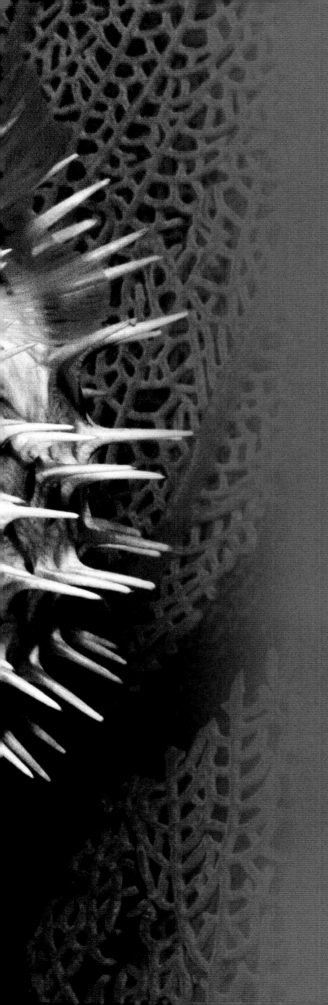

HOW
ANIMALS
WORK

◄ ANIMALS AT WORK
The variety of animal lifestyles is immense,
ranging from powerful land predators that
chase down their prey, to invertebrates that
filter-feed while permanently fixed to the
seabed. Animals have equally diverse methods
for protecting themselves against their
enemies – this porcupine fish has inflated its
body to scare off a predator. This section
reveals the defence and feeding strategies
many animals use and examines their life
processes, including how they reproduce and
develop. It also explains how animals move,
perceive the world, and conduct themselves
over the course of their lives.

ANATOMY

The structure of any living thing is called its anatomy. Animals are made up of cells, which are specialized to carry out different tasks. Simple animals are made up of a few types of cells. In advanced animals, identical cells are grouped into tissues that join together to form an organ. Organs are linked in a body system. Body systems are supported by either an internal or external skeleton.

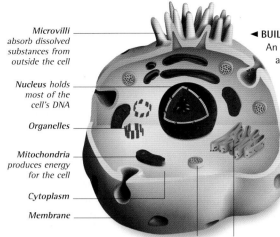

Microvilli *absorb dissolved substances from outside the cell*

Nucleus *holds most of the cell's DNA*

Organelles

Mitochondria *produces energy for the cell*

Cytoplasm

Membrane

Organelle   *Organelles*

◄ BUILDING BLOCK
An animal cell is held together by a flexible membrane. Inside is a jelly-like fluid called cytoplasm. This contains structures called organelles, which carry out different tasks in the cell. The nucleus is the most important organelle. It contains molecules of a chemical called DNA (deoxyribonucleic acid). These hold the instructions for everything the cell does.

INSIDE AN ELEPHANT ►
Internally, all mammals are very similar. The elephant's flexible, bony skeleton supports the weight of its organs and provides points of attachment for the muscles. Like all mammals, an elephant has a large, well-developed brain. Its heart and lungs are located in the thorax, the cavity between the neck and the abdomen. The kidneys, intestines, and reproductive organs lie in the abdomen to the rear.

ANIMAL BODY SYSTEMS

Body systems carry out all the processes essential for an animal to live. The nervous system responds to stimuli and triggers movement. Food is broken down by the digestive system, which also removes waste. The respiratory system uses oxygen to release food energy, and it expels carbon dioxide. Gases are carried by blood in the circulatory system. The reproductive system allows animals to produce young.

Simple body systems
Like most simple invertebrates, flatworms do not have respiratory organs or a circulatory system. Their digestive system has just one opening, the mouth, and their reproductive systems usually have both female organs (ovaries) and male organs (testes and genitals).

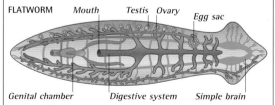

FLATWORM   *Mouth*   *Testis* *Ovary*
                                              Egg sac

Genital chamber   *Digestive system*   *Simple brain*

Arthropod body systems
Most arthropods, such as crayfish, have complex sensory organs and an elaborate nervous system to coordinate the movements of their limbs. Their digestive system is open at the mouth and tail. Blood flows partly through vessels and partly through spaces in the body. Oxygen is supplied to the body via tracheae or organs, such as gills.

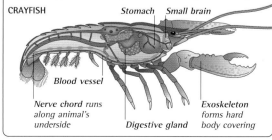

CRAYFISH   *Stomach*   *Small brain*

Blood vessel

Nerve chord runs along animal's underside   *Digestive gland*   *Exoskeleton forms hard body covering*

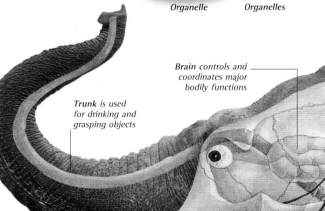

Skull *protects the brain and major sensory organs*

Brain *controls and coordinates major bodily functions*

Trunk *is used for drinking and grasping objects*

Blood vessels *carry blood to every part of the body*

Mouth *and nostrils (at the end of the trunk), breathe in oxygen, which flows to the lungs. The mouth is also linked to the digestive system*

Lungs, *part of the respiratory system, contain air sacs with thin walls so that oxygen can pass into the blood and carbon dioxide can pass out*

Heart, *part of the circulatory system, pumps blood around the body*

Skin *is a protective covering, and is the body's largest organ*

Limbs *are coordinated for movement*

OXYGEN FROM WATER ▲
Rotifers are simple microscopic marine animals. Like other simple animals, most of which live in water, their bodies contain only a few cells. Oxygen in the water simply seeps into the rotifer's cells, so it has no need for a circulatory system. At the same time, carbon dioxide escapes in the other direction.

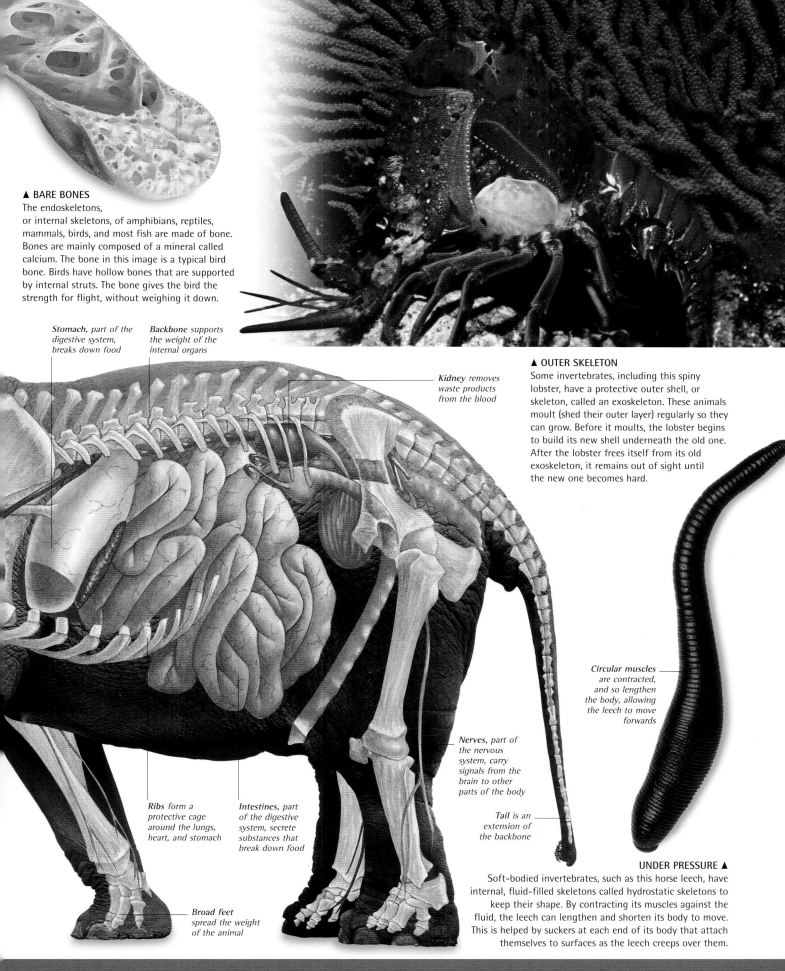

▲ BARE BONES
The endoskeletons,
or internal skeletons, of amphibians, reptiles,
mammals, birds, and most fish are made of bone.
Bones are mainly composed of a mineral called
calcium. The bone in this image is a typical bird
bone. Birds have hollow bones that are supported
by internal struts. The bone gives the bird the
strength for flight, without weighing it down.

Stomach, part of the digestive system, breaks down food

Backbone supports the weight of the internal organs

Kidney removes waste products from the blood

▲ OUTER SKELETON
Some invertebrates, including this spiny
lobster, have a protective outer shell, or
skeleton, called an exoskeleton. These animals
moult (shed their outer layer) regularly so they
can grow. Before it moults, the lobster begins
to build its new shell underneath the old one.
After the lobster frees itself from its old
exoskeleton, it remains out of sight until
the new one becomes hard.

Circular muscles are contracted, and so lengthen the body, allowing the leech to move forwards

Nerves, part of the nervous system, carry signals from the brain to other parts of the body

Ribs form a protective cage around the lungs, heart, and stomach

Intestines, part of the digestive system, secrete substances that break down food

Tail is an extension of the backbone

Broad feet spread the weight of the animal

UNDER PRESSURE ▲
Soft-bodied invertebrates, such as this horse leech, have
internal, fluid-filled skeletons called hydrostatic skeletons to
keep their shape. By contracting its muscles against the
fluid, the leech can lengthen and shorten its body to move.
This is helped by suckers at each end of its body that attach
themselves to surfaces as the leech creeps over them.

FIND OUT MORE ▶▶ Animal Characteristics **10–11** • Invertebrates **78–79** • Movement **28–29** • Reproduction **44–45**

Wing hinges, reducing air resistance in upstroke

Curved section of primary feathers generates lift

Primary feathers produce the power for flight as the bird brings its wing downwards

Tail feathers are a rudder for steering and airbrake for landing

Wing feathers are spread for maximum lift

▲ TAKING FLIGHT
Like many birds, a pigeon uses its light, flexible wings to fly. The wings are moved up and down by two sets of powerful muscles called the pectoralis and coracoideus muscles. These are attached to the bird's breastbone. By contracting its pectoralis muscles, the pigeon's wings flap down, giving the bird lift and propelling it forward. The coracoideus muscles pull the wings back up.

MOVEMENT

Animals move to track down prey, seek out mates, or escape predators. Most movement is controlled by the brain, which sends signals via the nervous system to groups of tissues called muscles. The muscles contract against a skeleton, moving the jointed limbs connected to them. An animal's limbs are adapted for its lifestyle. Some animals have legs for walking, running, and jumping, while some have fins or flippers for swimming. Other animals have wings for flying or gliding.

Tail is used to steer the cat through the air

Neck is straight, holding the head up so the cat can judge the distance

Hind limbs are at full stretch

Curved back acts like a spring

Powerful hind limbs produce energy for the jump

▲ LEAPING AND LANDING
A cat must coordinate its senses and muscles when it jumps. First, it judges the distance of the leap accurately so it can unleash the correct amount of force, which is stored in its muscles. Then, it uses the powerful thrust from its hind legs and its springlike backbone, to provide energy for the jump. While in the air, the cat uses its tail to maintain its balance so it can land safely.

Joint gives the limb flexibility

AERODYNAMICS OF THE WING

Air travelling over the curved upper surface of a bird's wing travels slightly further than air moving under the lower surface, so it travels faster. The slow-moving air exerts greater pressure beneath the wing, generating lift.

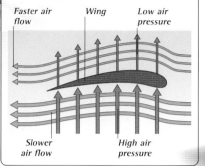

Faster air flow   Wing   Low air pressure

Slower air flow   High air pressure

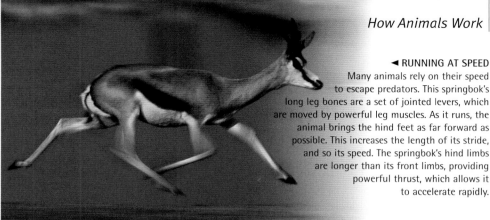

◄ **RUNNING AT SPEED**
Many animals rely on their speed to escape predators. This springbok's long leg bones are a set of jointed levers, which are moved by powerful leg muscles. As it runs, the animal brings the hind feet as far forward as possible. This increases the length of its stride, and so its speed. The springbok's hind limbs are longer than its front limbs, providing powerful thrust, which allows it to accelerate rapidly.

Shoulder acts like a shock absorber as the cat lands

Front legs are stretched forward to anticipate landing

Hind limbs are brought forward so that they are ready to provide thrust for the next movement

SWIMMING TECHNIQUES

Many fish swim by a series of S-shaped curves that travel along their bodies, pushing away the surrounding water and propelling the fish forwards. To turn, the fins are tilted at an angle to the flow of water. The water presses on the fins, exerting a force that turns the body.

Rolling
A dorsal fin along its back keeps a fish in an upright position. To roll on its own axis in one direction, the fish presses its dorsal fin in the opposite direction.

Rising and diving
To rise, stay level, or dive, a fish varies the angle of its pelvic fins and pectoral fins, which are along the sides of its body. The fish raises these fins to dive, and lowers them to rise.

Steering
The caudal fin is used for steering. By moving the caudal fin to the left, the fish steers itself to the right. Moving the tail to the right causes the fish to turn left.

◄ **EXOSKELETON MOVEMENT**
Animals with exoskeletons have several pairs of jointed limbs. Crabs have five pairs of legs. Each leg is made up of a series of sections, which are attached at joints. Pairs of muscles attached to the inner surface of each joint allow the crab to bend and move its limbs. Crabs use eight of their limbs for walking sideways. The two front limbs are modified into claws for feeding and defence.

JET PROPULSION ►
Some jellyfish simply float on the surface of the sea and drift with the tides, but others, such as this brown sea nettle, move using a form of jet propulsion. To move, the jellyfish contracts a ring of muscle around the edge of its bell-shaped body. This forces water out under the bell, propelling the jellyfish in the opposite direction. As the muscles on the edge of the bell relax, it fills with water again.

FIND OUT MORE ►► Anatomy **26–27** • Birds **192–193** • Fish **126–127** • Hoofed Mammals **289** • Jellyfish **84**

SENSES

Animals use their senses to gather information about their surroundings so they can mate, avoid danger, find food, and communicate. Senses also provide animals with information about their own bodies – for example, whether they are too hot or too cold. All the information is processed by the nervous system, which tells their bodies how to respond. Many species have senses that are more acute than our own, and some animals have senses that humans do not possess.

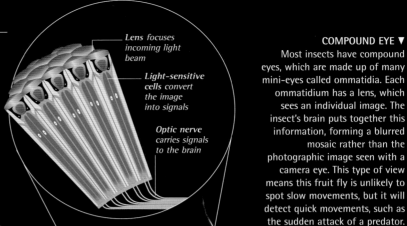

Lens *focuses incoming light beam*

Light-sensitive cells *convert the image into signals*

Optic nerve *carries signals to the brain*

COMPOUND EYE ▼

Most insects have compound eyes, which are made up of many mini-eyes called ommatidia. Each ommatidium has a lens, which sees an individual image. The insect's brain puts together this information, forming a blurred mosaic rather than the photographic image seen with a camera eye. This type of view means this fruit fly is unlikely to spot slow movements, but it will detect quick movements, such as the sudden attack of a predator.

CAMERA EYE

Vertebrates' eyes work like a camera, using a lens to focus light and form an image. Light bounces off objects and enters the eye through the cornea. The lens focuses the light on the retina, where an image is formed upside down. The retina converts the light rays into nerve signals, which leave the eye along optic nerves and travel to the brain, where an upright image is formed.

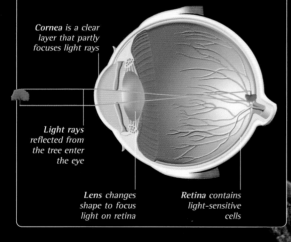

Cornea *is a clear layer that partly focuses light rays*

Light rays *reflected from the tree enter the eye*

Lens *changes shape to focus light on retina*

Retina *contains light-sensitive cells*

Maxillary palp *detects airborne chemicals*

Proboscis *has sensors for tasting and recognizing different foods*

Some leg bristles *are taste sensors*

▲ SNIFFER DOG

Animals with a sense of smell have the ability to detect chemicals that are present in the air or in water. Many animals use scent to mark territory and attract mates. Predators use scent to locate prey. Dogs have an acute sense of smell, and can be trained to detect even small traces of substances, for example, illegal drugs.

TASTING THE AIR ▶

Some reptiles, such as this tegu lizard, are equipped with a sensory device called a Jacobson's organ. Located in the roof of the animal's mouth, it can detect traces of chemical substances in the air, such as those left by potential prey. A reptile's tongue flicks in and out constantly, sampling the air and transferring these chemicals to this sensitive organ.

Tongue collects scent molecules

Wing has sensors that detect the wind

Antenna detects chemical scents carried in the air

HEARING

All sounds have a certain pitch. A high-pitched sound, such as a whistle, makes the air vibrate backwards and forwards more times each second than a low-pitched sound, such as that produced by a truck engine. The number of vibrations per second is called the frequency of the sound and is measured in hertz. This chart shows that humans cannot hear sounds with frequencies above 20,000 hertz, or below about 30 hertz. Bats hear a much wider range of frequencies. Dolphins only hear high frequency sounds.

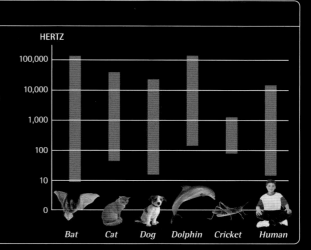

HERTZ

100,000	
10,000	
1,000	
100	
10	
0	

Bat Cat Dog Dolphin Cricket Human

Ears are much larger than those of other foxes

◀ SOUND FUNNEL

Hearing is the ability to detect sound waves. Some animals rely on this sense to communicate and hunt. Fennec foxes live in the Sahara and hunt at night, when the air is cool. Their large ears act like funnels to collect sound waves. The waves are focused on a membrane inside the ear called the eardrum, which vibrates when it picks up sound. The fennec fox can swivel its ears so that it can pinpoint the exact location of its prey.

Leg has bristles that are sensitive to touch

Fleshy tentacles surround the nostrils

TOUCHING TENTACLES ▶

The star-nosed mole from North America lives in total darkness in underground tunnels. This creature uses its 22 pink, fleshy nose-tentacles to feel its way around, touching as many as 12 objects per second. The super-sensitive tentacles can locate and identify even the tiniest prey by touch.

FIND OUT MORE ▶▶ Bats 254–255 • Communication 34–35 • Deserts 58–59 • Insects 97 • Sharks 131

BEHAVIOUR

Everything an animal does, and the way in which it does it, makes up its behaviour. An animal's behaviour enables it to increase its chances of survival and find a mate. Some behaviour is instinctive, which means it is programmed by an animal's genes and does not have to be learned. Animals also have varying degrees of natural intelligence, which allows them to learn specific kinds of behaviour, either from members of their species, or from good or bad experiences.

Squirrels learn to use teeth and clawed feet to undo catches on the cage

◄ LEARNED BEHAVIOUR
Animals associate the actions they carry out with the results of those actions. Some animals can learn complicated tasks if their endeavours are rewarded. These grey squirrels have learned to steal peanuts from this bird feeder. Through a combination of intelligence and physical agility, they undo catches so they can reach the food.

Grass is long and flexible

Heavy stone is used as a hammer

Ostrich eggshells are exceptionally thick

Beak is used to knot and weave grasses together

▲ TOOL USER
Some animals learn to use simple tools in order to feed. The shell of an ostrich egg is too thick for this Egyptian vulture to crack open with its beak. Instead, it uses heavy stones to smash the egg. If there are no stones nearby, the bird flies off in search of one that is suitable.

Pipit works tirelessly to feed the oversized chick

◄ NATURAL PARENT
Pipits are genetically programmed to respond to a gaping red beak by feeding it. Maternal instinct in this meadow pipit is so strong it feeds the cuckoo even though it is too large to be its own chick. Some cuckoos have lost the instinct to build their own nests, so they lay their eggs in the nests of other birds.

HUNTING IN A PACK ▲
African wild dogs hunt in packs of about 30 individuals. By working together they can catch and kill prey that would be too large for a single dog to tackle. Although they have a natural instinct to stay together in social groups, the young animals must learn how to hunt cooperatively from the older dogs. One dog leads the pack, while the others follow. They chase their unfortunate victim until it is too exhausted to run, and once they catch their prey, the dogs force it to the ground and devour it.

Paper cell is the work of several cooperating wasps

Queen wasp lays eggs

◄ WEAVING A NEST
Although vitelline masked weaver birds are born with a natural instinct to construct their hanging nests, they need to practise their construction methods. The nest is built on a swing-shaped hoop made from a grass stalk, around which the rest of the nest is woven and knotted from grass leaves. Early attempts at nest-building often fall to pieces, but this determined species of bird eventually perfects its technique.

▲ SOCIAL INSECTS
Paper wasps are born with a natural instinct to cooperate in nest-building. Led by a queen wasp, the worker wasps toil tirelessly to construct a safe environment in which young wasps can develop. The workers also take collective responsibility for the feeding of the young.

Lateral line has pressure sensors that allow instant coordinated movement

SAFETY IN NUMBERS ►
The shoaling behaviour of some fish, such as these blue-striped snappers, makes it difficult for a predator to isolate and catch a single fish among a fast-moving group that constantly changes direction. A predator may be confused by the apparent size of the moving object; also, there are more pairs of eyes on the lookout for an attacker. Shoaling depends on a high level of coordinated movement, which is achieved through acute vision and sensory systems in the fish that respond instantly to even the slightest movements around them.

FIND OUT MORE ►► Animal Homes 48–49 • Carnivores 38 • Cuckoos 218 • Fish 126–127 • Wasps 113 • Weavers 235

COMMUNICATION

Animals communicate by sending out signals that are recognized and understood by other animals. These signals include sounds, vibrations, displays of colour, the use of scent, and even dancing. Communication has many uses. It can help an animal to find a mate, threaten rivals, defend territory, warn other animals of danger, and to keep in touch with the family group. Some young animals use special signals to demand food from their parents.

NORMAL COLOUR

BREEDING COLOUR

ATTRACTING A MATE ▲
When the breeding season arrives in spring, the male stickleback undergoes a colour change. His throat and belly turn bright red, his eyes become clear, and silver scales appear on his back. These colours tell females that he wishes to mate, and they also warn other males to stay away. However, by becoming more brightly coloured, the stickleback risks being seen more easily by predators.

▲ WARNING CALL
Howler monkeys live in small troops (groups) of about six members in the rainforests of Belize. Each troop has its own territory, which it defends from other troops by howling to warn them off. This call is the loudest sound produced by any land mammal, and can be heard more than 3 km (2 miles) away. The howlers make the sound by forcing air through a large hollow bone in their throat called the hyoid.

◄ KEEPING IN CONTACT
Some whales, including this southern right whale, produce sounds, known as songs, which can travel long distances through water. The exact meaning of whale song is not fully understood, but they may be used to attract mates, and probably allow whales to keep in contact with each other in vast areas of ocean. Human activity in the oceans, with the use of sonar technology and noisy boat engines, may prevent whales from communicating.

▲ FEED ME!
Nestlings, such as these skylark chicks, tell a parent they want food by stretching their necks and gaping their beaks, which are brightly coloured to attract attention. The behaviour of the chicks stimulates the instinct of the adult to feed them. In some species, such as great tits, parents can go on up to 900 hunting trips each day to feed their demanding brood.

Cornicles are at the rear end

WATCH OUT! ▶
Some animals release chemical signals called pheromones, which are detected by other members of the same species. When an aphid spots a predatory ladybird, it secretes an alarm pheromone from small tubes, called cornicles, to warn the rest of the colony. Other aphids detect the signal with their antennae and make their escape.

◀ BACK OFF!
Animals show aggression to other members of their species when competing for food, shelter, or mates. Animals may also be aggressive towards other species that are threatening them. By hissing, baring its sharp teeth, and raising its coat hairs, this African serval cat may scare off an aggressor without either animal being hurt.

◀ WAGGLE DANCE
Honeybees use a complicated system of dances to communicate with each other. When a worker bee finds a rich supply of food, it returns to the hive and performs a figure-of-eight dance on the hive comb, waggling its behind. Other bees then follow the dance. The angle of the dance in relation to the position of the Sun in the sky, and the speed at which the dance is performed, tell all the other bees where to find the food and how far away it is.

LEAVING MESSAGES ▲
Black bears communicate with each other by marking objects, such as trees, with their scent. They usually do this by standing on their two hind legs and rubbing the objects with their backs, shoulders, and the back of their heads. They also bite and claw the objects. Each bear has its own scent, which reveals whether or not it is ready to mate, and possibly its mood.

FIND OUT MORE ▶▶ Bears **274–275** • Bees **112** • Behaviour **32–33** • Senses **30–31** • Whales **282–283**

COPPER SHARK

The copper shark (also known as a bronze whaler), is an active predator of bony fish. This species forms groups that follow the annual migrations of sardines, travelling north along the eastern and western coasts of South Africa. Before they strike, the sharks allow other predators, such as dolphins, tuna, and yellowtails, to herd the sardines into a concentrated shoal, called a bait ball. The waiting predators then charge at the silvery mass of fish, snatching mouthfuls as they pass through it.

Scientific name: *Carcharhinus brachyurus*

Order: Carcharhiniformes (ground sharks)

Class: Chondrichthyes (cartilaginous fish)

Distribution: Tropical and temperate seas

Status: Not threatened

Maximum length: 3.25 m (11 ft)

Maximum weight: 305 kg (672 lb)

Food: Bony fish, cephalopods, smaller sharks, and rays

Reproduction: Viviparous, which means the embryos are nourished with a placenta and the females give birth to live young

No. of young: Between 13 and 20 pups

FIND OUT MORE ▶▶ Bony Fish **134** • Carnivores **38** • Dolphins **286–287** • Gamefish **146–147** • Sharks **131**

CARNIVORES

Animals that feed on other animals are called carnivores. Many of them chase or ambush prey, killing it with their sharp beaks, teeth, talons, or claws. Some carnivores, including snakes, scorpions, and spiders, use venom to subdue victims so they die quickly, without injuring their attacker in a struggle. Other carnivores do not kill their prey outright. They inflict a wound and feed on its blood. Animal flesh is high in energy, so many carnivores can survive for long intervals between meals.

A LION'S FEEDING FEATURES ▶
Like all big cats, lions have dagger-shaped canine teeth. Combined with powerful jaw muscles that deliver a devastating bite, and a wide gape when the jaws are open, a lion's canines are fearsome weapons that can quickly kill large animals, such as wildebeest. Carnassial teeth, further back in the lion's jaw, have sharp ridges that are adapted for cutting flesh from bones.

Canines bite into flesh

Carnassial, or cheek, tooth

Large jaw

Water jet has a range of up to 1.5 m (5 ft)

◀ SNAKE HARMER
Undeterred by the cobra's threat display, this mongoose relies on speed and agility to overcome its adversary, killing the snake by biting its neck with razor-sharp teeth. Indian mongooses usually tackle less dangerous prey, such as mice. They also feed on eggs. When they were introduced to islands in the Pacific and the Caribbean to control rats, mongooses drove some ground-nesting birds to the verge of extinction by feeding on their eggs.

ANT ARMY ▶
Some ants overcome prey that is much larger than themselves by sheer weight of numbers, overwhelming animals, such as grasshoppers, then using powerful jaws to dismember them. They are the most abundant carnivores in the tropics – one hectare (2¹/₂ acres) of rainforest can contain eight million ants.

FIREPOWER ▶
Archerfish lurk below the surface of tropical streams waiting to ambush insects crawling on leaves that overhang the water. Once it spots its victim, the fish shoots water from its mouth, knocking the insect into the stream, where it becomes easy prey.

◀ BLOOD SUCKER
Leeches give a painless bite, so victims do not realize that the parasite is feeding on their blood, which is an easily digestible, protein-rich food. The biting leech injects a protein called hirudin, which stops blood clotting so that its meal flows freely. When the leech stops feeding the wound continues to bleed.

FIND OUT MORE ▶▶ Big Cats **268** • Carnivorous Mammals **264** • Mongooses **271** • Omnivores **40** • Scavengers **41**

HERBIVORES

Animals that eat plants are called herbivores. Plant food is sometimes low in nutrients. Seeds can be packed with energy-rich food, but other parts of plants, such as stems and leaves, contain fewer nutrients that animals can use. To survive, some animals eat almost continuously. Most herbivores have bacteria in their guts that helps to break down the plants' tough cell walls.

Large molars to crush and grind leaves and branches

◄ ELEPHANT TEETH
The skull of the African savanna elephant reveals the grinding molars that this herbivore uses to crush plant food. Hard ridges on the surfaces of these teeth wear at a different rate from the rest of the teeth. This prevents the molars from being worn smooth by continuous chewing.

NUT CRACKER ►
The most nutritious parts of seeds are usually protected by a hard seed coat. Parrots have specialized features that allow them to penetrate the outer layer. The pointed tip of a parrot's beak can exert tremendous pressure, cracking open the seed and exposing the edible kernel. The sharp edges of the beak are used to cut food items. Parrots also use their feet to grasp and manipulate seeds.

FUSSY EATER ►
Some herbivores have a highly specialized diet. This means they can live only in places where their food is available, making these animals vulnerable to extinction if they lose their habitat. This golden bamboo lemur feeds exclusively on a type of giant bamboo that contains levels of cyanide that would kill most mammals. However, the lemur is immune to the poison.

Long neck gives the giraffe a feeding advantage

▲ GRAZING YAK
Wild yaks graze on low-growing grasses, mosses, and lichens that grow in high, bleak pastures. Like other ruminants, or cud-chewers, the yak partially digests its food before regurgitating it and chewing it a second time. The yak then swallows the food again. Eventually the food passes through the animal's four-chambered stomach, where bacteria helps the yak to digest the plant material.

▲ HIGH BROWSER
Giraffes are the only African mammals that can reach the succulent upper foliage of the acacia tree, so they have no competitors for food. These herbivores use their long, muscular tongues to grip hold of the plant, and their grooved teeth to strip off the leaves. Giraffes spend about 20 hours per day feeding on up to 68 kg (150 lb) of food.

FIND OUT MORE ►► Anatomy 26–27 • Ecology 14–15 • Giraffes 299 • Hoofed Mammals 289 • Parrots 216–217

Curved tusks may be attractive to females

OMNIVORES

Animals that eat both plants and other animals are called omnivores. This flexible diet allows omnivorous species to colonize a wide range of habitats. They can also switch between food sources according to the season. Most omnivores have specially adapted feeding features that help them to consume their mixed diet. For example, most bears have large canine teeth for biting into flesh, and rounded molars for crushing and grinding plant food.

◄ A HEARTY BREAKFAST
The barbirusa lives in groups in the forests of Indonesia, where it relies on its excellent hearing and acute sense of smell to find food, mainly in the morning. The barbirusa usually feeds on fruit, fungi, nuts and insect larvae. If it can catch them, a barbirusa will also eat rodents.

Anemone tentacles protect the clown fish from predators

BEAR NECESSITIES ►
Grizzly bears eat large animal prey when they can catch it, but take advantage of any food that is seasonally plentiful, including new plant shoots in spring and berries in autumn. Some also catch salmon as they migrate up rivers to spawn. This varied diet helps bears to build up their fat reserves for their long winter sleep.

Powerful, pointed beak for killing prey and picking up seeds

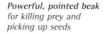

RICH PICKINGS ►
Clown fish are covered with a slime that makes them immune to the stinging tentacles of sea anemones. They hover among the waving tentacles, waiting for the sea anemone to paralyse and eat prey, then these fish help themselves to the leftovers. Clown fish also feed on algae, as well as microscopic sea plants called phytoplankton, and minute sea animals called zooplankton.

▲ CROW SKULL
Crows are among the most successful omnivores in the bird world. One of the reasons for their success is their all-purpose beak. It is sharply pointed, allowing the bird to pick up small food items, such as seeds. The beak is also long, so the crow can grab and hold large prey, such as mice, birds, and frogs.

FIND OUT MORE ►► Bears 274–275 • Crows 230 • Pigs 293

SCAVENGERS

Scavengers depend on the skills of other animals to catch and kill food for them, as they prefer to feed on the remains of prey that is left behind by predators. The boldest scavengers will sometimes steal food from the hunters. Species with a scavenging lifestyle can be very adaptable, often sharing human habitats and living on waste food that we leave behind.

▲ VERSATILE SCAVENGERS
Hyenas, such as these spotted hyenas, have powerful jaw muscles and strong teeth. These features allow them to crush the bones of discarded animal prey. Hyenas eat everything that is left, except hooves and horns. Although these animals specialize in feeding on carrion (dead animals), they sometimes also hunt for live prey.

Clown fish may lure other animals towards the stinging tentacles

▲ GREEDY VULTURES
Vultures, including lappet-faced vultures, soar high in the sky or perch on trees to scour the ground for dead animals. They also watch each other and when one bird finds a corpse, the others soon descend and crowd around it, squabbling for a share. A vulture's hooked, sharp-edged bill is adapted for ripping through tough skin and slicing flesh.

FIND OUT MORE ▶▶ Birds of Prey 206–207 • Carnivores 38 • Racoons 277

DEFENCE

All animals need a strategy to avoid being attacked and eaten. Even large cats, such as lions, are vulnerable to predators, especially when they are infants. Many hoofed mammals depend on watchfulness and speed to escape hungry predators. Slower animals may defend themselves with armour or spines. Some species rely on deception, using colour patterns that resemble dangerous species that predators learn to avoid. Others may blend in with their surroundings.

Squid has a streamlined shape for fast swimming

Ink squirts into the water

A PRICKLY PROSPECT ▶

A porcupine's body bristles with long, hard, sharp-tipped spines, or quills. This creature raises and rattles its quills to warn away predators, such as leopards, hyenas, and bobcats. If the attacker persists, the porcupine runs backwards into it, driving the quills into its face or body, where they work their way deep into the flesh. The quills are extremely difficult to remove from the wounds and they can cause infections.

▲ CLOUD OF INK

Most cephalopods, including many species of squid, have an ink gland linked to their gut. If they feel threatened, they release a cloud of ink into the water to confuse attackers. Under the cover of this cloud, the creature jets away to safety. Some squid also produce poisons. Predators soon learn to avoid those particular species.

◀ BODY ARMOUR

A hairy armadillo cannot outrun a predator, but overlapping plates on its body provide it with an effective suit of armour. When it tucks its head into its chest and rolls itself up, the armadillo's soft, vulnerable body parts are completely protected. Most attackers, unable to prise open their prey, eventually give up trying to eat the armadillo.

▲ IRRITATING HAIRS

Slow-moving tiger moth caterpillars use their stiff, sharp hairs to deter predators. The hairs stick in the attacker's flesh, eyes, or throat, causing discomfort. Some species of caterpillar have hairs that are coated with irritating chemicals, which cause rashes on the hands of any humans that handle them.

Bristles put off hungry predators

PLAYING DEAD ▶

When all else fails, some animals simply pretend to be dead when predators grab them. A Virginia opossum becomes limp and motionless if it is caught. However, if its attacker's attention is diverted for a moment, it will spring into life and scuttle away to safety. This defence behaviour, which is also used by some snakes and beetles, is often called playing possum.

Folded wings match the shape and pattern of surrounding leaves

LEAF MIMIC ▶

The camouflage pattern of this dead leaf butterfly provides effective protection if the insect behaves like an autumn leaf. To do this, it must sit in the correct position on the twig, matching the arrangement of the real leaves and remaining still. Camouflaged animals, such as this species, become conspicuous if they move away from their natural surroundings.

◀ LARGER THAN LIFE

If a toad is threatened by a grass snake it undergoes an alarming change, inflating its body, standing on tiptoe, and swaying from side to side. This startled snake may decide that its potential victim is too big to swallow and it might look elsewhere for its meal. Some toad species can produce poison to defend themselves.

FIND OUT MORE ▶▶ Armadillos **251** • Cephalopods **89** • Colubrids **187** • Hoofed Mammals **289** • Possums **246**

REPRODUCTION

Animals reproduce in two ways. In asexual reproduction, a parent may split into two, or part of its body may break away to become a new individual. In sexual reproduction, a male sex cell (sperm) and a female sex cell (ovum) unite in a process called fertilization. Fertilization produces an organism called an embryo, which grows into a new animal. Many animals that reproduce sexually perform rituals to attract a mate.

◄ BUDDING HYDRA
Hydras, which are tiny animals that live in ponds usually reproduce asexually. A swelling, called a bud, forms the side of the parent's body. Ove time, the bud develops a mouth and tentacles, so that it can f independently. Eventual the new individual split away from the parent.

Tentacles are used to capture prey

◄ IMPRESSING THE LADIES
Rituals performed to attract a mate during the breeding season are called courtship. Most birds, including this riflebird, have fixed courtship displays that ensure they attract a mate of the same species. Male riflebirds fan out their wings and bob up and down, moving their heads from side to side. The females then choose the male they feel has presented the most impressive display.

HEAD BANGERS ►
During the breeding season, larger male Spanish ibexes with the bigger horns usually have their pick of the females. Males of the same size compete for mates, rearing up on their hind legs and butting heads. These contests normally end with the weaker male bowing out before either animal is seriously injured.

Size of horns is an indication of age and dominance

Strong neck muscles support heavy horns

Powerful legs are used to rear up in a threat display

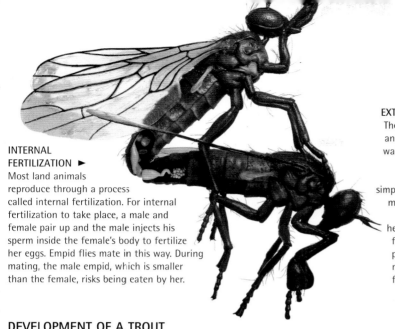

INTERNAL FERTILIZATION ►

Most land animals reproduce through a process called internal fertilization. For internal fertilization to take place, a male and female pair up and the male injects his sperm inside the female's body to fertilize her eggs. Empid flies mate in this way. During mating, the male empid, which is smaller than the female, risks being eaten by her.

EXTERNAL FERTILIZATION ►

The silver salmon, like many animals that live or mate in water, reproduces through a process called external fertilization. The female simply lays her eggs, then the male passes over them and releases sperm, as shown here. Fertilization outside a female's body is a random process. Only a few of the millions of sperm released fertilize some of the eggs.

DEVELOPMENT OF A TROUT

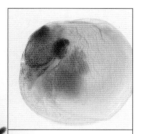

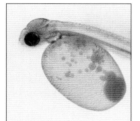

EYED EGG
After fertilization, and depending on the temperature of the water, a multi-celled embryo begins to develop inside a trout's egg. The embryo soon grows features, such as eyes. These can be seen through this egg as two black dots.

ALEVIN
The eggs hatch into tiny fish called alevins. They do not have mouths for feeding. Instead, the alevins absorb nutrients from a yolk sac that is attached to their stomachs. It takes several weeks for the alevins to consume the yolk.

SEXUAL MATURITY
After it has absorbed all the yolk, the young trout, called a fry, looks like a mini adult. The fry must find its own food, which fuels its growth, and after one to four years the trout reaches maturity. It is then able to reproduce, starting the cycle again.

▲ SHELLED ANIMALS

Many reptile embryos and all bird embryos develop inside a protective, shelled egg. While birds incubate their eggs in a nest by using the warmth from their bodies, turtles keep their eggs warm by laying them on rotting vegetation or burying them in sand. Young turtles use a special egg tooth on the front of their beak to break through the shell.

GESTATION PERIOD ►

If a female's egg has been fertilized internally, it is either laid to hatch later, or it is retained inside the mother while it begins to develop into a young animal. Most mammalian embryos become a foetus that grows inside the mother's uterus. The period of development between fertilization and birth is called the gestation period. For gorillas, the gestation period lasts between 250 and 290 days.

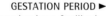

Uterus sits in the female's pelvic area

Foetus develops inside the mother's uterus

FIND OUT MORE ►► Gorillas **262** • Mammals **240–241** • Placental Mammals **247** • Reptiles **168–169** • Sheep **300**

PARENTING

Different animals give different levels of care to their offspring. Some animals produce vast numbers of eggs, which hatch into young that must fend for themselves immediately. Normally, very few of them survive to become adults. Other species produce fewer young, but the parents defend and feed them, often at great risk to themselves. This form of parenting usually increases the chances of the offspring surviving to adulthood.

Transparent body hides larva from predators

▲ OFF AT SEA
The female crab holds her fertilized eggs close to her in a spongy mass. She keeps them healthy by splashing them with water. Once the crab eggs hatch into larvae, the mother no longer takes care of her young, and they drift away in the ocean currents as part of plankton. The larvae go through a process of metamorphosis, in which they change form numerous times before they acquire adult characteristics and move back to the seashore.

MOUTH BROODER ►
Mouthbrooders, such as this yellowhead jawfish, are a group of fish that care for their eggs and young in their mouth and throat cavities. Even after they hatch, the young fry hide in their parent's mouth if they feel threatened. Once the danger has passed, the adult blows its babies from its mouth, so that they can swim nearby.

FOOD FOR THE BIRDS ►
Not only do egrets provide their young with food, they also help them to digest it. Like many other birds, the parent first eats the food, then thrusts its beak into a chick's throat, and regurgitates the partially digested food. When the chicks grow stronger, the adult drops undigested food into the nest, and the young compete to get the greater share.

Chick waits for its food

Youngster is not harmed by its mother's jaws

◄ BY THE NECK
The female hamster is an extremely attentive mother. If danger threatens, she carries each of her babies away to safety, either by putting them into pouches in her cheeks, or by lying them across a toothless area in her jaws. Female hamsters produce two or three litters per year. Each litter contains up to eight young.

▲ GROUP RESPONSIBILITY
Musk oxen live in herds of up to 100 individuals in Greenland and northern Canada. When wolves threaten the herd, the adults form a defensive circle around the young, facing their attackers with their horns. The adults also huddle around the young to keep them warm, shielding them from the icy Arctic wind.

MOTHER'S MILK ▶
All mammals suckle their offspring on milk, which is a high-energy food that provides the essential nutrients that young animals need in their early stages of growth. Suckling develops a close bond between the mother and her offspring. Many large mammals, such as these topi from East Africa, suckle their young for up to a year.

▲ PARENT BUG
Most invertebrates lay their eggs and then abandon them. Earwigs are an exception to this rule. In autumn, the female earwig lays her eggs in soil, tending them through the winter, and licking each one regularly to remove mould. When the young hatch in spring, their mother feeds them often and the family stays together for several months.

FIND OUT MORE ▶▶ Invertebrates **78–79** • Mammals **240–241** • Oceans **74–75** • Reproduction **44–45**

ANIMAL HOMES

Animals need somewhere to live that provides them with shelter from bad weather, a safe refuge from predators, and a place to raise their young. Some species make homes in natural features, such as caves or holes in trees. Several mammals excavate a home underground. Many animals build elaborate nests. This is a job with two parts – collecting the materials and fashioning them into finished homes.

▲ BAT CAVE
Caves provide bats with a dry home where there is very little temperature variation, whatever the weather outside. They use echolocation, bouncing sound waves off the cave walls, to find their way around in the darkness, and at dusk they go outside to feed. When thousands of bats roost in a single cave, vast piles of droppings accumulate on the cave floor.

MOUSE NEST ►
The American harvest mouse weaves a spherical nest, made of chewed grass, leaves, and stems. Each nest is the size of a tennis ball. Sitting about 60 cm (2 ft) above the ground, it is supported by the stems of grasses. The mouse uses its prehensile (grasping) tail, which can curl around grass stalks, as an extra foot to help it move around as it constructs its home.

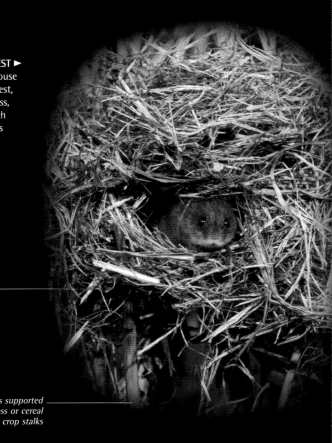

Woven grasses provide good heat insulation for young

Nest is supported by grass or cereal crop stalks

◄ BORROWED HOME
Unlike other crabs, hermit crabs have soft shells, so they have to find empty, hard shells in which they can live and hide from predators. Shells that have been outgrown and shed by other creatures can be difficult to find, so hermit crabs often fight for the right to an abandoned shell.

Crab reverses its body into the shell

BURROWING RODENTS ►
Naked mole rats of east Africa excavate extensive underground tunnels. These lead to the central chamber in which the colony of mole rats lives. The queen mole rat, whose only role is to produce young, surrounds herself with worker mole rats. The workers dig the tunnels. They also forage for roots and tubers, and defend the young from intruders.

BIRDS' NESTS

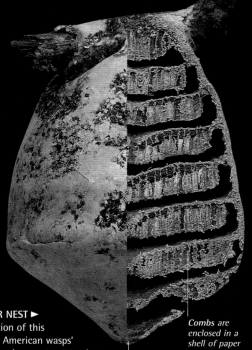

PAPER NEST ▶
A section of this
South American wasps'
nest has been cut out to show
the inside. The nest hangs from a
tree branch. It is built from plant
fibres, which adult wasps collect
and chew into a paste that
hardens into paper. The queen
starts the nest and worker wasps
extend it, building layers of
combs in which they rear their
young. The new combs are added
at the bottom.

*Combs are
enclosed in a
shell of paper*

Entrance hole

WOVEN HOMES
African weaver birds build
hanging nests, which are
made from grass stems and
suspended from thorn tree
branches. The nests are built
by the males, which often
construct several nests for
different females. Weaver
birds nest in noisy colonies.

ON THE GROUND
Glaucous-winged gulls of
the western United States
prefer to nest in low sites.
First, they scrape the ground
clean, then they build up
a ring of vegetation.
Sometimes the adult bird
starts several nests, but they
only complete and use one.

HOME WITH A VIEW
An African white-backed
vulture's nest is a wide
platform made of sticks;
it has space for the
fledglings to stretch their
wings as they learn to fly.
The nest is an excellent
viewing point from which
the parent can spot food.

*Hollow trunk
provides shelter,
and conceals owl
from predators*

*Adult bird's
mottled brown
plumage matches
the tree trunk*

*Young owl spends
most of its time in
the hollow*

HOLLOW HOME ▶
Like many owls, the screech owls of North, Central,
and South America live in forested areas and make
use of hollow trees as nest sites. This means that
they avoid the laborious process of nest-building.
The nest cavities, which are 2–6 m (6½–19½ ft)
above the ground, are usually found in deciduous
trees, such as elms, sycamores, and maples.

FIND OUT MORE ▶▶ Bats 254–255 • Behaviour 32–33 • Birds 192–193 • Caves 67 • Mice 304 • Owls 220–221

MIGRATION

Billions of animals are on the move at any one time, making journeys called migrations from one place to another. Migrating animals include insects, fish, amphibians, reptiles, birds, and mammals. These animals find their way by using their instincts, familiar landmarks, the Earth's magnetic field, or the position of the Sun and stars. Animals usually migrate to find food, places to breed, or to escape icy winters or scorching summers. Some migrations take place regularly every year; others take place occasionally.

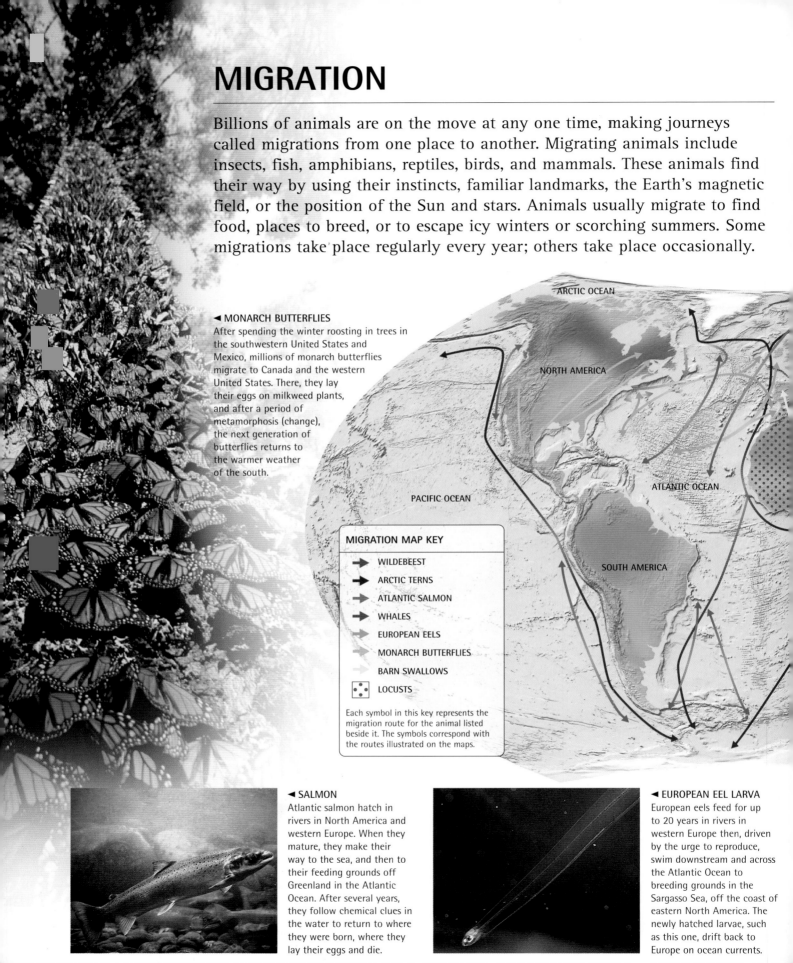

◄ MONARCH BUTTERFLIES
After spending the winter roosting in trees in the southwestern United States and Mexico, millions of monarch butterflies migrate to Canada and the western United States. There, they lay their eggs on milkweed plants, and after a period of metamorphosis (change), the next generation of butterflies returns to the warmer weather of the south.

ARCTIC OCEAN

NORTH AMERICA

PACIFIC OCEAN

ATLANTIC OCEAN

SOUTH AMERICA

MIGRATION MAP KEY

→ WILDEBEEST

→ ARCTIC TERNS

→ ATLANTIC SALMON

→ WHALES

→ EUROPEAN EELS

→ MONARCH BUTTERFLIES

→ BARN SWALLOWS

⬚ LOCUSTS

Each symbol in this key represents the migration route for the animal listed beside it. The symbols correspond with the routes illustrated on the maps.

◄ SALMON
Atlantic salmon hatch in rivers in North America and western Europe. When they mature, they make their way to the sea, and then to their feeding grounds off Greenland in the Atlantic Ocean. After several years, they follow chemical clues in the water to return to where they were born, where they lay their eggs and die.

◄ EUROPEAN EEL LARVA
European eels feed for up to 20 years in rivers in western Europe then, driven by the urge to reproduce, swim downstream and across the Atlantic Ocean to breeding grounds in the Sargasso Sea, off the coast of eastern North America. The newly hatched larvae, such as this one, drift back to Europe on ocean currents.

◄ **ARCTIC TERN**
The Arctic tern migrates further than any other bird, flying from one end of the globe to the other, and back again. The tern nests near the Arctic Circle during the summer in the northern hemisphere, then the bird migrates 12,000 km (7,500 miles) south to feed and to enjoy the summer in the southern hemisphere.

◄ **SWALLOWS**
Swallows spend the winter feeding in the warm climate of southern Africa. In the spring, they migrate to their breeding sites in northern Europe, often returning to the nests they used the previous year. When the adult birds migrate south again, they go before their young, leaving them to find their own way to Africa.

WILDEBEEST ►
At the end of the year, before the start of the wet season, herds of wildebeest set off south across the open plains of east Africa in search of water and fresh grass. These animals are able to sense rain up to 100 km (62 miles) away. In spring, once the rains are over, the herds set off west and north to their summer feeding grounds.

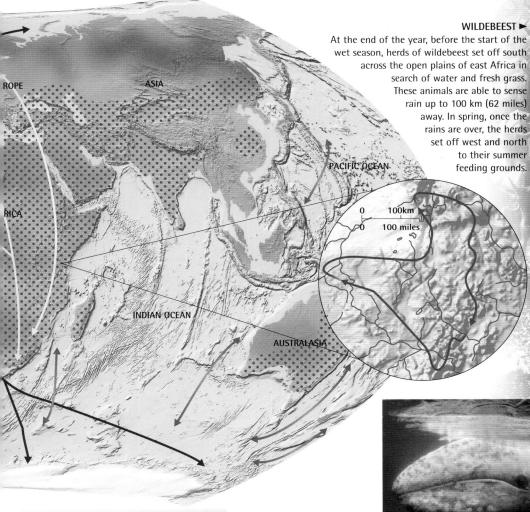

ROPE

ASIA

RICA

PACIFIC OCEAN

0	100km
0	100 miles

INDIAN OCEAN

AUSTRALASIA

◄ **LOCUSTS**
Locust migration is an occasional event. It occurs when food becomes scarce due to locusts overcrowding one area. Travelling up to 3,200 km (2,000 miles) in one year, swarms of locusts follow the prevailing winds, eating every plant in their path. Sometimes, they cause human famines by wiping out swathes of food crops.

▲ **GREY WHALE**
Many large whales feed in cold polar waters, where there is plenty of food, but migrate to warmer areas in the tropics to breed. The grey whale travels from the Arctic to the coast of Mexico. It feeds intensively before the long journey to build up stores of blubber, as food is harder to find in the warmer, tropical waters.

FIND OUT MORE ►► Butterflies 110–111 • Deserts 58–59 • Eels 138 • Salmon 145 • Whales 282–283

ANIMAL HABITATS

◄ **LIFE IN THE FROZEN NORTH**
Like other animals that inhabit the Arctic, the polar bear is superbly adapted to life in the freezing cold. Its long body fur and thick layer of blubber keep it warm on the shifting pack ice. Animals inhabit every part of the Earth, from the icy polar regions and high mountain tops, to the vast oceans and warm, wet rainforests. Wherever they live, animals interact with each other and their surroundings to produce complex, constantly changing environments, called habitats.

◄ GRASSLANDS
Grasslands support big, mobile herds of grazing animals, which are hunted by predators, such as lions and wolves. They also have large populations of smaller animals, such as rodents and insects.

◄ DESERTS
Deserts are dry and dusty, and usually very hot by day. Water is scarce, but many desert animals can survive for long periods without it. The most numerous animals are insects, spiders, scorpions, and reptiles.

◄ RAINFORESTS
Near the equator, a permanently warm, wet climate encourages the growth of lush rainforests. Rainforests are home to an enormous variety of species, including monkeys, parrots, insects, and amphibians.

◄ DECIDUOUS FORESTS
In regions with short, cold winters, deciduous forest trees shed their leaves in autumn and grow fresh ones each spring. Some animals hibernate, or sleep, through the winter, and many birds migrate to warmer regions.

◄ CONIFEROUS FORESTS
The coldest forests are dominated by evergreen, cone-bearing trees like pines and spruces, which can survive long, snowy winters and short summers. The forests are home to insects, birds of prey, and bears.

◄ MOUNTAINS
The higher slopes of mountains are cold and often almost barren, with no trees and a limited variety of plant and animal life. Some animals, such as mountain goats, are specialized for life in this harsh habitat.

HABITATS

All wild animals are adapted to live in particular types of places, or habitats. An Arctic fox, for example, is adapted for living on the frozen tundra, while a camel is specialized for life in deserts. The nature of any habitat is defined by factors such as climate, rock type, and whether it is land or water. These affect the plants that can grow, if any, and this in turn defines many habitats, for example forests and grasslands.

HABITATS OF THE WORLD ►
The major habitats of the world are heavily influenced by the climate. Deserts, for example, occur only in areas with low rainfall, while coral reefs grow only in warm, shallow parts of oceans. The climate of any land habitat is controlled by its distance from the equator and the way moisture carrying winds blow off the oceans.

KEY
- Grassland
- Desert
- Rainforest
- Deciduous forest
- Coniferous forest
- Mountains
- Polar region
- Fresh water
- Coral reef

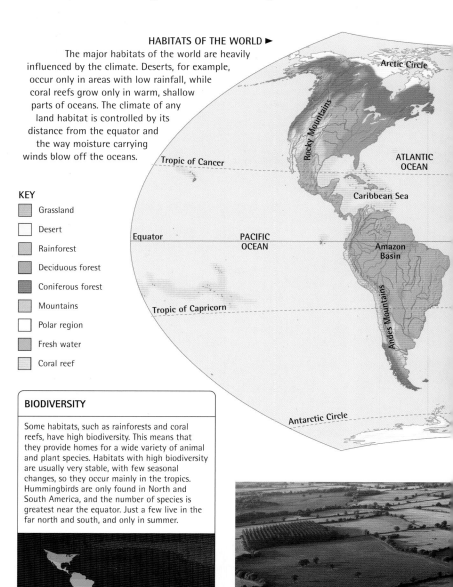

Arctic Circle

Rocky Mountains

Tropic of Cancer

ATLANTIC OCEAN

Caribbean Sea

Equator

PACIFIC OCEAN

Amazon Basin

Andes Mountains

Tropic of Capricorn

Antarctic Circle

BIODIVERSITY

Some habitats, such as rainforests and coral reefs, have high biodiversity. This means that they provide homes for a wide variety of animal and plant species. Habitats with high biodiversity are usually very stable, with few seasonal changes, so they occur mainly in the tropics. Hummingbirds are only found in North and South America, and the number of species is greatest near the equator. Just a few live in the far north and south, and only in summer.

Number of hummingbird species	3	155	60
	10	165	20
	55	110	1

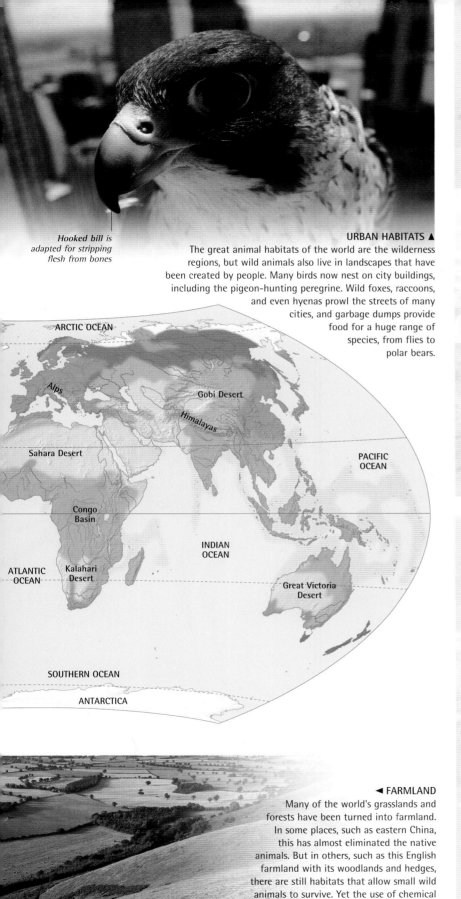

Hooked bill is adapted for stripping flesh from bones

URBAN HABITATS ▲

The great animal habitats of the world are the wilderness regions, but wild animals also live in landscapes that have been created by people. Many birds now nest on city buildings, including the pigeon-hunting peregrine. Wild foxes, raccoons, and even hyenas prowl the streets of many cities, and garbage dumps provide food for a huge range of species, from flies to polar bears.

CAVES ►
Most inland cave systems are formed in limestone rock, which is dissolved by rainwater draining through it. They are used as refuges and breeding sites by bats, cave swifts, and some insects.

POLAR REGIONS ►
In the Arctic, the short summer attracts huge numbers of birds and grazing animals north to breed on the flowering tundra. Few animals live there all year round. In the Antarctic, most animals live in, or on, the sea.

FRESH WATERS ►
Mountain streams and lakes are usually cool and unpolluted. Lowland waters are warmer, with a lot of dissolved nutrients and plants. They contain animals ranging from insects and shrimps to fish and crocodiles.

COASTS ►
Coastal animals have to survive battering waves and rising and falling tides, but the abundant food makes the dangers worthwhile. Sheltered beaches conceal a rich diversity of burrowing shellfish and worms.

CORAL REEFS ►
Reef-building corals live in partnership with tiny algae that can make food. Corals thrive in warm, shallow seas, where they build up complex reef systems that support communities of shellfish, fish, and other animals.

OCEANS ►
The oceans are very deep, but most fish and other ocean animals live near the surface, where they depend on the food made by floating algae. These algae are most abundant in cold, cloudy oceans and shallow coastal waters.

◄ FARMLAND
Many of the world's grasslands and forests have been turned into farmland. In some places, such as eastern China, this has almost eliminated the native animals. But in others, such as this English farmland with its woodlands and hedges, there are still habitats that allow small wild animals to survive. Yet the use of chemical pesticides makes even these landscapes hostile to wildlife.

FIND OUT MORE ►► Deserts 58–59 • Grasslands 56–57 • Mountains 66–67 • Oceans 74–75 • Rainforests 60–61

GRASSLANDS

Natural grasslands grow in continental regions that are too dry for forests to grow, but not dry enough to be deserts. There are two main types: tropical savannas, which have wet and dry seasons, and temperate prairies and steppes, which have hot summers and very cold winters. Grass can survive being grazed close to the ground by animals, but most tree seedlings are destroyed. So grazing helps stop grasslands becoming woodland.

Long wings allow the bird to soar over the plains

◄ SNAKE CATCHER
The long-legged secretary bird of the African savanna is a specialized grassland hawk that hunts by striding over the ground looking for insects, lizards, mice, and snakes. The grass fires that rage across the savanna in the dry season often attract secretary birds. They seize any small animals as they try to flee the flames.

Scaly legs protect against snake bites

◄ INSECT PREY
Tropical grasslands swarm with ants and termites, which live in huge colonies in anthills and termite mounds. Some eat grass seeds, while others gather grass, chew it up, and use it as compost to grow crops of edible fungus. The giant anteater of South America rips into termite mounds with its claws, and uses its long, sticky tongue to catch the insects.

Snout is long and tube-shaped

BURROWING BIRD ►
As trees are scarce on grasslands, many birds nest on the ground. These include the burrowing owl of the American prairies, which usually takes over the abandoned burrow of a rabbit or a ground squirrel. If it cannot find a vacant burrow it digs its own, using its bill and long legs. Unlike most owls, it is active by day.

◄ BUILT FOR SPEED

Many grazers are big, long-legged animals, able to roam widely to find fresh grass. Some make regular seasonal migrations between good grazing areas. Since there is nowhere to hide on the open grasslands, animals like this plains zebra are built for speed and endurance so that they can escape their enemies. But grassland hunters like the lion are also adapted to run fast and often win the chase.

Horns are used for defence and fighting

GRASSLAND BUTTERFLY ►

Many small plants grow among the grasses, and these are vital to insects. For example, European large blue butterflies feed on the nectar of wild thyme and lay their eggs on the plants. The eggs hatch into caterpillars that eat the thyme flowers, and are then carried into the nests of grassland ants, which mistake them for ant grubs. There the caterpillars prey on the real ant grubs until they are ready to become butterflies.

GRAZING HERD ►

Grass is plentiful, but it is not very nourishing. Grazing animals, including American bison, must spend much time eating to get the nutrients they need. They have large stomachs and digestive systems that can process huge quantities of grass. Despite this, there is enough grass to allow hundreds of animals to feed together. This means that they can live in herds for protection against predators, such as wolves.

◄ RECYCLING GANG

Grazing herds produce vast amounts of dung, which is recycled into plant nutrients by millions of microscopic fungi and bacteria. These nutrients make the ground fertile, and fuel the growth of more grass. The mixture of half-digested grass and microbes in the dung can also be used as food by other animals, such as the armies of dung beetles that collect it, roll it into balls, and bury it to feed their young.

LEAF-EATERS ►

Grassland vegetation is dominated by grasses and other small, soft-stemmed plants, but some trees and shrubs grow too. They provide food for specialized browsing animals. On the African savanna these include giraffes, which crop the foliage of tall acacia trees, and the gerenuk – a gazelle that stands on its hind legs to reach the leaves of tall shrubs.

FIND OUT MORE ►► Anteaters **250** • Birds of Prey **206–207** • Butterflies **110–111** • Owls **220–221** • Zebras **291**

DESERTS

Most deserts are in hot regions, where the Sun rapidly dries up any rain. However, deserts also exist in colder areas where it rarely rains, such as the Gobi Desert in central Asia. Much desert ground is bare rock and sand, but some plants and seeds survive the droughts, sprouting during any rare rainfall. These provide food for plant-eating animals, such as rodents, which are preyed on by hunters like cats and foxes.

DEADLY VENOM ►
The scaly skins of snakes and other reptiles prevent them from drying out, so they are well suited to desert life. They are able to survive for long periods without food. However, desert prey is so scarce that they must be sure of killing any animals they catch. This is why desert snakes, such as this desert horned viper, are armed with powerful venom.

Scales form a tough, waterproof layer over the skin

Thick fur on crown acts as insulation from the Sun

Long eyelashes keep dust out of the camel's eyes

Nostrils can be sealed against windblown sand

▲ DUNE DWELLER
This web-footed gecko has membranes between its toes that stop it sinking into soft, dry desert sand. Other animals have special adaptations to help them move across the dunes. These include sidewinder snakes, which coil over over the sand, and legless skinks, such as the sandfish, a snake-like lizard that swims through it.

SURVIVING THE SUN ►
Large desert animals often have nowhere to hide during the day, so they must be able to survive for hours in the intense heat of the Sun. A camel can last for weeks without water, and lose up to a third of its body weight. But when it does drink, it may gulp down as much as 136 litres (30 gallons) of water in just a few hours.

Tough lips can deal with thorny vegetation

◄ NOMADIC GRAZERS
Large grazing animals, such as these southern African gemsbok, have to roam over huge areas of desert to find enough food. These animals are able to travel long distances in the searing heat. They also have an instinct for finding the plants that spring up after rainstorms.

▼ MOBILE WATER SUPPLY
Oases provide vital water for many desert animals. In southwest Africa, male namaqua sandgrouse fly vast distances to gather water for their young. They wade into pools, soak up water in their belly plumage, and fly home like sponges on wings. The chicks then drink the water that runs off the adult's feathers.

UNDERGROUND REFUGE ►
Some desert animals escape the intense heat by spending the day in cool, dark burrows, where the temperature remains comfortable. Small mammals, such as these jerboas, often build underground seed stores. These work like natural air conditioners, soaking up moisture from the air in the burrow at night, and releasing it during the day.

Belly feathers are specially adapted to soak up water

Eye pupils open wide at night to let in more light

Tufted ears can swivel to pinpoint sound from any direction

NECTAR-FEEDING SUNBIRD ▼
Many deserts have fringes of scrubland, where regular seasonal rain allows a much wider variety of plants to grow. Some of these plants have spectacular flowers that attract nectar-feeding birds, such as this South African collared sunbird. As the birds flit from one flower to the next, they carry the pollen that fertilizes the flowers.

NIGHT HUNTER ►
Most desert carnivores are quite small, because food is hard to find. They usually hunt at night, when their prey is active, so they have well-developed senses to locate their targets in the dark. Desert foxes and small cats, such as this Arabian caracal, have large eyes for hunting by starlight, and huge ears that detect the slightest rustle or squeak in the gloom.

Sandy coat acts as camouflage by day

Male sunbird sucks up nectar from the flower

Aloe flowers are adapted to attract birds rather than insects

FIND OUT MORE ►► Grasslands 56–57 • Reptiles 168–169 • Senses 30–31

GREEN CANOPY ▲
The treetops form a continuous green canopy about 20 m (65 ft) above the forest floor. This is dotted with emergent trees, which grow even taller than those around them. The canopy provides a rich, high-level habitat for tree-climbing animals, such as monkeys and sloths, as well as birds like toucans, parrots, and eagles.

RAINFORESTS

As air rises over land near the equator, it draws warm, moist air in from the oceans. This also rises, cooling to form large clouds that drench the ground in heavy rain throughout the year. This warm, wet climate is ideal for trees to grow, and they cover the land in thick, tropical rainforests. The trees carry broad, strong leaves all year round, and there is always a plentiful supply of food for the huge variety of animals.

SHADY UNDERSTOREY ▲
Below the canopy is the understorey, which is made up of smaller trees, shrubs, and a tangle of creepers trailing from the canopy above. It is a dark, humid environment, and is home to a wide range of animals, including lemurs, jaguars, tarantulas, and iguanas.

◄ GLEAMING BLUE
Sunlit forest clearings glitter with the flashing wings of butterflies, such as the blue morphos of South America. The canopy and understorey swarm with butterfly and moth caterpillars, stick insects, and other leaf-eating invertebrates, as well as sap-sucking bugs. These are prey to birds, frogs, and lizards.

CLIMBING FROG ▲
Many rainforest frogs spend their lives up trees, hunting insects. Their large toe-pads stick to the glossy leaves of the forest trees. Some lay eggs in the tiny pools that form in plants growing on branches. Most are well camouflaged, like this duck-billed tree frog.

GROUND LEVEL ▲
Near the forest floor a layer of shrubby undergrowth struggles to survive in the dim light. The forest floor itself is covered with a layer of fallen leaves and other plant debris, and is inhabited by frogs, snakes, spiders, and millions of tiny insects and microbes.

Armoured body protects a fighting beetle from damage

◄ HEAVYWEIGHT FIGHTER
Rainforests are the home of an amazing variety of beetles. Scientists once found at least 600 unknown species of beetle on a single type of rainforest tree. Many are very big, for example the Hercules beetle, which lives in the forests of Central America. Males can be up to 18 cm (7 in) long. They use their long horns to fight over females.

▲ FRUIT LOVERS
Tropical rainforest trees can produce fruit at any time, so many forest animals such as birds, monkeys, and fruit bats feed on fruit throughout the year. Each tree fruits at a different time, so fruit-eaters, such as these Malaysian blue-crowned hanging parrots, spend their day on the move, searching the forest for a ripe, juicy meal.

FOREST MONKEY ▶
The most abundant food in the rainforest is leaves, but they have far less food value than fruit or meat. Most monkeys, such as the Indonesian long-tailed macaque, have a varied diet of leaves, fruit, and flowers. Specially adapted animals, including sloths, can live entirely on leaves.

CANOPY KILLER ▶
Tall trees in the rainforests of the Philippines provide perches for the watchful Philippine eagle. This fearsome hunter usually preys on monkeys and other animals in the treetops, swooping down to rip them from the branches with its powerful talons. It is now extremely rare, because most of its native forests have been cut down.

◄ GLOWING FEATHERS
The orange-bellied leafbird lives in mountain rainforests in southeast Asia, where it forages in the trees for insects, fruit, and nectar. The vivid plumage of the males makes them more eye-catching in the shady understorey, enhancing their courtship displays and improving their chances of breeding.

◄ SLENDER HUNTER
Small animals that live and nest in the rainforest trees are preyed upon by tree snakes, such as this green cat snake. The permanently warm rainforest climate allows snakes and other ectothermic (cold-blooded) animals to stay active all year round. Snakes in more seasonal climates often spend part of the year hibernating, hidden away from the cold.

◄ SEED SPREADER
Most rainforest mammals live in the trees, but the South American tapir roams the forest floor looking for juicy leaves and fallen fruit. As it feeds it swallows a lot of seeds. They pass through its gut and are dumped with its dung in another part of the forest, where they grow into new trees. Many tree species rely on tapirs to spread their seed like this.

Silver scales make the pacu glint like a coin

◄ FLOATING FEAST
Even fish benefit from the fruit crop of tropical rainforests. In South America, the pacu, or silver dollarfish, often eats the fruit that falls from trees overhanging the river bank. When rainforest rivers like the Amazon flood during rainy seasons, fish are able to swim among the trees and gather food from their submerged foliage.

FIND OUT MORE ▶▶ Beetles **106–107** • Butterflies **110–111** • Hoofed Mammals **289** • Parrots **216–217** • Primates **256**

CLOUDED LEOPARD

The clouded leopard is an agile climber. It uses its long tail to help it keep its balance as it leaps from tree to tree in the dense rainforests of southeast Asia. The clouded leopard is the smallest of the big cats. Its distinctive coat, with irregular cloud shapes on a tawny, grey, or silver background, give the leopard its name. It is now at risk of extinction, mainly due to the loss of its habitat through deforestation. It has also been hunted for its distinctive fur, and for its teeth and bones, which, like those of the tiger, are used in traditional Chinese medicine.

Scientific name: *Neofelis nebulosa*

Order: Carnivora (carnivores)

Class: Mammalia (mammals)

Distribution: Southeast Asia

Status: Vulnerable

Length: 60–110 cm (22–36 in)

Weight: 16–23 kg (35–51 lb)

Food: Reptiles, birds, and smaller mammals, including monkeys and wild boar

Number of young: 2–4 in a litter

FIND OUT MORE ▸▸ Big Cats **268** • Mammals **240–241** • Rainforests **60–61**

DECIDUOUS FORESTS

Deciduous forests flourish in temperate regions with warm summers and cold winters. Deciduous trees, such as oak, beech, and maple, have thin, broad leaves that are shed every autumn. They are replaced with a new set of leaves each spring. The lives of the animals that live in these deciduous forests are controlled by the seasons too. In spring, insects hatch out and migrating birds arrive. In autumn, animals gorge on food to prepare for winter.

◄ SPRING FEVER
Spring is a time of frenzied activity in deciduous forests. Millions of caterpillars hatch out to feast on the tender new leaves. Insect-eating birds, such as this pied flycatcher, return from the tropics to breed, and they feed their chicks on the abundant caterpillars. Predators, such as sparrowhawks, also breed in spring, when their prey is plentiful and their young have time to learn their hunting skills before winter.

HARD WINTER ▲
In winter, food is scarce. Some animals hide away or migrate to warmer regions, but others stay active in the forest. Meat-eaters, such as foxes, can catch small animals or scavenge from carcasses, but plant-eaters, including these fallow deer, may have problems finding enough to eat beneath the snow. Some die, providing more food for scavengers.

▼ CHILLING DOWN
Many birds leave the forest in winter and fly to the tropics where they can find food. Small animals cannot do this, so some survive by falling into a deep sleep called hibernation. The European hazel dormouse curls up in a well-insulated nest near the forest floor. Its body temperature falls and its heartbeat slows right down to save energy until it wakes up in spring.

SPOTTY SALAMANDER ►
The leaves that fall in autumn rot down to create rich soils. These support plants, fungi, and small animals such as earthworms, slugs, and beetles. Ground-living animals, such as this salamander, find plenty to eat in spring, summer, and autumn, but in winter they hide underground, away from the bitter cold.

Skin has brightly coloured pattern to warn predators of poisons in skin

FIND OUT MORE ►► Deer **298** • Rodents **302** • Salamanders **164–165**

CONIFEROUS FORESTS

In the cold northern forests, the short summers and long winters favour evergreen trees with tough, frost-proof needles instead of leaves. The trees bear their seeds in woody cones and are known as conifers. Coniferous forests are harsh habitats for animals, so there are fewer species than in the warmer forests to the south. Many animals are well adapted for the cold, with thick fur or feathers that allow them to stay active through the snowbound winters.

Male has reddish plumage; female is grey-green

SEEDS PULLED FROM CONE

Bill crosses at the tip

▲ FOREST HAWK
Like other hunters, the northern goshawk can usually find plenty of prey, because many small animals, such as squirrels, voles, and snowshoe hares, stay active in winter. The goshawk has relatively short, rounded wings, and a long tail, giving it the ability to swerve between branches at high speed.

Pine cones are glossy green when young

TIMBER DRILL ▶
Insects spend the winters hidden from the cold, emerging in huge numbers in summer. Swarms of blood-sucking flies fill the air, and armies of moth caterpillars strip the foliage from trees. Female wood wasps, such as this one, drill into timber with their sharp tails and lay their eggs. The wasp grubs live in the timber for up to three years, before emerging as winged adults.

Ears are tufted and pointed

▲ CONE CRACKER
Most of the birds that spend the summer in coniferous forests fly south to find food in winter. The red crossbill is a specialized finch that usually stays behind to feed on the seeds of conifers, such as spruce and pine. Its strange crossed bill is adapted for prising the cone scales apart, so it can scoop out the seeds with its tongue.

▶ SITTING TARGET
The red squirrels of northern Europe and Asia are conifer specialists. In winter, they feed high in the trees, stripping the cones to get at their seeds. As they do so they risk being seized by hungry goshawks, which pluck them from the branches, or by agile, pine martens hunting through the treetops.

FIND OUT MORE ▶▶ Adaptation **18** • Birds of Prey **206–207** • Finches **236** • Squirrels **303** • Wasps **113** • Weasels **277**

MOUNTAINS

High mountains are harsh habitats for animals. The rock is constantly being eroded (worn away) by rain and frost, because the climate is wetter and colder than in the lowlands. This creates craggy landscapes with thin soils, often covered by snow. Forest often grows on the lower slopes, but above the tree line (the highest point at which trees can grow) the trees are replaced by scrub and then alpine grassland. The animals also become more scarce and specialized, and some species are very rare.

Dense fur is camouflaged to blend with rocks and snow

◄ HIMALAYAN HUNTERS
Powerful predators are scarce on high mountains, because large prey is hard to find. They have to roam widely to find enough food, and often survive by scavenging. Many also live at lower altitudes, but the snow leopard of central Asia is a mountain specialist. It has a thick coat to keep out the cold, and a large cavity inside its nose that helps warm up the air that it breathes. Together they enable this big cat to live in snowbound regions with temperatures that plunge to -40°C (-40°F) in winter.

Thick tail is very long to improve balance on precipices

▲ ETHIOPIAN WOLVES
Mountain ranges that are surrounded by lowlands are like islands of wildlife. The animals that live in these areas are cut off from others of their kind, and they often evolve (develop) in unique ways. They include the Ethiopian wolf, the rarest species of dog on Earth. It lives in the mountains of Ethiopia, where fewer than 450 survive on the icy, open grasslands high above the tree line.

CRAG JUMPER ►
Mountain goats are specialized for living on cliffs and crags, and they are famous for being agile and sure-footed. Some species are solitary, and defend rare pockets of good grazing land as their own feeding territories. Others, such as the chamois of southern Europe, live in flocks that have to range over large areas to find enough food, and often migrate down the mountains to escape the winter snow.

FIND OUT MORE ►► Big Cats **268** • Birds of Prey **206–207** • Dogs **272** • Migration **50–51** • Sheep **300** • Wolves **273**

Sharp eyes can spot food from high in the sky

▲ RIDING THE WIND
The lammergeier of European, Asian, and African mountains is one of the most skilful mountain fliers. It spends hours in the air, soaring on rising air currents with barely a wingbeat as it searches for the carcasses of animals that have lost the fight for survival in the harsh mountain climate.

▲ MOUNTAIN BEAUTY
Mountain grasslands are often bright with flowers in summer. These attract nectar-feeding animals, such as hummingbirds and butterflies. The Apollo butterfly lives in the European Alps, where it often feeds in high, rocky pastures. It spends a lot of its time basking to keep warm, holding its body close to the bare rocks that soak up the Sun's rays.

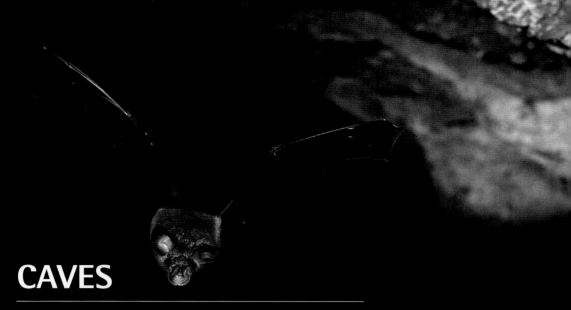

CAVES

Rainwater seeping down through cracks in limestone rock dissolves it like sugar, creating networks of tunnels, caverns, and underground rivers in limestone regions. These caves contain very little food for animals, because plants cannot grow in the dark. But they provide safe refuges for some animals, which leave the caves to find food elsewhere. Caves are insulated from the extreme heat and cold outside, so they make ideal breeding nurseries for animals such as bats and cave swifts.

▲ DAYTIME RETREAT
Bats navigate through caves using echolocation. As they fly they produce streams of high-pitched clicks. Echoes bounce off the rock walls, so that the bats can avoid them in the total darkness. This allows species like this Australian horseshoe bat to remain in dark caves by day and fly out to hunt at night.

◄ CAVE CRICKET
Colonies of bats and cave-breeding birds produce masses of dung, which provides food for cave-dwelling insects. These include cave crickets, which feel their way through the darkness with their extremely long, hair-like antennae. Like most animals that live in caves, these crickets will eat almost anything, including all kinds of debris, hibernating butterflies and moths, and even other cave crickets.

Body is humpbacked and wingless

Antennae are a cave cricket's main sense organs

Long legs allow the cricket to jump and climb

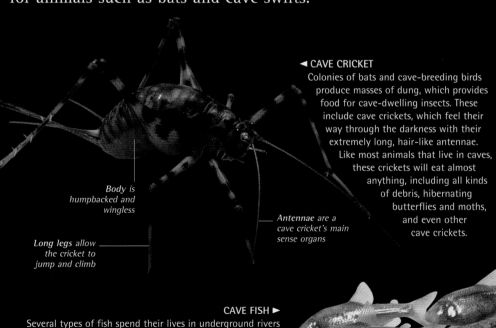

CAVE FISH ►
Several types of fish spend their lives in underground rivers and pools. They feed on edible debris and small animals that have been washed into the cave from the world outside. Some species, including these blind cave characins, have been living and breeding in the total darkness of caves for hundreds of years. Over time they have lost their eyes and skin colour, and their blood shows red through their transparent scales.

FIND OUT MORE ►► Adaptation **18–19** • Animal Homes **48–49** • Bats **254–255**

CHINSTRAP PENGUINS

These penguins are at home in some of the coldest and roughest seas in the world. Icebergs and pack ice offer the species a safe resting place between fishing trips, but if the floating ice spreads too far, it can prevent the birds from diving to feed. Each pair usually raises two young.

Scientific name: *Pygoscelis antarctica*	**Weight:** 3–4.5 kg (6½–10 lb)
Order: Sphenisciformes (penguins)	**Food:** Krill (shrimp-like crustaceans); a few fish
Class: Aves (birds)	**Reproduction:** Breeds in crowded colonies; each pair builds a nest from stones, bones, and feathers
Distribution: Seas and oceans all around Antarctica, as far north as the southern tip of South America	
	Number of young: 2
Status: Common	
Length: 71–76 cm (28–30 in)	FIND OUT MORE ▸▸ Penguins **195** • Polar Regions **70**

Strong wings enable snow geese to fly for hours on end

Big beak is adapted for gathering plant food

◄ MIGRATING SNOW GEESE
When the snow melts in spring, the Arctic tundra bursts into life. Tough plants start growing and flowering, and flies and other insects hatch in their millions. Vast numbers of geese, swans, and wading birds migrate north to nest and feed their chicks on the plants and swarming insect life. Snow geese may fly up to 3,500 km (2,000 miles) from the Gulf of Mexico, to nest in huge colonies on the islands of Arctic Canada.

POLAR REGIONS

In the polar regions, low temperatures prevent all the snow from melting in summer, and vast ice sheets have been created that cover most of Greenland and Antarctica. These areas are almost lifeless, and all the polar animals live either on the fringes of the ice sheets in the tundra, where the snow does melt in summer, or in the oceans. In winter, both the tundra and ocean surface freeze up, forcing most of the animals to migrate to warmer regions.

▲ ICE PROWLERS
Many animals leave the polar regions in winter, but in the Arctic the winter ice makes life easier for polar bears. As the ocean surface freezes, the bears can move out onto the sea ice to hunt seals. They are often trailed by Arctic foxes hoping to scavenge scraps from the remains of bear kills. Both have extremely thick fur to keep out the cold.

▲ OCEAN HUNTER
The icy oceans around Antarctica are rich in nutrients, providing food for a variety of fish, whales, penguins, seabirds, and seals. They include the Weddell seal, which hunts for fish beneath the sea ice. It bites holes in the ice so it can come to the surface to breathe, so most Weddell seals suffer from damaged teeth. Most other Antarctic seals hunt on the edge of the sea ice.

▲ SNOW COVER
Lemmings and other small animals can survive Arctic winters by feeding in their burrows under the snow, which insulates them from the bitterly cold winds. They are also hidden from airborne enemies like snowy owls. Yet they are not completely safe. They can be caught by weasels that are slim enough to chase them through their runs.

FIND OUT MORE ▶▶ Bears **274–275** • Chinstrap Penguins **68–69** • Migration **50–51** • Seals **280–281** • Wildfowl **202–203**

FRESH WATER

Rain falling on the land flows back to the sea as streams and rivers, and gathers in ponds, lakes, and swampy wetlands. These freshwater habitats are home to insects, fish, birds, amphibians, and mammals. Mountain streams and lakes are cool, pure, and beautifully clear, but they do not contain large numbers of plants and animals. The warmer, more fertile waters of lowland rivers and lakes can support more animals, but the diversity of species is often quite limited.

Wingspan can be up to 2.5 m (8¼ ft) across

▲ TOP PREDATOR
In autumn, thousands of American bald eagles gather on Alaskan rivers to prey on the Pacific salmon swimming upriver to breed. After they spawn, the fish are exhausted. The eagles can just wade into the shallows, seize them in their powerful talons, and carry them off.

FRESHWATER CRUSTACEAN ▶
Waters that contain a lot of dissolved calcium (lime) are ideal for shell-building creatures, such as snails, water fleas, shrimps, and this freshwater crayfish. These abundant animals provide plenty of food for fish, such as trout, which are caught by bigger predators like otters. Streams and lakes with very little calcium support fewer animals.

SALTWATER SHRIMP

In hot regions, lake water can evaporate quickly. This increases the saltiness of the water to create salt lakes. Very few animals can live in these lakes, but they often occur in vast numbers, like the brine shrimps that swarm in the Great Salt Lake of Utah, United States.

◀ FRESHWATER BREEDER
Most amphibians, such as this Australian brown-striped frog, depend on fresh water for breeding. The females lay their eggs in the water, and the males fertilize the eggs as they are laid. Their young start life as swimming tadpoles, but eventually they develop legs and are able to live and hunt on land.

FLY STRIKE ▶
Many large freshwater fish are voracious predators of smaller fish, insects, and other aquatic animals. This American largemouth bass is targeting a dragonfly perched on a waterlily flower. When big fish like this are introduced to lakes by humans, to stock the water for fishing, they can destroy many other fish. For example, the Nile perch was introduced to Africa's Lake Victoria in the 1960s, and has made hundreds of small, local species extinct.

FIND OUT MORE ▶▶ Birds of Prey **206–207** • Crustaceans **117** • Dragonflies **100** • Gamefish **146–147** • Frogs **160–161**

COASTS

The frontier between the land and the sea can be a violent, dangerous place for animals to live. Storm waves smash into exposed, rocky shores, crumbling them into stones and sand. The water sweeps these away and deposits them on sheltered shores as shingle banks and sandy beaches. The two types of shore are inhabited by different types of animals, which must also survive being covered and exposed twice a day by the rising and falling tide.

▲ BEACH PARTY

Seabirds, sea turtles, and seals live at sea, but they must return to land to lay their eggs or have young. These Cape fur seals, which live in southern Africa and Australia, form breeding colonies on beaches. After a female gives birth to a pup, she mates with the male in whose territory she has settled. When the pups are old enough the colonies break up.

◄ COASTAL BIRDS

Huge numbers of burrowing molluscs, worms, and other animals live buried in the soft sand or mud of quiet beaches. They are eaten by shorebirds, such as these dunlin, which use their long bills to probe for prey. When the tide rises they gather in flocks above the tide line, waiting for the water to ebb away so they can start feeding again.

BENEATH THE BEACH

A beach may look almost deserted, but there may be millions of animals hidden in the sand. They include molluscs, such as cockles and sand gapers; worms, such as lugworms and ragworms; and crustaceans, such as the masked crab. Some gather food from the sand, while others strain food fragments from the water when the tide comes in.

Shells clamp shut when the mussels are left high and dry

◄ SHELL PROTECTION

Many of the animals that live on exposed rocky shores spend their adult lives clinging to the rock. These barnacle-encrusted mussels have tough shells to protect them from wave-tossed stones, and to stop them drying up when the tide goes out. When the tide comes in again, the two halves of the shell open so the animal can filter food from the water.

1. Ribbon worm
2. Tellins
3. Sea mouse
4. Razor shell
5. Cockle
6. Ragworm
7. Peacock worm
8. Masked crab
9. Sea potato
10. Lugworm
11. Sand gaper
12. Sand mason worm

FIND OUT MORE ▶▶ Crabs 120 • Ecology 14–15 • Molluscs 86 • Oceans 74–75 • Seals 280–281 • Shorebirds 212–213

CORAL REEFS

Tropical coral reefs are created by simple marine animals that live in colonies supported by rocky limestone skeletons. Microscopic organisms called algae live in the corals, and make food using sunlight. This allows them to live in clear, warm water where nutrients are scarce. The food produced by the reef supports an amazing variety of fish, molluscs, and other animals, making coral reefs some of the richest of all marine habitats.

▲ DAZZLING DIVERSITY
The array of animals living on a reef includes many types of coral, fish, crustaceans, crabs, sea slugs, starfish, and sea urchins. Each species has developed specialized ways of living on the reef, so that they do not compete with each other. The total number of any one species on a reef is usually quite small, but the diversity of species is often astounding.

FEEDING PARTNERS ▶
Each individual coral resembles a sea anemone, with stinging tentacles for snaring tiny animals drifting in the water. When corals digest their prey, they pass some of the nutrients to the algae that live within their bodies. Meanwhile the algae manufacture different types of nutrients using solar energy, just as plants do, and this process provides the corals with most of their food.

▲ MALDIVES ATOLL
Many islands in the Indian Ocean and south Pacific are surrounded by coral reefs. Some ancient volcanic islands have sunk over time, but their reefs have continue to grow upwards to create ring-shaped coral atolls, such as this one. The outer edges of the reef rise like sheer cliffs from the deep, dark-blue ocean water, but the inner edges slope gently into a shallow central lagoon that is lined with gleaming coral sand.

REEF PATROL ▶
The deeper water on the outside of a reef is patrolled by powerful predators, such as sharks and barracudas, which are attracted by the shoaling fish and other prey. This hammerhead shark may also hunt in the shallow waters on the landward side of the reef. It uses sensors on its wing-shaped head to detect stingrays buried in the sand.

FIND OUT MORE ▶▶ Coral Reef Fish 148–149 • Corals 81 • Sea Anemones 81 • Sharks 131 • Sponges 80

OCEANS

The oceans cover more than three-quarters of the Earth, and have an average depth of more than 3.7 km (2.3 miles). Most ocean animals live in the sunlit zone near the surface. This is because their food supply depends on tiny floating algae that make food using the energy of the Sun. Few animals live in the dark depths of the ocean as it is freezing cold, the water pressure is immense, and there is little food.

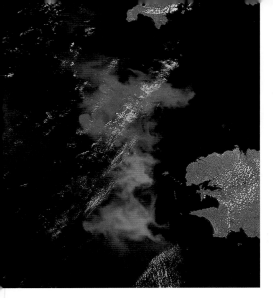

▲ TEEMING WITH LIFE
Some ocean waters contain more plant nutrients than others. These are absorbed by floating algae, which multiply to cover vast areas. This view from space shows one of these blooms of algae in the North Atlantic, off northern France. The cloudy green waters of such regions are much richer in food than the clear blue oceans of the tropics.

MICROLIFE ▶
The microscopic floating algae in oceans are eaten by tiny, drifting animals. Many of these, including this larval locust lobster, are the young forms of animals that live on the coast or seabed. Many larvae do not survive to adulthood – they are eaten by fish, jellyfish, shellfish, and even whales.

Nostrils and other sensory organs guide the shark to plankton swarms

Jellyfish gather plankton using their stinging tentacles

Gill rakers protect the delicate gills and snare the plankton

▲ OCEAN MAMMAL
The oceans contain so much food that some air-breathing mammals have adapted to live in them. They include whales and dolphins, which spend their entire lives in the oceans, and seals, which feed in the oceans but breed on land or floating ice. This New Zealand fur seal is hunting for fish in a coastal kelp forest of giant seaweed.

PLANKTON SWARMS ▶
Cloudy green waters are thick with microscopic algae and animals, known as plankton. They attract specialized plankton-feeders, such as the basking shark, one of the biggest fish in the sea. As it ploughs through a plankton swarm with its mouth wide open, it strains the water through the huge gill slits in its cheeks, gathering its tiny prey by the million.

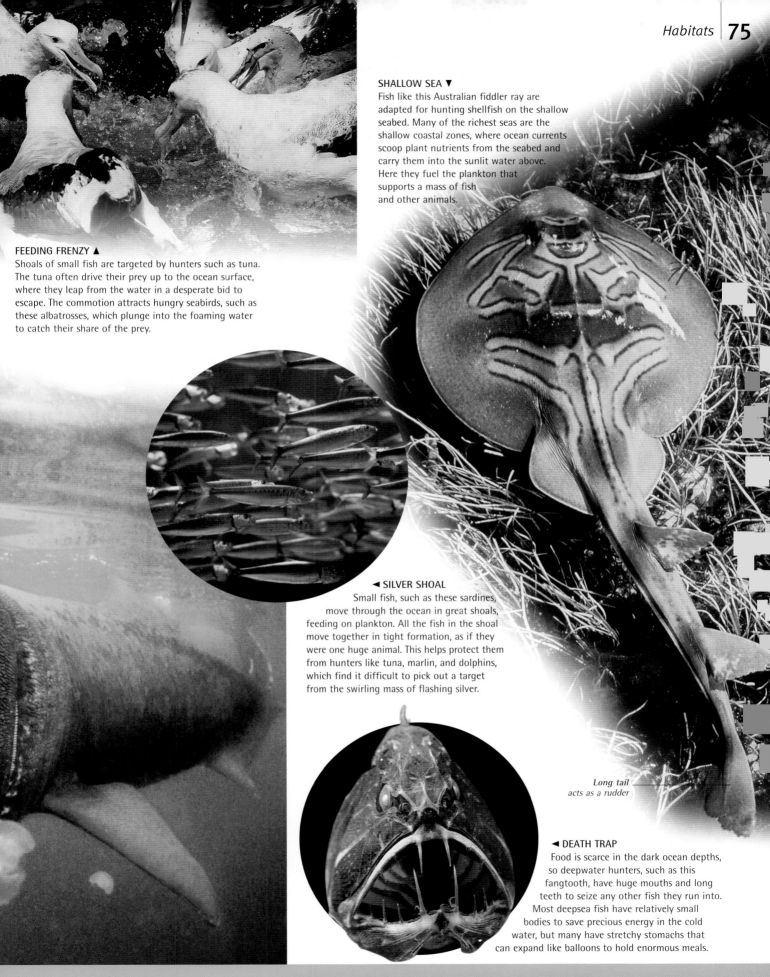

FEEDING FRENZY ▲
Shoals of small fish are targeted by hunters such as tuna.
The tuna often drive their prey up to the ocean surface,
where they leap from the water in a desperate bid to
escape. The commotion attracts hungry seabirds, such as
these albatrosses, which plunge into the foaming water
to catch their share of the prey.

SHALLOW SEA ▼
Fish like this Australian fiddler ray are
adapted for hunting shellfish on the shallow
seabed. Many of the richest seas are the
shallow coastal zones, where ocean currents
scoop plant nutrients from the seabed and
carry them into the sunlit water above.
Here they fuel the plankton that
supports a mass of fish
and other animals.

◄ SILVER SHOAL
Small fish, such as these sardines,
move through the ocean in great shoals,
feeding on plankton. All the fish in the shoal
move together in tight formation, as if they
were one huge animal. This helps protect them
from hunters like tuna, marlin, and dolphins,
which find it difficult to pick out a target
from the swirling mass of flashing silver.

*Long tail
acts as a rudder*

◄ DEATH TRAP
Food is scarce in the dark ocean depths,
so deepwater hunters, such as this
fangtooth, have huge mouths and long
teeth to seize any other fish they run into.
Most deepsea fish have relatively small
bodies to save precious energy in the cold
water, but many have stretchy stomachs that
can expand like balloons to hold enormous meals.

FIND OUT MORE ▸▸ Albatrosses **197** • Deepsea Fish **154–155** • Rays **130** • Seals **280–281** • Sharks **131** • Whales **282–283**

INVERTEBRATES

◄ BRIGHTLY COLOURED BUTTERFLY
Monarch butterflies feed on flower nectar and are well known for their long-distance migrations across North and Central America. Butterflies belong to a group of animals called insects. They are also invertebrates (animals without backbones). Invertebrates are the most numerous animals on Earth, and many species are still waiting to be discovered.

INVERTEBRATES

Invertebrates are animals that do not have a backbone, or bones of any kind. They are much more varied than vertebrates (animals with backbones), and make up over 95 per cent of all animal species. Invertebrates live in every kind of habitat, but are most common in the sea. Many are microscopic, but the largest are over 18 m (60 ft) long. Most invertebrates change shape as they grow up – a process called metamorphosis.

◄ TEEMING LIFE
Using their long tentacles, these hydromedusa jellyfish catch small animals near the surface of the open sea. Vast numbers of invertebrates drift with ocean currents, forming a mass of life called plankton. Some, including jellyfish, feed on smaller creatures around them. Others feed on tiny plant-like organisms called algae.

Transparent bell opens and closes, pushing the jellyfish through the water

◄ EARLY INVERTEBRATE
This fossil was left by a trilobite - an invertebrate that lived on the seabed over 400 million years ago. Trilobites were a widespread group of animals, with hard outer parts that fossilized easily. The first invertebrates were soft-bodied, which means that they left far fewer remains – the oldest known are from Australia, and are at least 550 million years old.

Body case has joints to allow movement of muscles underneath

▼ SKELETONS AND SHELLS
Invertebrates do not have bones, but many of them have other ways of supporting their bodies. The body of an earthworm is hydrostatic - it is kept firm by body fluid. Molluscs, such as this scallop, have hard shells, while arthropods, such as this beetle, have a body case called an exoskeleton. This consists of hard plates that meet at flexible joints.

SCARAB BEETLE

Smooth saddle is located near the head end of the worm

Hinged shell protects the soft body of the mollusc

COMMON EARTHWORM

Fluid-filled segments and muscle keep the worm firm

QUEEN SCALLOP

MAJOR INVERTEBRATE GROUPS

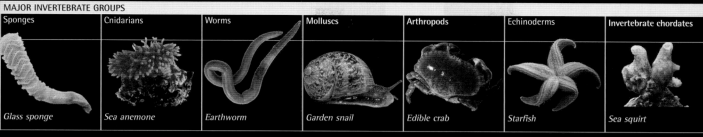

Sponges	Cnidarians	Worms	Molluscs	Arthropods	Echinoderms	Invertebrate chordates
Glass sponge	*Sea anemone*	*Earthworm*	*Garden snail*	*Edible crab*	*Starfish*	*Sea squirt*

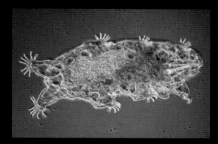

◄ MICRO-ANIMAL

This eight-legged invertebrate, called a tardigrade or water bear, is so small that it is visible only with a microscope. Despite being tiny, it has simple eyes and a brain, and can clamber about to find food. Because it is so minute, it can live in the smallest of habitats, such as the film of moisture that surrounds individual specks of soil. There are many other invertebrates that are microscopic.

Adult sea squirt has a bag-shaped body

◄ INVERTEBRATE CHORDATES

Sea squirts are invertebrates that have a strengthening rod that runs down their bodies. The rod, called a notochord, is also found in the embryos of vertebrates. As a vertebrate embryo grows, the notochord is replaced by the backbone. Animals that have a notochord at some point in their life cycle are called chordates.

METAMORPHOSIS

YOUNG
After feeding and growing for several weeks, this silk moth caterpillar has stopped eating and started to spin a silk cocoon. Inside the cocoon, its body will change into that of an adult moth. This change between the two stages in a silk moth's life is called metamorphosis.

ADULT
Unlike a caterpillar, the adult silk moth has working reproductive organs and two pairs of wings. It has tube-like mouthparts, instead of jaws, but it rarely feeds. Its job is to find a mate, so that it can reproduce and help the species to spread.

Carapace (hard shield) covers the crab's back

Compound eyes on stalks give all-round vision

Eggs are held in place by the crab's tail until they hatch out as tiny larvae

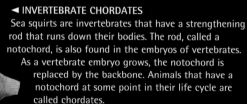

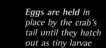

PARENTAL CARE

The velvet crab guards a clutch of eggs, which she carries beneath her body. This kind of behaviour is unusual in invertebrates, because most abandon their eggs, leaving their young to fend for themselves. Crabs carry their eggs until they have hatched, but some invertebrates – such as spiders and scorpions – carry their young on their backs until they are ready to start living on their own.

Large pincer claws raised to guard clutch of eggs

FIND OUT MORE ▸▸I Anatomy **26–27** • Arthropods **90** • Classification **308–309** • Crustaceans **117** • Insects **97**

SPONGES

Among the world's simplest animals, sponges are invertebrates that spend their adult lives fastened in one place. They feed by pumping water through their bodies to filter out any food that it contains. Their bodies are reinforced by a mesh of tiny fibres that gives them a spongy feel. Some live in fresh water, but most grow in the sea. The smallest are as tiny as a full stop, but the largest can be 2 m (6½ ft) wide.

HOW SPONGES FEED

Sponges feed by sucking in water through hundreds of pores, called ostia. Collar cells inside the sponge act like tiny pumps to create a current of water. As the water flows through the cells, they filter out food, such as minute plants and animals. The filtered water leaves through the osculum – a vent-like opening.

Water passes out through osculum (vent)

Collar cells collect food

Tube-shaped body attached to a stalk

Pore allows sea water to travel through the sponge

BODY OF A SIMPLE SPONGE

Glass-like spicules form a hollow lattice

GLASS SPONGE SKELETON

BATH SPONGE SKELETON

▲ SPONGE SKELETONS

Sponges have internal skeletons made from protein fibres, and specks of minerals called spicules. Glass sponges have brittle skeletons, because their spicules are made of silica – a mineral found in glass. Bath sponges are unusual in not having spicules. The fibres of a bath sponge are elastic, so the sponge regains its shape after it has been squeezed.

Shape of sponge is kept firm by a mesh of fibres

Water is expelled through the top of each vase

Sponge holds fast to rocks and filters food from the water

▲ TROPICAL VASE SPONGE

Some sponges are flat, but this tropical vase sponge looks like a collection of pipes, reaching up to 1 m (3⅓ ft) high. Its specialized shape gives it a large surface area through which to filter food from the surrounding water. There are over 5,000 kinds of sponges, and they are particularly common in sea caves and on coral reefs.

SPONGE BURROWS ►

Tiny sponges have bored into this shell, to keep out of harm's way. Although most sponges are soft, some of the smallest kinds can bore through shells, coral, and even solid rock. They do this by releasing an acid, which dissolves hard substances. Burrowing sponges help to consolidate reefs by breaking dead coral into small fragments, which slowly pack together.

Small holes bored into an oyster shell by individual sponges

FIND OUT MORE ►► Coral Reef Fish **148–149** • Coral Reefs **73** • Invertebrates **78–79**

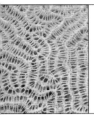

BRAIN CORAL
This coral often resembles a rounded boulder, 1 m (3⅓ ft) or more across, and is covered with winding grooves, like a brain. It can grow on the seaward edges of reefs, because it can withstand the pounding surf.

STAGHORN CORAL
The tips of this branched coral are rounded or spiky. One of the fastest-growing corals, it increases by up to 15 cm (6 in) a year. It needs lots of light and breaks quite easily, so it grows in the sheltered parts of reefs.

MUSHROOM CORAL
Unlike most reef-building corals, this type consists of a single polyp. It can be over 10 cm (4 in) across and lies on the reef or the seabed. If it is flipped over by the waves, it uses its tentacles to pull itself the right way up.

ORGAN-PIPE CORAL
In this coral, the polyps live in parallel rows, encased in tubes that look like tiny organ pipes. The living polyps are green, but the tubes that form their protective cases are made of a dark red limestone.

CORALS

Although they resemble plants, corals are simple sea-dwelling animals. They have soft bodies, known as polyps, and stinging tentacles. Many live in groups, called colonies, and grow calcium-rich cases for protection. These slowly build up to form reefs. Corals belong to a group of animals called cnidarians.

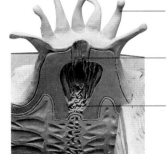

Tentacles are armed with stinging cells

Mouth can stretch wide to swallow food

Body cavity where food is digested and absorbed

▲ CORAL POLYP
Coral polyps have hollow bodies, with a single opening, the mouth, at the top. This is surrounded by a ring of stinging tentacles, which catch and pass food through the mouth to the body cavity below. At the base of the polyp is the hard cup, or case, within which it grows.

CORAL REEF ▲
Most reef-building corals live in clear seas, in parts of the world where the temperature never drops below 20°C (68°F). Coral reefs can be thousands of years old, and they are the richest habitats in the sea. The Great Barrier Reef, off Australia's east coast, is a single reef over 2,000 km (1,250 miles) long.

FIND OUT MORE ▶▶ Coral Reefs **73** • Invertebrates **78–79** • Jellyfish **84** • Sea Anemones **81**

SEA ANEMONES

Sea anemones are cnidarians – a group of invertebrates that have hollow bodies and a ring of stinging tentacles. However, unlike corals, they do not build cases, and they are usually solitary. Some species bury themselves in sand, but most use a strong sucker to fasten themselves to rocks or reefs.

Mediterranean anemone has thick tentacles with violet tips

Beadlet anemone can be green, red, or brown

Plumose anemone has a tuft of very fine tentacles

TENTACLE TRAP ▶
With their tentacles stretched out, these sea anemones are ready to trap any animals that come nearby. If one tentacle touches something edible, others quickly fold over the food, inflicting thousands of simultaneous stings. At low tide, many shoreline anemones pull in their tentacles, to prevent their bodies from drying out.

FIND OUT MORE ▶▶ Invertebrates **78–79** • Jellyfish **84**

ANTARCTIC JELLYFISH

Expanding the pink folds of its umbrella-shaped bell, this huge Antarctic jellyfish gently propels itself along under the ice of the Antarctic Ocean. It feeds on the seabed, as well as in the surface waters, killing small animals with the stinging cells on its tentacles. Competition for food is fierce in these icy waters. The long, cord-like tentacles of this jellyfish have been torn away from the bell by another predator, such as a sea anemone.

Scientific name: *Desmonema glaciale*

Order: Semaeostomeae (saucer-shaped jellyfish)

Class: Scyphozoa (jellyfish)

Distribution: On the Antarctic continental shelf, around the Antarctic peninsula, South Orkney Islands, and South Georgia island

Diameter: Bell up to 1 m (3⅓ ft) across

Length: Tentacles up to 9 m (30 ft)

Food: Feeds by day and at night on free-swimming and bottom-dwelling prey, including small fish, starfish, and worms

Life cycle: Life cycle follows several stages, including egg, swimming larva, anchored polyp, and free-swimming medusa (bell)

FIND OUT MORE ▸▸ Invertebrates 78–79 • Jellyfish 84 • Movement 28–29

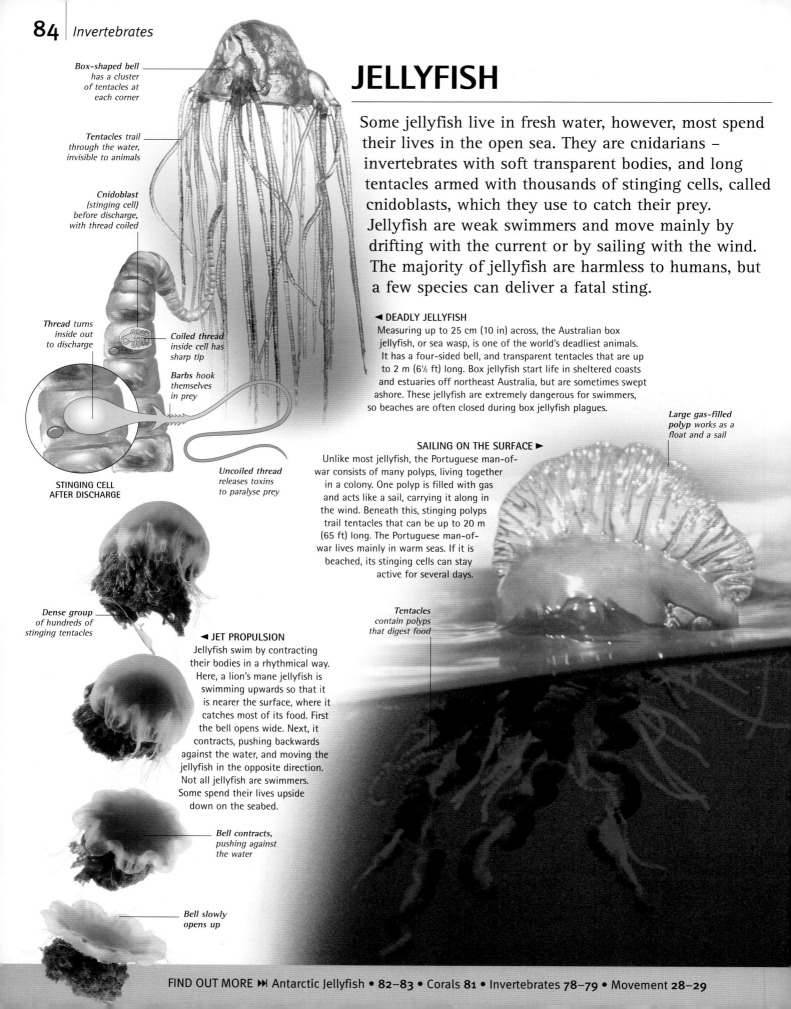

Box-shaped bell
has a cluster
of tentacles at
each corner

Tentacles trail
through the water,
invisible to animals

Cnidoblast
(stinging cell)
before discharge,
with thread coiled

Thread turns
inside out
to discharge

Coiled thread
inside cell has
sharp tip

Barbs hook
themselves
in prey

**STINGING CELL
AFTER DISCHARGE**

Uncoiled thread
releases toxins
to paralyse prey

Dense group
of hundreds of
stinging tentacles

JELLYFISH

Some jellyfish live in fresh water, however, most spend their lives in the open sea. They are cnidarians – invertebrates with soft transparent bodies, and long tentacles armed with thousands of stinging cells, called cnidoblasts, which they use to catch their prey. Jellyfish are weak swimmers and move mainly by drifting with the current or by sailing with the wind. The majority of jellyfish are harmless to humans, but a few species can deliver a fatal sting.

◄ DEADLY JELLYFISH
Measuring up to 25 cm (10 in) across, the Australian box jellyfish, or sea wasp, is one of the world's deadliest animals. It has a four-sided bell, and transparent tentacles that are up to 2 m (6½ ft) long. Box jellyfish start life in sheltered coasts and estuaries off northeast Australia, but are sometimes swept ashore. These jellyfish are extremely dangerous for swimmers, so beaches are often closed during box jellyfish plagues.

SAILING ON THE SURFACE ►
Unlike most jellyfish, the Portuguese man-of-war consists of many polyps, living together in a colony. One polyp is filled with gas and acts like a sail, carrying it along in the wind. Beneath this, stinging polyps trail tentacles that can be up to 20 m (65 ft) long. The Portuguese man-of-war lives mainly in warm seas. If it is beached, its stinging cells can stay active for several days.

Large gas-filled
polyp works as a
float and a sail

Tentacles
contain polyps
that digest food

◄ JET PROPULSION
Jellyfish swim by contracting their bodies in a rhythmical way. Here, a lion's mane jellyfish is swimming upwards so that it is nearer the surface, where it catches most of its food. First the bell opens wide. Next, it contracts, pushing backwards against the water, and moving the jellyfish in the opposite direction. Not all jellyfish are swimmers. Some spend their lives upside down on the seabed.

Bell contracts,
pushing against
the water

Bell slowly
opens up

FIND OUT MORE ▸▸ Antarctic Jellyfish • 82–83 • Corals 81 • Invertebrates 78–79 • Movement 28–29

WORMS

A worm is a long, soft-bodied invertebrate without any legs. Earthworms and roundworms have cylindrical bodies, but flatworms look more like ribbons. Worms live in many different habitats, and most of them need to stay moist to survive. Some feed on decaying plant remains, but others are active hunters. Many worms are parasites, living inside animals larger than themselves.

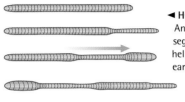

◄ HOW EARTHWORMS MOVE
An earthworm's body is divided into segments. Each segment has muscles that run around and along it, which help the worm to change its shape. To move forwards, the earthworm stretches out the segments near its head. Then, it bunches up the segments further back, and repeats this process until the rest of the body catches up. Small bristles, called chaetae, on each segment give the worm a good grip in the soil.

BURROWING EARTHWORM ▲
As this earthworm burrows into the soil, it helps air and rain to reach the roots of plants. It eats its way through the soil, digesting waste matter. Some kinds of earthworm also collect dead leaves on the surface, dragging them underground. Earthworms are among the world's most useful animals. They help plant remains to decompose (break down) and spread nutrients, making the soil more fertile.

UNDERWATER WORMS

PEANUT WORM
This smooth-bodied worm burrows in the seabed in shallow waters. It collects small particles of food, using mouthparts that work like an inflatable trunk. There are 350 kinds of peanut worm and they form a group (phylum) of their own.

MEDICINAL LEECH
The leech has a segmented body, like an earthworm, but it is flattened, with a sucker at each end. Leeches are parasites and live in ponds and damp places, feeding by sucking blood. This species is sometimes used in medicine to draw off excess blood.

RAGWORM
This common and very active worm lives in shallow seawater. It has a segmented body, sharp jaws, and leg-like flaps called parapodia that work like two rows of paddles. Ragworms swim well and hunt other animals in sand and mud.

PEACOCK FANWORM
Fanworms live in muddy sand close to the shore. They protect themselves by building a tube from mud and mucus, and feed by spreading out a crown of fan-like tentacles. When threatened, the worm pulls its tentacles into the tube.

Head

New section grows in neck region

Body surface absorbs food

Mature sections can contain 100,000 eggs

◄ ADULT TAPEWORM
Tapeworms are parasitic flatworms that spend their adult lives in the intestines of mammals and other vertebrates, clinging on with suckers and hooks. They do not have mouths, but absorb food through the surface of their body. The body sections each contain many eggs and, as the tail segments break away, their eggs are carried out of the host's body with the faeces.

ROUNDWORM ►
Also known as nematodes, roundworms have cylindrical bodies with tapered ends, and a tough body covering called a cuticle. Many live in water or in soil, but there are also parasitic species that cause serious diseases in humans. Scientists have identified over 20,000 roundworm species, but there may be many more.

FIND OUT MORE ►► Anatomy **26–27** • Invertebrates **78–79**

MOLLUSCS

There are about 100,000 mollusc species, ranging from tiny snails to giant squid. Most of these soft-bodied invertebrates have shells, and many feed by using a rough tongue called a radula. Apart from cephalopods, molluscs are usually slow movers, and some spend their adult lives fastened in one place. For most molluscs, home is in fresh water or in the sea, although slugs and snails live on land. Prehistoric molluscs, such as ammonites, are often found as fossils.

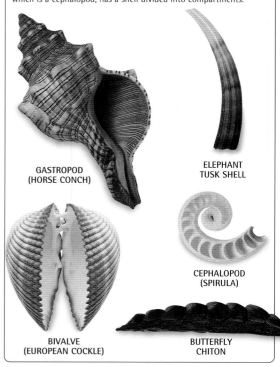

MOLLUSC SHELL SHAPES

Molluscs are divided into groups, with shells of different shapes. Gastropods, such the trapezium horse conch, usually have a spiral shell with a single opening. The tusk shell is similar, but is open at both ends. A bivalve, such as the cockle, has two halves. The butterfly chiton's shell has eight separate plates, and the spirula, which is a cephalopod, has a shell divided into compartments.

GASTROPOD (HORSE CONCH)

ELEPHANT TUSK SHELL

CEPHALOPOD (SPIRULA)

BIVALVE (EUROPEAN COCKLE)

BUTTERFLY CHITON

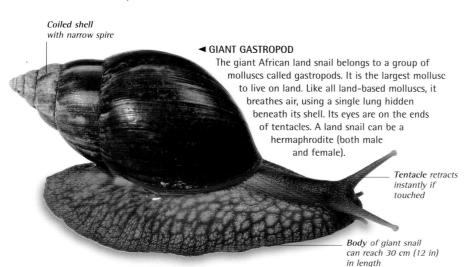

Coiled shell with narrow spire

◀ **GIANT GASTROPOD**

The giant African land snail belongs to a group of molluscs called gastropods. It is the largest mollusc to live on land. Like all land-based molluscs, it breathes air, using a single lung hidden beneath its shell. Its eyes are on the ends of tentacles. A land snail can be a hermaphrodite (both male and female).

Tentacle retracts instantly if touched

Body of giant snail can reach 30 cm (12 in) in length

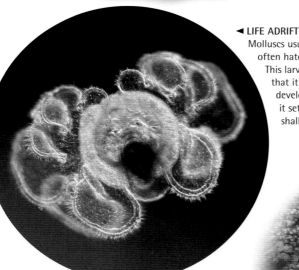

◀ **LIFE ADRIFT**

Molluscs usually start life as eggs. Those that live in water often hatch out as larvae, which live among the plankton. This larva, belonging to a sea snail, has transparent flaps that it uses to swim. As the larva grows, it slowly develops the beginnings of a shell. When this happens, it settles out of the water, and takes up life in the shallows near the shore.

Coral reef is a good grazing ground for sea slugs

Colourful gills cover a large surface area for collecting oxygen

MOLLUSCS WITHOUT SHELLS ▶

These brightly coloured sea slugs do not have shells, and breathe through raised finger-like gills along their backs. They crawl over seaweed and coral, using their radulas to scrape up small plants and animals. Some sea slugs use camouflage to protect themselves, while others deter predators with poisonous chemicals stored in their skin.

FIND OUT MORE ▶▶ Bivalves **88** • Cephalopods **89** • Gastropods **87**

Simple eye at tip of each longer tentacle

Short tentacle

Foot contains muscles that move the snail

GASTROPODS

Gastropods are the largest group of molluscs. The group includes slugs and snails, and they are the only molluscs that are found in water and on land. They move by creeping on a sucker-like foot. Snails have coiled, spiral shells, and some have a hard body flap that works like a door, shutting them inside. Slugs do not usually have shells. Land snails are mostly vegetarians, but many sea snails are predators.

◄ UNDERNEATH A SNAIL
The muscular foot of this brown garden snail is a feature of all gastropods. As it crawls, the snail secretes a layer of sticky slime, leaving a trail behind it. Its head, with four tentacles extended, leads the way. Many of its vital organs – including its heart, lung, and stomach – are safely tucked away inside its shell.

KILLER CONES ►
The textile cone is a predatory sea snail. It has a specialized tongue, or radula, that is tipped with a hollow tooth containing poison. This weapon works like a harpoon, flicking out in a split-second, paralysing the victim, and dragging it towards the mouth of the cone. Cone shells are extremely venomous – some species have been known to kill humans that have picked them up on beaches and reefs in tropical waters.

Breathing hole leads to lung

Tentacles help slug to find food

SLIPPERY SLUG ▲
This European land slug is built in the same way as a snail, although it does not have an external shell. Slugs need moist conditions to survive. Many hide away during the day, and come out to feed after dark, when the air is cooler. Some slugs eat plants, while others are predators, eating soft-bodied animals, including different kinds of slug.

SUMMER SHUT-DOWN ►
On land, molluscs have to be careful not to let themselves dry out. During hot weather, land snails often climb up plants, and then seal themselves inside their shells to retain moisture. They can remain dormant like this for months, becoming active within hours if it rains. Slugs cannot do this because their shells are internal. Instead, they shelter in damp places or burrow into the soil.

Flattened tentacle with eye at base

Lung located beneath widest part of shell

▲ GRAZING POND SNAIL
This great pond snail is feeding on an underwater plant, using tiny tooth-like structures, called denticles, on its radula. Instead of biting, the teeth work more like a strip of sandpaper, scraping away pieces of food. Snails often graze on microscopic algae growing on the surface of stones and rocks. As they feed, they leave zigzag markings that indicate where they have been at work.

▲ RASPING RADULA
This electron microscope image shows a snail's radula, which has hundreds of tiny curved denticles. They are the ideal shape for scraping plants and algae, and new denticles grow throughout the snail's life. Predatory sea snails, such as whelks, use their denticles to attack other animals.

FIND OUT MORE ►► Invertebrates 78–79 • Molluscs 86

BIVALVES

Bivalves are molluscs that have shells with two parts, known as valves, joined by a hinge. Most bivalves have powerful muscles that can shut their shells tight, sealing them inside. These invertebrates live in shallow water, and on rocky or muddy shores. Some can move slowly, but many – including oysters and mussels – are fixed in place throughout their adult lives. They filter food from the water around them through mucus-covered gills.

Diver's weight is about a third that of a giant clam

Two-part shell is open and rests on its hinge, surrounded by corals

BIVALVES ON THE MOVE

Scallops are among the few bivalves that can swim. They normally rest on the seabed, with their shells slightly open. If a predator touches them, they snap their shells together, squirting out a jet of water that pushes them along. To sense danger, scallops use small tentacles, and many tiny eyes, which line the edges of their shells.

Shell is hinged and can snap open and shut

Simple eyes sense shadows cast by starfish and other predators

Valves clap together, forcing out a jet of water

QUEEN SCALLOP

Scallop opens shell and pumps water through the gills to feed

LIVING DRILL ▶

Some bivalves have sharp-edged shells, which they use to bore into their surroundings. Shipworms drill through wood, but piddocks bore through soft rocks, and even telephone cables on the seabed. These molluscs have wormlike bodies and live in burrows which protect them. To feed, they extend a tube from their burrow and draw in water.

Piddock's burrow may be up to 15 cm (6 in) long

Empty shell, left behind after piddock's death

◀ FARMED OYSTER

Oysters are molluscs that attach themselves to rocks. They have long been cultivated as food, and for their pearls. These gems form around specks of grit that get trapped inside an oyster's body. The oyster envelops the grit with mother-of-pearl, or nacre – the same substance that lines the inside of its shell. Natural pearls, like the one shown here, usually have an irregular shape.

▲ LIVING IN THE LIGHT

The giant clam is the world's largest bivalve, weighing over 200 kg (440 lb). This massive example is wedged in among the corals on a reef. In daylight, the clam opens up to expose its colourful lips, which contain millions of microscopic organisms called algae. The sunlight enables the algae to make food by photosynthesis, and the clam takes a share of this food supply.

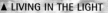

FIND OUT MORE ▶▶ Coasts **72** • Coral Reefs **73** • Invertebrates **78–79** • Molluscs **86**

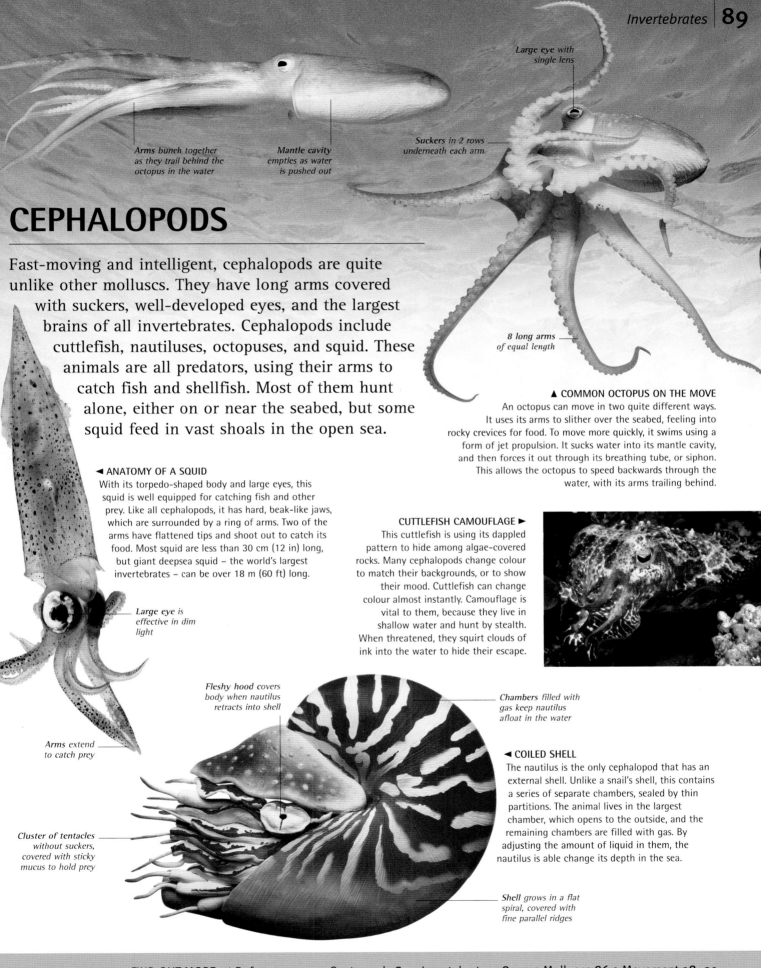

Large eye with
single lens

Arms bunch together
as they trail behind the
octopus in the water

Mantle cavity
empties as water
is pushed out

Suckers in 2 rows
underneath each arm

CEPHALOPODS

Fast-moving and intelligent, cephalopods are quite
unlike other molluscs. They have long arms covered
with suckers, well-developed eyes, and the largest
brains of all invertebrates. Cephalopods include
cuttlefish, nautiluses, octopuses, and squid. These
animals are all predators, using their arms to
catch fish and shellfish. Most of them hunt
alone, either on or near the seabed, but some
squid feed in vast shoals in the open sea.

8 long arms
of equal length

◄ ANATOMY OF A SQUID
With its torpedo-shaped body and large eyes, this
squid is well equipped for catching fish and other
prey. Like all cephalopods, it has hard, beak-like jaws,
which are surrounded by a ring of arms. Two of the
arms have flattened tips and shoot out to catch its
food. Most squid are less than 30 cm (12 in) long,
but giant deepsea squid – the world's largest
invertebrates – can be over 18 m (60 ft) long.

▲ COMMON OCTOPUS ON THE MOVE
An octopus can move in two quite different ways.
It uses its arms to slither over the seabed, feeling into
rocky crevices for food. To move more quickly, it swims using a
form of jet propulsion. It sucks water into its mantle cavity,
and then forces it out through its breathing tube, or siphon.
This allows the octopus to speed backwards through the
water, with its arms trailing behind.

CUTTLEFISH CAMOUFLAGE ►
This cuttlefish is using its dappled
pattern to hide among algae-covered
rocks. Many cephalopods change colour
to match their backgrounds, or to show
their mood. Cuttlefish can change
colour almost instantly. Camouflage is
vital to them, because they live in
shallow water and hunt by stealth.
When threatened, they squirt clouds of
ink into the water to hide their escape.

Large eye is
effective in dim
light

Fleshy hood covers
body when nautilus
retracts into shell

Chambers filled with
gas keep nautilus
afloat in the water

Arms extend
to catch prey

◄ COILED SHELL
The nautilus is the only cephalopod that has an
external shell. Unlike a snail's shell, this contains
a series of separate chambers, sealed by thin
partitions. The animal lives in the largest
chamber, which opens to the outside, and the
remaining chambers are filled with gas. By
adjusting the amount of liquid in them, the
nautilus is able change its depth in the sea.

Cluster of tentacles
without suckers,
covered with sticky
mucus to hold prey

Shell grows in a flat
spiral, covered with
fine parallel ridges

FIND OUT MORE ►► Defence **42–43** • Gastropods **87** • Invertebrates **78–79** • Molluscs **86** • Movement **28–29**

ARTHROPODS

With over a million known species, arthropods are the biggest group of animals on Earth, and they live in every imaginable habitat. They include arachnids, insects, crustaceans, centipedes, and millipedes. Arthropods have a tough body case, called an exoskeleton. Their bodies are divided up into segments, and they have legs with flexible joints.

▼ LIVING IN A CASE
A lobster's exoskeleton covers the whole of its body, including its antennae and its eyes. As with all arthropods, it is built of tough plates, which meet at flexible joints. Land-dwelling arthropods, such as spiders and caterpillars, have thin exoskeletons, but those of some water-dwelling arthropods, including this lobster, are much thicker and very strong.

Main antennae can be as long as the lobster's body

Short antenna

Tail fan works like a paddle for rapid movement

Hinged segments allow abdomen to bend up or down

Carapace (hard shield) covers the front of the lobster's body

Jointed legs combine flexibility with strength

Heavy pincers used for crushing crabs and other prey

Compound eyes contain many separate mini-eyes

Antennae sense vibrations and chemicals in the air

Long sheath covers the mosquito's mouthparts

◄ SENSE ORGANS
Despite its small size, a mosquito, like many arthropods, has elaborate sense organs. These include compound eyes to help it to navigate and antennae to enable it to pinpoint food. Male mosquitoes also use their antennae to find females, by sensing the vibrations they make as they fly. Mosquitoes are covered in sensory bristles, which detect anything moving nearby.

MOULTING TARANTULA ►
This tarantula is in the process of moulting (shedding its exoskeleton). Unlike human skin, an arthropod's exoskeleton cannot grow in step with its owner. Instead, the arthropod moults from time to time, replacing its exoskeleton with a new one that forms underneath. The spider pulls its body out of the old exoskeleton, leaving an empty skin. At first, the new exoskeleton is soft, but it hardens within a few hours.

◄ LEGS AND MOVEMENT
Arthropods are the only invertebrates that have reinforced, jointed legs. A millipede's many pairs of legs look the same, and they work in the same way to move it along. The legs of other arthropods work in different ways. Lobsters have a pair of pincers for collecting food, four pairs of legs for walking, and several pairs of paddles for swimming. Insects have six legs, and many of them have two pairs of wings.

FIND OUT MORE ▶▶ Centipedes **116** • Crustaceans **117** • Insects **97** • Senses **30–31**

ARACHNIDS

Arachnids are the second-largest group of arthropods after insects. This group of invertebrates includes spiders, scorpions, harvestmen, ticks, and mites. Most are hunters, biting or stinging to subdue their prey, but ticks suck blood, and mites often feed on plants and other foods. Arachnids have eight legs and a body that is divided into two parts.

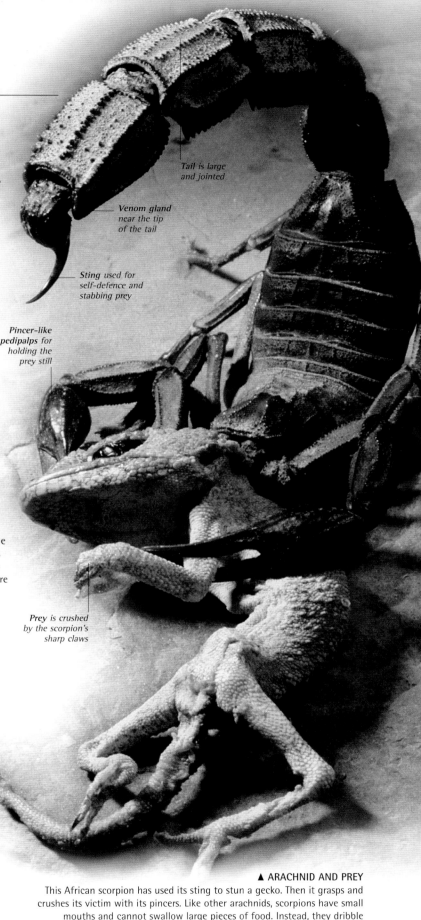

Tail is large and jointed

Venom gland near the tip of the tail

Sting used for self-defence and stabbing prey

Pincer-like pedipalps for holding the prey still

Prey is crushed by the scorpion's sharp claws

Spinnerets at rear of abdomen

8 simple eyes arranged in 2 rows of 4

Feet end in tiny hooks

Cephalothorax is covered by a hard shield

Pedipalps (limb-like mouthparts) handle food

▲ ARACHNID ANATOMY
The front of an arachnid's body is the cephalothorax. It bears the animal's mouthparts and fangs, as well as its legs. The rear section, or abdomen, contains the digestive system. This wolf spider's abdomen is rounded and covered in hairs. The spinnerets – small nozzles that produce the spider's silk – are located at the spider's rear end.

◄ MOTHER SPIDER
Compared to some invertebrates, many arachnids are devoted parents. This female nursery web spider has laid her eggs and wrapped them in a cocoon made of silk. She watches over the eggs until they hatch, keeping predators and parasites at bay.

Egg sac suspended from a rock by silk threads

◄ TINY SWIMMERS
Most arachnids breathe air and live on land. However, ten per cent of mites are found in ponds and lakes. These tiny swimmers take their oxygen from the water, and they speed through it on feathery legs. Most water mites are only a few millimetres long, but they are often brightly coloured, making them easy to see with the naked eye.

▲ ARACHNID AND PREY
This African scorpion has used its sting to stun a gecko. Then it grasps and crushes its victim with its pincers. Like other arachnids, scorpions have small mouths and cannot swallow large pieces of food. Instead, they dribble digestive fluid onto their prey. As it dissolves, they suck it up. Many arachnids, including scorpions, can survive for months on one large meal.

FIND OUT MORE ▶▶ Harvestmen **95** • Horseshoe Crabs **96** • Mites **95** • Scorpions **94** • Sea Spiders **96** • Spiders **92**

SPIDERS

Spiders often make people feel uneasy, but their ability to catch insects can be very useful to humans. There are 40,000 species of spider and they belong to a group of arthropods called arachnids. They have eight jointed legs and a pair of poisonous fangs. Some species make webs to catch food, but many stalk their prey. They live in all habitats on land, except where it is very cold.

▲ HUNTING TARANTULA
Most spiders feed on insects, but some also catch vertebrates, such as frogs, lizards, and roosting birds. This Mexican red-rumped tarantula has caught a grasshopper, and is starting to feed. Tarantulas move slowly, and they catch their prey by stealth, feeling for food as they inch their way around. They hide in burrows by day, and come out to hunt at night.

Small outer eyes detect moving prey up to 25 cm (10 in) away

Large central eyes are used to judge distances before making a jump

Hindlegs can push off swiftly, powered by body fluid under pressure

▲ TRAPDOOR SPIDER
Instead of hunting in the open like other spiders, this South African trapdoor spider lurks in a silk-lined burrow, which is covered by a camouflaged lid. If an insect walks past, the spider senses the vibrations. It flicks open the lid, bites the prey and drags it below ground. Then it closes the lid to eat its meal.

▲ HUNTING BY SIGHT
Most spiders have eight eyes, but rather poor vision. Jumping spiders, however, have excellent eyesight. They have two extra-large eyes that face forwards and give them an excellent view of their prey. This spider scans its surroundings, poised to spring. As it pounces on its prey, it can leap up to 40 times its own body length – a distance that can be up to 60 cm (2 ft). Jumping spiders usually hunt during the day.

Legspan of tarantulas can reach 28 cm (11 in)

◄ BITING SPIDER
Although all spiders have a poisonous bite, only a few are dangerous to humans. This black widow spider, from North America, is highly venomous, but it usually hides if disturbed. The Sydney funnel-web spider, which comes from Australia, is larger and can be aggressive. Wandering males of this species are more likely to bite humans during the breeding season.

TARANTULA CLAWS

Hairs on legs are used to sense vibrations

▲ GIANT HAIRY SPIDER
Tarantulas, such as this brightly coloured species from Central America, are the world's largest spiders. They are covered with velvety hairs, and have strong legs, and blunt feet with a pair of small claws. Most tarantulas live in burrows, and catch prey by biting downward with venom-filled fangs.

TARANTULA FANGS

FIND OUT MORE ▶▶ Arachnids **91** • Arthropods **90** • Defence **42–43** • Invertebrates **78–79** • Web-making Spiders **93**

WEB-MAKING SPIDERS

All spiders make silk, but only some kinds can weave it into webs to ensnare their prey. The most common web-makers build spiral webs, or orbs, but in the world of spiders, there are many other web designs. Once a web is complete, the spider waits patiently in it for its catch. Trapped in an intricate framework, which combines strong, stretchy, and sticky types of silk, its victims have little chance of escape.

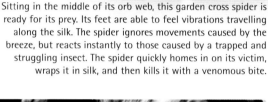

MAKING AN ORB WEB

STARTING OUT
An orb-web spider starts to spin a web by stretching a single line of silk between two supports. It then hangs a loop of silk below this line, walks halfway along the loop, and lowers itself on another thread. Once it has reached something solid, it pulls the thread tight.

MAKING THE FRAME
The spider's next task is to complete the frame around the outside of the web. When this is in place, it crosses the frame from one side to another, adding lots of extra spokes, which give the web greater strength. So far, all these elements are made of non-sticky silk.

STICKY SPIRAL
The spider now moves to the centre of the web. Working its way outwards, it builds a temporary non-sticky spiral to hold the spokes in place. Finally, it works its way back inwards, eating up the first spiral, and replacing it with a much denser spiral of sticky threads to trap prey.

▲ ORB-WEAVING SPIDER
Sitting in the middle of its orb web, this garden cross spider is ready for its prey. Its feet are able to feel vibrations travelling along the silk. The spider ignores movements caused by the breeze, but reacts instantly to those caused by a trapped and struggling insect. The spider quickly homes in on its victim, wraps it in silk, and then kills it with a venomous bite.

▲ HOW SPIDERS SPIN SILK
This magnified image shows threads of silk emerging from the body of an orb-weaving wasp spider. Spiders make silk in their abdomens, and it emerges through special nozzles called spinnerets. At first, the silk is liquid, but it hardens as it is stretched by the spider's legs. Spiders make several types of silk, which they use to protect their eggs and make webs.

Spider sits in a funnel-shaped lair, with its legs resting on the web

Strands of silk are woven together to form a sheet

Web can be up to 30 cm (12 in) across

◄ SHEET WEBS
From the safety of its lair, this sheet-web spider waits for food to come its way. Unlike an orb-weaver's web, this one is made of non-sticky silk, and it looks like a small sheet of silk laid over the surface of plants. The funnel-shaped lair is often located at one end of the web. Sheet webs are common in grassy places, but some are found in quiet corners indoors.

FIND OUT MORE ▶▶ Arachnids **91** • Arthropods **90** • Invertebrates **78–79** • Spiders **92**

SCORPIONS

Armed with pincer-like pedipalps and a poisonous sting, scorpions are nocturnal predators, living mainly in warm parts of the world. The largest of these arachnids grows to 20 cm (8 in) long, but buthid scorpions, which are smaller, have stronger venom. Scorpions feed on spiders, insects, and other small animals, which they catch and kill with their pincers. They use their stings for self-defence and to paralyse larger prey.

Sting arches over back to defend the scorpion

Flat body can slip into crevices and under stones

Newly born young have pale bodies

Pedipalps (limb-like mouthparts) grip and crush small animals

STING IN THE TAIL ▶
To defend itself, this desert scorpion is arching its segmented tail, ready to sting. The sting is at the tail's tip. A scorpion's body also consists of a cephalothorax (combined head and thorax), four pairs of walking legs, and a pair of pedipalps in the form of pincers. Its eyes are near the centre of the head, but its vision is poor.

▲ LIVE YOUNG
Unlike most other arachnids, which lay eggs, scorpions give birth to live young. The young resemble miniature versions of their parents, and spend the first part of their lives riding on their mother's back. After the young have moulted for the first time, they take up life on their own. Adult scorpions live and hunt alone, and come together only when they need to breed.

Front legs are long and whip-like and used to sense food and surroundings

Jagged pedipalps catch and tear up insect prey

Large pedipalps used to grasp scorpion's mating partner

Sting kept out of the way of the scorpion's partner

WHIP-SCORPION ▲
Whip-scorpions are not true scorpions, as they do not have stings. Tailless species, such as this one, have extra-long front legs, which they use as feelers to find their food. Instead of pincers, they have spiky leg-like pedipalps that can fold up like penknives to grip their prey. Whip-scorpions can move quickly, in a sideways motion.

◀ COURTSHIP DANCE
As they prepare for an elaborate courtship dance, the male scorpion's pedipalps reach out to clasp those of the female. As the dance nears its end, the male deposits a package of sperm called a spermatophore on the ground. He guides the female's abdomen into position over the sperm, so that her egg cells can be fertilized and develop into young.

MITES

Mites are eight-legged arachnids that look like tiny spiders. However, mites differ from spiders in many ways. Their tiny bodies do not have clear divisions, they never spin webs, and they live on a much wider range of food. Many mite species live on plants, among dead leaves, or in household dust. Other mites are parasites, fastening themselves to another animal to feed.

VELVET MITE ▶
Despite its small size, this bright red mite is easy to spot as it scuttles over walls or along garden paths. Like all mites, it starts life as a six-legged larva, but has eight legs once it becomes adult. Velvet mite larvae live as parasites on other arthropods. When they grow up, they feed on other small animals and their eggs.

Sensory hairs cover hard body case

▲ MICRO-MITE
Many mites are so minute that they can be seen only with a microscope. This house dust mite lives indoors, on bedding and on floors, and it feeds on the flakes of dead skin. The mite itself does not bite, but its droppings can trigger off asthma in people who suffer from allergies. Even smaller mites live on the human body.

BLOOD-SUCKER ▼
Ticks are large mites that feed on blood, by clinging on to their victims with their mouthparts. As this sheep tick feeds, its body swells and becomes as large as a grape. Ticks can take days to suck up a meal, but when they have finished they drop off the body of their animal host. Some ticks spread diseases that affect humans.

SHEEP TICK BEFORE FEEDING   SHEEP TICK AFTER FEEDING

FIND OUT MORE ▶▶ Arachnids **91** • Arthropods **90** • Invertebrates **78–79** • Spiders **92–93**

HARVESTMEN

It is easy to mistake harvestmen for spiders because they have eight long and slender legs. However, harvestmen have pear-shaped bodies and two eyes, which are often raised up on a small bump, giving them an all-round view. Some harvestmen are hunters, while others scavenge, feeding on dead remains. They live in a variety of habitats, and are usually seen in late summer.

Pedipalps flank the small mouth

◀ LONG LEGS
A harvestman's legs are usually much longer than its body. The second pair of legs is often the longest, and is used as antennae. If caught, a harvestman can jettison its other legs, but it needs these to survive. The rest of the body is compact, with slender jaws, and tiny leg-like pedipalps on either side of the mouth.

Legs are usually bent at the knee, so the body stays close to the ground

FIND OUT MORE ▶▶ Arachnids **91** • Arthropods **90** • Invertebrates **78–79** • Scavengers **41** • Spiders **92–93**

SEA SPIDERS

Despite their name, sea spiders are not true spiders. They are long-legged invertebrates that live in shallow water and on the deep seabed. They usually have eight legs – although some have up to twelve – and the largest are over 75 cm (30 in) across. They move slowly, and feed on small animals, such as corals, that cannot run or swim away. Sea spiders begin life as larvae, and metamorphose (change) as they grow up.

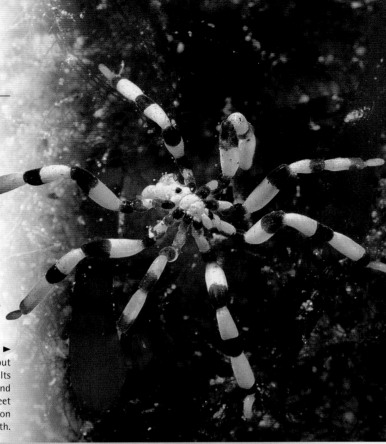

AUSTRALIAN SEA SPIDER ▶
With its bright markings, this sea spider stands out against weed-covered rocks in the Southern Ocean. Its legs are long and slender, but the body is small and stubby. Sea spiders cling to their prey with their feet and tear off small pieces from it using tiny pincers on either side of their mouth.

FIND OUT MORE ▶▶ Arthropods **90** • Coral Reefs **73** • Invertebrates **78–79** • Spiders **92**

HORSESHOE CRABS

Also known as king crabs, these armoured marine arthropods resemble helmets with spiky tails. Their mouthparts and legs are hidden under a domed shield, or carapace, which protects them from attack. Horseshoe crabs feed on small animals on the seabed, but once a year they crawl out of the water to mate and lay their eggs. There are only four species of these unusual animals. The largest kind grows up to 60 cm (2 ft) long.

TOTAL PROTECTION ▲
A horseshoe crab's carapace, or shell, hides all the softer parts of its body. The front part of the shield covers the head and mouthparts, and carries a pair of compound eyes. The hinged rear section covers its abdomen. If the animal is overturned, it can flip itself over again, using its stiff tail.

◀ BREEDING TIME
Every spring, horseshoe crabs gather on muddy beaches in the eastern United States to mate and lay their eggs. Each female digs a hole above the low-tide line, and the male fertilizes the eggs as they are laid. The female covers up the eggs, before crawling back into the sea. When the young hatch, they have a carapace, but only the beginnings of a tail.

Head shield with widely spaced compound eyes

◀ FOSSIL HORSESHOE CRAB
Horseshoe crabs have changed little in over 400 million years. This fossilized specimen lived in the Jurassic Period – the time when the dinosaurs ruled life on Earth. Horseshoe crabs are not true crabs – they are more closely related to arachnids, the animal group that includes spiders, scorpions, and mites.

FIND OUT MORE ▶▶ Arachnids **91** • Arthropods **90** • Crabs **120** • Spiders **92** • Scorpions **94**

INSECTS

For sheer variety of species, insects are by far the most successful animals on Earth. This success is due to their small size, their varied diets, their well-developed nervous systems, and their ability to fly. Nearly one million species have been identified by scientists, and even more are waiting to be discovered. They live in every habitat on dry land and in fresh water.

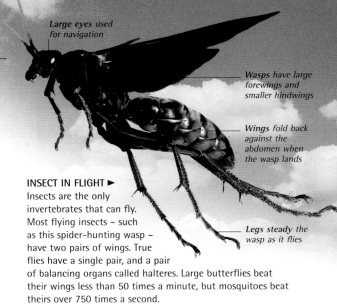

Large eyes used for navigation

Wasps have large forewings and smaller hindwings

Wings fold back against the abdomen when the wasp lands

Legs steady the wasp as it flies

INSECT IN FLIGHT ▶
Insects are the only invertebrates that can fly. Most flying insects – such as this spider-hunting wasp – have two pairs of wings. True flies have a single pair, and a pair of balancing organs called halteres. Large butterflies beat their wings less than 50 times a minute, but mosquitoes beat theirs over 750 times a second.

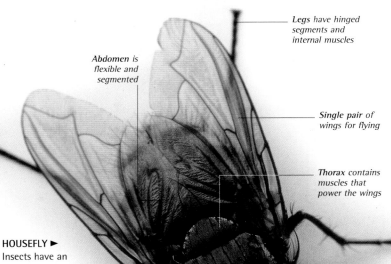

Abdomen is flexible and segmented

Legs have hinged segments and internal muscles

Single pair of wings for flying

Thorax contains muscles that power the wings

HOUSEFLY ▶
Insects have an external skeleton or body case. A housefly's body is divided into the head, thorax, and abdomen. The head has single pair of antennae, and two compound eyes. The thorax has six legs and, in most adults, one or two pairs of wings. Inside the abdomen are the digestive and reproductive organs.

Compound eyes are divided into many sections, each with its own lens

Sensory hairs cover the body

Short antennae on front of the head

Larva is wormlike, with 6 short legs and no wings

MEALWORM BEETLE LARVA

◀ CHANGING SHAPE
Nearly all insects undergo a process of metamorphosis (change) as they grow up. Some insects, such as this mealworm beetle, undergo complete metamorphosis: they develop from egg to larva to pupa to adult, with substantial changes at the pupa stage. Incomplete metamorphosis involves three stages of development, from egg to nymph to winged adult.

ADULT MEALWORM BEETLE

INSECT FEEDING TECHNIQUES

NECTAR-FEEDERS
Insects eat a huge range of foods, and their mouthparts have evolved in different ways to deal with different diets. A butterfly has a tubular proboscis (tongue), which it uses for sipping nectar from flowers. When it finishes, its tongue coils up beneath its head.

PLANT-EATERS
Scarab beetles feed on plants, dung, and decaying remains. Unlike butterflies, they have strong jaws for chewing their food. This beetle's jaws are dwarfed by three large horns on its head and its thorax. Males use these to fight with rivals during the breeding season.

BLOOD-SUCKERS
A mosquito's mouthparts work like a straw. When the mosquito bites, sharp-tipped stylets inside the outer sheath of its proboscis (feeding tube) are pushed into the victim's skin. If they hit a blood vessel, blood flows, enabling the mosquito to suck up a meal of blood.

FLUID-FEEDERS
A housefly's mouthparts work like a retractable sponge. To feed, the fly lowers the sponge and dribbles saliva over its food. The saliva dissolves the food, and the fly sucks up the nutritious fluid. The sponge folds away when the fly has finished feeding.

FIND OUT MORE ▶▶ Arthropods **90** • Beetles **106–107** • Butterflies **110–111** • Flies **108** • Senses **30–31**

HONEYPOT ANTS

Deep inside an ant colony, these worker ants hang from the ceiling in clusters, their abdomens swollen with food. Their job is to store sweet plant juices called nectar, which are gathered by other workers. In the arid outback region that these insects inhabit, the honeypots act as living larders for the ant colony. They are also prized as bush tucker by Australian aboriginals, who bite off the sacs of nectar.

Scientific name: *Camponotus inflatus*

Order: Hymenoptera (ants, bees, wasps, and relatives)

Class: Insecta (insects)

Distribution: Semi-arid areas of Australia

Status: Common within habitat

Size: Varies with the role of the ant – honeypot workers swell to the size of a grape

Food: Foraging ants collect fluids, such as nectar and honeydew, and feed them to large workers in the nest. In times of drought, these honeypots regurgitate food for other ants

Breeding activity: Eggs are laid only by the queen and the young are tended by workers. Mature colonies produce new queens, which fly off to mate and found new nests

Colonies: Nests are built in soil under groves of mulga trees (a type of acacia). Chambers deep in the nest house the honeypots

FIND OUT MORE ▶▶ Ants 114 • Arthropods 90 • Insects 97

DRAGONFLIES

With their slender bodies and transparent wings, dragonflies are among the most spectacular predators in the insect world. They hunt in the air, speeding after other flying insects, and catching them with their bristly legs. Dragonflies undergo incomplete metamorphosis. They have three stages of development – from egg to nymph to adult – and they shed their skin to enable growth. Their relatives, damselflies, are smaller.

▲ UNDERWATER NYMPH

Resting on a submerged plant stem, a young dragonfly waits for prey to come within range. Young dragonflies and damselflies are known as nymphs and live in water. They have slim bodies, well-developed legs, and special mouthparts called a mask, which can shoot out to grip their prey. Dragonfly nymphs can catch tadpoles and even small fish.

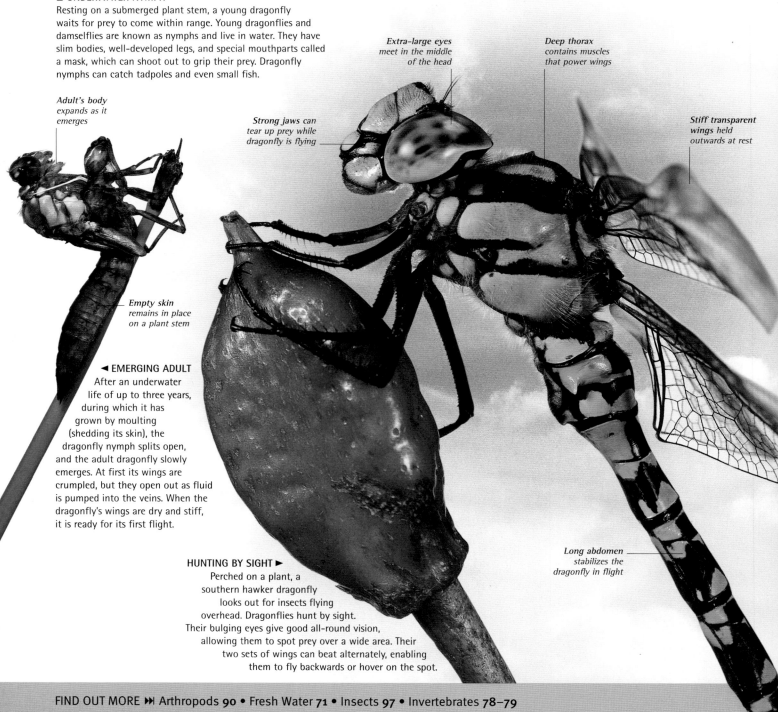

Extra-large eyes meet in the middle of the head

Deep thorax contains muscles that power wings

Strong jaws can tear up prey while dragonfly is flying

Stiff transparent wings held outwards at rest

Adult's body expands as it emerges

Empty skin remains in place on a plant stem

◄ EMERGING ADULT

After an underwater life of up to three years, during which it has grown by moulting (shedding its skin), the dragonfly nymph splits open, and the adult dragonfly slowly emerges. At first its wings are crumpled, but they open out as fluid is pumped into the veins. When the dragonfly's wings are dry and stiff, it is ready for its first flight.

HUNTING BY SIGHT ►

Perched on a plant, a southern hawker dragonfly looks out for insects flying overhead. Dragonflies hunt by sight. Their bulging eyes give good all-round vision, allowing them to spot prey over a wide area. Their two sets of wings can beat alternately, enabling them to fly backwards or hover on the spot.

Long abdomen stabilizes the dragonfly in flight

FIND OUT MORE ▶▶ Arthropods 90 • Fresh Water 71 • Insects 97 • Invertebrates 78–79

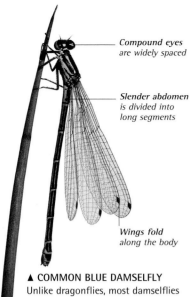

Compound eyes
are widely spaced

Slender abdomen
is divided into
long segments

Wings fold
along the body

▲ COMMON BLUE DAMSELFLY
Unlike dragonflies, most damselflies
fold their wings back when they are
at rest. This common blue damselfly
is smaller than most dragonflies, and
flies more slowly. Damselflies eat a
wide range of insects and other small
animals, snatching them from plants,
rather than catching them in the air.

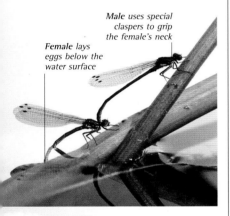

Male uses special
claspers to grip
the female's neck

Female lays
eggs below the
water surface

▲ LAYING EGGS
The male damselfly clasps the female's neck
before mating, and maintains his grip while
she finds a suitable place to lay her eggs.
Using the tip of her abdomen, the female
slits open the stems of submerged plants, and
lays her eggs inside. Once she has finished, the
male and female damselflies take
off in tandem, and seek another
spot to mate again.

Two pairs of
wings, which span
up to 10 cm (4 in)

MAYFLIES

Mayflies are insects that have a remarkably short adult life. The young grow up in rivers, streams, and lakes, where they eat plant and animal material. The adults cannot feed, and usually survive for less than a day. Adult mayflies emerge from the water in spring and summer, fluttering over the water's surface in swarms. They mate in midair, and the females drop their eggs into the water below. Once this task is finished, the adults die.

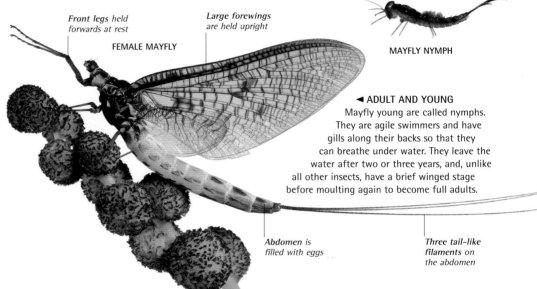

Front legs held
forwards at rest

Large forewings
are held upright

FEMALE MAYFLY

MAYFLY NYMPH

◄ ADULT AND YOUNG
Mayfly young are called nymphs.
They are agile swimmers and have
gills along their backs so that they
can breathe under water. They leave the
water after two or three years, and, unlike
all other insects, have a brief winged stage
before moulting again to become full adults.

Abdomen is
filled with eggs

Three tail-like
filaments on
the abdomen

FIND OUT MORE ▶▶ Arthropods **90** • Fresh Water **71** • Insects **97**

STONEFLIES

Like dragonflies and mayflies, stoneflies are insects that spend the early part of their lives in water. The young live in streams and lakes, where they feed mainly on underwater plants. Adult stoneflies are poor fliers, and rarely stray far from the water's edge. They spend most of their time on waterside rocks or crawling among plants. The adults eat very little, and live for just a few weeks.

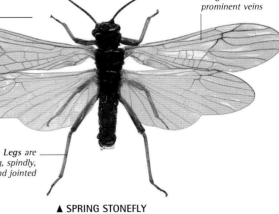

Antennae can be as
long as the body

Translucent
wings with
prominent veins

Legs are
long, spindly,
and jointed

▲ SPRING STONEFLY
This adult spring stonefly has a thickset body
and two pairs of wings, which can fold flat
over its back. The females of some species
run across the water's surface after they have
mated, scattering their eggs behind them.
Young stoneflies, called nymphs, resemble
young mayflies, but have two tails.

GRASSHOPPERS

With their extra-large back legs, grasshoppers and their close relatives, crickets, are among the insect world's best jumpers. Most kinds can fly, and some form huge swarms that travel over 100 km (60 miles) a day. Grasshoppers feed on leaves, and live on or near the ground. They are often well camouflaged, but males make loud mating calls. Crickets are better climbers, they are often nocturnal, and they may feed on animals as well as plants.

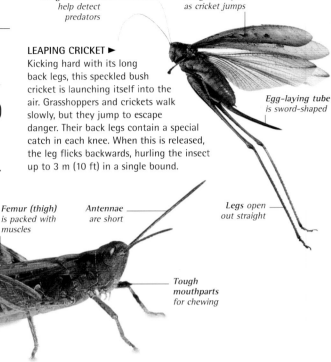

LEAPING CRICKET ▶
Kicking hard with its long back legs, this speckled bush cricket is launching itself into the air. Grasshoppers and crickets walk slowly, but they jump to escape danger. Their back legs contain a special catch in each knee. When this is released, the leg flicks backwards, hurling the insect up to 3 m (10 ft) in a single bound.

Long antennae help detect predators

Wings are open as cricket jumps

Egg-laying tube is sword-shaped

Legs open out straight

Femur (thigh) is packed with muscles

Antennae are short

Wings fold back along the body

Tough mouthparts for chewing

▲ COMMON FIELD GRASSHOPPER
The common field grasshopper has a long body with a rounded head, six jointed legs, and two pairs of wings. Its tough forewings protect its hindwings when it moves about on the ground. The hind legs are specially adapted for jumping, with an extra-large femur (thigh).

▲ ATTRACTING A MATE
As it sits on a blade of grass, this male stripe-winged grasshopper rubs its back legs against its hindwings to attract a mate. This method of making sound is called stridulation, and each species of grasshopper has its own call. Crickets rub their wings together to stridulate.

LOCUST

◀ LOCUST SWARM IN SENEGAL, AFRICA
In desert regions, a species of grasshopper called a locust can form gigantic swarms if the weather is unusually wet. Locusts breed rapidly, covering the ground with their young. When the food starts to run out, the swarm flies off to find more. A large swarm can contain over 10 billion insects – the biggest known gathering of insect life on Earth.

FIND OUT MORE ▶▶ Arthropods **90** • Communication **34–35** • Deserts **58–59** • Insects **97** • Migration **50–51** • Movement **28–29**

PRAYING MANTISES

With their front legs clasped together, these predatory insects look like someone at prayer. This is part of an efficient hunting technique. When a mantis hunts, it waits for other insects to come within its range, then makes a strike. Most mantises can fly, but they usually lurk in plants. They live worldwide, but are most common in warm climates.

Head can swivel in all directions

Spiny front legs are gripping prey

STEALTH POSITION

CAPTURING PREY

FEEDING MANTIS

▲ MAKING A KILL

Praying mantises are stealthy and patient hunters. Spotting a fly, this one stretches out and gets ready to attack. It suddenly lunges forwards, reaching out with its spiny front legs, which fold around the insect and snap shut. Once the mantis has caught its prey, it starts to feed immediately.

FIND OUT MORE ▶▶ Arthropods **90** • Insects **97** • Invertebrates **78–79**

STICK INSECTS

For stick insects, camouflage is the key to survival. These long-bodied leaf-eaters spend their lives in trees, and they use camouflage to hide from birds and other predators. They feed and move about at night – during the day, they keep perfectly still to avoid being seen. Females are usually larger than the males and often do not have wings. Leaf insects are close relatives of stick insects.

Male Macleay's spectre looks like dried leaves

Broad abdomen resembles a leaf blade

Legs are camouflaged by leaf-like flaps

Spiny green nymph resembles a smooth twig

HIDDEN FROM VIEW ▶
Clustered on a leafy branch, several stick insects blend in well with their surroundings. Some stick insects are smooth and slender, while others, such as the Macleay's spectre at the top of this image, have spines that mimic prickly plant stems. Natives of tropical regions, both of these larger species of stick insects are popular for breeding as pets.

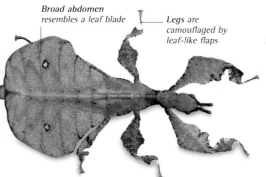

▲ LEAF INSECT

Leaf insects have flat bodies and leaf-like flaps on their legs. Their camouflage is excellent, with spots and blotches, and raised ridges resembling leaf veins. Leaf insect eggs do not need to be fertilized by a male and are simply dropped on the ground by the female.

FIND OUT MORE ▶▶ Arthropods **90** • Insects **97** • Invertebrates **78–79**

Armoured thorax is used by males to ram their rivals

Spiracles can expel air to make a hissing sound

Egg case is deposited in a crevice before the eggs hatch

COCKROACHES

Cockroaches are scavenging insects that thrive in warm parts of the world. Like other arthropods, they have segmented bodies and jointed legs. Their bodies are flat, which helps them to squeeze into tight spaces and, although they have two pairs of wings, they usually sprint away from danger. Some species are indoor pests, but most live in forests and other natural habitats.

Antennae are used for finding food

▲ WINGLESS COCKROACH
Measuring up to 9 cm (3½ in) long, the Madagascan hissing cockroach has no wings and cannot fly. If it is threatened, it hisses by squeezing air through spiracles (openings) in its abdomen. Males also hiss during courtship, to encourage females to mate. Females keep their eggs inside their bodies until the young have hatched.

◄ RAPID REPRODUCER
This female American cockroach is carrying a case containing a batch of eggs. During her lifetime, she may produce up to 50 cases, each containing a dozen or more eggs. In warm habitats – and in centrally heated buildings – her young can start breeding at just 10 weeks old. These cockroaches are widespread household pests. Because they breed so rapidly, they can be difficult to control.

Tough forewings fold over softer hindwings

FIND OUT MORE ▶▶ Arthropods **90** • Insects **97** • Scavengers **41**

ANT LIONS

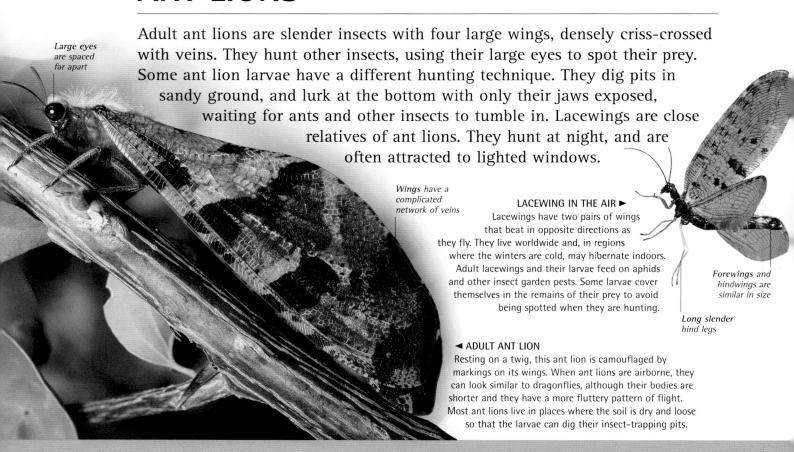

Large eyes are spaced far apart

Adult ant lions are slender insects with four large wings, densely criss-crossed with veins. They hunt other insects, using their large eyes to spot their prey. Some ant lion larvae have a different hunting technique. They dig pits in sandy ground, and lurk at the bottom with only their jaws exposed, waiting for ants and other insects to tumble in. Lacewings are close relatives of ant lions. They hunt at night, and are often attracted to lighted windows.

Wings have a complicated network of veins

LACEWING IN THE AIR ►
Lacewings have two pairs of wings that beat in opposite directions as they fly. They live worldwide and, in regions where the winters are cold, may hibernate indoors. Adult lacewings and their larvae feed on aphids and other insect garden pests. Some larvae cover themselves in the remains of their prey to avoid being spotted when they are hunting.

Forewings and hindwings are similar in size

Long slender hind legs

◄ ADULT ANT LION
Resting on a twig, this ant lion is camouflaged by markings on its wings. When ant lions are airborne, they can look similar to dragonflies, although their bodies are shorter and they have a more fluttery pattern of flight. Most ant lions live in places where the soil is dry and loose so that the larvae can dig their insect-trapping pits.

FIND OUT MORE ▶▶ Defence **42–43** • Dragonflies **100** • Insects **97**

TRUE BUGS

When people talk about bugs, they often mean any insect. However, true bugs are a group of insects with piercing mouthparts and two pairs of wings. Like other insects, true bugs are arthropods, and there are over 80,000 species. Some feed on other animals or their blood, but many more feed on plants, often sucking up their sap. True bugs live in all kinds of habitats, from forests to fresh water, and a few even skate over the surface of the sea.

WATER BUGS

BACKSWIMMER
Hanging upside down below the surface of a lake or pond, a backswimmer lies in wait for an insect to crash-land. Sensing the ripples made by its struggles, it uses its oar-like back legs to row towards its victim. It grasps its prey with its front legs and stabs it with its mouthparts.

GIANT WATER BUG
These ferocious freshwater predators can measure up to 10 cm (4 in) long, and can catch frogs and fish. They lurk in muddy water, and grab their prey with their powerful front legs. Breeding females may glue their eggs onto the males' backs, for protection until they hatch.

PONDSKATER
Pondskaters live on the surface of ponds and streams. They attack small animals that have fallen in. A pondskater's feet have water-repellent hairs to stop them breaking through the surface film. Relatives called ocean striders live on the open sea.

WATER SCORPION
Like all water bugs, the water scorpion breathes air. It takes the air in through a long tube, or siphon, which protrudes from the rear end of its body. To take a breath, it swims up to the surface, and hangs upside down with the tip of the tube in contact with the surface.

Large eyes are spaced far apart

Hard thorax carries head and wings

Drum-like tymbal located on each side of abdomen

BIG BUG ▶
This giant cicada, from southeast Asia, is one of the world's largest bugs. It can be as long as an adult human hand. Like all cicadas, it has a broad body, and a wide head with a bug-eyed look. Male cicadas have a pair of sound-producing organs on their abdomen called tymbals, which make loud screeching or whining calls. In still conditions, these can be heard over 1 km (⅔ mile) away. Young cicadas feed on the sap of underground roots.

Forewings are larger than the hindwings

◀ ADULT APHID AND YOUNG
Most insects reproduce by laying eggs, but aphids often give birth to live young. These tiny, soft-bodied bugs live by sucking sap. Aphids can reproduce sexually but, in spring and summer, wingless females also produce large numbers of young without mating. Aphid populations increase rapidly, and are a major problem for farmers and gardeners, because they spread plant diseases.

Aphids often have a covering of wax

WINGLESS FEMALE APHID

YOUNG APHID

Spiny thorax hides head and body tucked in below

BUG DEFENCE ▶
Perched on a twig, these South American thorn bugs use camouflage to hide from sharp-eyed birds. A spine on their thorax gives them their thorn-like shape. It also makes them difficult to swallow if a bird sees through their disguise. Thorn bugs usually feed in groups, and they often face the same way, making their camouflage even more convincing.

Wings folded along sides

FIND OUT MORE ▶▶ Arthropods 90 • Defence 42–43 • Insects 97 • Reproduction 44–45

BEETLES

Beetles make up nearly a quarter of all the animals on Earth. There are almost 400,000 species, ranging from tropical giants that measure over 15 cm (6 in) long to minute specimens that are barely visible to humans. Like other insects, beetles are arthropods. The adults have extra-tough bodies and hardened forewings called elytra, which close over the hindwings to form a protective case. Many beetles are plant-eaters, but some are predators and scavengers.

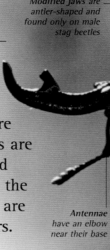

Modified jaws are antler-shaped and found only on male stag beetles

Antennae have an elbow near their base

Beetle grips his opponent by the thorax

Male's antennae are fan-shaped

Elytra (forewings) remain still during flight

Hindwings are normally stowed away against abdomen

Soft hindwing unfolds to full size before take-off

Powerful legs are segmented

▲ COCKCHAFER IN FLIGHT

Like most beetles, this cockchafer beetle has a stout body and two pairs of wings. Its elytra (forewings) are tough and hard, covering its hindwings when it is on the ground. Male cockchafers have short antennae, with segments that open up like tiny fans. Their legs are all similar in size, and they have hooked feet that help the beetle cling to plants and leaves.

BEETLE VARIETIES

COMMON TIGER BEETLE
This long-legged predator is a fast mover and lives in open, sunny habitats, where it hunts other insects and spiders. There are 2,000 species of tiger beetle. Adults have sickle-shaped jaws and well-developed eyes. The larvae ambush prey from burrows in dry ground.

GIANT LONGHORN BEETLE
The giant longhorn beetle takes its name from its extra long antennae. There are over 30,000 species of longhorn beetle, and many adults are brightly coloured. They are usually found in woods, where their larvae bore into dead wood and living trees.

JEWELLED FROG BEETLE
This beetle lives in the tropics and is one of over 35,000 species of leaf beetle. Many are brightly coloured, with an iridescent (metallic) sheen. Found all over the world, leaf beetles grow up on a diet of leaves or roots. Many species, such as the Colorado beetle, are pests.

AUSTRALIAN JEWEL WEEVIL
This weevil is a member of the animal kingdom's largest family, which consists of over 50,000 species. Using its long rostrum (snout), with small jaws at its tip, a weevil feeds on plants, often chewing deep inside them to lay its eggs. Many weevils are agricultural pests.

GREAT DIVING BEETLE
One of 3,500 species of diving beetle, the smooth and streamlined great diving beetle lives in ponds and lakes, where it hunts worms, insects, and small fish. It has hair-fringed hindlegs that work like oars, and it breathes under water by storing air beneath its elytra.

Mixing chamber in beetle's abdomen contains chemicals

Bright colours warn other animals to avoid the beetle

GLOW-WORM ▶
Curving her abdomen upwards, this female glow-worm is using light to attract a mate. The tip of the beetle's abdomen has special luminous segments that produce their own light after dark. Female glow-worms have no wings. They hide in grass, signalling to the males as they fly overhead. If a female glow-worm is disturbed, her light quickly goes out.

BOMBARDIER BEETLE ▲
At the first sign of danger, many beetles run or fly away. The bombardier beetle is different, because it squirts a jet of toxic chemicals from the tip of its abdomen. The chemicals are hot and acidic, and they explode with an audible crack. The beetle can spray the jet in any direction, giving unsuspecting predators a nasty surprise.

Female ladybird lays her eggs in batches on leaves

Adult colours develop once the exoskeleton has hardened

THE LIFE CYCLE OF A LADYBIRD ▶
All beetles – including this seven-spot ladybird – develop by complete metamorphosis, changing shape completely as they grow. The female ladybird lays its eggs on plants. These hatch out into wingless larvae, which feed on aphids. After about four weeks, each larva turns into a pupa. Inside, its body is broken down and rebuilt. About a week later, the pupa splits and an adult ladybird emerges.

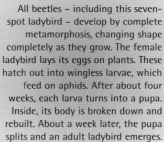

Eggs hatch after about a week

Newly emerged adult has a soft exoskeleton and wings

Larva moults (sheds its skin) several times as it grows

Pupa forms on the underside of a leaf

◀ DUELLING STAG BEETLES
Using its impressive-looking antlers, a male stag beetle lifts a rival off its feet. The antlers are specially enlarged mouthparts, and they can open and close like a pair of tweezers. Male stag beetles fight over females during the breeding season. These tussles look dangerous, but the loser rarely suffers any lasting harm.

Cylindrical body with mottled elytra

Wooden beam has been attacked by deathwatch beetles

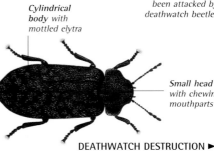

Small head with chewing mouthparts

SCARAB BEETLE
Revered by the ancient Egyptians, scarab beetles grow up to 17 cm (6½ in) long. Solidly built, they range in colour from black to gold or green. There are about 16,500 species, and they dispose of natural waste by feeding on plants, dead animals, and dung.

DEVIL'S COACH HORSE
Unlike most beetles, the devil's coach horse has a long, flexible abdomen and short elytra. If threatened, it curves its abdomen upwards, as though preparing to sting. Its family – the rove beetles – contains about 30,000 species. Larger species hunt or scavenge at night.

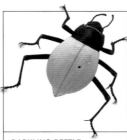

DARKLING BEETLE
Common in deserts and other dry places, darkling beetles – like this example from the Namib Desert in Africa – have domed bodies and long legs. There are about 17,000 species in this family, most of which feed on dead plants, dry animal remains, or stored food.

DEATHWATCH DESTRUCTION ▶
The deathwatch beetle chews it way through wooden beams in old buildings, sometimes weakening them so much that they collapse. Beetle pests also damage stored food and crops. Among them are cotton boll weevils, which lay waste to cotton fields; and colorado beetles, which attack potato plants.

FIND OUT MORE ▶▶ Arthropods **90–91** • Insects **97** • Scavengers **41**

Single pair of transparent wings

Large compound eyes cover most of the fly's head

Segmented abdomen covered with tough hairs

Mouthparts are sponge-like and fold away underneath head

Haltere helps to balance fly when in flight

Feet can grip smooth surfaces

FLIES

Unlike most flying insects, true flies have only one pair of fully functioning wings. However, they are often fast and agile in the air. Many flies can hover; others can fly backwards, or even upside down. There are over 120,000 species of true flies, with a wide variety of habitats and lifestyles. Some flies pollinate flowers, while others suck blood or feed on plants. Many flies carry diseases to other animals.

▲ TYPICAL TRUE FLY
The house fly is one of the world's most widespread insects. Its forewings are usually transparent and slender, with a small number of veins. Flies have modified hindwings called halteres – knob-shaped organs that help them balance in the air. They also have very short antennae and bodies covered with bristles.

MAJOR FLY FAMILIES

BEE-FLY
With their round, furry bodies, these flies resemble bumblebees, but they have only one pair of wings. The adults have long tongues and feed on nectar, hovering in front of flowers.

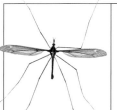

CRANE FLY
These flies, also called daddy-long-legs, have very long, trailing legs, and slender wings that can be up to 10 cm (4 in) from tip to tip. Their larvae develop in soil and mud.

MOSQUITO
Female mosquitoes use their needle-like mouthparts to suck blood. In warm parts of the world, the females of some species spread malaria – one of the most dangerous diseases.

HOVER FLY
With its black and yellow bands, a hover fly resembles a wasp. Adults feed on flower pollen and nectar. These superb fliers can hover over their favourite plants to keep rivals away.

TACHINID FLY
This brightly coloured species of tachinid fly comes from New Guinea. It spends the first part of its life as a parasite, feeding on other insects. Tachinid flies are used to to control insect pests.

◄ HOUSE FLY LARVAE
Flies develop by complete metamorphosis, which means that they change shape completely as they grow up. These house fly larvae, or maggots, do not have eyes or legs. They feed on rotting matter, and burrow their way through their food. In warm weather, they can turn into adult flies after just 10 days.

Maggots have a pointed head and blunt rear

Bristles sense any air currents as the fly feeds

Wings will start to beat almost instantly if the fly is disturbed

LIQUID FOOD ►
With the jointed mouthparts that are typical of arthropods, this house fly feeds on leftover food. Instead of chewing, it dissolves its food by bathing it in saliva containing digestive enzymes. Then it uses its mouthparts like a sponge to suck up the mixture of saliva and dissolved foods.

Hairs on fly's legs and feet can spread bacteria

Pad produces cocktail of digestive juices

FIND OUT MORE ▶▶ Bees **112** • Insects **97** • Wasps **113**

Small head with biting mouthparts

Body is flattened sideways

FLEAS

Fleas are highly specialized parasites that feed on the blood of mammals and birds. Each species of flea has its favourite type of animal, known as a host, to feed on. They are small insects, and do | not have any wings, but they can jump many times their own length using their powerful back legs. Flea larvae, which look like tiny worms, grow up in nests and bedding, and feed on adult flea droppings and dried blood. Fleas can spread diseases when they bite.

▲ GIANT LEAPS
The long hind legs of this flea work like a catapult to propel it high into the air. They do this by releasing stored tension in their leg muscles. Some fleas can jump over 30 cm (12 in) – a huge distance for insects that are only a few millimetres long. Fleas jump to climb onto their hosts, or to move from one host to another. Once they are safely aboard, they move by scuttling through their victim's feathers or fur.

LEG MUSCLES CROSS-SECTION

FLEAS AND DISEASE

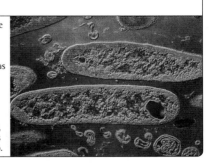

These bacteria cause bubonic plague – a disease that killed millions of people in the past, and that continues to claim lives. Rats can carry plague bacteria, which rat fleas may pass on to humans when they bite. Bubonic plague is treatable with antibiotics, but the best way to prevent it is to keep rats under control. Fleas also spread internal parasites. The dog flea, for example, spreads tapeworms that affect dogs and cats, and sometimes people too.

FIND OUT MORE ▶▶ Arthropods 90 • Insects 97 • Mice 304 • Invertebrates 78–79

Single human hair

Body is broad and flattened

LICE

Lice are blood-sucking parasites, but they spend their whole lives aboard their victims. They are wingless insects that move slowly, clinging to fur or feathers with their strong claws. Lice attack mammals and birds, and one kind – the head louse – is a common parasite of humans. Most species infect one kind of animal, and never suck blood from anything else.

Powerful legs each have a single claw

◄ HUMAN HEAD LOUSE
The human head louse has curved claws that grip hairs very tightly, making it extremely difficult to dislodge. It has a small head, and a large abdomen that swells up and turns dark when it feeds. Head lice are more common in children than adults, and they live even in the cleanest hair. They can be killed with specially medicated shampoo.

STARTING LIFE ▶
Fastened to a human hair, this head louse egg, or nit, is just starting to hatch. The young louse is about to crawl out of the hinged top of the egg. Female lice lay their eggs one by one, fixing them in place with a glue-like substance. Each egg takes about nine days to hatch.

FIND OUT MORE ▶▶ Arthropods 90 • Insects 97 • Invertebrates 78–79

BUTTERFLIES

With over 160,000 species, butterflies and moths make up the third largest group of insects. Unlike other insects, they are completely covered with microscopic scales. Moth scales are generally dark, but butterflies are often beautifully coloured. Adult butterflies and moths feed on nectar and other sugary liquids, but their caterpillars usually feed on leaves. They live all over the world, especially in warm places, and some species migrate long distances to breed.

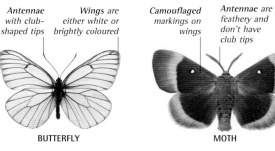

Antennae with club-shaped tips *Wings are either white or brightly coloured*

BUTTERFLY

Camouflaged markings on wings *Antennae are feathery and don't have club tips*

MOTH

BUTTERFLY OR MOTH? ▲
Butterflies always fly by day, and most are brightly coloured. They usually have club-shaped antennae, and rest with their wings held up. There are exceptions, but moths are often drab, and most of them fly after dark. Their antennae are usually feathery, and many species rest with their wings held flat.

Wings are covered by a mosaic of tiny scales

Forewings are larger than hindwings

MICROGRAPH OF SCALES ON WINGS

Antennae are used to track down flowers

SWALLOWTAIL BUTTERFLY ▶
Like all butterflies, this tiger swallowtail has two pairs of wings, slender antennae, and a tube-shaped proboscis. It has six long legs, which it uses to perch on flowers. Some butterflies, called nymphalids, stand on just four legs. Their front legs are tiny, and they hold them off the ground, pressed against their bodies.

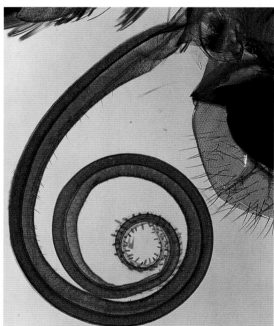

▲ ROLL-UP MOUTHPARTS
An adult butterfly or moth has mouthparts in the form of a tubular proboscis, carried like a coiled-up spring. This can be uncoiled and used like a drinking straw to sip sugary liquids from flowers and rotting fruit.

BUTTERFLY RECORDS

SMALLEST
The wingspan of the western pygmy blue can be as little as 1 cm (⅜ in), making it the world's smallest-known butterfly. It lives in the western United States, as well as in Central and South America, and it has been introduced into Hawaii.

LARGEST
With a wingspan of up to 0.3 m (1 ft), the rare Queen Alexandra's birdwing is the largest butterfly in the world. It lives in the forests of New Guinea, and its caterpillar feeds on climbing vines. When it flies, it flaps its wings and glides.

Eyespots frighten predators

WARNING SIGNS ▲
If it is in danger, this io moth tries to frighten off its attacker by revealing two staring eyespots. These markings can startle predators, allowing the moth to escape. Some butterflies, such as the monarch, are brightly coloured to indicate that they are poisonous.

MINIATURE MOTH ►
Plume moths have spindly legs and slender feather-like wings. Their wingspan can be less than 1.5 cm (⅔ in) and although they are widespread, they often go unnoticed. Many moths are even smaller, which makes them very hard to spot. These tiny insects are called micromoths. Micromoths are extremely common, and they include some significant crop pests.

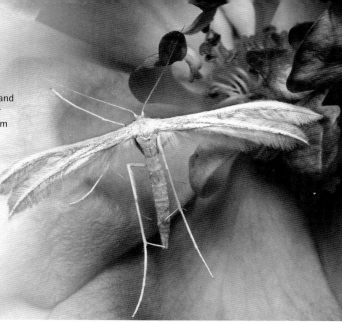

Wings harden allowing butterfly to fly away

Egg is laid on a milk parsley plant

▲ A NEW BUTTERFLY
Butterflies and moths grow up by means of a process called complete metamorphosis. A common swallowtail lays her eggs singly on food plants. After a caterpillar hatches, it grows quickly, shedding its skin frequently. It then stops feeding, moults again, and forms a chrysalis, or pupa, from which the adult butterfly later emerges.

Newly hatched caterpillar feeds on the egg's shell

Adult butterfly breaks open the pupa and crawls out

Caterpillar's colours become brighter as it grows

Pupa anchored in place while, inside, the body changes

MOTH MIGRATION

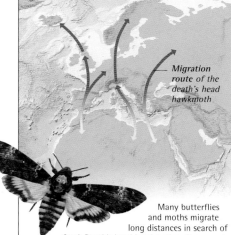

Migration route of the death's head hawkmoth

Many butterflies and moths migrate long distances in search of food. Death's head hawkmoths often spend the winter in North Africa, flying northwards in spring. They can reach as far as the Arctic Circle, a distance of over 2,000 km (1,240 miles). During their migration, these moths mate and lay eggs. The parents often die after breeding, leaving their young to complete the return journey.

GREATEST MIGRANT
The monarch butterfly is the world's greatest insect migrant. Every year, millions of these butterflies fly north to breed, across Mexico and the United States to Canada. Their young cover up to 3,500 km (2,175 miles) on the return journey.

NOISIEST
Most butterflies are silent, but male cracker butterflies make a clicking noise with their wings as they fly. It is loudest during the breeding season, when males skirmish in midair. These butterflies live in the forests of Central and South America.

GREATEST PEST
The small white butterfly lays its eggs on cabbages, cauliflowers, and related plants. Its caterpillars can ruin crops if they are left unchecked. The small white butterfly has spread from Europe to many other parts of the world.

MOST WIDESPREAD
The painted lady is found in all the world's continents except Antarctica. It is a tireless migrant, travelling long distances to breed. Its caterpillars feed on a wide range of common plants, including thistles, nettles, and brambles.

RAREST
The atala hairstreak was once common in Florida, but disappeared during the 1940s. It later returned to the United States from the Caribbean islands. Many butterflies have become rare as a result of climate change, pollution, and loss of habitat.

FIND OUT MORE ▶▶ Grasslands 56–57 • Insects 97 • Invertebrates 78–79 • Migration 50–51 • Mountains 66

BEES

Bees are close relatives of wasps and ants. Together they make up the second-largest group of insects, after beetles, and they live all over the world. Bees get their food from the nectar and pollen of flowers. As bees feed, pollen is carried from one flower to another on their bodies, helping to fertilize plants and create seeds. Some bees spend their lives on their own, but bumblebees and honeybees live in large groups called colonies. In most colonies life revolves around a single female, the queen.

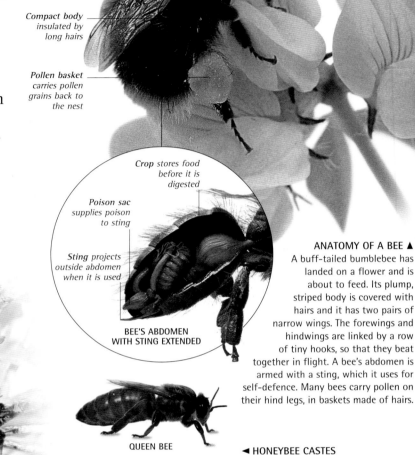

Long forewings *hooked to shorter hindwings*

Compact body *insulated by long hairs*

Pollen basket *carries pollen grains back to the nest*

Crop *stores food before it is digested*

Poison sac *supplies poison to sting*

Sting *projects outside abdomen when it is used*

BEE'S ABDOMEN WITH STING EXTENDED

ANATOMY OF A BEE ▲
A buff-tailed bumblebee has landed on a flower and is about to feed. Its plump, striped body is covered with hairs and it has two pairs of narrow wings. The forewings and hindwings are linked by a row of tiny hooks, so that they beat together in flight. A bee's abdomen is armed with a sting, which it uses for self-defence. Many bees carry pollen on their hind legs, in baskets made of hairs.

QUEEN BEE

DRONE BEE

WORKER BEE

◄ HONEYBEE CASTES
A honeybee colony contains three types, or castes, of bee. The queen has a longer body than other bees and is the only member of the colony to lay eggs. Male bees that mate with her are called drones. Workers are females that carry out all the tasks that keep the colony running. Although they are unable to lay eggs themselves, they tend the young, and build and protect the nest. They also gather nectar and pollen, and make honey – the colony's winter food.

Honeybee workers cluster around the queen

▲ SWARMING BEES
When a honeybee nest becomes too crowded, the existing queen may fly off, taking many workers with her and leaving a new queen in the nest. The swarm often settles on a branch, while scouts search for a new nesting site. Beekeepers collect honeybee swarms to install in their hives.

SOLITARY LEAFCUTTER BEE ►
The leafcutter bee lives and breeds on its own, laying its eggs in hollow plant stems. It wraps each egg in a piece of leaf, which it cuts out with its jaws. The leafy parcel contains a supply of pollen, which the grub eats once it has hatched. Many other solitary bees lay their eggs in burrows underground, or in tunnels in dead wood.

FIND OUT MORE ►► Ants **114** • Communication **34–35** • Insects **97** • Wasps **113**

WASPS

Some wasps are aggressive, and carry a powerful sting. But wasps are useful to humans, because they help to control the numbers of insects that may be pests. Social wasps live in large groups, raising their young in nests. The adult wasps forage for insects, and then feed them to their young. Other wasps are solitary. Some grow up on plants, inside swellings called galls. Many others start their lives as parasites.

Abdomen curves as egg laying begins

▲ LIVING DRILL
This female giant ichneumon wasp has located the larva of another insect, using her keen sense of smell. Gripping a branch with her legs, she will drill through the wood with her sharp-tipped ovipositor (egg-laying tube), to lay an egg on the larva's body. When the egg hatches, the young wasp larva will gradually eat its host.

◀ COMMON WASP
Wasps usually have slender bodies, well-developed antennae, and a narrow waist. They have two pairs of wings, which beat together when they fly. Social wasps, such as this one, have strong jaws that are used to chew material for nests and food for their young. Many wasps have bright markings.

Jointed legs attached to the thorax

Slender waist links the thorax and the abdomen

Parasitic wasp grubs in centre of gall

MAKING A WASPS' NEST

STARTING THE NEST
This wasp queen has started to build a nest, using fibres of dead wood. She chews the fibres, mixing them with saliva to turn them into a paste. Next, she spreads out the paste to make paper walls, which are curved, like tiny cups. The entire nest hangs from a papery stalk.

ADDING LAYERS
Work continues as the queen builds further walls around the nest. They are separated by narrow gaps that are filled with air. The air helps to keep the nest warm, just like insulation inside the walls of a house. When four or five walls are complete, the queen moves inside.

▲ GALLS AND GRUBS
This fruit-like swelling is a gall – an abnormal growth on a plant, triggered off by living things, such as insects. Gall wasp grubs living inside were using it for food and protection. However, the grubs of a parasitic wasp have hatched out and eaten the gall wasp grubs.

EGG CHAMBERS
The queen works upside down to build a layer of cells inside the nest. She lays an egg in each one, and feeds the grubs once they have hatched. They quickly grow up into workers. The queen can now concentrate on breeding, while the worker wasps expand the nest.

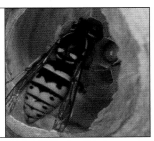

Bold stripes warn other animals to keep away

DIGGER WASP ▶
Flicking her antennae, this digger wasp scuttles across the ground, searching for cockroaches. The adult wasp feeds on the nectar from flowers, but needs to provide a food store for her larvae. When she catches a cockroach, she paralyses it with her sting and drags it into a burrow. She lays an egg on the body, which, when it hatches, feeds on the cockroach.

MAKING ROOM
The workers gradually tear down the innermost walls and build new ones around the outside. By the end of the summer, the nest could be 20 cm (8 in) across, with up to 5,000 workers, all of them offspring of the original queen.

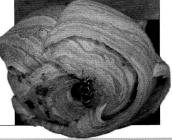

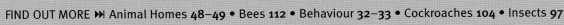

FIND OUT MORE ▶▶ Animal Homes **48–49** • Bees **112** • Behaviour **32–33** • Cockroaches **104** • Insects **97**

ANTS

Ants are social insects that live together in groups called colonies. Whether their colony is small or millions strong, the ants divide the work between them. The queen lays eggs throughout her life, while non-breeding female workers gather food and care for the young. Workers are wingless but, from time to time, winged males and queens swarm – they fly off to breed and start new nests.

Antennae have an elbow near the base

Thorax is long and slender

Strong jaws can grasp and carry prey

Abdomen can squirt acid to protect ant

Network of chambers inside plant stem

▲ ANT PLANT

This ant plant, from southeast Asia, is like a living hotel. Its swollen stem is riddled with hollow chambers, which ants use as their home. The ants eat sugary nectar produced by the plant's flowers, and in return, they protect the plant from leaf-eating animals. The ants also leave droppings inside the plant, which the plant uses as fertilizer to help it to grow.

◄ WOOD ANT WORKER

A worker ant has the segmented body typical of arthropods. It has a rounded abdomen and a long thorax that ends in a narrow waist. This wood ant has well-developed eyes, but other ants have poor sight. Ants have sensitive antennae, and find food mainly by smell. Their feet leave trails of special scents called pheromones, which lead them back to their nests.

Hooked feet provide good grip

Piece of leaf cut from a tree

Thorns grow at the base of acacia leaves

◄ DEFENCE FORCE

For these bull-thorn acacia ants, the hollow thorns of the acacia tree make an ideal home. Here, they live and breed, ferociously attacking any other animals that touch the twigs or leaves. The tree provides them with nectar and nutritious oil. The ants enter the thorns through small holes, which sometimes whistle in the wind.

Ant carries the leaf pieces in its jaws

Small worker rides on the leaves

LEAFCUTTER ANTS ►

Dwarfed by their loads, these leafcutter ants carry pieces of leaf back to their underground nest. They will use the leaves to grow a special fungus that they eat. Other ants usually eat a wider range of food, including seeds and other insects. Army and driver ants pour across the ground in fast-moving swarms, attacking any animal that is too slow to get away.

Ants emerge from a hole at the base of the thorn

FIND OUT MORE ►► Anteaters **250** • Arthropods **90** • Bees **112** • Carnivores **38** • Honeypot Ants **98–99** • Insects **97**

TERMITES

Termites are insects that resemble ants, although they are not closely related, and they feed in a different way. They are strict vegetarians, preferring dead leaves and wood to plants that are green and still alive. Termites live in colonies, and some species build the largest and most impressive nests in the insect world. Termites live in warm regions, where they are regarded as a pest. If they feed on wooden structures, they can cause them to collapse.

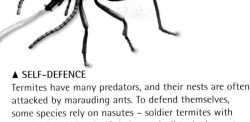

Nozzle formed by modified jaws

▲ SELF-DEFENCE
Termites have many predators, and their nests are often attacked by marauding ants. To defend themselves, some species rely on nasutes – soldier termites with nozzle-shaped heads. If their nest is disturbed, nasutes squirt a sticky fluid over their attackers, tangling them in threads of the glue-like liquid.

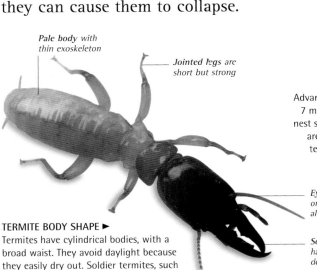

Pale body with thin exoskeleton

Jointed legs are short but strong

Eyes are small or missing altogether

Soldiers often have well-developed jaws

TERMITE BODY SHAPE ▶
Termites have cylindrical bodies, with a broad waist. They avoid daylight because they easily dry out. Soldier termites, such as this one, defend the nest, while workers forage for food and build the nest. The queen can be up to 8 cm (3 in) long. She spends her entire life inside the nest, laying up to 30,000 eggs a day.

Solid walls of sun-dried mud

Ventilation chimney keeps nest cool

INSECT ARCHITECTURE ▶
Advanced termites make mound-shaped mud nests up to 7 m (23 ft) high. This cross-section of a funnel-shaped nest shows an interior with ventilation ducts, a nursery area, and a special underground garden, where the termites grow a type of fungus on rotting wood. They harvest this and use it as food.

Nest extends above and below ground

TERMITE BUILDING STYLES

NEST WITH A ROOF
This termite nest is shaped like a mushroom, with a central pillar and several overlapping roofs. Nests like these are found in the forests of tropical Africa, where almost every day brings downpours of heavy rain. The sloping roofs help to throw off the water, keeping the termites dry.

NEST IN A TREE
In the forests of South America, many termites build ball-shaped nests and fasten them to tree trunks and branches. The nests are made of carton – a mixture of termite droppings and saliva, which resembles cardboard when it dries. Abandoned nests provide homes for snakes and birds.

PILLAR NEST
This termite nest in the Northern Territory of Australia is made of mud that has hardened in the sunshine. It is tall and narrow, with flat sides facing east and west. This keeps the nest warm when the sun rises and sets, but helps it to stay cool at midday, when the sun is high overhead.

1 *Access route to water underneath nest*

2 *Nursery area containing eggs and young*

3 *Royal cell containing queen*

4 *Chambers where termites live*

FIND OUT MORE ▸▸ Animal Homes **48–49** • Ants **114** • Grasslands **56–57** • Insects **97**

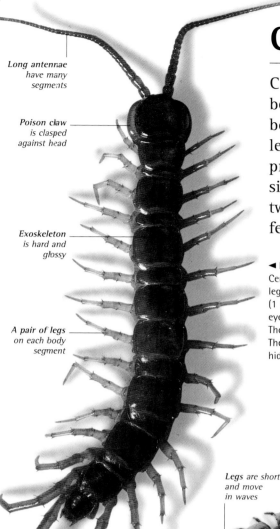

Long antennae have many segments

Poison claw is clasped against head

Exoskeleton is hard and glossy

A pair of legs on each body segment

CENTIPEDES

Centipedes look very different from other arthropods because they have long bodies, with a pair of legs on each body segment. Centipedes can have up to 180 pairs of legs, although most have far fewer than this. They are predators, and kill their prey with poison claws on either side of their head. Millipedes are similar, but they have two pairs of legs on each body segment and are scavengers, feeding on rotting plants and fungi.

◄ FAST RUNNER
Centipedes are fast runners – some long-legged species can sprint at nearly 2 kph (1 mph). Most centipedes have poor eyesight, and some have no eyes at all. They use their long antennae to find prey. Their flat bodies are an ideal shape for hiding under logs and stones.

SUBTERRANEAN CENTIPEDE ►
Geophilid centipedes, such as this one, live and hunt among fallen leaves and in the soil. Pale, long, and thread-like, they have dozens of tiny legs. These centipedes are very flexible and can twist and turn like snakes, helping them to slip through small spaces and crevices as they search for prey, such as mites and other soil-dwelling arthropods.

Body is segmented and flat

Legs are short and move in waves

Long antennae used to find prey in soil

◄ MILLIPEDE MOVEMENT
Like all millipedes, this flat-backed millipede has two pairs of legs on each body segment. From a distance, it looks like a centipede, but it moves slowly, and does not have poison claws. Millipedes can have up to 375 pairs of legs. Many species – including this one – do not have eyes, and find their way by smell and touch.

ABOUT TO CURL UP

CURLED UP

▲ SELF-DEFENCE
This pill millipede is not armed with a bite or sting to defend itself. If it is threatened or attacked, it rolls up in a ball and waits until the danger has passed. This species has a very short body for a millipede, so it can tuck its legs up inside its exoskeleton. Longer millipedes often coil up if they are touched, and some ooze toxic chemicals from their bodies.

Mouse has been paralysed and killed by venom

GIANT CENTIPEDE ►
Using its poison claws, this giant centipede has killed a mouse. Giant centipedes live in the tropics. They are sometimes brightly coloured, and they can grow up to 30 cm (12 in) long. Like other centipedes, they stalk and ambush their prey by night. The powerful venom in their bite can be dangerous for humans.

FIND OUT MORE ►► Arthropods 90 • Defence 42–43 • Invertebrates 78–79 • Mice 304 • Scavengers 41

CRUSTACEANS

This varied group of invertebrates includes crabs, lobsters, shrimps, krill, barnacles, and water fleas. Crustaceans take their name from their body case. In larger species, it is reinforced with chalky minerals, turning it into a hard crust. Compared to other arthropods, crustaceans are scarce on land, but very common in fresh water and the sea. They range in size from microscopic copepods to giant crabs that are several metres across.

Tough body case protects the soft parts of the body

LAND CRUSTACEAN ▲
Woodlice are the only crustaceans that are completely at home on land. Their bodies dry out easily, so they stay in damp places, feeding at night. Female woodlice carry their eggs in a pouch beneath their abdomen. The young are carried for several days after they have hatched, so that they stay moist. Some crabs also live on land, however, they return to water to breed.

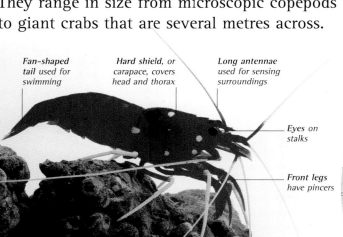

Fan-shaped tail used for swimming

Hard shield, or carapace, covers head and thorax

Long antennae used for sensing surroundings

Eyes on stalks

Front legs have pincers

▲ CRUSTACEAN BODY CASE
Like all arthropods, crustaceans have an exoske eton, or body case. This cleaner shrimp's exoskeleton is transparent and paper-thin, but those of crabs and lobsters are thicker and heavier. Crustaceans also have two pairs of antennae, and compound eyes on stalks. They use their many pairs of legs for walking, swimming, and for picking up food.

Adult copepod has long antennae

Young shrimp larva has spines and long tail

Mature crab larva with well-developed legs

◄ LIFE AFLOAT
Near the surface of the sea, vast numbers of young crustaceans spend their lives adrift. They form part of the plankton – a mass of small animals that are a vital food for fish, whales, and some seals. Crustacean larvae hatch from eggs. They look very different from their parents, and they usually feed in a different way. Like most invertebrates, they slowly metamorphose (change) as they grow up.

Legs can be retracted inside the exoskeleton

◄ FEEDING BARNACLE
Surrounded by brightly coloured corals, this barnacle is using its legs to collect food. A barnacle's exoskeleton resembles a shell. It opens up so the barnacle can extend its legs, and closes when they retract. This is particularly useful for barnacles on rocky coasts, where they are often pounded by the waves.

FIND OUT MORE ▶▶ Arthropods **90** • Coasts **72** • Corals **81** • Fresh Water **71** • Oceans **74–75** • Senses **30–31**

ROBBER CRAB

This large land crab has clambered up a palm tree to nip off a coconut with its powerful pincers. On the ground, the crab will then pound it open to feed on the flesh. Robber, or coconut, crabs are scavengers, roaming beaches at night in search of food. Unlike other hermit crabs, the adults have a hard shell covering their abdomen. Robber crabs are the largest arthropods to live on land, but are threatened by intensive hunting.

Scientific name: *Birgus latro*

Order: Decapoda (crabs and relatives)

Class: Crustacea (crustaceans)

Distribution: Oceanic islands in the Western Pacific and eastern Indian oceans,

Status: Uncommon in part of their range

Length: Legspan up to 1 m (3⅓ ft)

Weight: Up to 4 kg (9 lb)

Food: Emerge at night from daytime burrows to scavenge for coconuts, leaves, fruit, and the remains of animals, including crustaceans

Breeding activity: Takes place between June and September. Each female releases several hundred eggs into the sea

Life cycle: Larval stage is spent in the sea. When they return to land, young crabs live in gastropod (sea snail) shells or broken coconut shells until they are about 2.5 cm (1 in) across

FIND OUT MORE ▶▶ Arthropods **90** • Crabs **120** • Crustaceans **117**

CRABS

Crabs belong to the arthropod group called crustaceans. Most crabs have broad bodies, with a short, curved abdomen hidden away on the underside, and a tough carapace (hard case) covering the head and thorax. They have eight legs for walking, plus another pair that end in pincers. They use the pincers to handle food, and for defence if attacked. Crabs are predators and scavengers, and most species live on coasts and mudflats.

Stalk has compound eye at its tip

Abdomen is hidden inside a mollusc shell

BORROWED SHELL ▲
Unlike most crabs, hermit crabs have a long body with a soft curved abdomen, which makes them vulnerable to attack. To protect themselves, they live in empty mollusc shells. This common hermit crab will quickly outgrow its shell and swap it for a larger one. Hermit crabs are scavengers that feed along the tideline.

Long walking legs are attached to the thorax in pairs

Heavy pincers can crack open mollusc shells

Jointed back legs are used for walking

Abdomen tucked away beneath the crab's body

▲ POWERFUL PINCERS
With its extra-thick exoskeleton and two powerful pincers, an adult edible crab can weigh over 1 kg (2¼ lb). Like most crustaceans, young crabs drift in open water as larvae. They slowly metamorphose (change shape), before settling down among rocks and in sediment on the seafloor.

Giant claw attracts females

Feeding claws used to scrape up sediment and pass to mouth

▲ SPIDER CRAB
Spider crabs have pear-shaped bodies, small pincers, and long, slender legs. Giant spider crabs are the world's largest crustaceans, with a legspan of up to 3.5 m (11 ft), and they live in the deep sea. Some spider crabs attach camouflage items, such as shells and seaweed, to spiny hooks on their carapace.

MALE FIDDLER CRABS ▶
Locked together by their claws, two male fiddler crabs fight at low tide. Fiddler crabs live in mangrove swamps, where they dig burrows in the mud. Males have one small claw, which they use for feeding, and one giant claw, which they use for fighting and for attracting female crabs.

FIND OUT MORE ▸▸ Animal Homes **48–49** • Crustaceans **117** • Robber Crab **118–119**

LOBSTERS

Measuring up to 1 m (3⅓ ft) long, lobsters are heavy-bodied crustaceans that live on the seabed. They have eight walking legs, and a front pair that often ends in heavy claws. Lobsters are predators, scenting food with their long antennae, and using their claws to crack open animals with body cases and shells. Their smaller relatives, shrimps, are similar in shape, but live in fresh and brackish water, as well as salt water.

Antennae branch
out at the front
of the head

Forward-facing
eyes are used for
spotting prey

Lobster follows
the one in front

Antennae can be
longer than the
lobster's body

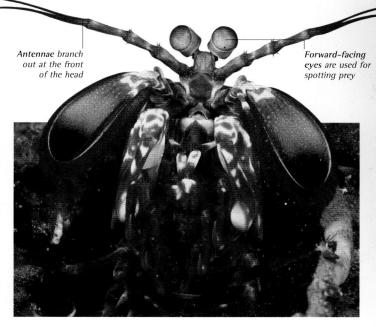

▲ MANTIS SHRIMP
Peering through the water with its large, bright eyes, a mantis shrimp lies in wait for its prey. If an animal comes within range, this formidable crustacean strikes out swiftly with its powerful front legs to spear and slice its prey. Mantis shrimps may grow up to 35 cm (14 in) long, and can cut through a human finger.

Legs on thorax
are used for
filter-feeding

▲ ANTARCTIC KRILL
Antarctic krill are shrimp-like animals that inhabit the Southern Ocean. They live around the ice and in the open water, where they form enormous swarms that can weigh over a million tonnes. Krill have bristly legs, which are used like sieves to collect plankton from the water. Krill are an essential food for many marine animals, including fish, penguins, seals, and whales.

LOBSTERS ON THE MOVE ▲
Moving in a single file, these spiny lobsters are migrating across the seabed near the coast of Florida. They spend the winter in deep water, and the summer in coral reefs close to the shore. Although they have small claws, their bodies have sharp edges and spines, providing them with excellent protection from predators.

◄ CRUSHING AND CUTTING
A common lobster's two claws are different in shape, and it uses each of them in different ways. Its powerful right claw has blunt teeth, ideal for smashing open shells. Its slimmer left claw has sharp teeth and is used for slicing up softer food, such as dead fish. Lobsters normally move by walking, but if they sense danger they flick their tail, speeding backwards through the water.

FIND OUT MORE ►► Anatomy **26–27** • Arthropods **90** • Crustaceans **117** • Migration **50–51** • Oceans **74–75**

◄ TUBE FEET
Reaching out into the water, the tube feet of this common Atlantic starfish will grip anything solid that they touch. All echinoderms have feet that are arranged in rows on their bodies. Tube feet are flexible, and they are filled with body fluid. By changing the pressure of this fluid, an echinoderm can make them extend or retract.

Foot ends in a sticky sucker

Arms braced against the seabed

Feet are arranged in rows underneath each arm

Protective spines cover upper surface of the body

ECHINODERMS

This group of invertebrates includes starfish, sea urchins, and sea cucumbers, as well as rarer animals such as feather stars. Outwardly, echinoderms are not very similar, but they all have chalky skeletons and body parts that are arranged in groups of five. Echinoderms live in the sea, but, apart from feather stars, few of them can swim. Instead, they use tiny, sucker-tipped feet to creep over rocks, reefs, or the seabed.

▲ PRISED APART
This common starfish is using its tube feet to open a mussel's shell. The feet grip the two halves of the shell, and slowly pull them apart. When the halves of the shell start to separate, the starfish turns its stomach inside out and pushes it into the shell to digest the mussel's soft parts. The starfish then pulls its stomach back into its own body.

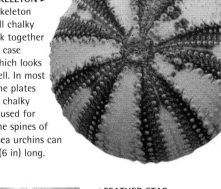

SEA URCHIN SKELETON ►
A sea urchin's skeleton is made of small chalky plates. They lock together to make a rigid case called a test, which looks like a round shell. In most echinoderms, the plates are armed with chalky spines that are used for self-defence. The spines of some kinds of sea urchins can be over 15 cm (6 in) long.

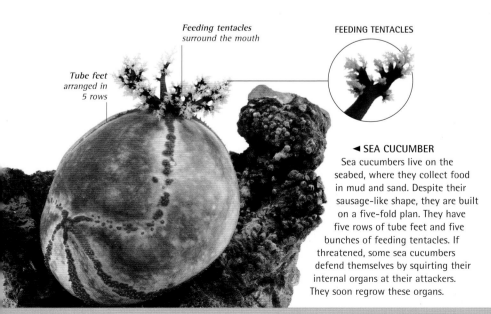

Feeding tentacles surround the mouth

FEEDING TENTACLES

Tube feet arranged in 5 rows

◄ SEA CUCUMBER
Sea cucumbers live on the seabed, where they collect food in mud and sand. Despite their sausage-like shape, they are built on a five-fold plan. They have five rows of tube feet and five bunches of feeding tentacles. If threatened, some sea cucumbers defend themselves by squirting their internal organs at their attackers. They soon regrow these organs.

◄ FEATHER STAR
These feather stars, from an Australian coral reef, have many graceful arms that beat up and down when they swim. Their mouths face upwards, and they use their arms to collect specks of floating food. Feather stars belong to an ancient group of echinoderms called crinoids, which were once some of the commonest animals in the sea. Like all crinoids, they begin life anchored to the seabed on a flexible stalk.

FIND OUT MORE ►► Anatomy 26–27 • Coral Reefs 73 • Invertebrates 78–79

STARFISH

Starfish are easier to recognize than other echinoderms because of their unique shape. Most species have five arms, and they include some of the most colourful animals in the sea. They move slowly, and feed mainly on mussels, corals, and other animals that cannot crawl or swim away. Brittlestars are similar to true starfish, but they are scavengers.

Common sunstar has up to 12 arms

Brittlestar's arms are fragile and break easily

Spiny starfish has long arms with large spines

Common starfish has 5 arms and an orange body

New arms growing from a single old one

◄ GROWING NEW ARMS
If a starfish loses an arm, the missing limb slowly regenerates (grows back). Normally, the severed arm dies, but in some starfish it can survive to take up life on its own. The arm of this Pacific starfish is regenerating to make a complete new animal. Its four new arms will take several months to become fully grown.

CORAL KILLER ►
The crown-of-thorns starfish has long, poisonous spines, and it feeds on corals in the Pacific Ocean. Sometimes, large numbers of these starfish swamp coral reefs, leaving them dead and barren. These starfish plagues usually subside, allowing the coral to recover.

STARFISH SHAPES ▲
True starfish have star-shaped or cushion-shaped bodies, depending on the length of their arms. Their arms can bend, but slowly, and not very far. Brittlestars have thin, flexible arms, and bodies with a central disc. Unlike starfish, they can hook their arms around solid objects to pull themselves along. Starfish and brittlestars are often covered with spines.

FIND OUT MORE ►► Ecology 14–15 • Coral Reefs 73 • Echinoderms 122 • Invertebrates 78–79

SEA URCHINS

Sharp spines protect rows of tube feet

Most sea urchins live on rocks and reefs, where they scrape off plants and small animals with a set of downward-pointing jaws. Some irregularly shaped species live on the seabed, and feed by burrowing through sediment or collecting food on the bottom. When sea urchins die, their empty skeletons, or tests, are often washed up on the shore. In living urchins, the test is surrounded by rows of tube feet and chalky spines.

▲ LIVING IN A CASE
The common sea urchin's hollow test contains hundreds of separate plates, with five sets of spines, and five sets of holes for its tube feet. The urchin uses its spines and tube feet to move, and to cling or wedge itself onto rocks. It also uses its feet to pass food into its mouth, which is underneath its body and contains a set of five jaws.

STARTING LIFE ►
Smaller than a pinhead, this sea urchin larva will spend several weeks drifting close to the surface of the sea. As the larva matures, it metamorphoses (changes shape). This magnified image shows its skeleton beginning to form. Eventually, it takes on its adult shape and settles down on a rock or reef. Some echinoderms produce larvae, while others release eggs and sperm into the water.

FIND OUT MORE ►► Coasts 72 • Coral Reefs 73 • Echinoderms 122 • Invertebrates 78–79

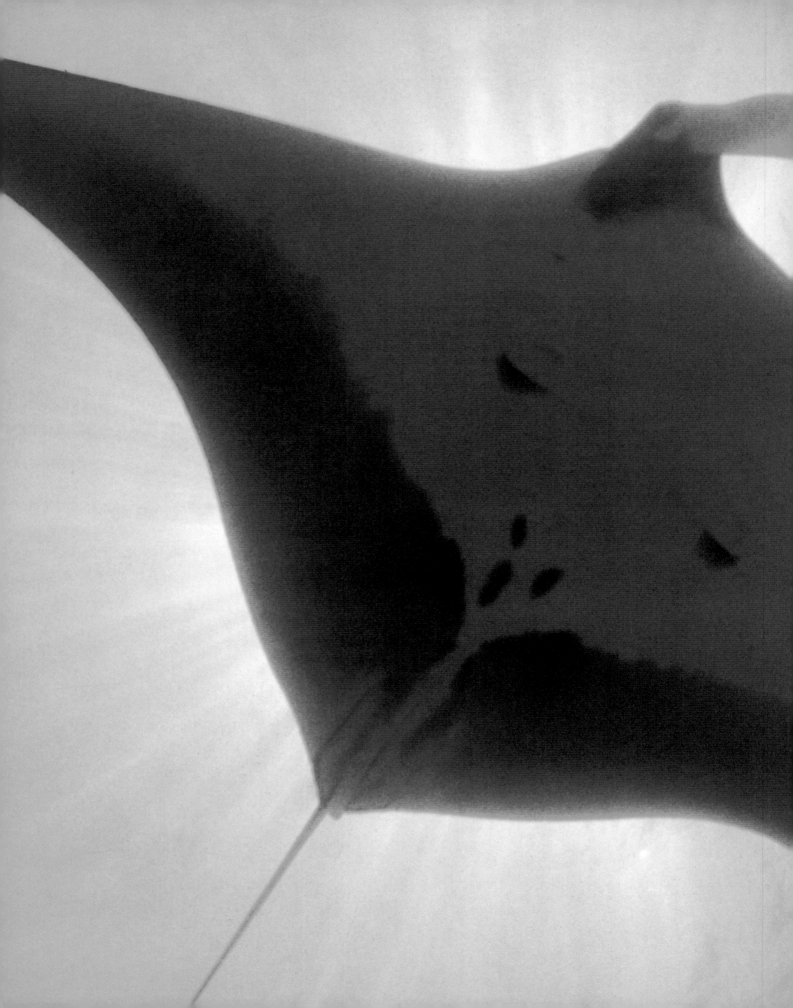

FISH

◄ GENTLE GIANT
A manta ray slowly swims through the sunlit surface waters of the open ocean, flapping its fins like the wings of a giant bird. The manta belongs to a group of fish called cartilaginous fish. The two other groups are jawless fish and bony fish. Fish are the largest group of vertebrates (animals with backbones), and were the first to appear on Earth. Most fish live in either fresh water or the sea, but a few species can move between both habitats.

FISH

Fish are vertebrates (animals with backbones) that live and swim in water. Most fish breathe by using gills. There are four different groups of fish: two groups of jawless fish; cartilaginous fish (sharks, rays, and chimaeras); and bony fish. These groups have similarities, but they are only distantly related. Fish are found in all aquatic environments and there are at least 24,000 living species.

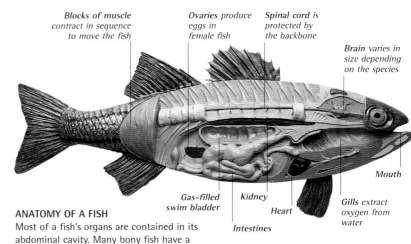

Blocks of muscle contract in sequence to move the fish

Ovaries produce eggs in female fish

Spinal cord is protected by the backbone

Brain varies in size depending on the species

Mouth

Gas-filled swim bladder

Kidney

Heart

Gills extract oxygen from water

Intestines

ANATOMY OF A FISH

Most of a fish's organs are contained in its abdominal cavity. Many bony fish have a balloon-like swim bladder, which fills with gas to control their buoyancy (ability to float). Sharks have a large, oil-filled liver to keep them buoyant. Fish use their kidneys and gills to get rid of waste products.

Slimy skin and scales protect the fish from infection

FISH GROUPS

Jawless fish	Cartilaginous fish	Bony fish
Lamprey	Thornback ray	Cichlid
Hagfish		

HOW FISH SWIM ▶

Fish need to generate considerable force to move through water. The fastest fish have streamlined bodies and powerful muscles. Bundles of muscles along the backbone contract in waves, from front to back, curving the body and moving the tail from side to side. Some fish also use their pectoral fins to row themselves along.

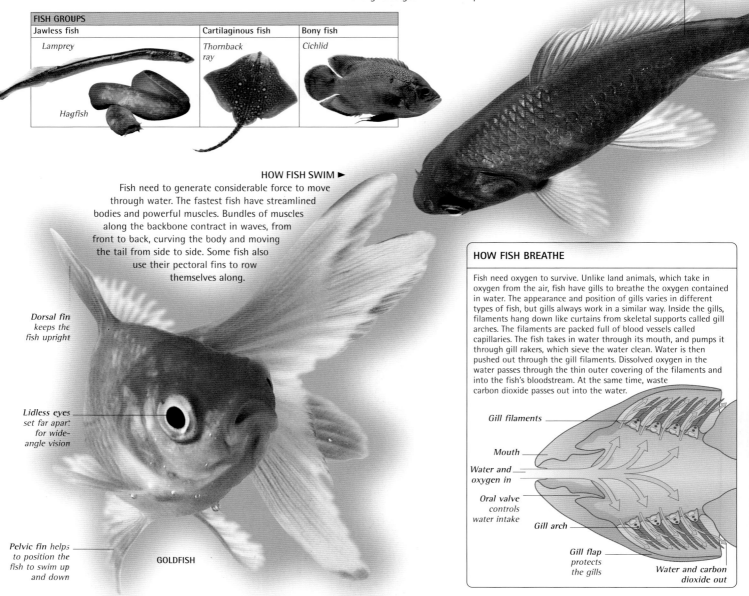

Dorsal fin keeps the fish upright

Lidless eyes set far apart for wide-angle vision

Pelvic fin helps to position the fish to swim up and down

GOLDFISH

HOW FISH BREATHE

Fish need oxygen to survive. Unlike land animals, which take in oxygen from the air, fish have gills to breathe the oxygen contained in water. The appearance and position of gills varies in different types of fish, but gills always work in a similar way. Inside the gills, filaments hang down like curtains from skeletal supports called gill arches. The filaments are packed full of blood vessels called capillaries. The fish takes in water through its mouth, and pumps it through gill rakers, which sieve the water clean. Water is then pushed out through the gill filaments. Dissolved oxygen in the water passes through the thin outer covering of the filaments and into the fish's bloodstream. At the same time, waste carbon dioxide passes out into the water.

Gill filaments

Mouth

Water and oxygen in

Oral valve controls water intake

Gill arch

Gill flap protects the gills

Water and carbon dioxide out

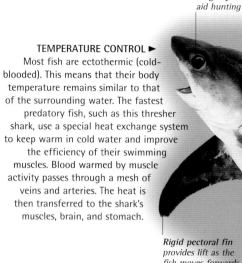

Large eyes
aid hunting

**Long, scythe-shaped
tail** is used to trap
and stun prey

TEMPERATURE CONTROL ▶
Most fish are ectothermic (cold-
blooded). This means that their body
temperature remains similar to that
of the surrounding water. The fastest
predatory fish, such as this thresher
shark, use a special heat exchange system
to keep warm in cold water and improve
the efficiency of their swimming
muscles. Blood warmed by muscle
activity passes through a mesh of
veins and arteries. The heat is
then transferred to the shark's
muscles, brain, and stomach.

Triangular dorsal fin
balances the fish as its
tail thrusts sideways

Rigid pectoral fin
provides lift as the
fish moves forwards

Streamlined head
eases movement
through the water

Pectoral fin is
used to steady
and angle the fish

Pelvic fin stabilizes
the fish's body

Tail moves from
side to side to
propel the fish
through the water

Caudal or tail fin
has 2 lobes (parts)
on a goldfish

FIN SHAPES

▲ BODY SHAPE
The Australian leafy sea dragon lives a quiet life among seaweed,
camouflaged by its strange shape and leaf-like skin extensions. Over
time, fish have developed different body shapes that are designed to suit
particular habitats or lifestyles. This means they no longer have the
normal streamlined body shape of most fish, which helps them slide
easily through the water.

LUMPSUCKER FISH
The lumpsucker is a good example
of a fish that has developed other
uses for its fins, besides swimming
and staying upright in the water.
It uses its sucker-like pelvic fins
to cling to shallow, wave-washed
rocks. The female lays her eggs
on the rocks, out of reach of
predatory fish, and the male
guards them until they hatch.

SIAMESE FIGHTING FISH
These fish have large, flamboyant
fins that are almost useless for
swimming. The brightly coloured
fins are used by males to attract
a mate. Breeders of this tropical
aquarium fish have produced
varieties with extra-large fins.
Although the fish are only 6 cm
(2 in) long, the males fight
fiercely – sometimes to the death.

TRIPOD FISH
The soft mud covering large areas
of the deepsea floor makes it
tricky for predatory fish to lie in
wait for their prey. Tripod fish
have overcome this by supporting
themselves above the mud on
their amazingly long fins. They
can remain motionless for hours
until their prey swims close
enough to be snapped up.

FIND OUT MORE ▶▶ Anatomy 26–27 • Classification 308–309 • Movement 28–29 • Oceans 74–75

JAWLESS FISH

Fossils show us that the earliest fish living around 450 to 360 million years ago did not have jaws. The only remaining survivors of this group of jawless, or agnathan, fish are around 50 species of hagfish and 38 species of lamprey. Instead of a normal mouth, these eel-like fish have a round suction disc armed with small, sharp teeth. Lampreys are parasites that feed on living fish. Hagfish are scavengers that feed on rotting carcasses.

◄ HAGFISH
A hagfish can tie its body in a knot because it has a simple flexible rod called a notochord instead of a rigid backbone. The knot helps to anchor the hagfish while it tears off flesh from dead fish or other rotting carcasses. Its flexibility can also help it wriggle free from predators. Hagfish eggs hatch into young that look like tiny adults.

Whisker-like barbels help the blind hagfish detect food

Big eyes help to find prey

Sucker-like mouth with rasping teeth

Pore-like gill slits in scaleless, slimy skin

▲ SEA LAMPREYS
Most lampreys live in the sea but migrate up rivers to lay eggs. The eggs hatch into worm-like larvae called ammocoetes that live in mud tunnels for around three years, feeding on organic debris. The larvae then metamorphose (change) into adults and swim downstream. Adults clamp onto living fish with their sucker-like mouths, scrape a hole in the prey, and eat blood, fluids, and flesh.

CARTILAGINOUS FISH

Rays, sharks, and chimaeras make up this relatively small but very successful group of fish. The huge whale shark, the manta ray, and the ferocious great white shark all belong to this group. Cartilaginous fish have skeletons made from bendy lightweight cartilage instead of bone. Most species have teeth that are continuously replaced. Their skin is covered with dermal denticles, which are overlapping scales that resemble tiny teeth.

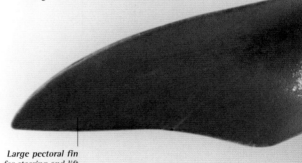

Large pectoral fin for steering and lift in the water

GHOST SHARK ►
The ploughnose or elephant fish, which is found off the coast of southern Australia, is a chimaera with an unusually long snout. Chimaeras, sometimes called ghost sharks, live in the deep ocean. There are over 30 known species, most of which have a long body and a bulky head that is covered with pores to help them sense prey. Their gill slits are not visible, unlike those of sharks and rays.

▲ ELECTRIC RAY
Like most rays, the marbled electric ray lives on the seabed, where its flat body is well camouflaged. Electric rays have an unusual second line of defence. If touched, the muscles in their pectoral fins produce an electric shock that is powerful enough to kill other fish and stun a human. Most fish lay eggs, but many species of ray give birth to live young.

FIND OUT MORE ►► Fish **126–127** • Scavengers **41**

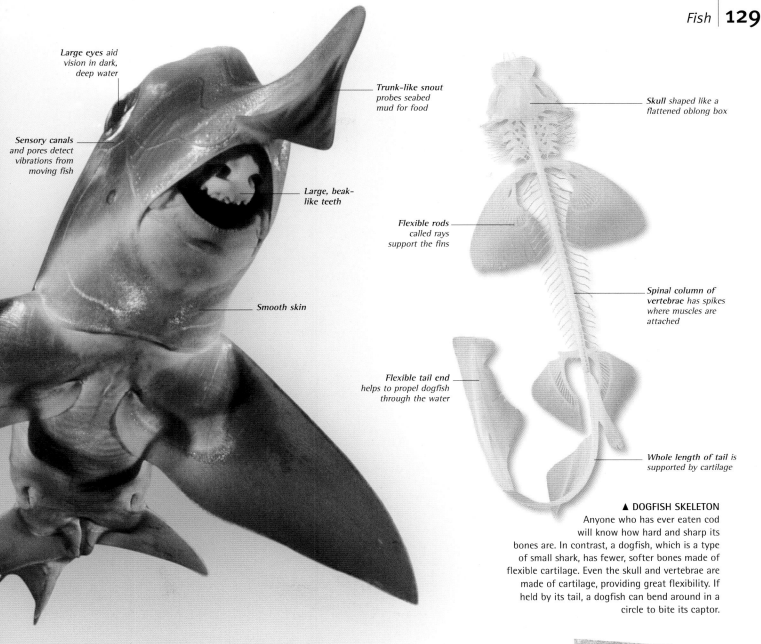

Large eyes *aid vision in dark, deep water*

Sensory canals *and pores detect vibrations from moving fish*

Trunk-like snout *probes seabed mud for food*

Large, beak-like teeth

Smooth skin

Skull *shaped like a flattened oblong box*

Flexible rods *called rays support the fins*

Spinal column of vertebrae *has spikes where muscles are attached*

Flexible tail end *helps to propel dogfish through the water*

Whole length of tail *is supported by cartilage*

▲ DOGFISH SKELETON
Anyone who has ever eaten cod will know how hard and sharp its bones are. In contrast, a dogfish, which is a type of small shark, has fewer, softer bones made of flexible cartilage. Even the skull and vertebrae are made of cartilage, providing great flexibility. If held by its tail, a dogfish can bend around in a circle to bite its captor.

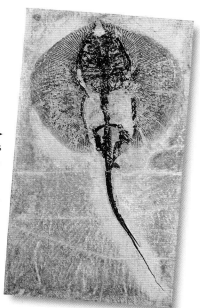

SHARK AND RAY ANCESTOR ▶
Complete fossilized skeletons or impressions of sharks and rays, such as this *Heliobatis* stingray, are unusual because, unlike bone, cartilage is too soft to fossilize well. However, fossils of cartilaginous fish have been found in rocks nearly 400 million years old. Some of these remains look remarkably similar to modern species. Sharks' teeth are often found in fossils, as they are harder than cartilage.

▲ SHARK SHAPE
The blacktip reef shark has all the features of a typical shark. Its pointed head, underslung mouth, and streamlined body reduce water resistance so that it can cut quickly through the ocean. The shark's asymmetrical tail is designed to provide lift as it swims along. Like most sharks, the blacktip reef shark has five external gill slits and bears live young.

FIND OUT MORE ▶▶ Anatomy **26–27** • Fish **126–127** • Oceans **74–75** • Rays **130** • Sharks **131**

RAYS

Rays are the largest group of cartilaginous fish and include skates, stingrays, electric rays, and the huge plankton-eating manta ray. A ray has a flat body with large, wing-shaped pectoral fins joined to its head. There are more than 450 different kinds of ray, and most live in the oceans. They live on or close to the seabed and eat fish, crabs, and worms that they dig out from the sediment.

Pectoral fins used like wings for swimming

Snout has nostrils to help detect hidden prey

Mouth contains broad, flat teeth for crushing mollusc shells

5 gill slits open on the underside

Eyes are well developed and raised up on top of the head

Spiracle (breathing hole) takes in water when ray is on seabed

UNDERSIDE OF RAY

Camouflaged back has spines along the middle

TOPSIDE OF RAY

DAPPLED BACK ▶
The distinctive dappled patterns on the back of this undulate ray help it to blend in with the gravel and sand of the seabed. The undulate ray is not fished commercially, but it is sometimes caught by trawlers. Its ornate appearance means that it is often kept in aquariums. Many rays bear live young, but the undulate ray lays large, brown, oblong egg capsules.

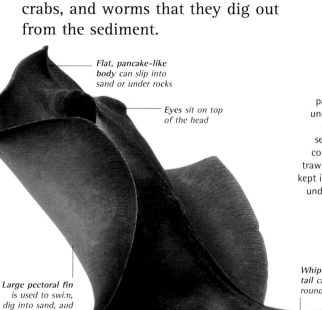

Flat, pancake-like body can slip into sand or under rocks

Eyes sit on top of the head

Large pectoral fin is used to swim, dig into sand, and hold down prey

Whip-like, flexible tail can bend right round to sting prey

Serrated, venomous spine used in self-defence

◀ A PAINFUL STING
Like other rays, a stingray is camouflaged to hide from predators. If attacked, it can defend itself with its long, barbed tail. The sting is extremely painful to humans if the ray is stepped on. However, stingrays are not aggressive and in Grand Cayman in the Caribbean, divers often swim with them. The rare giant freshwater stingray, which grows up to 2 m (6½ ft) across, is found in rivers in Borneo, Thailand, and Australia.

Triangular dorsal fin resembles a shark's fin

Broad pectoral fin joined to the head

Saw snout armed with bony teeth

SAWFISH ▶
A sawfish looks like a flattened shark, but it is actually an elongated ray found in tropical coastal waters and estuaries. The long, flat, saw-like snout is used to slash through shoals of fish, and to rummage through mud and sand for buried fish and invertebrates, such as shellfish.

Spiracle (breathing hole) takes in water when sawfish is on the seabed

Small eyes on sides of the head

FIND OUT MORE ▶▶ Cartilaginous Fish **128–129** • Oceans **74–75**

SHARKS

There are about 350 species of sharks living in the oceans. A few species, such as the bullshark, swim into estuaries and up rivers. Sharks are cartilaginous fish that range in size from the pygmy shark, which is 25 cm (10 in) long, to the 12 m (39 ft) whale shark. They are superb hunters and track their prey by sight, smell, and by detecting the electricity produced by moving fish. Only a few sharks are known to attack humans, but all should be treated with caution and respect.

Snout contains deep pores that sense tiny electric signals given out by moving fish

Nostrils aid the shark's excellent sense of smell

Head and snout are cone-shaped and push easily through water

Serrated triangular teeth are designed to tear chunks of flesh from prey

Pectoral fins are long, curved, and stiff, helping to lift the shark in the water

Pale underside provides camouflage against the bright water surface above

GREAT WHITE SHARK ▶
The great white shark is the most feared of all sharks due to its large size and reputation as a man-eater. However, most attacks on humans are cases of mistaken identity. To a shark, swimmers resemble seals and surfers lying on boards look like turtles. During an attack, a great white will slam into its victim with its snout lifted up to expose its sharp, cutting teeth.

◀ BIRTH AND GROWTH
Most sharks and rays give birth to live young but many smaller sharks lay eggs, each of which is protected by a tough egg case. Dogfish egg cases have long tendrils to cling to seaweed. Each baby grows inside its case for 6-9 months, then breaks out and swims away. Empty egg cases are known as mermaid's purses and are often washed up onto beaches.

MERMAID'S PURSE

ADULT DOGFISH

JAWS AND TEETH

Sharks have several rows of hard teeth, lying one behind the other. Only the outermost rows are used at any one time; the rest lie flat in the shark's jaws. The extra teeth move forwards as the front teeth break or fall out. Individual teeth can be replaced every 8–15 days. Different sharks have different-shaped teeth, according to diet.

Jagged razor-sharp teeth to bite chunks out of prey

JAWS OF A TIGER SHARK

Upper jaw cartilage

Jaw joint opens wide

Lower jaw cartilage

Replacement teeth gradually straighten

Teeth in use are upright

Mako shark's teeth are dagger-like to hold slippery prey

BLUE SHARK ▲
The torpedo-shaped blue shark regularly swims thousands of kilometres on long-distance migrations. Those living in the North Atlantic follow ocean currents in a clockwise loop. In the Pacific, they move north and south with the seasons. Blue sharks can dive to a depth of several hundred metres as they feed on fish and squid.

FIND OUT MORE ▶▶ Cartilaginous Fish **128–129** • Copper Shark **36–37** • Dangerous Fish **152–153** • Whale Shark **132–133**

WHALE SHARK

Whale sharks are the world's largest species of fish. Despite their great size and fearsome appearance, they are harmless to humans. A whale shark's mouth may be up to 1 m (3⅓ ft) wide and contains 300 rows of tiny hooked teeth – even though it does not chew or bite its food. It feeds by filtering plankton, small crustaceans, and fish from the water as it swims along with its mouth wide open.

Scientific name: *Rhincodon typus*

Order: Orectolobiformes (carpet sharks)

Class: Chondrichthyes (cartilaginous fish)

Distribution: In tropical waters worldwide

Status: Vulnerable

Length: 12–14 m (39–46 ft)

Weight: Over 12 tonnes (11¾ tons)

Food: Sieves over 6,000 litres (1,500 gallons) of water an hour through its gills, filtering out small shrimps and plankton

Breeding activity: Mates and reproduces at 30 years old; most adults are solitary

Number of young: May be hundreds; females give birth to live pups; newborns are 60 cm (2 ft) long

FIND OUT MORE ▸▸ Cartilaginous Fish **128–129** • Oceans **74–75** • Sharks **131**

BONY FISH

Bony fish make up the largest group of fish. Their skeletons are made almost entirely of strong, light bone. Most bony fish have a gas-filled swim bladder that allows them to control their buoyancy (ability to float). Many of the fish in this group lay thousands to millions of eggs straight into the water, where they float until they hatch into larvae. The larvae then develop into adults. Some species, such as seahorses, lay fewer eggs and protect them until they hatch.

BONY FISH SKELETON ▶

Like other vertebrates, this Atlantic cod has a skull, backbone, and ribs, but its skeleton also includes numerous flexible bones that support the fins and allow the fish to make intricate movements. Strong spines extend from the vertebrae. These overlap with other spines that extend from the base of each fin. The fins are supported by flexible fin rays, as in this cod, or by hard spines.

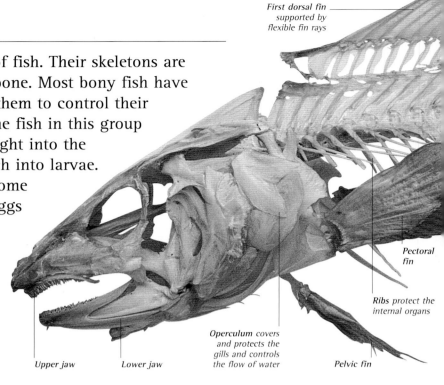

First dorsal fin supported by flexible fin rays

Pectoral fin

Ribs protect the internal organs

Upper jaw   *Lower jaw*   *Operculum covers and protects the gills and controls the flow of water*   *Pelvic fin*

First dorsal fin with sharp spines

▲ SPINY-RAYED FISH

Many bony fish, such as this freshwater perch, have sharp spines as well as flexible rays in their first dorsal and anal fins. Over half the known species of fish are spiny-rayed. Counting spines and rays can help to identify closely related species of fish. Spines can make it difficult for predators to swallow spiny-rayed fish.

BONY FISH SCALES ▶

Most bony fish, including this goldfish, are covered with lightweight overlapping scales that protect their skin and help them slide through the water. The scales are made of thin bone and provide flexible armour against infection and injury. The age of some fish can be calculated by counting growth rings on the fish's scales.

OVERLAPPING SCALES

Lateral line shape can be used to help identify fish

Scales along the lateral line have open pores

◀ LATERAL LINE

Trevallys and many other types of bony fish live in large shoals for safety. The shoal can move in perfect unison through the water, as each fish senses its neighbours using its lateral line – a system of sense organs arranged in a canal along the head and sides of each fish. The sense organs pick up vibrations created by the fish as they move.

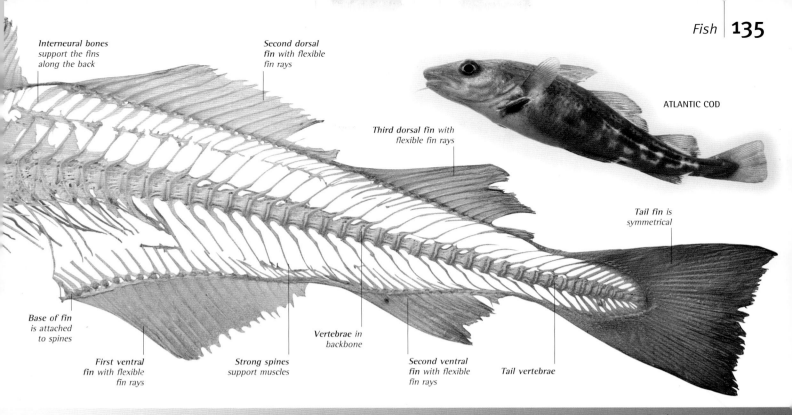

Interneural bones
support the fins
along the back

Second dorsal
fin with flexible
fin rays

Third dorsal fin with
flexible fin rays

ATLANTIC COD

Tail fin is
symmetrical

Base of fin
is attached
to spines

First ventral
fin with flexible
fin rays

Strong spines
support muscles

Vertebrae in
backbone

Second ventral
fin with flexible
fin rays

Tail vertebrae

FIND OUT MORE ▸▸ Anatomy **26-27** • Cod **140** • Fish **126–127** • Oceans **74–75** • Seahorses **144**

FLESHY-FINNED FISH

Coelacanths and lungfish are the only living representatives of an ancient group of bony fish called fleshy-finned fish, or lobefins. The fins of fleshy-finned fish are on the ends of stumpy limbs. Strong muscles inside the limbs are attached to the skeleton. Ancestors of this group of fish developed true limbs and evolved into early four-legged land animals. Fleshy-finned fish were common in Devonian times, around 400 to 350 million years ago. Today, only eight species are known.

LIVING FOSSIL ▲
Coelacanths were thought to have died out over 65 million years ago. Then, in 1938, a single specimen was discovered off the coast of South Africa in the Indian Ocean. The fish live in deep water, on steep rocky reefs, and in caves. They are fierce predators that grow to nearly 2 m (6½ ft) long, but breed slowly and are endangered by fishing. A second species was discovered near Indonesia in 1990.

Mouth gulps in air
to swim bladder
used as lung

LUNGFISH ▶
The Australian lungfish lives in deep pools or rivers and normally breathes with its gills. However, it can use its swim bladder like a primitive lung to take in oxygen from the air if the water becomes stagnant. African and South American lungfish live in small pools that often dry up. They have small gills but breathe air all the time through a pair of lungs.

Long, fleshy fin is
used to walk along
the river or lake bed

Large scales made
of a hard tooth-
like substance

FIND OUT MORE ▸▸ Evolution **16–17** • Fish **126–127**

STURGEON

Prehistoric-looking sturgeon belong to a group of primitive ray-finned bony fish in which only the skull (or parts of it) and some fin supports are made of bone. The rest of the skeleton, including the backbone, is made mainly of cartilage. Sturgeon live in coastal waters around Europe and North America and migrate up rivers to lay their eggs. Other primitive ray-finned fish include freshwater paddlefish, gars, bichirs, and bowfin.

Elongated snout with mouth and sensory barbels underneath

Rows of bony scutes (shield-shaped hard plates) embedded in scaleless skin

BELUGA STURGEON ▲
The beluga sturgeon is the largest fish to enter fresh water and reaches a length of at least 5 m (16 ft) and a weight of around 1,500 kg (3,300 lb). Larger beluga may have existed but most are now much smaller due to overfishing for caviar. Adults spend most of their life in the sea but swim up rivers to lay eggs. Beluga can live for over 100 years.

CLOSE-UP OF STURGEON SKIN

SINGLE STURGEON SCUTE

Long shark-like tail fin

◄ PADDLEFISH
The North American paddlefish grows up to 1.5 m (5 ft) long and lives mainly in the Mississippi river system. Its strange flat snout is nearly as long as its body and contains electroreceptors that sense objects in the deep, dark rivers in which it lives. The rare Chinese paddlefish lives in the Yangtze river. Paddlefish are also a source of caviar.

Skin patterned on head and snout

Mouth is gaping and almost toothless

Flabby gills with long gill rakers used to strain food from water

Long jaws armed with sharp teeth for seizing prey

Smooth, scaleless skin

LONG-NOSED GAR ►
Another primitive ray-finned fish is the long-nosed gar of eastern North America, which lives in fresh water. With its needle-sharp teeth and long jaws, the long-nosed gar resembles a miniature alligator. The fish waits motionless in rivers and lakes, hidden by vegetation, then grabs passing prey with lightning speed.

FIND OUT MORE ▶▶ Bony Fish 134–135 • Fresh Water 71

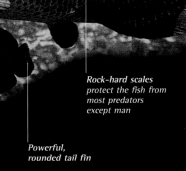

Shark-like tail fin with backbone turning up into upper lobe

GIANT ARAPAIMA ▶
The arapaima or pirarucu from the Amazon River in South America is one of the world's largest freshwater fish, growing up to 2.5 m (8¹/₂ ft) long. A fearsome predator, it can grab large fish and even birds. However, it is a gentle parent. Eggs and newly hatched young are guarded carefully by both mother and father. Unfortunately, when river waters are low, the fish can be caught easily and they are now rare.

Rock-hard scales protect the fish from most predators except man

Streamlined dark green body

Powerful, rounded tail fin

BONY-TONGUED FISH

Tropical freshwater rivers and lakes are home to a group of ancient fish known as bony tongues – so named because they have small, sharp teeth on the tongue and the roof of the mouth. Most fish in this group live in oxygen-poor swamps and stagnant water and can use their swim bladders as primitive lungs to take in extra oxygen from the air. A diverse group, bony-tongued fish include the arapaima, knifefish, and elephantnose fish.

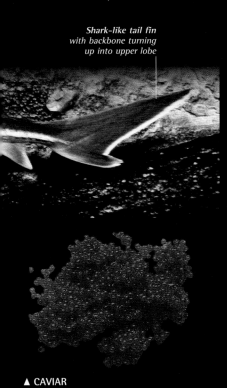

▲ CAVIAR
Sturgeon are famous because their unshed eggs are made into an expensive delicacy called caviar. The most prized caviar comes from the beluga, which is found mainly in the Caspian and Black seas in Eastern Europe. Large fish produce 100-200 kg (220-440 lbs) of caviar. A cheaper substitute caviar is produced from lumpfish roe (eggs).

◀ CLOWN KNIFEFISH
The narrow body of the clown knifefish helps it slip easily through the dense tropical underwater vegetation of Southeast Asia. A knifefish has no separate tail fin. It moves by rippling its unusually long anal fin, while keeping its body straight. The knifefish's swim bladder doubles as a breathing organ, and it often rises to the surface of the water to take air.

Body is hump-shaped, flat, and silvery

Long anal fin undulates to enable fish to swim backwards and forwards

Skin markings give this species its common name of clown knifefish

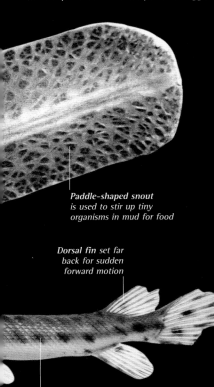

Paddle-shaped snout is used to stir up tiny organisms in mud for food

Dorsal fin set far back for sudden forward motion

Hard, diamond-shaped scales made of enamel-like substance called ganoin

ELECTRICAL ELEPHANTNOSE FISH ▶
The African elephantnose fish can produce weak electrical signals that act like radar, bouncing off objects and sending back echoes, to help it find its way around murky rivers and lakes. It has an unusually large brain in relation to its body size, to interpret the signals it receives back. The fish's downward-curving fleshy nose is used to probe the river or lake bottom in search of food.

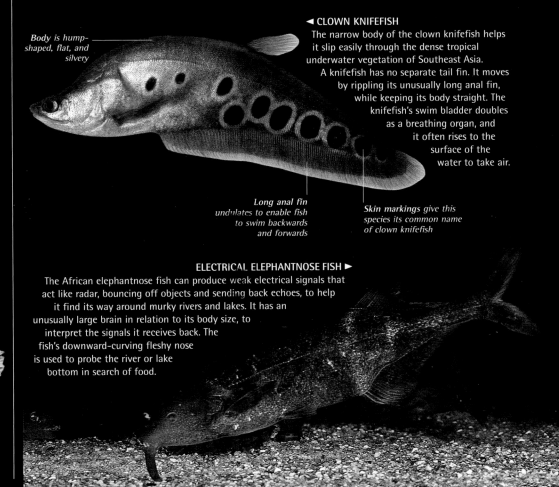

FIND OUT MORE ▶▶ Bony Fish **134–135** • Fresh Water **71** • Senses **30–31**

EELS

Eels have long, snake-like, flexible bodies, and most have slippery, scaleless skin. True eels include morays, congers, snake eels, freshwater eels, and deepsea eels. Most eels live in the sea, but some live in fresh water. Those that live in fresh water return to the sea to spawn (breed). There are over 700 species of eel, all of which start life as transparent larva. The larvae look so different from the adults that they were once thought to be a separate species.

Tough skin is often brightly patterned

Powerful jaws look ferocious, but eels rarely bite humans

Black and white markings help to camouflage eel

Needle-sharp teeth to seize and hold captured prey

◄ MORAY EEL
Moray eels are common on coral reefs and in rocky areas in tropical oceans. During the day, a moray remains hidden with only its head sticking out from a hole or crevice, but it may make a sudden lunge to catch a passing fish. At dusk, the eel emerges to hunt farther afield. Its long, thin body allows it to slip in and out of the coral on the reef, rooting out small fish.

◄ ZEBRA MORAY EEL
The zebra moray has strong pebble-like teeth for crushing hard crabs, molluscs, and sea urchins. It uses its excellent sense of smell to locate its prey. Like other moray eels, it has one long fin running along the rear half of its body. It swims by bending its body in a series of snake-like curves.

RIBBON EEL ►
A ribbon eel has leaf-like nostril flaps and chin barbels, which give it the appearance of a miniature dragon. Male ribbon eels are bright blue with yellow fins, females are yellow, and young ones are nearly black. This unusual species of moray eel can change sex – males become yellow and turn into females. These large females then produce lots of eggs.

Jaws constantly open and close so that the eel can breathe

Thin, flat body can measure up to 1.2 m (4 ft) long

ELVERS ►
European and North American freshwater eels spawn just once in the deep ocean and then die. Their eggs hatch into transparent leaf-shaped larvae called leptocephalus larvae, which drift inshore on ocean currents. Near the coast, the larvae change shape and become tiny transparent eels called elvers. These swim and wriggle their way into river mouths and then upstream into fresh water.

Slimy skin

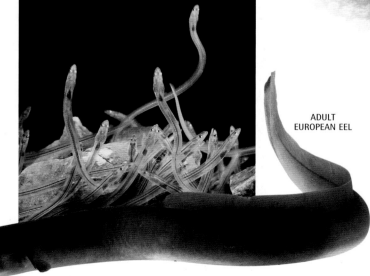

ADULT EUROPEAN EEL

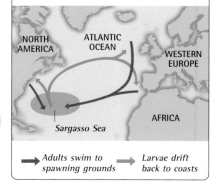

MIGRATION OF SPAWNING EELS

Freshwater eels live for many years in rivers and lakes before swimming thousands of kilometres to spawn in or near the Sargasso Sea. How they find their way there is still not fully understood. The larvae are carried back to river mouths in ocean currents. The European species reaches the coasts of Europe in about one year.

NORTH AMERICA
ATLANTIC OCEAN
WESTERN EUROPE
AFRICA
Sargasso Sea

→ *Adults swim to spawning grounds*   → *Larvae drift back to coasts*

FIND OUT MORE ▸▸ Coral Reefs 73 • Coral Reef Fish 148–149 • Migration 50–51 • Reproduction 44–45

◄ **ANCHOVETA SHOAL**
Huge shoals of tiny anchovetas feed off the coast of Peru in South America. Cold, nutrient-rich ocean currents rise to the ocean's surface and encourage the growth of plankton – the anchovetas' food. Periodically, a pattern of weather called El Niño stops these currents rising, so the plankton don't grow and the number of anchovetas is greatly reduced. Anchovetas are also affected by overfishing.

HERRINGS

Silvery, streamlined herrings live in the open ocean in huge shoals. The fish swim along with their mouths wide open, and feed by filtering tiny crustaceans from plankton floating in the water. For hundreds of years, herrings and their relatives have been a source of food, oil, fertilizer, and animal feed for millions of people around the world. Herrings are a vital link in many ocean food chains, and sharks, birds, seals, and whales all follow migrating shoals.

Single dorsal fin — *Large, silvery scales on body*

Forked tail for fast swimming
NORTH ATLANTIC HERRING

SARDINE

THE HERRING FAMILY ▲
There are over 360 species of herring and their smaller relatives, and they are found worldwide. Most herring species, including pilchards, sprats, anchovies, and anchovetas, lay thousands of eggs in traditional ocean spawning areas. Shads, however, migrate upriver to spawn. After hatching, the larvae drift in ocean currents, and many young fish are caught and sold as whitebait.

NORTHEAST ATLANTIC HERRING STOCKS

In 1977, the herring stocks in the northeast Atlantic collapsed as a result of intensive modern fishing methods. In 1965, the total catch was around 3.5 million tonnes and UK landings, as shown here, were around 100,000 tonnes. By 1977, this figure had dropped to 40,000 tonnes. Herring fishing was banned. The fishery reopened in 1983, but recovery has been slow.

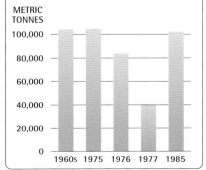

METRIC TONNES: 100,000 / 80,000 / 60,000 / 40,000 / 20,000 / 0 — 1960s 1975 1976 1977 1985

SARDINE FISHING ►
Spanish fishermen use bright lights to attract a shoal of sardines. Sardines are an important commercial catch in the Mediterranean and North Atlantic. The name sardine does not refer to one species of fish. If you open a can of sardines, you may be eating sprats in Norway, pilchards in Portugal, and young herrings or pilchards in North America.

CANNED SARDINES

FIND OUT MORE ►► Bony Fish 134–135 • Fish 126–127 • Oceans 74–75

COD

Cod are among the best-known marine fish in the northern hemisphere, and one of the world's most important commercial fish. Relatives of the cod include haddock, whiting, hake, and pollock. These fish live in cool waters in the North Atlantic Ocean and the Baltic and Barents seas. Cod feed on fish (such as herrings), crabs, worms, and molluscs. In turn, they are an important food for seals, dolphins, seabirds, and fish, such as halibut.

COMMERCIAL COD FISHING ▲
Modern fishing boats can catch entire shoals of cod at a time. Cod is a popular food in many countries, and has been heavily overfished. It was once the most plentiful fish in the North Atlantic, but stocks collapsed in 1992. Most cod in the North Sea are now under five years old because most of the older, larger fish have been caught.

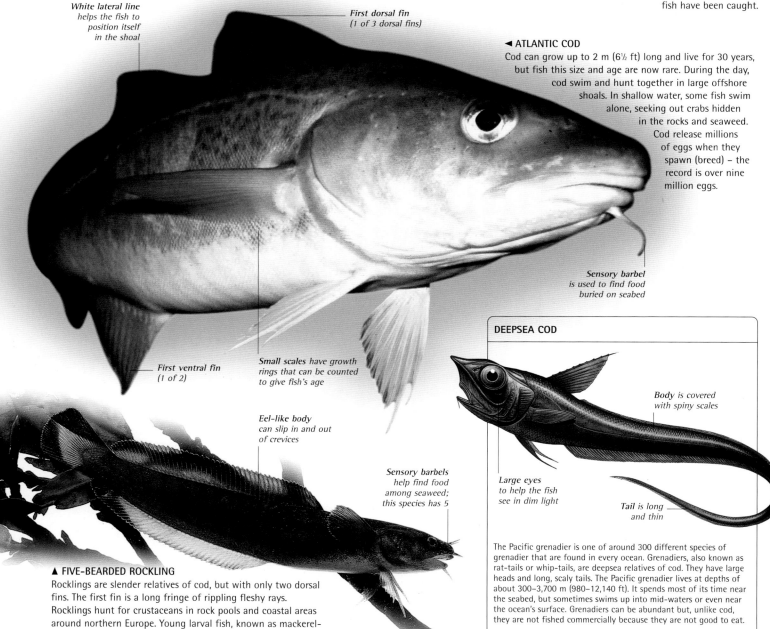

White lateral line
helps the fish to position itself in the shoal

First dorsal fin
(1 of 3 dorsal fins)

◄ ATLANTIC COD
Cod can grow up to 2 m (6½ ft) long and live for 30 years, but fish this size and age are now rare. During the day, cod swim and hunt together in large offshore shoals. In shallow water, some fish swim alone, seeking out crabs hidden in the rocks and seaweed. Cod release millions of eggs when they spawn (breed) – the record is over nine million eggs.

Sensory barbel
is used to find food buried on seabed

First ventral fin
(1 of 2)

Small scales have growth rings that can be counted to give fish's age

Eel-like body can slip in and out of crevices

Sensory barbels help find food among seaweed; this species has 5

DEEPSEA COD

Body is covered with spiny scales

Large eyes to help the fish see in dim light

Tail is long and thin

The Pacific grenadier is one of around 300 different species of grenadier that are found in every ocean. Grenadiers, also known as rat-tails or whip-tails, are deepsea relatives of cod. They have large heads and long, scaly tails. The Pacific grenadier lives at depths of about 300–3,700 m (980–12,140 ft). It spends most of its time near the seabed, but sometimes swims up into mid-waters or even near the ocean's surface. Grenadiers can be abundant but, unlike cod, they are not fished commercially because they are not good to eat.

▲ FIVE-BEARDED ROCKLING
Rocklings are slender relatives of cod, but with only two dorsal fins. The first fin is a long fringe of rippling fleshy rays. Rocklings hunt for crustaceans in rock pools and coastal areas around northern Europe. Young larval fish, known as mackerel-midge, float at the surface and are often eaten by seabirds.

FIND OUT MORE ▸▸ Bony Fish **134** • Deepsea Fish **154–155** • Oceans **74–75**

FLATFISH

Flatfish are found in all the world's oceans. They lie at the bottom of the sea, hiding from predators and feeding on small fish, molluscs, crabs, and worms. Young fish hatch from eggs floating in plankton, and swim down to the seabed to live on mud, sand, or rock. There are about 540 known species of flatfish, including plaice, sole, halibut, flounder, and turbot.

Long dorsal fin extends along body to head

Eyes on right side of body

Eyeless left side faces the seabed

Muscles and blood vessels are visible on the underside of the plaice

Skin pattern matches speckled grains of sand on the seabed

CAMOUFLAGED TURBOT ▲
Turbot are one of the largest flatfish, measuring up to 1 m (3⅓ ft). They can be difficult to spot, because they are able to change colour quickly and blend in with their surroundings. Turbot also hide by burrowing into sand, leaving only their eyes showing. Both eyes are on the left side, making them left-eyed, like their close relatives, brill.

PLAICE ▲
The plaice is a common European flatfish. Both its eyes are on the right side of its body and it lies on the seabed on its sightless left side. Its patterned upper surface blends in with the seabed, providing good camouflage. Plaice are most active at night when they hunt for shellfish. Adults have extra teeth in their throat to crush shells.

White underside faces the seabed

LIFE CYCLE OF A SOLE

THIRTEEN DAY-OLD LARVA
Like all flatfish, a young sole starts life with a rounded body and one eye on either side of its head. Gradually, an amazing metamorphosis (change) takes place. The eye on its left side moves around the head to join the eye on the right. The fish also becomes thin and flat.

TWENTY-EIGHT DAY-OLD LARVA
At first, a sole swims near the seabed but, by the time it is a month old, it settles its flattened body on the seafloor with its eyeless side facing down. By this stage, the sole's mouth has moved around to the top. The fish's skin is still semi-transparent, so its bones and organs can be seen.

YEAR-OLD SOLE
The skin on the sole's upper side soon develops pigment (colour) and becomes much darker. By the time the sole is a year old, it can control its colour pattern. Young fish live mostly in sheltered estuaries, at river mouths. The fish move into deeper waters as they grow.

MOVING EYES ▲
The Californian halibut is normally left-eyed but in some populations almost half the halibut have their eyes on the right side. This is because the eyes can move either onto the left or right side of the head as the fish grows up. This large flatfish can grow to 1.5 metres (5 ft) long.

FIND OUT MORE ▸▸ Bony Fish **134–135** • Fish **126–127** • Oceans **74–75**

Operculum covers gills

Long dorsal fin has a strong spine at the front and many soft rays

Mouth can be stuck out for grubbing through mud for food

Tail fin is fork-shaped

Mouth barbels are used to find food in murky waters

Large scales reflect light, giving the fish a shiny metallic sheen

CARP

Carp belong to one of the largest groups of freshwater fish, known as the cyprinids. There are over 1,500 different species in this group, including goldfish, minnows, tench, bream, and roach, and they are found in North America, Europe, Africa, and Asia. Carp and their relatives have an internal bony structure called the Weberian apparatus that connects the swim bladder and inner ear, giving them superb hearing.

▲ COMMON EUROPEAN CARP
Carp are native to Europe and Asia, but they have been successfully introduced to many other parts of the world. A carp has no teeth in its jaws. Instead it has a grinding pad further back in its mouth, and blunt pharyngeal teeth, which are located in its throat. It uses these teeth to mash up plants and small invertebrates. Carp are often kept in ponds as ornamental fish, and they are also raised on fish farms for food.

MOOR GOLDFISH

COMET SHUBUNKIN

BITTERLING REPRODUCTION ▶
Female bitterlings lay their eggs inside a freshwater mussel through a tube called an ovipositor. Sperm released by the male is sucked into the mussel with the water the mussel uses to breathe and feed. The eggs hatch and the young bitterlings grow in this safe living nursery, without harming the mussel.

Long ovipositor inserts eggs inside mussel shell

▲ ORNAMENTAL CARP
Carp and goldfish have been kept as pets for centuries. Many varieties with different colours and shapes have been produced through selective breeding, including moor goldfish, which have bulging eyes; multi-coloured comets; and mirror carp, which have just a few large scales. Koi carp, which live for many years, are especially valuable.

MIRROR CARP

FIND OUT MORE ▶▶ Bony Fish **134–135** • Fresh Water **71** • Molluscs **86** • Reproduction **44–45**

CATFISH

There are over 2,200 species of catfish. Most are freshwater species, and they are found on every continent except Antarctica. Catfish take their name from the long barbels on their heads, which look like a cat's whiskers. These feelers are covered in taste buds and help the fish find food in murky waters. Walking catfish are able to move from one body of water to another, using their stiff pectoral fins.

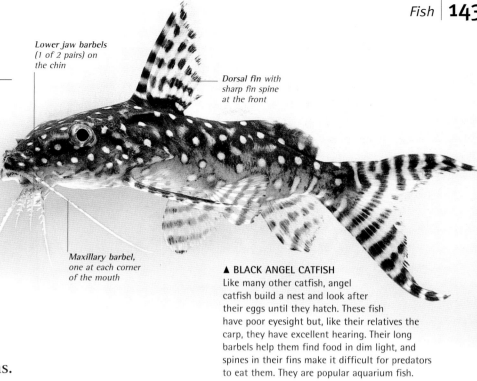

Lower jaw barbels (1 of 2 pairs) on the chin

Dorsal fin with sharp fin spine at the front

Maxillary barbel, one at each corner of the mouth

▲ BLACK ANGEL CATFISH
Like many other catfish, angel catfish build a nest and look after their eggs until they hatch. These fish have poor eyesight but, like their relatives the carp, they have excellent hearing. Their long barbels help them find food in dim light, and spines in their fins make it difficult for predators to eat them. They are popular aquarium fish.

AQUARIUM FISH ►
Corydoras catfish are often found in aquariums because they are small, attractive, and easy to keep. They only grow to around 10 cm (4 in) long. Like most catfish, they have tough, leathery, scaleless skin. The natural home of the leopard corydoras is in small tributaries in the lower part of the Amazon River in South America.

▲ WELS CATFISH
Most catfish live in warm tropical waters, but the largest species in the world, the wels catfish, comes from Eastern and Central Europe. It grows to at least 3 m (10 ft) long, and some have been estimated to be 5 m (16½ ft) in length. These ferocious predators eat water birds, mammals, and fish – there are even tales of large catfish eating dogs.

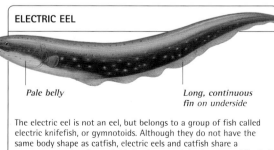

ELECTRIC EEL

Pale belly

Long, continuous fin on underside

The electric eel is not an eel, but belongs to a group of fish called electric knifefish, or gymnotoids. Although they do not have the same body shape as catfish, electric eels and catfish share a common ancestor. Gymnotoids live in warm inland waters of Central and South America. They can produce and sense weak electric signals that allow them to navigate and find food. The electric eel can also produce an electrical discharge strong enough to stun or kill another fish for eating, or even knock over a human.

▲ STRIPED MARINE CATFISH
Around 30 species of catfish live in the sea. Striped catfish are one of the commonest marine catfish. They live on coral reefs in the Indian and Pacific oceans. The young swim together in tight shoals as protection against predatory fish. Divers are wary of these fish because, like most catfish, they have sharp spines in their dorsal and pectoral fins that contain a mild venom.

FIND OUT MORE ►► Carp **142** • Defence **42–43** • Fresh Water **71**

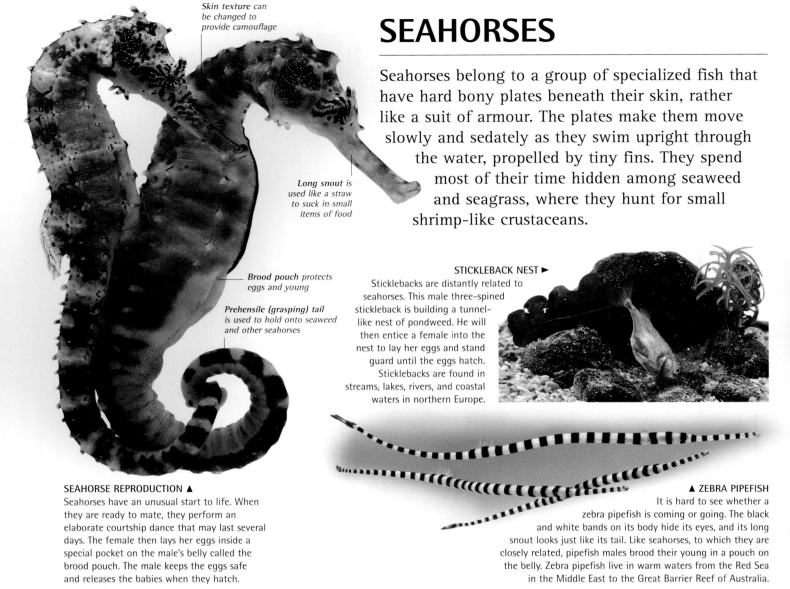

Skin texture can be changed to provide camouflage

Long snout is used like a straw to suck in small items of food

Brood pouch protects eggs and young

Prehensile (grasping) tail is used to hold onto seaweed and other seahorses

SEAHORSES

Seahorses belong to a group of specialized fish that have hard bony plates beneath their skin, rather like a suit of armour. The plates make them move slowly and sedately as they swim upright through the water, propelled by tiny fins. They spend most of their time hidden among seaweed and seagrass, where they hunt for small shrimp-like crustaceans.

STICKLEBACK NEST ▶
Sticklebacks are distantly related to seahorses. This male three-spined stickleback is building a tunnel-like nest of pondweed. He will then entice a female into the nest to lay her eggs and stand guard until the eggs hatch. Sticklebacks are found in streams, lakes, rivers, and coastal waters in northern Europe.

SEAHORSE REPRODUCTION ▲
Seahorses have an unusual start to life. When they are ready to mate, they perform an elaborate courtship dance that may last several days. The female then lays her eggs inside a special pocket on the male's belly called the brood pouch. The male keeps the eggs safe and releases the babies when they hatch.

▲ ZEBRA PIPEFISH
It is hard to see whether a zebra pipefish is coming or going. The black and white bands on its body hide its eyes, and its long snout looks just like its tail. Like seahorses, to which they are closely related, pipefish males brood their young in a pouch on the belly. Zebra pipefish live in warm waters from the Red Sea in the Middle East to the Great Barrier Reef of Australia.

FIND OUT MORE ▶▶ Defence 42–43 • Parenting 46–47 • Reproduction 44–45

CICHLIDS

Cichlids are a large group of freshwater fish that may contain as many as 2,000 different species. Cichlids live mainly in lakes in tropical parts of Africa, India, and South America. Many African lakes contain their own particular species of cichlid that are not found anywhere else in the world. Unlike many other fish, cichlids take great care of their young, and some even use their mouths as a nursery for their babies.

▲ MOUTH BROODERS
Most African cichlids are mouth brooders. After laying her eggs, the female (or occasionally the male) gathers them into her mouth and keeps them safe until they hatch. The fry (baby fish) are let out to feed, but are collected at night or if danger threatens. After two to three weeks the fry swim off and the female can eat again.

FIND OUT MORE ▶▶ Fresh Water 71 • Parenting 46–47

SALMON

Some salmon populations live in land-locked lakes and spend their whole lives in fresh water. However, many species make amazing migrations from their ocean feeding grounds in the Atlantic and Pacific oceans back to their home rivers to spawn (breed). Fish that move between salt water and fresh water like this are called anadromous fish. Most salmon, and their close relatives, trout and char, live in the northern hemisphere.

Streamlined head and body for fast swimming

Dorsal fin in the middle of the back

Adipose (fleshy) fin is characteristic of all salmon and trout

▲ SOCKEYE SALMON MIGRATION
During their spawning runs up North American and Alaskan rivers, sockeye salmon use powerful thrusts of the tail to leap up waterfalls. Before spawning they spend several years at sea, feeding greedily on other fish to build up their strength. Special ladders are sometimes built to help the salmon get past obstacles on the river, such as dams.

▲ STREAMLINED SALMON
The Atlantic salmon has a powerful, streamlined body and a large tail for long-distance swimming. During their lives, salmon hatched in European rivers may travel right across the Atlantic Ocean to rich feeding grounds off the coast of Greenland. Salmon is a popular food, but wild salmon are becoming increasingly rare as a result of damming, which prevents the fish from swimming upstream to breed, and illegal netting.

Red coloration develops over the salmon's body before spawning

Hump develops on the male salmon's back

Hooked upper jaw

▲ BREEDING SOCKEYE SALMON
During the breeding season, sockeye salmon change colour, and the males grow longer jaws and humps on their backs as they swim upriver to shallow spawning grounds. When they reach their destination, the females dig a nest called a redd in the gravel of the river bed, and lay their sticky eggs. The eggs are quickly fertilized by the males. Exhausted by their long journey and the effort of spawning, the adult salmon soon die.

◄ SALMON EGGS
Salmon eggs hatch into tiny young fish called alevins. At first, the alevins remain attached to a round yolk sac from which they absorb food. When this has gone, they swim out of the nest to look for food. Many alevins are eaten, but the survivors develop into young salmon that are called parr. When they finally reach the sea, the fish are a beautiful silvery colour and are known as smoults.

FIND OUT MORE ►► Fish **126–127** • Fresh Water **71** • Migration **50–51** • Oceans **74–75** • Reproduction **44–45**

GAMEFISH

Most gamefish are fast, strong predators that put up a challenging fight when fishermen are trying to catch them. Like all fish, they have two different kinds of muscles for swimming. Dark red muscles are used for steady cruising, while strong white muscles are for short bursts of speed. Tuna, which swim long distances, have mainly red muscle and dark flesh. Pike, which swim quickly over short distances, have mainly white muscle and pale flesh.

Dorsal fin

▲ FAST SWIMMER

A bluefin tuna is perfectly designed for fast swimming. It has a torpedo-shaped body that slips easily through the water and a stiff, sickle-shaped tail that helps it gain maximum speed. It can also fold down its dorsal fin to give its body an even more streamlined shape. In short bursts, a bluefin tuna can swim at speeds of up to 70 kph (44 mph).

FIGHTING MARLIN ▶

Blue marlin are admired by anglers for the way they put up a tremendous fight when they are hooked, often making spectacular leaps out of the water. These huge fish live in the open ocean and may weigh over 800 kg (1,760 lb). Marlin have streamlined bodies that help them swim fast. They feed on other fish, such as mackerel, tuna, and squid.

Bill-like upper jaw may be used to stun prey

Short lower jaw helps marlin to gulp down fish

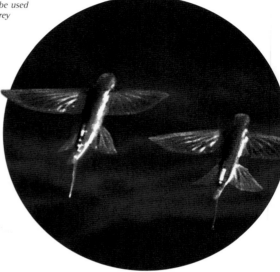

▲ FLYINGFISH

Flyingfish live close to the ocean's surface. If a flyingfish is chased by a large predatory fish, it shoots out of the water, opens its large pectoral fins, and glides above the surface. This means that when fishermen spot flying fish, they can tell that a gamefish, such as a marlin, may be nearby. A noisy boat may also make flying fish take to the air.

Smooth, streamlined body

FASTEST SHARK ▲

The shortfin mako, which belongs to a group of sharks called mackerel sharks, is thought to be the world's fastest shark. If caught on a fishing line, it can leap up to 6 m (20 ft) above the sea's surface at an estimated speed of 75 kph (47 mph). The shortfin mako has sharp, dagger-like teeth that help it to stab and grip slippery, fast-moving prey, such as mackerel, tuna, and squid.

▲ LARGEMOUTH BASS

Largemouth bass are originally from North America, but they have been introduced into other countries for sport fishing. In the United States, popular contests are held to catch the heaviest bass – big ones can weigh over 11 kg (24¼ lb). As its name suggests, this type of bass has a very large mouth and is a greedy predator in lakes and rivers. In some countries where it has been introduced, it has become a pest because it eats other gamefish. Largemouth bass lay their eggs in a gravel nest and the male guards the eggs and the young fry.

Large pectoral fin helps the fish manoeuvre through vegetation

Ventral fin is near the tail to help give the fish a burst of speed when hunting

▲ NORTHERN PIKE

The northern pike is a popular freshwater gamefish in North America and Europe. It has soft fins that can be angled in different directions so that it can hang motionless in the water. It hunts by lying in wait among water weeds, and then bursts out from its hiding place like a torpedo to grab its prey. It feeds mainly on other fish, but it also eats insects, frogs, and animals swimming on the water's surface, such as water voles and young waterfowl.

Large tail to help the pike make short bursts of speed

Bright stripe along the side gives the rainbow trout its name

Back has many small, dark spots

RAINBOW TROUT ▶

Most trout prefer to live in cool, clear running water, but rainbow trout are less fussy. These fish are native to North America, but they have been introduced into lakes and reservoirs throughout the world for anglers to catch. Rainbow trout are predators. They often rise to the surface to catch insects, so they are mostly caught by anglers who fly-fish using hooks disguised with tiny feathers to look like floating insects.

FIND OUT MORE ▶▶ Fish 126–127 • Fresh Water 71 • Sharks 131

CORAL REEF FISH

Coral reef fish live on, in, and around tropical coral reefs. Many reef fish have bright colours and patterns that help them to find each other, disguise themselves, or scare away predators. A coral reef provides fish with plenty of food and places to live. A few fish eat the coral itself, but most feed on other plants and animals. A coral reef may be home to hundreds of different species of fish.

SANDY PATCHES ►
At night, twinspot or clown wrasse stay safe from predators by wriggling down into sandy patches near the reef and hiding there until dawn. Young fish, like the ones shown here, have bright clown-like colours, but change colour and pattern as they grow into adults.

◄ GRAZING PARROTFISH
Parrotfish spend their day grazing on the reef. Their teeth are joined together to form a strong, parrot-like beak, which is used to scrape algae off corals and rock. Without the parrotfish – and other grazers such as surgeonfish – the reef would quickly become overgrown with seaweed. The huge bumphead parrotfish uses its mouth to grind up and eat the coral itself, which is passed out as sand.

PARROTFISH SKULL

◄ PLANKTON-PICKERS
During the daytime, swarms of golden anthias fish swim around just above the surface of the reef. They feed by picking plankton (tiny floating animals and plants) from the water with their mouths. Small, colourful damselfish feed in the same way. In the evening, all the plankton-pickers move closer to the reef, ready to hide among the coral when it gets dark. They come out again at dawn.

JUVENILE ANGELFISH

ADULT ANGELFISH

EMPEROR ANGELFISH ▲
Adult emperor angelfish are patterned with bold yellow and blue stripes. In contrast, young fish that are less than about 13 cm (5 in) long are dark blue with white circles and curves. Adult males defend their territory (the area of the reef in which they live), and attack and chase away other males. However, they ignore young angelfish – probably because they do not recognize them as their own kind.

COLOURFUL REEF FISH

MANDARIN FISH
Mandarin fish live among broken coral and sand in shallow areas of coral reefs. Although they are pretty, mandarin fish are covered in a horrible-tasting slime, so few fish eat them. Predators recognize their bright pattern and avoid them.

BUTTERFLY FISH
Many different kinds of butterfly fish, such as this yellowtail butterfly fish, are found on coral reefs. All butterfly fish are similar in shape, but each species has its own colourful pattern. The patterns help the fish to recognize each other.

HUMPBACK GROUPER
The spotty humpback grouper hunts small fish and crustaceans close to the reef. It is now rare on many reefs because it is caught by fishermen for food. Young groupers, which are deep purple, are also caught and sold as aquarium fish.

CLOWN TRIGGERFISH
The bright patterns of the clown triggerfish make it easy to recognize. However, from a distance its spotty pattern blends in with the reef. Dark colours hide the triggerfish's eyes so that a predator cannot tell which end of the fish is which.

◄ PREDATORY FISH
This spotted moray eel has made its home inside an old pipe. It will hide until suitable prey is in reach, and then launch a surprise attack. Once caught, its prey will find it difficult to escape from the eel's sharp, fang-like teeth. Although moray eels are fierce predators, they will not venture out to hunt until dark in case they are caught by larger predators, such as sharks.

NOCTURNAL REEF FISH ►
Soldierfish are nocturnal, which means they only come out at night when there are fewer predators. Their large eyes help them to see in the dark and snap up minute sea creatures called zooplankton. Although they look bright in the beam of a torch, their reddish colour does not show up in the dark. During the day they hide in caves or under coral.

Large mouth opens and closes as the moray breathes

HELPFUL FISH ►
This blue-spotted grouper is having its teeth cleaned by a small, blue-striped cleaner wrasse. The wrasse picks parasites off the grouper's skin and gills, and also eats dead skin and scraps of food. The grouper would normally eat a fish this size but will not harm the wrasse. This kind of relationship, which helps both partners, is called symbiosis.

Cleaner wrasse feeding on scraps in a grouper's mouth

FIND OUT MORE ►► Coral Reefs 73 • Corals 81 • Defence 42–43 • Ecology 14–15 • Scavengers 41

RED-SPOTTED BLENNY

A blenny is the name given to any fish of the family Blenniidae – a large group containing around 350 small fish found near rocky shores or on coral reefs. Most blennies have long scaleless bodies and a continuous dorsal fin. Their wedge-shaped heads contain tiny comb-like teeth, which they use to scrape algae from rocks. Some blennies, such as this red-spotted blenny, have fleshy filaments above their eyes.

Scientific name: *Istiblennius chrysopilos*

Order: Perciformes (perch-like fishes)

Class: Actinopterygii (ray-finned fishes)

Distribution: Tropical or temperate waters in the Atlantic, Indian, and Pacific oceans

Status: Some species may become vulnerable as they are collected for the aquarium trade

Length: Up to 45 cm (18 in) but most blennies are under 15 cm (6 in)

Food: Algae scraped from rocks; small invertebrates, such as molluscs

Breeding activity: Males usually change colour during the breeding season to attract a female and warn off other males

Number of young: Females lay around 100 eggs, which are usually guarded by the male until they hatch

FIND OUT MORE ▶▶ Coral Reef Fish 148–149 • Coral Reefs 73

DANGEROUS FISH

In both ocean and freshwater habitats, fish must use skill and deception to survive and hide from predators. Many use camouflage to conceal themselves, but others arm themselves with sharp spines or poisons. Most fish use these weapons to defend themselves, and when humans are stung or bitten it is because the fish feels threatened. On extremely rare occasions, some fish, such as large sharks, may attack humans.

▲ MAN-EATING SHARK

The tropical tiger shark is one of the world's most feared sharks, and is considered to be as dangerous or even more dangerous than the great white shark. It has been known to attack divers, swimmers, and boats. Its prey includes fish, birds, lobsters, and mammals, and it may also eat rubbish, such as wood and metal. The shark has a large head and a streamlined body. Young sharks are marked with vertical, tiger-like stripes, which fade as the sharks grow to adulthood.

Strong skull supports powerful jaws with sharp, interlocking teeth

Skin has silvery flecks with red on the belly

SKULL

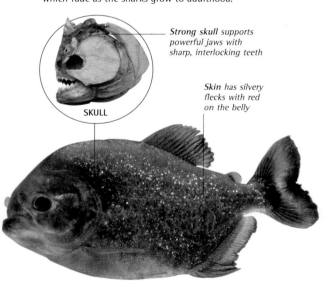

▲ PIRANHA FISH

Red piranhas live in South American rivers. They eat small fish, insects, and fruit and are not usually dangerous to people. However, blood or body fluids from a wounded animal can cause the fish to go into a feeding frenzy. In this state, a shoal of piranha can kill a large animal, such as an antelope, and strip it to a skeleton in minutes. Humans may be similarly attacked. Red piranhas are usually dark blue-brown with a silvery sheen and a red belly, which gives the fish its name.

▼ BARRACUDA SHOAL

Barracuda are fast-moving predators with needle-sharp teeth. They usually swim in shoals near the surface of warm tropical seas. This helps to protect them from predators bigger than themselves, such as sharks. Large great barracuda adults are usually solitary. Very occasionally, one of these lone fish may attack a human when they mistake a hand or a shiny watch for a silvery fish.

Elongated head has powerful jaws and knifelike teeth

SKULL

Long, streamlined body

Tentacle and
eye stripe disguise eyes to confuse predators

Venomous fin spine

Large pectoral fin
with venomous spines

Large tail
helps fish dart forwards to snap up prey

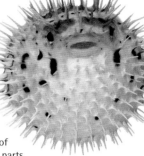

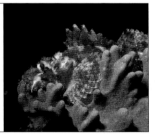

PORCUPINE FISH ▲

The porcupine fish is a kind of puffer fish. If threatened, it gulps in water so that it looks like a prickly football. Puffer fish are only dangerous to humans when eaten. They contain a deadly poison called tetrodotoxin. A single fish contains enough poison to kill 30 people. In spite of this, non-poisonous parts of the fish are eaten as a delicacy in Japan.

INFLATED
PORCUPINE FISH

◄ VENOMOUS FISH

Tropical lionfish are brightly coloured with elegant but venomous spiky fins. Their red and white stripes warn predators not to attack them. On land, wasps use the same sort of colours to warn of their sting. Because they are easily spotted, lionfish are less dangerous to divers and swimmers than well-camouflaged scorpionfish or stonefish.

CAMOUFLAGED FISH

SCORPIONFISH
Scorpionfish live on coral reefs. Their camouflage allows them to hide on the seabed and snap up any passing fish. Sharp spines on their fins can inject a painful poison. However, like most venomous fish, they are not aggressive and only use their poison in self-defence.

STONEFISH
As their name suggests, stonefish resemble knobbly rocks and are invisible until they move. They are the most venomous fish known. If a human treads on one or handles one in a net, they may be stung by its spiny fins. The sting is incredibly painful and is often fatal.

WEEVERFISH
Weeverfish lie partly buried low down on sandy beaches in Europe. Anyone stepping on a weeverfish may be injected with poison from its spiny black dorsal fin. Although very painful, the sting is not usually life-threatening.

FIND OUT MORE ►► Coral Reefs **73** • Coral Reef Fish **148–149** • Defence **42–43** • Oceans **74–75** • Sharks **131**

DEEPSEA FISH

Most deepsea fish never have any contact with either the seabed or the ocean's surface. They spend their lives swimming and floating in deep, cold, dark water. Although there are some giant deepsea fish, such as the oarfish, most are very small because food is difficult to find. Many deepsea fish are black so that they do not show up in the luminescent (glowing) light produced by deepsea predator fish.

Pectoral fin is large and flipper-like

Photophores produce light by chemical reactions

DRAGONFISH PHOTOPHORES ▶
Sunlight cannot reach far down into the ocean, and below 500–1,000 m (1,640–3,280 ft) it is inky black. Dragonfish, however, produce their own light in organs called photophores that are dotted along their sides. This bluish light is called bioluminescence. Deepsea fish can recognize the light patterns produced by different fish.

Lure is luminescent and attracts prey

Large tail fin helps the fish to move quickly

Luminescent lure is wiggled to attract prey

Needle-like teeth grasp fish attracted to the lure

Hinge-like jaws open wide to swallow large prey

BLACK DEVIL ANGLERFISH

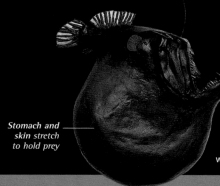

Stomach and skin stretch to hold prey

◀ BLACK DEVIL ANGLERFISH
The black devil anglerfish is only about 13 cm (5 in) long, but it is a ferocious predator. Anglerfish lure their prey within reach by fishing with a luminous rod. The rod is a modified fin spine, and is jerked up and down above the angler's large mouth. If a fish swims within reach, the angler grabs it with its long, dagger-like teeth.

▲ DEEPSEA ANGLERFISH
In the inky black depths of the ocean, it can be difficult to find a mate. When a male deepsea anglerfish finds a female, he attaches himself to her with his teeth and becomes a parasite. He can then fertilize her eggs whenever she lays them. The male is smaller than the female, and causes her little damage during this process.

SEA LEVEL

SUBLITTORAL ZONE SEA LEVEL
TO 200 m (650 ft)

1,000 m (3,280 ft)

BATHYAL ZONE
200–2,000 m (650–6,560 ft)

2,000 m (6,560 ft)

SWALLOWER EEL ▲
The swallower eel has an enormous mouth in relation to its size. It can open its jaws so wide that it can swallow fish that are bigger than itself. This is important because it lives below 1,000 m (3,280 ft) where food is scarce. The tip of its thin tail is luminous and may be dangled close to its open mouth to lure fish.

Teeth are numerous but tiny

Luminous (glowing) mouth may help attract shrimps

▲ MEGAMOUTH SHARK
The massive megamouth shark can grow to at least 5 m (16 ft) long and yet it was not discovered until 1976. This is because it spends much of its time in deep water, rarely coming to the surface, so only a few have ever been seen. It feeds by filtering tiny shrimps and other plankton from huge mouthfuls of water.

DEEPSEA ZONES ►
Many marine animals live in or on the seabed but others spend their whole lives swimming or floating in mid-water. All the animals shown on this page have a preferred depth range or zone where they live. Few animals live in the deepest, hadal zone. However, the sublittoral and bathyal zones teem with animals and plants.

3,000 m (9,840 ft)

◄ HATCHETFISH
Hatchetfish can make themselves almost invisible to predators. They are so thin that they are difficult to see head-on, and they keep very still. Predators looking up toward the ocean's lighter surface cannot see a hatchetfish's silhouette because the hatchetfish has a silvery belly. Its eyes face upward to spot predators swimming above it.

NAUTILE SUBMERSIBLE

NAUTILE

4,000 m (13,120 ft)

ABYSSAL ZONE
2,000–6,000 m (6,560–19,680 ft)

◄ HYDROTHERMAL VENT
Hydrothermal vents are places where hot water full of minerals gushes up through the seafloor. Vents are found 2,000–3,000 m (6,560–9,840 ft) down on mid-ocean ridges where there is volcanic activity. Worms, shellfish, and shrimps thrive in the warm water and provide food for strange-looking fish called eelpouts and brotulids.

Minerals colour the water like smoke

5,000 m (16,400 ft)

▲ OARFISH
The oarfish resembles a giant eel with bright red fins and a crest of long rays on its head. Oarfish can grow to 11 m (36 ft) long and, in the past, were thought to be dangerous sea serpents. They eat small shrimps, fish, and squid, and live in tropical and temperate waters worldwide at depths of around 1,000 m (3,280 ft).

Giant tube worms live on food made by bacteria

EELPOUT VENT FISH

6,000 m (19,680 ft)

HADAL ZONE
6,000 m (19,680 ft) AND DEEPER

FIND OUT MORE ▸▸ Defence 42–43 • Sharks 131 • Oceans 74–75

AMPHIBIANS

◀ LEADING A DOUBLE LIFE
The red-eyed tree frog inhabits the rainforests of Central America, and its moist skin is well suited to this warm, damp habitat. Like all amphibians, it is an ectothermic (cold-blooded) animal. Most amphibians can function both on land and in water – the name amphibian comes from the Greek words "amphi" and "bios", meaning "double life".

AMPHIBIANS

Amphibians are divided into three groups: frogs and toads; newts and salamanders; and caecilians. They are ectothermic (cold-blooded) creatures, which means their body temperature changes with their surroundings. They also have naked, moist skin that lacks feathers, hair, or scales. Most amphibians breed in water, where they lay eggs that develop into larvae. During the larval stage, amphibians breathe through gills; as adults, they develop lungs for breathing on land.

Pattern of markings are unique to this particular individual

Warning colours on the hands, feet, and belly

Hind legs are much longer than the forelegs

Skin is kept moist by mucus from special glands

Bulbous eyes sit on top of the head

FROG AND TOAD FEATURES ▲
Frogs and toads are the most easily recognized amphibians because they have such a distinctive body shape. Like this Oriental fire-bellied toad, they have tailless, squat bodies with long hind legs. They also have large, bulging eyes and wide mouths. Their skin is thin and porous, which means water and air can pass through it. Many amphibians are able to breathe through their skin as well as their lungs.

Eyes are adapted for seeing above and below the water

Body curves upwards upon entering the water

AMPHIBIANS

Frogs and toads

Tinker reed frog

Salamanders and newts

Marbled newt

Caecilians

Linnaeus's caecilian

Mouth gulps air before swimming off

IN AND OUT OF THE WATER ▲
Water plays a vital role in this northern leopard frog's life. Like many amphibians, this species needs to keep its body moist so that oxygen and carbon dioxide can pass through its skin easily, allowing the frog to breathe. Most amphibians require a watery environment to mate and to lay and fertilize their eggs. This is because their eggs have no shell to stop them from drying out. The newly hatched tadpoles pass through various stages in the water before they move onto the land.

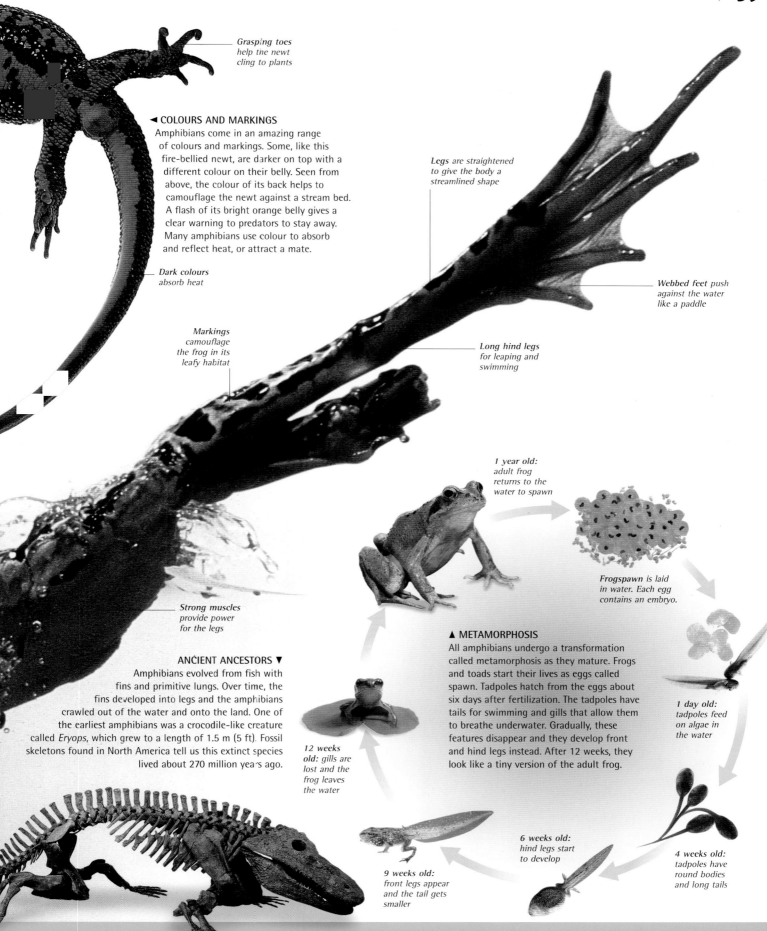

Grasping toes *help the newt cling to plants*

◄ **COLOURS AND MARKINGS**
Amphibians come in an amazing range of colours and markings. Some, like this fire-bellied newt, are darker on top with a different colour on their belly. Seen from above, the colour of its back helps to camouflage the newt against a stream bed. A flash of its bright orange belly gives a clear warning to predators to stay away. Many amphibians use colour to absorb and reflect heat, or attract a mate.

Dark colours *absorb heat*

Markings *camouflage the frog in its leafy habitat*

Legs *are straightened to give the body a streamlined shape*

Webbed feet *push against the water like a paddle*

Long hind legs *for leaping and swimming*

Strong muscles *provide power for the legs*

ANCIENT ANCESTORS ▼
Amphibians evolved from fish with fins and primitive lungs. Over time, the fins developed into legs and the amphibians crawled out of the water and onto the land. One of the earliest amphibians was a crocodile-like creature called *Eryops*, which grew to a length of 1.5 m (5 ft). Fossil skeletons found in North America tell us this extinct species lived about 270 million years ago.

1 year old: adult frog returns to the water to spawn

Frogspawn is laid in water. Each egg contains an embryo.

▲ **METAMORPHOSIS**
All amphibians undergo a transformation called metamorphosis as they mature. Frogs and toads start their lives as eggs called spawn. Tadpoles hatch from the eggs about six days after fertilization. The tadpoles have tails for swimming and gills that allow them to breathe underwater. Gradually, these features disappear and they develop front and hind legs instead. After 12 weeks, they look like a tiny version of the adult frog.

12 weeks old: gills are lost and the frog leaves the water

1 day old: tadpoles feed on algae in the water

4 weeks old: tadpoles have round bodies and long tails

6 weeks old: hind legs start to develop

9 weeks old: front legs appear and the tail gets smaller

FIND OUT MORE ▶▶ Evolution **16–17** • Fleshy-finned Fish **135** • Reproduction **44–45**

Large orbit, or eye socket, protects the eye

Skull is large but light

Pre-sacral, or shortened, vertebrae

Urostyle

Sacral vertebra

Elongated ankle bone

FROGS

With more than 4,500 known species, the frogs and toads form the largest of the three groups of amphibians. They live in an astounding range of habitats – in lakes, marshes, and other wet places, as well as grasslands, mountains, and even deserts. There are no clear differences between frogs and toads, but frogs generally have smooth skin and are found in or near water. Most toads live on land and have warty skins.

◀ BARE BONES
This American bullfrog skeleton shows some of the characteristic skull and skeletal features of frogs. They all have large eye sockets, a broad skull, and a short spine with ten vertebrae or less. The earliest frogs had short tails but, as these animals evolved, the tails gradually disappeared. All that remains is the urostyle. This is a peculiar rod-like bone formed from fused tail vertebrae. This amphibian's long hind legs have elongated ankle bones that allow the legs to fold when the bullfrog is at rest.

Eardrum, or tympanic membrane

Male frogs are generally smaller than females

Eye has moveable eyelids and tears to keep it moist

Inflated air sac of stretchy skin

▲ MATING EMBRACE
When mating, frogs and toads join in an embrace called amplexus. Male European common frogs grasp the female just behind her forelegs; in other species, the male may hold its mate in front of her hind legs. As the female releases her eggs, the male fertilizes them with his sperm. The fertilized eggs, called spawn, are left in the water and develop into tadpoles.

◀ MATING CALL
Male frogs and toads make croaking noises to attract a mate. They produce these sounds by inflating and deflating vocal sacs in their throats. Each frog and toad has its own distinctive croak, so the calls of this gladiator frog will only attract females from its own species.

MALE MIDWIFE ▶
The male midwife toad from western Europe shows a unique form of parental care. The female lays a string of up to 50 eggs, which are transferred to the male during mating. The male winds the string around his hind legs in a bundle. After three weeks of carrying them around, the male takes the eggs back to a pond where they hatch.

FROG AND TOAD DEFENCE

HIDING OUT
This Asian horned frog is perfectly concealed against the leaf litter of the forest floor. Not only is it the same colour, but the points on its nose and above its eyes resemble the tips of leaves. Many other frogs and toads also use camouflage to hide from predators and prey.

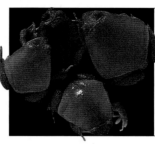

RED ALERT
The bold colouring of the Madagascan tomato frog acts as a warning to would-be predators that the frog is poisonous and should be left alone. Like many other species of frog, the tomato frog is endangered and is at risk of becoming extinct.

DEADLY DART FROGS
The most colourful amphibians are the tiny poison dart frogs of Central and South America. Native American people in the Amazon Basin collect toxins from the skin of these frogs. They apply the poison to the tips of the arrows and darts that they use to hunt.

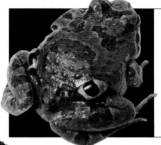

SUDDEN SHOCK
The Chilean four-eyed frog has a pair of glandular markings on its flanks that resemble eyes. When it feels safe and secure, its thighs cover the false eyes. If the frog is threatened, it suddenly exposes the eyespots, which startle its unsuspecting enemy.

Many legs make light work of whipping up the foam nest

Foam protects the eggs and keeps them moist

Sticky tongue flips out from the frog's mouth

▲ WHIPPING UP A FROTH
Perched on tree branches that overhang water, South African grey tree frogs use their hind legs to whip up mucus into a foamy nest. The frogs lay their fertilized eggs inside the froth, which stops the eggs from drying out in the sun. After they hatch, the tadpoles drop into the water below, where they feed and eventually develop into frogs.

Insect prey has no chance of escape once it gets stuck to the frog's tongue

Frog launches itself towards its prey

Strong hind legs propel the frog forwards

Bundle of eggs wound round the toad's hind legs

LAUNCHING AN ATTACK ▲
Leaping towards a woodlouse, this European common frog has very little time to judge accurately the distance it needs to jump. The frog must also flick out its long, sticky tongue at just the right moment to catch its prey. Frogs tend to pursue fast-moving insects, such as flies and crickets, so they only get one chance to snap them up. The frogs are usually quick enough to catch their prey, but if they miss, their meal escapes, and they will have wasted energy without any reward.

Webbed feet push against the ground

Warty skin is characteristic of many toads

FIND OUT MORE ▶▶ Amphibians **158–159** • Defence **42–43** • Golden Toads **162–163**

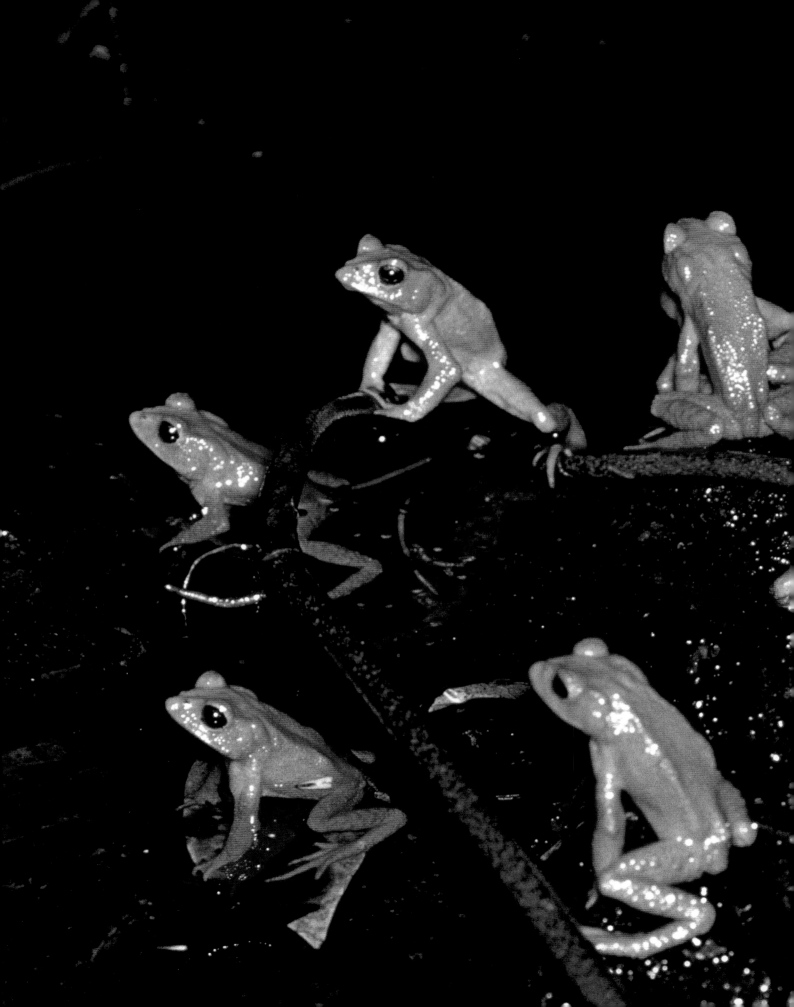

GOLDEN TOADS

Gatherings of these golden toads are a thing of the past. Scientists believe they have been driven to extinction by increased levels of ultraviolet radiation and climate change, which may have weakened the immune systems of these toads, leaving them vulnerable to disease.

Scientific name: *Bufo periglenes*

Order: Anura (frogs and toads)

Class: Amphibia (amphibians)

Distribution: Monteverde Cloud Forest, Costa Rica

Status: Has not been seen since 1989 and is believed to be extinct

Length: Females 42–56 mm (1½–2 in); males 39–48 mm (1½–1¾ in)

Colour: Males are a very striking orange. Females are black with scarlet blotches edged in yellow

Food: Insects

Reproduction: Males and females gather around small, temporary pools during the rainy season. Mating produces between 200 and 400 eggs, which may take five weeks to reach adulthood

FIND OUT MORE ▸▸ Amphibians **158–159** • Frogs **160–161**

SALAMANDERS

There are about 360 species of salamanders and newts. These slender, tailed amphibians are shy creatures that inhabit damp places, mainly in the cool, temperate regions of the northern hemisphere. Most species undergo metamorphosis (change of physical form), but a small number of aquatic salamanders keep their larval features in adulthood, particularly their external gills and fins.

MATING RITUAL ▶
Great crested newts perform an elaborate underwater mating ritual. First, the male swims in front of the female to show off its colourful belly. Raising the crest on his back and lashing his tail, he then fans chemicals called pheromones towards the female to get her attention. Finally, the male deposits his sperm on the pond or stream bed and guides the female over it so that her eggs can be fertilized.

Broad tail wafts pheremones from the male towards the female

ON ALL FOURS ▶
The fire salamander walks slowly on land. Like most other salamanders, its legs move in a sequence of alternate and opposite steps. The salamander lifts and moves the front foot of one side of its body forwards at the same time as the hind foot on the other side of its body. For a quick burst of speed, the salamander whips its long tail from side to side. This swishing action increases with its walking speed.

Underside is colourful and patterned

Skin on the topside is dark brown and warty

Left front foot is pushing the body forwards

Female newt is attracted by the pheromones and the male's mating dance

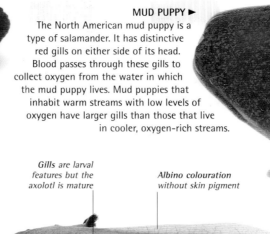

MUD PUPPY ►
The North American mud puppy is a type of salamander. It has distinctive red gills on either side of its head. Blood passes through these gills to collect oxygen from the water in which the mud puppy lives. Mud puppies that inhabit warm streams with low levels of oxygen have larger gills than those that live in cooler, oxygen-rich streams.

Worm is clamped between the salamander's jaws

▲ MEAL FOR ONE
Land-dwelling salamanders, such as this Oriental striped salamander, rely on their eyesight when hunting for soft-bodied animals, such as this earthworm. Once the salamander spots its prey, it begins a slow approach, then makes a swift and sudden grab at its meal. Aquatic salamanders feed on tadpoles, snails, and small fish. They use their sense of smell to locate their prey.

Gills are larval features but the axolotl is mature

Albino colouration without skin pigment

Blood-rich gills obtain oxygen for respiration

Forelimbs are too weak for walking on land

▲ FOREVER YOUNG
The axolotl has a condition called neoteny. This means it is a sexually mature adult that can breed, yet it resembles a larva. It will never develop the land legs or body shape of other adult salamanders. Instead, the axolotl keeps its gills and lives a completely aquatic life. In the wild, axolotls are now found only in Lake Xochimilco in Mexico.

Right hind foot presses against the ground, pushing the body forwards

Left hind foot moves forwards at same time as the right front foot

Tail curves to help the salamander balance

FIND OUT MORE ▶▶ Amphibians 158–159 • Deciduous Forests 64

CAECILIANS

Caecilians are limbless, wormlike amphibians with needle-sharp teeth and a bony skeleton. Some live underground, where they use their pointed snouts and powerful skulls to burrow through the soil. Others live underwater. These aquatic species have a fin on their tail for swimming. About 170 species of caecilians are found in the tropical regions of Africa, Asia, and South America.

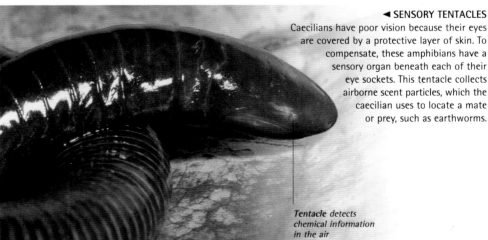

◄ SENSORY TENTACLES
Caecilians have poor vision because their eyes are covered by a protective layer of skin. To compensate, these amphibians have a sensory organ beneath each of their eye sockets. This tentacle collects airborne scent particles, which the caecilian uses to locate a mate or prey, such as earthworms.

Tentacle detects chemical information in the air

FIND OUT MORE ▶▶ Amphibians 158–159 • Senses 30–31 • Worms 85

REPTILES

◄ PATIENT HUNTER
The green tree python from New Guinea
and northernmost Australia hunts at night,
searching the branches of rainforest trees for
bats, sleeping birds, and other prey. Like all
reptiles, it is ectothermic (cold-blooded)
and has a scaly skin. Apart from snakes,
the reptiles include lizards, strong-jawed
crocodiles and alligators, and tortoises and
turtles, which have shells for protection.

REPTILES

Reptiles are ectothermic (cold-blooded) animals with scaly skin. There are about 8,000 species of reptiles, including crocodilians, lizards, snakes, turtles, and tuataras. Most reptiles, including those that live mainly in water, lay eggs on land, although some lizards and snakes give birth to live young. Reptiles with legs have a sprawling gait because their limbs are jointed to the side, not below as in dinosaurs, mammals, and birds.

▲ PROTECTIVE SHELL

Like other tortoises and turtles, this starred tortoise from India has more than just ordinary skin to protect it. It also has a strong shell, which is made up of large plate-like scales, or scutes, on top of bone. The shell has two parts. The upper part is called the carapace, and the flatter part beneath the belly is called the plastron. The shell protects the reptile from its enemies and bad weather, but makes it a slow mover.

TEMPERATURE CONTROL ▶

Reptiles cannot generate heat internally. The temperature of their bodies is determined by the temperature of their surroundings. Each reptile has a preferred body temperature range that it needs to maintain to stay active. They keep their body temperature within this range through their behaviour. Like this ocellated lizard, reptiles bask in the sun to absorb warmth. As the day becomes hotter, the lizard retreats into the shade to cool down. By shuttling in and out of the shade, the lizard can keep its temperature relatively stable.

Forked tongue flicks in and out of the mouth constantly

Transparent scale covers the eye

Each scale is set in the epidermis (upper layer) of the skin

◀ SKIN DEEP

Like all reptiles, this red-tailed rat snake is covered in scaly skin. The scales, which are part of the outer layer of its skin, or epidermis, are toughened with keratin. This is the same horny substance that human fingernails are made from. The belly scales of most snakes form a series of wide overlapping plates. These help the snakes to slither smoothly across the ground. All reptiles replace their scales by shedding their outer skin. This allows room for the reptile to grow, and also replaces skin that is worn out.

Wide scales on belly

REPTILES				
Tuataras	Lizards	Snakes	Turtles	Crocodilians
Tuatara	Monitor lizard	Indian python	Leopard tortoise	Spectacled caiman

◀ SURVIVING SPECIES

This unusual reptile is called a tuatara. Although it may look like a lizard, it belongs to a different group of reptiles called rhynchocephalians. All other rhynchocephalians died out millions of years ago, and they are now found only as fossils. The two species that survive inhabit small islands off the coast of New Zealand. They grow slowly but can live to 100 years or more. Tuataras live among seabird colonies, eating insects and sometimes young chicks.

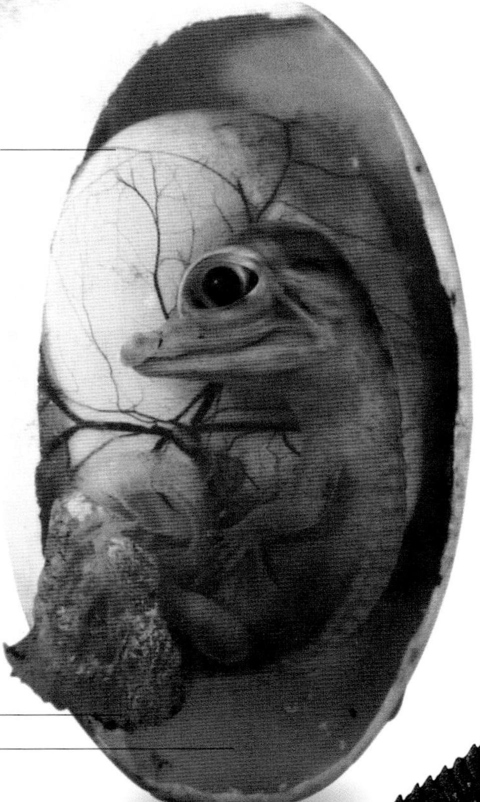

Strong legs are used for digging burrows

Amnion is full of fluid

REPTILIAN EGG ▶

Like all reptilian eggs, an alligator's egg contains everything the embryo needs to develop. The protective shell has tiny pores that allow oxygen to seep into the egg so the embryo can breathe. All animals need a watery environment for the early stages of their development, and this embryo is enclosed in a membrane called the amnion. The embryo draws nourishment from the yolk, while the albumen (egg white) cushions the embryo and provides it with extra water and protein. After an egg has been laid, it takes about 40 days for an alligator to hatch.

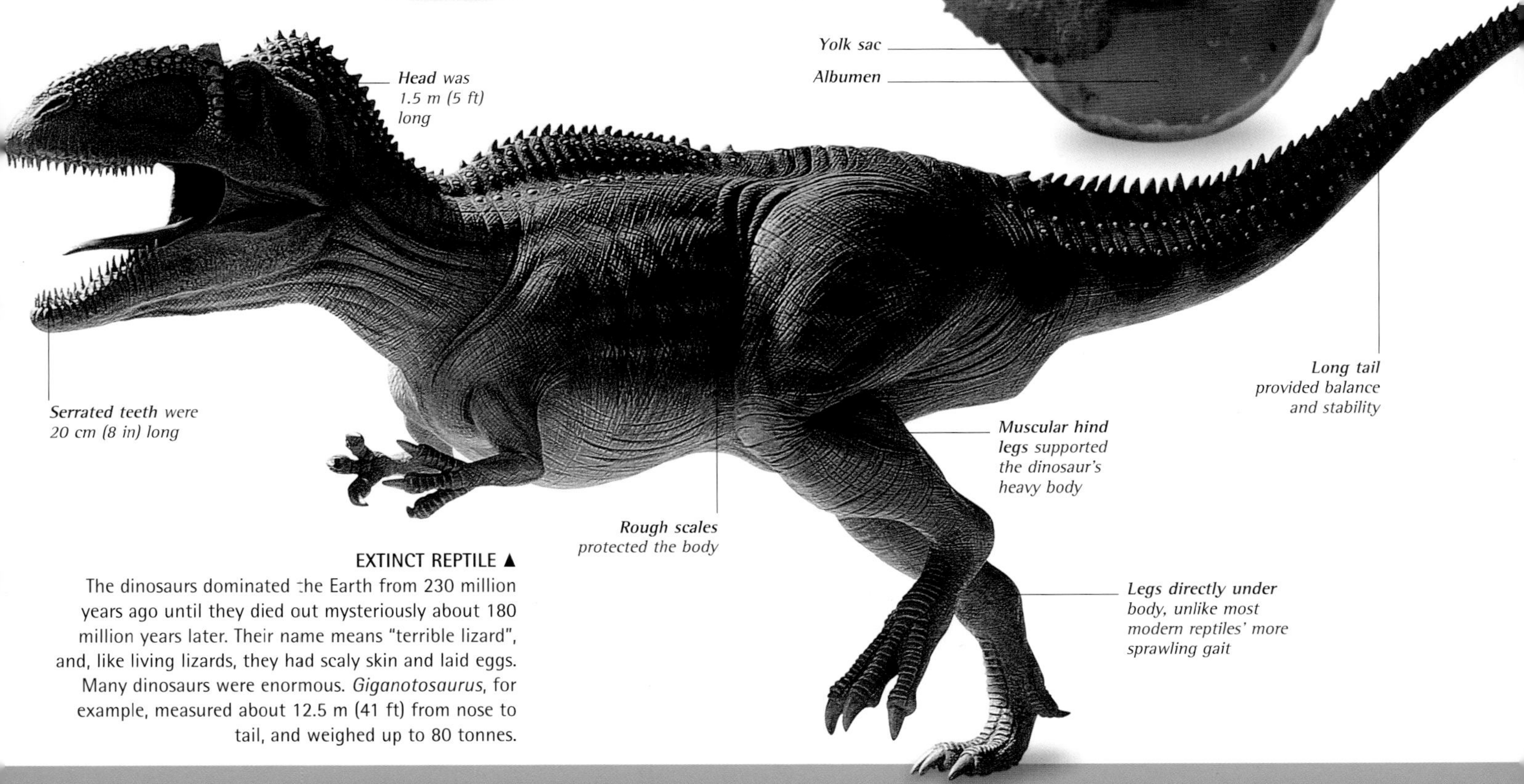

Yolk sac

Albumen

Head was 1.5 m (5 ft) long

Long tail provided balance and stability

Serrated teeth were 20 cm (8 in) long

Muscular hind legs supported the dinosaur's heavy body

Rough scales protected the body

Legs directly under body, unlike most modern reptiles' more sprawling gait

EXTINCT REPTILE ▲

The dinosaurs dominated the Earth from 230 million years ago until they died out mysteriously about 180 million years later. Their name means "terrible lizard", and, like living lizards, they had scaly skin and laid eggs. Many dinosaurs were enormous. *Giganotosaurus*, for example, measured about 12.5 m (41 ft) from nose to tail, and weighed up to 80 tonnes.

FIND OUT MORE ▶▶ Extinction **19** • Lizards **176** • Reproduction **44–45** • Snakes **184–185** • Turtles **170–171**

Carapace
(upper shell) is
streamlined

Plastron (lower
shell) protects
the belly

Front flippers
propel the turtle
forwards

▲ **LONG-HAUL SWIM**
Sea turtles are well adapted for their lives
in the warmer parts of the world's oceans.
They have powerful flippers and flat,
streamlined shells that allow them to glide
through the water with ease over long
distances. Some of them, such as this
green turtle, migrate up to 1,000 km
(620 miles) from their feeding grounds
to traditional nesting beaches.

TURTLES

Turtles are wide-bodied reptiles with shells that protect their soft
bodies from damage and attacks by predators. There are about
300 different species of turtle, most of which live in ponds and
rivers. Seven species live in the sea, while about 50 species,
known as tortoises, live on land. Land species tend to have
high, domed carapaces (upper shells). Those of aquatic turtles are
low and streamlined. All turtles use their sharp beaks to tear
up food, because they do not have teeth.

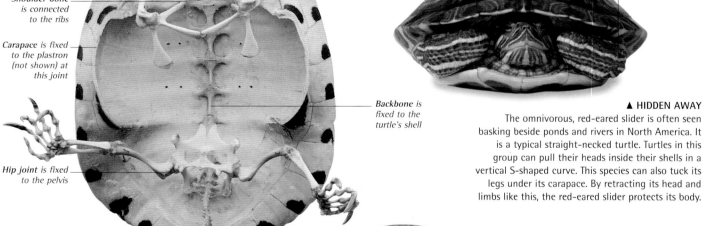

Shoulder bone
is connected
to the ribs

Carapace is fixed
to the plastron
(not shown) at
this joint

Hip joint is fixed
to the pelvis

Backbone is
fixed to the
turtle's shell

Leg tucks away
neatly under
the carapace

▲ **HIDDEN AWAY**
The omnivorous, red-eared slider is often seen
basking beside ponds and rivers in North America. It
is a typical straight-necked turtle. Turtles in this
group can pull their heads inside their shells in a
vertical S-shaped curve. This species can also tuck its
legs under its carapace. By retracting its head and
limbs like this, the red-eared slider protects its body.

INSIDE OUT ▲
A turtle's shell is part of its
skeleton. The shell has two distinct
layers. Horny plates, called scutes, form
the outer layer of the shell, although some
species have leathery skin instead. The inner
layer is made up of bony plates. Many of the
turtle's bones, including the ribs and the
backbone, are fused to the bony layer. The
pelvis and shoulders sit inside the rib cage.
All turtles have four limbs. Aquatic turtles
have either webbed feet or flippers, while
land species have short, club-shaped legs.

◄ **SKIN-COVERED SHELL**
The shell of this softshell turtle
has no horny scutes and feels like
leather. The bony layer underneath
is very lightweight, allowing the
turtle to move quickly underwater.
Softshells live in Africa, Asia, Indonesia,
and North America, and are usually found
half buried in mud in rivers and ponds, where
they hide from enemies and wait to ambush
passing prey. They can also be seen basking in the Sun.

Neck cannot be retracted inside the shell

Hind flippers are used to steer

◄ SNAKE-NECKED TURTLE

With its long neck, this carnivorous Australian turtle can snorkel for air from below the water's surface, and reach passing prey, such as frogs and fish, which it snaps up with a vicious bite. This species belongs to a group called the side-necked turtles. These turtles bend their neck and head sideways to fit under the edge of their carapace.

Worm-like lure on its tongue

Rugged shell deters predators

DEADLY DECOY ▲

The alligator snapping turtle is native to the southern United States. This fierce creature lurks at the bottom of ponds and slow-moving rivers, either stalking or ambushing anything it can catch – including other turtles. These turtles have a remarkable growth on their tongue that looks just like a pink worm. Passing fish are attracted to what looks like a tasty meal, only to find the reptile's powerful jaws closing around them.

▲ LAYING EGGS

All turtles lay their eggs on land, so the only time sea turtles leave the sea is to nest. The female loggerhead turtle lays her eggs in a specially dug hole on the beach, then fills in the hollow with sand to hide them. After about two months, the eggs hatch and the baby loggerheads scramble down to the water to begin their life at sea.

GALAPAGOS GIANT ▶

Weighing up to 185 kg (408 lb), the giant tortoise of the Galapagos Islands is the largest tortoise in the world. These herbivores have a tremendous capacity for storing water, which enables them to survive the long dry season on the islands. Giant tortoises live in small herds, with males fighting if necessary to establish dominance.

FIND OUT MORE ►► Hawksbill Turtle **172–173** • Reproduction **44–45** • Reptiles **168–169**

HAWKSBILL TURTLE

The hawksbill turtle takes its name from its sharp, beak-like jaw, which is an excellent tool for seeking out food on coral reefs. This species is best known for its stunning, mottled-brown carapace, which is often referred to as tortoiseshell. These distinctive markings have meant that the hawksbill's shell was highly prized, resulting in decades of hunting that led to a sharp decline in numbers. Although the hawksbill turtle is now a protected species, illegal trade in tortoiseshell still occurs.

Scientific name: *Eretmochelys imbricata*

Order: Chelonia (turtles)

Class: Reptilia (reptiles)

Distribution: Tropical coral reefs in the Atlantic, Pacific, and Indian Oceans

Status: Critically endangered

Length: 55-95 cm (22-37 in)

Weight: 55–80 kg (121–176 lb)

Food: Invertebrates, such as sponges, sea squirts, molluscs, and sea urchins

Reproduction: Mating often occurs in shallow waters near nesting beaches

Number of young: Females lay 2–6 clutches of eggs, averaging 130 eggs per clutch

FIND OUT MORE ►► Conservation 22–23 • Turtles 170–171

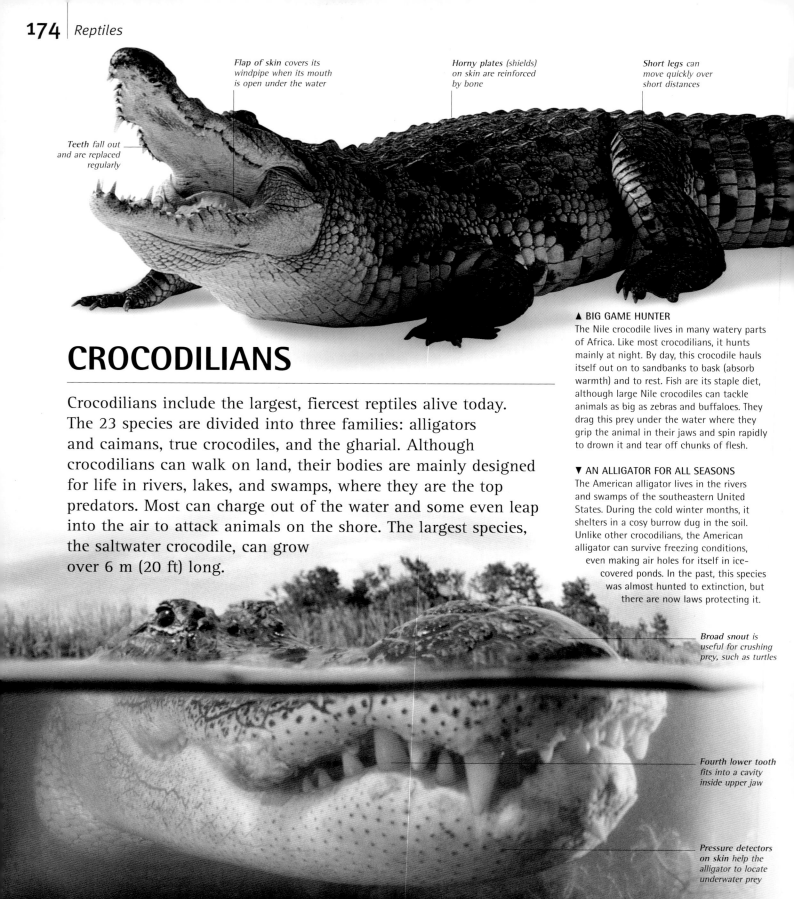

Teeth *fall out and are replaced regularly*

Flap of skin *covers its windpipe when its mouth is open under the water*

Horny plates *(shields) on skin are reinforced by bone*

Short legs *can move quickly over short distances*

CROCODILIANS

Crocodilians include the largest, fiercest reptiles alive today. The 23 species are divided into three families: alligators and caimans, true crocodiles, and the gharial. Although crocodilians can walk on land, their bodies are mainly designed for life in rivers, lakes, and swamps, where they are the top predators. Most can charge out of the water and some even leap into the air to attack animals on the shore. The largest species, the saltwater crocodile, can grow over 6 m (20 ft) long.

▲ BIG GAME HUNTER

The Nile crocodile lives in many watery parts of Africa. Like most crocodilians, it hunts mainly at night. By day, this crocodile hauls itself out on to sandbanks to bask (absorb warmth) and to rest. Fish are its staple diet, although large Nile crocodiles can tackle animals as big as zebras and buffaloes. They drag this prey under the water where they grip the animal in their jaws and spin rapidly to drown it and tear off chunks of flesh.

▼ AN ALLIGATOR FOR ALL SEASONS

The American alligator lives in the rivers and swamps of the southeastern United States. During the cold winter months, it shelters in a cosy burrow dug in the soil. Unlike other crocodilians, the American alligator can survive freezing conditions, even making air holes for itself in ice-covered ponds. In the past, this species was almost hunted to extinction, but there are now laws protecting it.

Broad snout *is useful for crushing prey, such as turtles*

Fourth lower tooth *fits into a cavity inside upper jaw*

Pressure detectors *on skin help the alligator to locate underwater prey*

Powerful tail can lash out either in attack or defence

▲ FEARSOME FISHER

The gharial – or gavial – lives in the rivers of southeast Asia, where it is a specialist fish-eater. Its long, narrow snout is lined with interlocking, razor-sharp teeth, which are ideal for holding struggling prey. The bulbous growth on the tip of the male's snout is called a ghara. Scientists think it may amplify the sounds the gharial makes during courtship.

Mother cracks egg open before carrying baby to the water

WHAT IS THE DIFFERENCE?

It is not always easy to tell the difference between a crocodile and an alligator. The best way is when their mouths are shut. There are also differences in bone structure that cannot be seen from the outside.

Crocodile When a crocodile's mouth is closed, some of the teeth in its lower jaw, especially the large fourth tooth, overlap the upper jaw on the outside. When viewed from above, crocodiles also tend to have longer, narrower snouts than alligators.

Alligator When alligators and caimans close their mouths, their lower teeth cannot be seen. Members of this family also tend to have shorter, broader snouts than crocodiles.

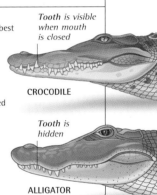

Tooth is visible when mouth is closed

CROCODILE

Tooth is hidden

ALLIGATOR

CARING PARENTS ▲

Like most crocodilians, Nile crocodiles are extremely attentive parents. The female lays her eggs in a hole that she digs in the ground, then covers them up with vegetation, and guards them closely until they are ready to hatch. When she hears chirping noises coming from the underground nest, the mother digs down to uncover the eggs. She may help crack the shells before gently carrying the babies down to the water's edge in her mouth.

Nostrils sit just above the water line

◄ WATER BABY

This young caiman is well adapted for its life in the rivers and wetlands of South America. Its eyes, nostrils, and ears are set high on its head so it can still see and breathe as it lies unseen in the water. Young caimans, like other young crocodilians, tend to stay close to their mother for protection. If they need to escape from predators, they sink underwater, where they cover their nostrils and ears with special flaps. An extra eyelid also moves across each eye to protect it.

FIND OUT MORE ▶▶ Conservation **22–23** • Parenting **46–47** • Reptiles **168–169**

LIZARDS

With about 4,500 species, lizards make up the largest, and most widespread, group of reptiles. Most lizards have slim bodies, large heads, four legs of a similar length, and a long tail. A small number of lizards have no limbs at all. Most species reproduce by laying eggs, although some give birth to live young. Lizards are mainly predators, eating insects and small mammals, which they crush with their pointed teeth.

▲ THERMAL DANCING
The shovel-snouted lizard lives on the burning sands of the Namib Desert in Africa. To cool down, it lifts two feet at a time off the hot sand. This cooling technique is known as thermal dancing. If the dance fails to cool the lizard, it burrows under the sand. Lizards thrive in deserts because they can live on less food than warm-blooded animals.

Legs sprawl to side of body

Tail has broken at a weak point

New tail is beginning to grow from the stump

Body bends as the lizard moves

Five claws on each foot

▲ A TAIL'S TALE
Some lizards can shed their tails deliberately to escape the clutches of a predator. The vertebrae (backbones) along their tails have built-in weak points where the tail can break off easily. As in the case of this tree skink, the tail soon begins to grow back. Eventually, it will look almost the same as the old tail on the outside but it will have a flexible tube of cartilage instead of bone on the inside.

▲ TIME FOR LUNCH
Most lizards are carnivores. They can be roughly divided into two different types of predators. There are those that actively search for prey, such as this European green lizard. The other group of carnivorous lizards sit and wait for their food to come near, then pounce on it. Of this type, the geckos are among the most useful to people, as they often feed on insects that find their way into houses in tropical climates.

▲ LEGLESS LIZARD
Although this slow worm looks like a snake or a worm, it is actually a legless lizard. Slow worms are active at night when they use their forked tongues to sense slow-moving prey, such as earthworms, slugs, and snails. In the cold winter months, the slow worm hibernates under soft soil, leaves, or tree roots. This lizard can live for several years, but it has many predators, including adders, rats, and kestrels.

Colouring helps the lizard blend in with its surroundings

FIND OUT MORE ▶▶ Defence 42–43 • Deserts 58–59 • Reptiles 168–169

IGUANAS

Iguanas are a diverse group of lizards that live in a variety of habitats from seashores to deserts, and from forests to grasslands. Large iguanas, such as the green and marine iguanas, are herbivores. Smaller iguanas, including the collared lizard and the anole lizards, are carnivores. Many iguanas have spines, crests, or loose flaps of skin that make them look bigger and fiercer to predators and rivals.

▲ OCEAN DWELLER
Marine iguanas feed on seaweed in the sea around the Galapagos Islands. They dive to depths of up to 15 m (49½ ft) in the cold water to reach their food, then bask in the sun to warm up. These iguanas swallow a lot of saltwater, so they have glands in their mouths that transfer the salt to their nostrils, where they can snort it out.

INTERESTING IGUANAS

HORNED LIZARD
This flat, wide-bodied lizard lives in the deserts of western North America where it feeds mainly on ants. A slow mover, the horned lizard relies on camouflage and its sharp spines for defence. If these fail, it squirts foul-tasting blood from its eyes.

COURTSHIP DISPLAY
Male anole lizards inflate their coloured dewlaps and bob their heads to attract females and intimidate rivals. These iguanas live in trees in the southeastern United States. They are sometimes referred to as American chameleons, though they are iguanas.

COLLARED LIZARD
The prominent black-and-white stripes on the back of the neck give this lizard its common name. Collared lizards live on the rocky terrain of the gullies and canyons of the western United States. They are extremely agile hunters and can sprint on two legs.

External eardrum detects airborne vibrations

Crest of modified scales runs along the back

◄ COMMON IGUANA
The common or green iguana is the largest iguana species. This male may eventually reach 2 m (6½ ft) in length, from head to tail. Common iguanas live in trees in Central and South America. Their long tails help them balance, while their feet are well designed for gripping the branches of trees. Iguanas often bask on branches that overhang water. If a predator comes near, this iguana drops into the pool or pond below and swims away to safety.

Long claw on toe provides a good grip when climbing

FIND OUT MORE ▸▸ Evolution 16–17 • Lizards 176 • Reproduction 44–45 • Reptiles 168–169

BASILISK LIZARD

Travelling at speeds of up to 12 kph (7.5 mph), the basilisk can swiftly cross a 400-m (1,174-ft) wide lake on its strong hind legs without sinking. Crossing water is one method of escaping from land predators, but this iguana can swim equally well and will sometimes stay submerged for long periods of time to avoid danger. The basilisk also moves about with great agility among the dense vegetation on the banks of tropical rivers and lakes.

Scientific name: *Basiliscus basiliscus*

Order: Squamata (snakes and lizards)

Class: Reptilia (reptiles)

Distribution: Central America

Status: Plentiful in the wild, but loss of habitat may impact the future of this species

Length: 76–80 cm (30–32 in)

Weight: 260–288 g (9–10 oz)

Food: Small mammals, crickets, grasshoppers, worms, and fruit

Reproduction: Female prepares hole and lays eggs, which are then covered. Incubation takes about three months

Number of young: Females lay up to 18 eggs

FIND OUT MORE ▶▶ Iguanas **177** •
Reptiles **168–169**

CHAMELEONS

Chameleons, which live mainly in the tropical forests of Africa and Madagascar, are well known for their ability to change the colour of their skin. They are the only lizards with zygodactyl feet, or pincers. These grasping feet are ideal for tree climbing. Chameleons use their remarkably long and sticky tongues to snap up insects – the tongue can extend to twice the length of the animal's body. A chameleon's eyes can move independently of each other, giving excellent all-round vision.

JACKSON'S CHAMELEON NATURAL COLOUR

Left eye is swivelling to look backwards

JACKSON'S CHAMELEON IN AN ANGRY MOOD

Right eye is looking forwards

Horns are unique to this particular species

▲ COLOUR CONSCIOUS

A chameleon uses its colour to camouflage itself from predators and prey, or to communicate with other chameleons. The light green colour of this Jackson's chameleon helps it to blend in well with its surroundings. Rival males show their anger with each other by darkening to a brownish colour. If neither male backs off, the chameleons interlock their horns, and each animal tries to throw the other off balance.

Tail helps it to balance on the branch

Tail can coil around branches to help the chameleon climb

MADAGASCAN MIXTURE

PANTHER CHAMELEON
The panther chameleon prefers to live in lightly wooded scrub, but it adapts well to non-natural habitats. The males can turn blazing shades of red and orange when challenging rivals, and they sometimes inflict serious injuries on each other during fights.

PARSON'S CHAMELEON
This rainforest-dweller is a slow mover that sits and waits to ambush passing prey. Parson's chameleons hibernate during the colder parts of the year. The males, which are larger and more colourful than the females, can be identified by the orange scales on their eyes.

OUSTALET'S CHAMELEON
This species is the largest of all the chameleons. Unusually for a chameleon, the male is less colourful than the female, but he becomes flushed with colour during courtship. The oustalet's chameleon lives high in trees in the hottest areas of Madagascar.

PYGMY CHAMELEON ▶
One of the world's smallest lizards, the pygmy chameleon grows to only 34 mm (1⅓ in). It is well camouflaged for its life among fallen leaves and low branches, where it feeds on tiny insects. With its short tail and tiny legs it cannot climb much higher. Pygmy chameleons are found in the rainforests of West and Central Africa.

FIND OUT MORE ▶▶ Defence **42–43** • Lizards **176** • Reptiles **168–169**

AGAMIDS

Sometimes referred to as dragons, agamids are related to the iguanas and chameleons. This group of lizards is distributed across Asia, Africa, and Australia, and come in a variety of shapes and sizes. Some rainforest-dwelling agamids can glide from tree to tree by spreading out flaps of skin between their bodies and forelimbs. Several others have enlarged scales, either all over their bodies or on their tails.

Butterfly will be a tasty snack for the hungry lizard

Tongue is used to help grab prey

Male's head becomes brightly coloured during breeding season

Spines make the lizard look more fearsome than it is

Lump resembles head when real head is lowered in defence

SOCIAL LIZARDS ▶
A long tail and lengthy limbs give this rock agama great balance and agility, so it has no trouble stretching for its prey. Rock agamas are social animals that live in small colonies headed by a dominant male. Some colonies have a dominant female. The males defend their colonies violently, biting rivals and lashing them with their tails.

▲ **THORNY DEVIL**
The thorny devil, or moloch, is found in many desert regions of Australia. This bizarre lizard is entirely covered with thorn-like spines. It may look scary, but it is completely harmless, except to the ants on which it preys. The thorny devil can consume 1,000 ants in one hour, flicking them up with with its tongue and crushing them with its specially adapted teeth.

Long legs for running and leaping after prey

DEFENCE STRATEGIES

FRILLED LIZARD
When threatened, the frilled lizard of Australia spreads out the large frill of skin around its shoulders. It also hisses, opens its mouth, and sometimes rushes towards the threat. If this bluff fails, the lizard will run away.

SPINY TAILED LIZARD
This agamid lives in rocky deserts in North Africa and western Asia. When disturbed, it retreats to cracks in rocks inflating its body so that it cannot be dislodged. It also lashes out with its thick, spiny tail.

HORN-HEADED LIZARD
The mountain horn-headed lizard has spines on its neck and back, and behind each eye. Horn-headed lizards are native to southeast Asia. They all live in trees and have strong claws for gripping on to branches.

BEARDED LIZARD
This lizard's beard is actually a patch of loose, prickly skin on its throat. To scare off predators, such as birds of prey and monitor lizards, this agamid flattens its body, inflates its beard, and opens its brightly coloured mouth.

ON TWO LEGS
The Chinese water dragon resembles a common iguana. It has a similar lifestyle too, even diving into water to escape attack. This agamid knows one extra trick. On land, it can stand up on its hind legs and scamper away.

FIND OUT MORE ▶▶ Iguanas 177 • Lizards 176 • Reptiles 168–169

GECKOS

Large head and wide jaw for seizing big prey

Geckos are small lizards with flat heads and large eyes. Typical geckos have no eyelids and many also have specialized feet that allow them to climb a variety of surfaces, including tree trunks and rock faces. Most geckos are nocturnal (night active), but a very small number are diurnal (day active). There are more than 1,000 species of gecko, each of which makes its own distinctive call to attract mates and to warn off rivals.

Tail breaks off easily when attacked

Toe pad has thousands of hairlike structures

▼ QUICK LICK

Like most geckos, this Madagascan day gecko does not have eyelids. Instead, its eyes are covered and protected by a transparent membrane called a spectacle. Unable to clean its eyes with tears, the gecko licks them with its tongue. As its name suggests, the Madagascan day gecko is active in the daytime. This species prefers to live in the lush green foliage of the Madagascan rainforests, where it is well camouflaged.

Long tongue extends as far as the eye

◄ GETTING A GRIP

The tokay gecko from southeast Asia can climb on smooth or vertical surfaces, and it can even hang upside down. Each pad on its toes has thousands of tiny hairs, and each hair has thousands of even smaller bumps on it. These can mesh with even minuscule irregularities on a surface, giving the gecko the grip it needs.

GALLERY OF GECKOS

LEOPARD GECKO
A native of the rocky deserts and dry grasslands of Central Asia, this gecko gets its name from its leopard-style colouring and markings. This lizard uses its tail to store food. When food is plentiful, the tail grows in size. It shrinks when food is scarce.

AFRICAN FAT-TAIL
This shy, docile creature stores fat in its tail, using it as an energy reserve during lean times. Male African fat-tailed geckos call out for mates by clicking their tongues against the roof of their mouths. This species lives for about 25 years.

RING-TAILED GECKO
Reaching lengths of 22 cm (8⅛ in), this is Australia's largest species of gecko. The ring-tailed gecko is also found in New Guinea and the Solomon Islands. It tends to live in tropical areas with high rainfall, as it needs a lot of moisture to survive.

FLYING GECKO
By spreading out flaps of skin along the side of its body and between its toes, Kuhl's flying gecko can glide from tree to tree in its rainforest habitat. This gecko is among six species of flying geckos that live in southeast Asia.

SANDFISH

Short legs are typical of skinks

Shiny scales are reinforced by small bones underneath

Shovel-shaped nose makes moving through sand easier

SKINKS

With nearly 1,300 species, skinks form the largest group of lizards. They are shy creatures and are found in the warmer regions of the world. They live mainly on the ground, sheltering among stones, in leaf litter, or even underground. Most skinks have short legs, with smooth shiny bodies covered in scales. Nearly half the skink family give birth to live young, rather than laying eggs.

SHINY SKINK ▲
The sandfish lives in the sandy deserts of North Africa and Arabia. Its smooth, shiny appearance and cylindrical shape are typical of most skinks. Although it often hunts on the desert surface, it can also dive beneath it, wriggling through the sand like a fish through water. In this way, the sandfish escapes predators, stalks prey, and avoids extreme temperatures.

TWO HEADS ARE BETTER THAN ONE ▶
The shingleback, or pinecone, or stump-tailed, skink lives in dry regions of Australia. This omnivorous creature spends most of its life sheltering in sandy burrows or in cracks in rocks. The shingleback has a long, stocky body with wrinkled scales. Its tail looks like its head, which confuses its enemies. By the time a predator has worked out which end of the reptile to attack, the shingleback has disappeared into the safety of its shelter.

End of tail is gripped in the lizard's mouth

BLUE-TONGUED SKINK ▶
The blue-tongued skink is native to Australia and the nearby islands of southeast Asia. It is much larger, more heavily built and slow-moving than other skinks. If threatened, it tries to alarm attackers by sticking out its vivid blue tongue, hissing, and flattening its body. Blue-tongued skinks are now popular as pets.

◀ PRICKLY COUSIN
The armadillo lizard of southern Africa is a girdle-tailed lizard, and is a close relative of skinks. If a predator comes near, the armadillo lizard grabs its tail in its jaws and curls up to present a mouthful of spines to the attacker. This prickly lizard lives in family groups in scrubland and rocky outcrops. Insects and spiders make up the bulk of its diet.

FIND OUT MORE ▶▶ Defence **42–43** • Deserts **58–59** • Lizards **176** • Reptiles **168–169**

MONITORS

Monitors are carnivorous lizards that live in Asia, Africa, and Australia. Armed with a keen sense of smell, long, sharp claws, and powerful jaws, they are versatile hunters that devour any live animal they can catch. Some species also eat carrion (dead animals). Most monitors are agile climbers and strong swimmers. This group of reptiles includes the world's largest lizard, the Komodo dragon, which can reach a length of 3 m (10 ft).

KOMODO DINNERTIME ▶
Komodo dragons hunt large animals including wild boar, deer, and water buffalo. They even eat other komodo dragons. These lizards usually wait to ambush prey, seizing it with their jaws. If the prey manages to escape at first, it soon dies from infections caused by bacteria in the komodo dragon's saliva.

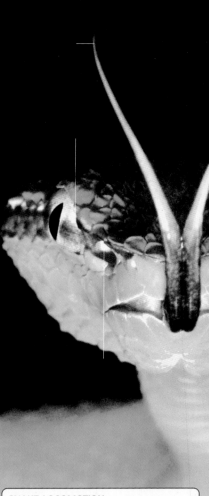

Forelimbs are used to force the rival to the ground

◀ WRESTLING REPTILES
At the beginning of the mating season, male monitors engage in ritual combat to win a mate. Using their tails for support, they wrestle each other in an upright position, grabbing their rivals and trying to push them to the ground. For some species, such as these Bengal monitors, it is a simple contest of strength and the loser walks away unharmed. The males of other species also bite each other, causing injuries.

Lower jaw has glands containing venom

▲ AMERICAN COUSIN
The gila monster is a large, heavy-bodied lizard that lives in the deserts of the southwest United States and Mexico. It is distantly related to the monitors, and is one of only two venomous lizards in the world. The venom, which is produced by glands in the gila monster's lower jaw, collects in grooves in the lizard's teeth. This toxin is not injected into the victim, but flows into its wounds as the lizard chews on it.

SNAKE LOCOMOTION

Snakes have several different ways of moving. The method used depends on the size of the snake and the surface on which it is travelling.

Linear movement This is a slow, straight-line motion used mainly by large, heavy snakes, such as boas. Each belly scale is lifted up, moved forward, and thrust down again.

Serpentine movement The snake glides forward maintaining the same wavy shape. The back of each wave is pressed against objects on the ground so the snake can wriggle along.

Concertina movement When moving through its tunnel, a burrowing snake anchors itself with wide loops, and uses its grip to push or pull the rest of its body along.

SNAKES

Snakes are long, thin reptiles with scaly skin and forked tongues. Their teeth cannot break up their food into small pieces so snakes must swallow their prey whole. There are about 3,000 species living in many different habitats on all continents except Antarctica. Over 800 snakes are venomous. They inject venom into their victims with specially adapted teeth called fangs. It is believed snakes evolved (developed) from lizards that lost the use of their legs.

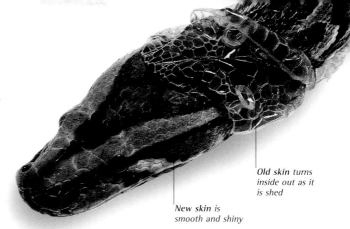

Old skin turns inside out as it is shed

New skin is smooth and shiny

▲ SHEDDING SKIN
Like all reptiles, this Burmese python sheds its outer, transparent layer of skin regularly as it grows. For snakes, this shedding, or sloughing, starts at the mouth. The snake rubs the side of its head along the ground to turn the skin back. It then slithers out of its old skin, leaving it behind in one piece.

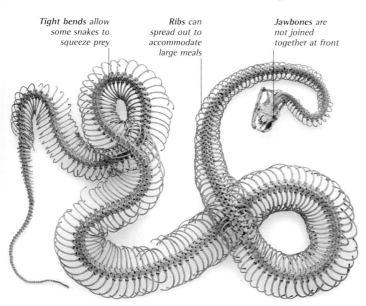

Tight bends allow some snakes to squeeze prey

Ribs can spread out to accommodate large meals

Jawbones are not joined together at front

▲ SNAKE SENSES
Snakes have unique sensory systems. The tongue is a highly sensitive organ of taste, smell, and touch. It collects airborne scent particles that are analysed in the roof of the mouth in a structure called the Jacobson's organ. Snakes do not have external ears and are deaf to airborne sounds, but they can sense vibrations. Some have sensors that detect heat from other animals.

FLEXIBLE SKELETON ▲
Depending on their length, snakes have between 180 and 400 vertebrae in their backbone. This gives their bodies strength and flexibility. Ribs attached to the vertebrae give shape to the body and provide anchorage for muscles. The jaws of snakes are loosely connected to each other, allowing the mouth to open wide enough to swallow large prey.

LETHAL INJECTIONS

Vipers are a group of venomous snakes. A viper's fangs lie against the roof of the mouth when they are not in use. As the viper bites, its upper jawbones rotate, bringing the fangs forward. At the same time, glands in the snake's jaws contract, squeezing venom down channels inside the fangs and out through holes at the tips. Cobras also have hollow fangs, but they are shorter and fixed in position.

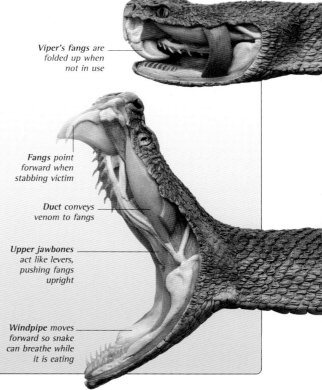

Viper's fangs are folded up when not in use

Fangs point forward when stabbing victim

Duct conveys venom to fangs

Upper jawbones act like levers, pushing fangs upright

Windpipe moves forward so snake can breathe while it is eating

Young snake samples the air with its Jacobson's organ

Snake eggs have tough, flexible shells

◄ NEW BEGINNINGS
This baby hognosed snake is checking out its surroundings before it leaves the security of its egg. It is in no hurry to leave, and may stay put for a few days. Young snakes break through their eggshell using a temporary egg tooth on the upper jaw. Some snakes, such as boas, give birth to live young instead of laying eggs.

FIND OUT MORE ▸▸ Anatomy **26–27** • Evolution **16–17** • Reptiles **168–169** • Senses **30–31**

BOAS

The world's largest snakes belong to the boa family, which includes the true boas and the pythons. Boas live mainly in the Americas and give birth to live young. Pythons are from Africa, Asia, and Australasia, and they lay eggs. Boas evolved (developed) from ancient lizard-like animals. They still display evidence of this, as they have tiny traces of hind legs. Boas constrict (squeeze) their prey to kill it.

Body is coiled around branches

Heat-sensitive pits help detect warm-blooded prey

Tail is raised to imitate the snake's head

Real head is pressed to the ground

▲ TREE BOAS

This Cook's tree boa is one of eight species of tree boa found throughout the American tropics. Tree boas are mainly nocturnal (active at night). An animal such as this can catch and constrict prey with the front of its body, while still clinging firmly to a branch with its tail. Adult tree boas mainly eat mammals and birds, while the young feed on lizards.

◄ DEFENSIVE TRICKS

The tail and head of the Calabar ground boa are very difficult to tell apart. If threatened, this snake can curl itself into a ball and raise its tail, while protecting its real head. This behaviour may confuse or deter potential predators. Native to the rainforests of Africa, this boa spends most of its time underground, hunting for mice and other mammals.

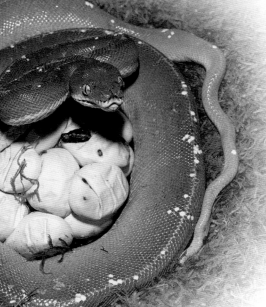

▲ INCUBATION

The green tree python is one of only a few snakes to look after its eggs once they are laid. The female wraps her body around the eggs and shivers her muscles, creating heat to speed up the development of the embryos. The mother does not feed during the seven weeks it takes the eggs to hatch. Green tree pythons, which are native to tropical Australia and nearby islands, have a similar lifestyle to tree boas.

DEADLY EMBRACE ►

Coiled around a caiman, this anaconda will squeeze its prey until it stops breathing. A native of South America, the anaconda is the world's heaviest snake, reaching 250 kg (551 lb). It lurks in swamps and slow-moving rivers, waiting to ambush its next meal. Female anacondas are larger than the males, and they may reach 10 m (33 ft) long.

FIND OUT MORE ▸▸ Carnivores 38 • Parenting 46–47 • Reptiles 168–169 • Snakes 184–185

MEXICAN
MILKSNAKE

*Red and black
are common
warning colours*

EASTERN
CORAL SNAKE

COLUBRIDS

More than two-thirds of all the world's snake species are colubrids. They come in a range of sizes, shapes, and colours. Some colubrids live in trees, while some live underground. Some species specialize in certain prey, and some eat any small animal they can catch. About one-third of the colubrids are mildly venomous. They use their solid fangs, which sit at the back of their mouths, to create a wound, in to which the venom runs.

▲ MIMICRY
Some varieties of milksnake resemble the deadly coral snakes of the cobra family. Milksnakes are harmless and may have evolved to mimic coral snakes and scare off predators. Although they do not have venom, milksnakes will defend themselves by biting an attacker. They also release a foul-smelling fluid.

FAKING DEATH ►
By lying on its back with its tongue hanging limply, this grass snake is pretending it is dead in the hope that a predator might lose interest in it. The grass snake will also hiss and produce a pungent smell to defend itself. Common across Europe, this non-venomous snake often hunts in water, feeding mainly on frogs and fish.

Underside of body turned upwards to mimic death

Skin on throat can stretch paper-thin

GOLDEN FLYING SNAKE ►
This mildly venomous snake from southeast Asia can glide from one tree to another. As it launches itself, the snake spreads out its ribs to flatten its body, and pulls in its underside to create a hollow underneath. This change of form gives the golden flying snake an aerodynamic shape.

Head is not much wider than the body

▲ BIG STRETCH
Common egg eaters from Africa have flexible jaws and can expand their mouths to swallow birds' eggs whole. This species has a specialized backbone to help their unusual feeding habit. Part of the backbone holds the egg in place in the snake's throat, while another part cuts through the shell and forces out the liquid inside. Eventually the snake spits out the eggshell. Egg eating snakes are at their most active in spring, fasting for the rest of the year.

COLUBRID GALLERY

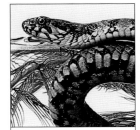

VIPERINE WATER SNAKE
This snake feeds primarily on fish. It is able to stay underwater without breathing for long periods, waiting to ambush passing prey. It often basks in the sun on land, partly because the heat helps with its digestion.

INDIGO SNAKE
Growing to 2.5 m (8⅓ ft), this harmless colubrid is North America's longest snake. A ground-dweller, it often shelters in tortoise burrows. The indigo is common in Mexico, but it is now quite rare in the United States.

MANGROVE SNAKE
Shown here in a threat posture, this striking tree-dweller from southeast Asia is mildly venomous. Mainly nocturnal (night active), it feeds on birds and their eggs as well as small mammals and other prey.

BROWN TREE SNAKE
This native of Australia and New Guinea has caused havoc since its introduction to the Pacific island of Guam. As well as killing many of Guam's unique forest birds, it often causes power cuts by climbing on power lines.

FIND OUT MORE ►► Defence 42–43 • Reptiles 168–169 • Snakes 184–185

COBRAS

The venomous cobra family includes sea snakes, coral snakes, and mambas, as well as the true cobras. The most characteristic cobras are those from Asia and Africa that rear up and spread their hoods. All cobras have hollow fangs fixed in position at the front of their mouths. Their deadly venom usually attacks the nervous system of their victims, and they use it to stun prey and to defend the snakes against predators, such as crocodiles.

Wide belly scales help the sea krait to move on land

Hood is extended fully

Windpipe extension allows the cobra to eat and breathe at the same time

HOODED SNAKE ▶

The Egyptian cobra seldom makes unprovoked attacks. When it is threatened, it raises the forepart of its body off the ground, erects the skin around its neck by extending the ribs behind its head, and makes a prolonged hissing sound. If the attacker persists, the snake will attack, sinking its venomous fangs into the aggressor. Once it sees a chance to escape, the Egyptian cobra flees.

▲ SEA SNAKES

More than 60 species of snake live in the tropical areas of the Pacific and Indian Oceans. They are divided into two groups: the true sea snakes and the sea kraits. All these sea-going snakes have flat, rudder-like tails and nostrils that can close under the water. Sea kraits such as this one can move on land, where they lay their eggs; true sea snakes are helpless out of water.

BLACK MAMBA ▶

Each of these male black mambas is fighting for dominance by trying to push the other to the ground in a test of strength. A black mamba can move at speeds of 22.5 kph (14 mph), making it the fastest snake in the world. They have keen eyesight so they can strike their victims with accuracy – a bite from a black mamba can kill a human in 20 minutes. Black mambas are in fact brown or greyish in colour.

MONOCLED COBRA

Until recently, most Asian cobras were thought to be variants of one species, the Indian, or spectacled, cobra. Now scientists have identified at least 11 separate species, including this monocled cobra from eastern Asia. The Asian cobra species are the snakes that are used in snake charming. Several of these cobras have eye-like markings on their hoods, warning predators to keep away.

Single eye-spot warns that the snake is dangerous

VIPERS

Vipers are venomous snakes with long fangs that fold into the mouth when not in use. Most vipers are wide-bodied, slow-moving predators that ambush their victims. They are divided into two groups: pit vipers and pitless, or true, vipers. Pit vipers, such as rattlesnakes, differ from the true vipers because they have heat-sensing pits between their eyes and nostrils. These pits, which are highly sensitive, help the vipers to detect prey, even if it is only a fraction of a degree warmer than the temperature surrounding them.

Rattle has six segments

VIPER VARIETY

SOUTHERN PACIFIC RATTLESNAKE
This rattlesnake lives in California and Mexico, primarily in grasslands and scrub. On warm days it hunts during the day, but when the days get too hot, it hunts at night. This species feeds on lizards, rodents, and birds.

PUFF ADDER
A heavy-bodied viper from Africa, this species bites readily. Its name comes from its habit of puffing and hissing through its nostrils, which it does to intimidate predators. Like many vipers, it does not move away when disturbed. It relies on its camouflage for protection.

AMERICAN COPPERHEAD
A relative of rattlesnakes, the American copperhead is native to the eastern United States, where it lives on a varied diet, ranging from small mammals and amphibians to insects. The copperhead vibrates its tail when it feels threatened, even though it has no rattle.

MALAYSIAN PIT VIPER
This pit viper from southeast Asia is usually found at the edges of forests and in clearings. Its venom is highly potent and the snake is quick to strike if it is disturbed.

Wide jaws have room for venom glands

Heat-sensitive pits detect infrared (heat) rays

Forked tongue picks up scents in the air

TAIL RATTLE ►
The rattlesnake's unique rattle makes a buzzing sound when the snake vibrates its tail, warning other animals not to approach it. The rattle is a non-living structure that is made up of loosely linked hollow scales. These scales are the remains of the tail left behind every time a rattlesnake sheds its skin. There are about 30 species of rattlesnake, most of which live in the United States or Mexico.

▲ BLENDING IN
The Gaboon viper is a highly patterned snake, but in its tropical woodland habitat it becomes almost invisible. A relative of the puff adder, this thick-bodied viper reaches lengths of 1.8 m (6 ft) and has fangs up to 4 cm (1⅗ in) long. Rodents and other small mammals are its prey. The Gaboon viper waits for its victims while partially hidden among leaves on the forest floor.

▲ MAKING TRACKS
Instead of moving like other snakes, Peringuey's adder, which comes from Africa, crosses loose, desert sand by sidewinding. Sidewinding is an efficient and rapid method of movement that stops the snake sinking into the sand. It involves just two or three points of the body momentarily touching the ground as the snake moves sideways, leaving behind characteristic J-shaped marks.

FIND OUT MORE ►► Deserts 58–59 • Reptiles 168–169 • Snakes 184–185

BIRDS

◄ GORGEOUS FEATHERS
Birds are the only animals alive today with feathers. They are directly descended from dinosaurs, some of which also had feathered bodies, and it is often suggested that birds are in fact living dinosaurs. Birds' plumage may be plain for camouflage or colourful for display purposes, as in this scarlet macaw from forests in Central and South America. The most common bird displays include those of males to impress potential partners.

BIRDS

With their often stunning colours, varied calls, beautiful songs, and ability to live worldwide in all habitats, birds are the most noticeable of all vertebrates (animals with backbones). There are nearly 10,000 species of bird, almost all of which can fly. They have several adaptations for flight, including wings, powerful breast muscles, feathers, and light skeletons. Birds reproduce by laying eggs, and many species build a nest for their eggs and young.

Primary feathers at the wingtips provide thrust and extra control

Secondary feathers along the inner part of the wing provide lift

FEATHERS ►
The feature that makes birds unique is that their bodies, wings, and tails are covered with feathers. A feather is made of a central shaft from which lots of barbs (branches) spread outwards in evenly spaced rows. The barbs lock together like the teeth of a zip, forming a flat surface all over the bird.

CLOSE-UP IMAGE OF A WING FEATHER

THE POWER OF FLIGHT
Birds, such as this European robin, are the best fliers of all animals. They can fly fast or slow, dive, hover, glide, and soar. Hummingbirds can even fly backwards. Flight enables birds to reach food and perch or nest above ground level. It is also a highly effective method of travel – many birds perform amazingly long migrations. Even flightless birds, for example ostriches, emus, and penguins, still possess wings and had ancestors that could fly.

Small body feathers provide a streamlined surface for flight and keep the bird warm

Tail helps the bird to steer in flight and balance when perched

Lower legs and feet are featherless in most birds

BILL SHAPES

SEED-EATER
Many birds, including this zebra finch from Australia, have short, cone-shaped bills suited to cracking seeds. All seed-eaters have grooves inside the upper part of their bills, in which seeds can be wedged to hold them tightly while they are split open.

FRUIT- AND NUT-EATER
Some larger parrots, such as this blue-fronted amazon from South American rainforests, have immensely powerful bills with a sharp hook at the tip. They use their bills to peel the thick skins off fruit and tear its sweet flesh into pieces, and to smash tough nuts apart.

NECTAR-FEEDER
A variety of birds, including hummingbirds and this scarlet-chested sunbird from Africa, specialize in drinking sugary nectar from flowers. Their bills are long, narrow, and often downcurved to help them probe the flowerheads. They may have long tongues, too.

FISH-EATER
The bill of this black-crowned night heron, which has a wide range in the world's warmer regions, is typical of fishing birds. It is long, strong, sharply pointed, and dagger-like in shape. Some fishing birds also have serrated bill edges, like saw blades, to grip their catch.

MEAT-EATER
This golden eagle's powerful, deeply hooked bill is like those of most birds of prey and owls. Very strong and with sharp cutting edges, it is capable of tearing into prey and slicing through skin or flesh. Vultures have the biggest bills of all, able to rip through tough hide.

Bill is light, flexible, and strong

Upper mandible of bill has a hole in each side for the nostrils

Lower mandible (hinged section) of the bill

Skull has a big eye socket

CROW SKELETON ▶
Birds have incredibly lightweight skeletons that reduce their body weight for flying. In most birds, their feathers weigh more than their entire skeleton. Many of their bones are hollow, with a honeycomb structure of criss-cross bony struts. This design gives a bird skeleton strength with a minimum of weight.

Neck is made up of many small, jointed bones

Ulna (a wing bone) is equivalent to the forearm of humans

Good eyesight is essential for flight and finding food

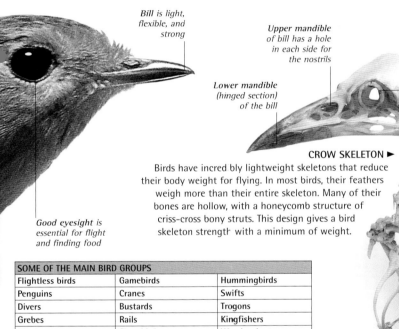

Pale eggs help parents to see them in the dark nest hole

SOME OF THE MAIN BIRD GROUPS		
Flightless birds	Gamebirds	Hummingbirds
Penguins	Cranes	Swifts
Divers	Bustards	Trogons
Grebes	Rails	Kingfishers
Albatrosses	Shorebirds	Woodpeckers
Pelicans	Parrots	Perching birds
Herons and storks	Cuckoos	The perching birds or songbirds is by far the largest group, with almost 6,000 species.
Flamingos	Pigeons	
Wildfowl	Owls	
Birds of prey	Nightjars	

Wide breastbone anchors the huge wing muscles

Knee is hidden among the feathers of a living bird

Tail bone

Goose takes oil from a gland near its tail to rub on its feathers to protect them

Bird's ankle is where the knee is in land animals

◀ PREENING
Birds must keep their plumage in tip-top condition because activities such as flight or swimming cause their feathers a lot of wear and tear. They do this by preening, like this red-breasted goose. To preen, a bird runs its bill through its feathers, zipping them back into shape and removing dirt, water, and parasites.

BIRD EGGS ▲
If female birds had to carry their young around, they would be far too heavy to fly. Instead, they lay eggs in which their offspring continue to develop outside their bodies. Eggs, such as these belonging to a blue tit, have strong shells to protect the babies inside. Birds build a wide variety of nests to hold their eggs and chicks, and they are beautifully crafted, complex structures in some species.

FIND OUT MORE • Animal Bodies 48–49 • Migration 50–51 • Waterfowl 201–211 • Perching Birds 226–227

*Tall neck helps
the bird spot danger
at long range*

*Male's plumage
is shaggy and
black and white*

*Massive legs have
strong muscles for
rapid acceleration*

*Large 2-toed
feet are suited
to sprinting*

FLIGHTLESS BIRDS

Some birds have lost the ability to fly. They include penguins, several ducks, many rails, a species of parrot, and a varied group of birds known as ratites. This group comprises the ostrich, emu, rheas, cassowaries, and kiwis. Ratites have powerful legs and big feet for walking and running. Their wings are small and weak, with loose, fluffy feathers that are useless for flight. It is thought that they are among the most ancient of all birds.

▲ BUILT FOR SPEED
These rival male ostriches are competing for territory and social status. The males that win these battles mate with most of the females in the surrounding area. Ostriches are found in Africa in open country. With little cover to hide in, they sprint to escape predators. They can run at 70 kph (45 mph) for long periods.

ROLE REVERSAL ►
The usual roles of the sexes are reversed in rheas, cassowaries, ostriches, and emus. Males, not females, play a large part in caring for the young. Having kept the eggs warm on his own, this male rhea of South America now has sole responsibility for looking after the brood of youngsters.

*Brood stays
close to their
father for
protection*

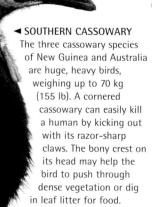

*Bony ridge,
or casque,
on the head*

◄ SOUTHERN CASSOWARY
The three cassowary species of New Guinea and Australia are huge, heavy birds, weighing up to 70 kg (155 lb). A cornered cassowary can easily kill a human by kicking out with its razor-sharp claws. The bony crest on its head may help the bird to push through dense vegetation or dig in leaf litter for food.

LIVING ON FOOT

BROWN KIWI
All four kiwi species live in the forests of New Zealand and nearby islands. Unlike other birds, a kiwi's nostrils are at the tip of its long bill. Kiwis are nocturnal. At night they shuffle along while sniffing and probing the soil to locate worms and other invertebrates.

EMU
The emu grows up to 1.9 m (6¼ ft) tall. It roams the Australian outback in search of seeds, berries, insect prey, and fresh water. If these become scarce, it may wander hundreds of kilometres to find new supplies.

FIND OUT MORE ■ Birds 192–193 ■ Conservation 211 ■ Penguins 195

Wings *are held out for balance when waddling on land*

All penguins *are grey or black above and white below*

Dense, fur-like *plumage lies over a thick layer of fat*

PENGUINS

Penguins are superbly adapted for life in the sea. Their compact, streamlined bodies are perfect for slipping through the water, and their thick coats of short, stiff feathers provide insulation against the cold. Penguins cannot fly because their wings have evolved (developed) to become flippers. They feed on fish, squid, and krill. All 17 species inhabit the southern hemisphere.

▲ HUGE COLONIES
Penguins are extremely social birds: their breeding colonies on rocky shores, ice, or snow are often vast. Those of some species, such as these Adélie penguins, may contain as many as half a million birds. Adélies breed in one of the world's harshest environments, on offshore islands and coasts in the Antarctic. Their nests are packed together, with each pair just out of pecking distance of its neighbours. Nesting so closely helps the adults and chicks to keep warm during snowstorms.

KING PENGUIN ►
The king penguin does not build a nest. Instead, it balances its single egg on top of its large webbed feet. Its feet are supplied with many small blood vessels that transfer heat to the egg. It takes 51–57 days for the egg to hatch, and the adults tend their chick for 10–13 months until it becomes fully independent.

JACKASS PENGUIN ►
Although penguins are most common in cold climates, they are not confined to the southern oceans around Antarctica. For example, the Galapagos penguin lives on the equator, and the jackass penguin occurs in South Africa. The jackass is named for its donkey-like, braying calls. Like most penguins, it lays two eggs, but if there is not enough food only one chick survives. Chicks hatch covered in soft down and cannot enter water until they grow waterproof adult feathers.

SPEED SWIMMING ►
With their plump bodies and webbed feet, penguins move much more efficiently in water than on land. They have several swimming techniques, including porpoising, in which they leap in and out of the sea at the surface. This macaroni penguin is flying underwater, flapping its wings to provide power.

FIND OUT MORE ► Chinstrap Penguins 68–69 • Evolution 16–17 • Polar Regions 70

Bold plumage appears only in the breeding season

Bill is pointed for snatching fish underwater

Nest is a simple platform fixed to water-dwelling plants

GREBES

These water-dwelling birds, and a group of similar, unrelated species called divers, have sharp, dagger-like bills for seizing fish and other aquatic prey. They have slender bodies and swim so low in the water that their backs may partially submerge. Superb swimmers, grebes can dive to great depths and remain underwater for several minutes. Grebes occur almost worldwide, but divers are found mainly in the northern hemisphere.

▲ FLOATING NEST
Divers and grebes, such as this red-necked grebe, build large nests of rotting vegetation that float on the water's surface. To stop the nests drifting away, they attach the structures to reeds or other aquatic plants. It is quite a struggle for the birds to haul themselves out of the water onto their nests because their legs are placed so far back on their bodies. This arrangement greatly increases thrust while swimming and diving, but both divers and grebes can hardly stand up or walk.

Chestnut-red neck feathers are spread in a fan

◄ WEED CEREMONY
Some grebes perform courtship dances, using ritual movements that vary from species to species. One of these great crested grebes has surfaced with a beakful of water weed plucked from the lake bed and is presenting it to its mate. In the next stage of the display, its partner also collects weed. The two birds rise up, breast to breast, and shake their heads from side to side.

Bird faces its partner and rises up out of the water

Strands of water weed are waved from the bill

▲ DEFENDING TERRITORY
In spring, divers establish fishing territories on large lakes to guarantee a regular supply of food. Breeding pairs, such as these great northern divers, defend their fishing rights against rivals. The male of each pair announces their ownership of part of the lake with wailing cries loud enough to be heard 1.6 km (1 mile) away. In winter, divers often move to the coast.

Adult grebe is about to pass food to its chick

CARING FOR CHICKS ►
For several weeks after hatching, grebe chicks, such as these baby pied-billed grebes, ride on their parents' back. In this way, they stay snug and are protected from predators. Grebes often eat small feathers, and feed them to their young. The feathers form a soft layer in the stomach. This layer is regularly brought back up and ejected through the bill. This may remove internal parasites, or it offer protection from swallowed fish bones.

ALBATROSSES

Albatrosses are large seabirds with extremely long wings for gliding low above the waves. The wandering albatross has the greatest wingspan of any bird, at up to 3.5 m (11 ft). Albatrosses travel huge distances across the oceans – sometimes right around the world. Most remain in the southern oceans, but some live in the northern Pacific. Almost all of the 21 albatross species are declining, and some face extinction, because every year thousands are accidentally caught on fishing hooks.

GLIDING ►
FLIGHT
Albatrosses save energy by soaring in and out of the hollows between the waves. Wind currents above the waves give them lift for almost no extra effort. As a result the great birds can glide for immense distances with scarcely a wing beat. This black-browed albatross is coming in to land.

Heavy body weighs 3–5 kg (6½–11 lbs)

Wing is held in place by a locking mechanism in the shoulder

Webbed feet are used to swim and to slow the albatross down when landing

Very long, narrow wings are suited to gliding and soaring

TUBENOSE ►
Albatrosses belong to a group of seabirds known as tubenoses, which also includes fulmars, shearwaters, and petrels. These species are named for the shape of their large nostrils, which sit on top of the bill as in this giant petrel, or along the side in albatrosses. Tubenoses have a good sense of smell, which they may use to locate mates, nesting burrows, young, or food.

Long nostrils are on the outside of the bill

Hooked bill is used for tearing meat off carcasses

◄ SLOW BREEDER
This yellow-nosed albatross is sitting on its single egg to keep it warm. Albatrosses are the slowest breeders of all birds. In about half of the albatross species, incubation and chick development takes up to a year. This is so long that the adults can breed only once every two years. Although albatrosses have very long lives, with an average lifespan of 30 years, they often do not start to breed until 10–15 years old.

▲ COURTSHIP BALLET
This pair of wandering albatrosses is engaging in a spectacular courtship display on the remote island of South Georgia in the Atlantic. These performances help to strengthen the bond between pairs. The birds bow to each other, clatter their bills, and dance round with open wings as if acting out a strange ballet.

PELICANS

Pelicans are the largest members of a group of water birds that includes cormorants, gannets, boobies, frigatebirds, and darters. All these species eat fish and are strong swimmers, with feet that are webbed between all four toes. Their fishing techniques range from high-speed underwater pursuits to dramatic plunge-dives. Many of these birds live at sea, but some pelicans, cormorants, and darters live in fresh water.

GREAT WHITE PELICAN ▶
Among the world's most unmistakable birds, pelicans have massive bills and huge feet. On the underside of a pelican's bill is a fold of saggy skin that can expand to create a large pouch. When dragged through water, the pouch acts like a fishing net, trapping any fish near the surface. A full pouch holds more than 13 kg (29 lb) of water and fish. Pelicans often hunt as a team, swimming in lines to herd fish into the shallows where there is no escape.

Throat pouch expands to scoop up fish

Long bill turns bright orange during the breeding season to attract a mate

Wings are long and broad for soaring and gliding

Dense plumage is completely water-repellent

Powerful legs are set far back on the body

Fully webbed feet are perfect for swimming, but clumsy on land

▲ RESTING ON ROCKS
Pelicans, including these brown pelicans, spend a good deal of time between fishing trips resting on rocks, sand banks, and other perches out of the water. Unlike other pelicans, brown pelicans are seabirds and do not feed at the surface. Instead, they dive from midair to seize fish. When they spot a fish, they fly as high as 10 m (30 ft), then fold their wings and hurtle into the sea.

DRYING TIME ▶
Unlike most water birds, cormorants lack waterproof plumage. When wet, their feathers get very heavy, which helps the birds to dive and stay underwater more easily. When out of water, cormorants perch with spread wings for long periods to dry off their wet feathers.

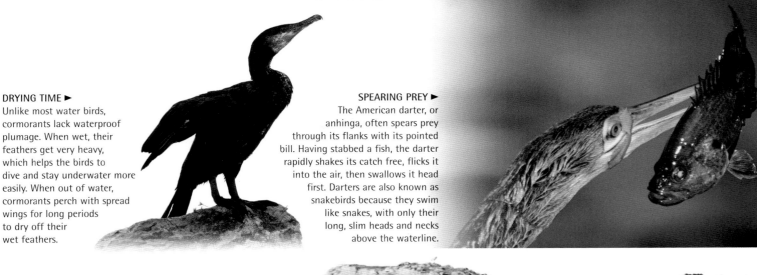

SPEARING PREY ▶
The American darter, or anhinga, often spears prey through its flanks with its pointed bill. Having stabbed a fish, the darter rapidly shakes its catch free, flicks it into the air, then swallows it head first. Darters are also known as snakebirds because they swim like snakes, with only their long, slim heads and necks above the waterline.

▲ CROWDED COLONY
Northern gannets nest in closely packed colonies on rocky islands in the North Atlantic. Each pair defends a tiny space around its nest from its neighbours. Fights are frequent, and the noisy calls of birds at a huge colony can be deafening. The adults may travel up to 200 km (125 miles) a day to find food for their young, making plunge-dives into shoals of fish.

SKY-POINTING DISPLAY ▶
Boobies are relatives of gannets and live in tropical oceans worldwide. Like gannets, they court each other and maintain their pair bonds with a complex language of displays at their breeding colonies. Here, a blue-footed booby is sky-pointing to its mate. Another display involves the booby lifting its bright blue feet one at a time in a slow dance, like a clown showing off a pair of oversized shoes.

BALLOON ATTRACTION ▶
Groups of male great frigatebirds entice passing females to land and mate with them by inflating their throat pouches into shiny red balloons. Great frigatebirds live in tropical areas of the Pacific, Atlantic, and Indian oceans, and breed on mostly uninhabited islands. They are superb fliers, using their aeronautical ability to chase other seabirds and steal their catches of fish.

FIND OUT MORE ▶ Animal Characteristics 10–11 • Coasts 72 • Oceans 74–75 • Reproduction 44–45

HERONS

Herons are birds of the waterside and shallow wetlands, although a few live in drier habitats. They have long legs and are often seen wading slowly in water and mud, looking for aquatic prey such as fish and frogs. The heron family includes egrets and bitterns. Storks are close relatives. Most species have long, graceful heads and necks, which are usually held back in an S-shape. When they spot prey, the birds suddenly shoot their necks out to seize their victim with their dagger-like bills.

Silvery white plumes develop on the bird's back in the breeding season

Long legs for wading into water

Long toes spread the bird's weight on soft mud

◄ ROOFTOP NESTS

White storks nest on church spires and other tall buildings throughout mainland Europe. Each spring, the storks return to the same nest sites from Africa, where they live in the winter. Many stories are associated with storks, such as the ancient legend that they deliver human babies.

HERONS AND THEIR RELATIVES

SNOWY EGRET

A number of slim herons, often with white plumage, are called egrets. To impress its mate in courtship displays, the snowy egret raises its delicate sprays of feathers. In the late 19th and early 20th centuries, many egrets were killed to provide plumes for women's hats.

SADDLE-BILLED STORK

This odd-looking bird lives in wetlands in tropical Africa. It has a huge multicoloured bill, with which it seizes large fish, crabs, frogs, and water beetles. Unlike many herons and other storks, it usually nests in separate pairs rather than packed together in colonies.

GOLIATH HERON

The largest of all the world's herons, this giant African bird stands up to 1.5 m (5 ft) tall and can tackle heavier prey than its smaller relatives. Usually it feeds alone or in pairs, spearing fish in lakes, rivers, or swamps. It may wade into water as deep as its belly.

FLAMINGOS

Flamingos are an ancient group of tall wading birds that evolved more than 10 million years ago. There are five species, which all live and breed in the tropics and subtropics, usually in salty or brackish water found in shallow lakes or coastal lagoons. Flamingos are specialist feeders that use their bills to sieve tiny organisms from the water.

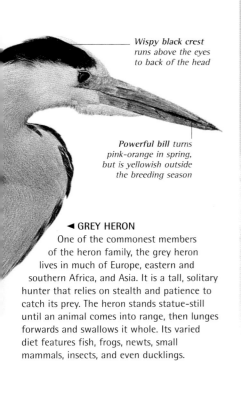

Wispy black crest runs above the eyes to back of the head

Powerful bill turns pink-orange in spring, but is yellowish outside the breeding season

◄ GREY HERON
One of the commonest members of the heron family, the grey heron lives in much of Europe, eastern and southern Africa, and Asia. It is a tall, solitary hunter that relies on stealth and patience to catch its prey. The heron stands statue-still until an animal comes into range, then lunges forwards and swallows it whole. Its varied diet features fish, frogs, newts, small mammals, insects, and even ducklings.

Small head and deep, downturned bill

Narrow wings with black and crimson feathers

LESSER FLAMINGO ►
Flamingos are highly social, and this species gathers in huge numbers in East Africa. Its colonies on the lakes of the Rift Valley, which may each contain more than a million birds, are counted among the world's greatest natural spectacles.

Pink colouring comes from pigments in the bird's food

Bare head prevents plumage getting dirty when eating meat

Hatchet bill for hacking into dead animals

Very long legs dangle behind the stork when in flight

▲ SCAVENGER STORK
The marabou stork lives in Africa, on grassy plains, in urban areas, and near water, and it survives mainly by scavenging. To find food, it soars effortlessly on its broad wings, like a bird of prey. Often several marabous turn up at an animal carcass, competing with vultures for the meat. Their large beaks easily slash through fur and skin, exposing the flesh inside. Marabou storks also kill live prey.

▲ FILTER FEEDER
A flamingo feeds by sweeping its bill upside down through the water. Its large, fleshy tongue acts like the piston of a pump, forcing water over rows of comblike teeth inside the bill. These trap small aquatic organisms, on which the bird lives. Greater flamingos, such as this one, eat mainly crustaceans. Other flamingos filter microscopic algae.

Legs are protected from salty or toxic water by their thick scales

▲ PARENTAL CARE
The Andean flamingo is one of three species of flamingo found on lakes high in the Andes mountains of South America. Like all flamingos, it makes a cylindrical nest of mud. The single chick is fed by both parents, which drip a nutritious, milk-like fluid from their bills into their offspring's bill.

Small webbed feet used for stirring up mud in search of food

WILDFOWL

Birds in this large group have broad, flattened bills, waterproof plumage, and webbed feet for swimming on fresh water or the sea. They include swans, geese, and ducks. Most swans – the largest wildfowl – have white plumage and brightly coloured bills. Geese spend a lot of time on dry land, feeding on crops or grazing. Ducks include many species that swim and dive for plant or animal food, and a few that can perch in trees.

White ring surrounds large dark eye

Broad bill with hard nail at the tip

MALE MANDARIN DUCK

FEMALE MANDARIN DUCK

Plumage has grey-brown streaks for camouflage

Strong legs for perching in trees where nest is made

Webbed feet to propel the duck through the water

◄ DULLER IS SAFER

Like all ducks, male and female mandarin ducks look very different. The male has boldly patterned plumage to attract a mate. The female has dull plumage that camouflages her from predators while she is incubating eggs. Ducks cannot fly when they moult (shed) their wing feathers, so at this dangerous time of the year, males acquire brown plumage to help them hide.

FEATHERED FOWL

SHELDUCK
This large duck feeds on muddy coasts and estuaries, sweeping its bill from side to side to find tiny snails and other aquatic animals. In late summer, large numbers of shelducks from northwestern Europe migrate to the North Sea region to moult.

PLUMED WHISTLING DUCK
Whistling ducks are named for their high-pitched calls, which are quite unlike the quacks, squeals, or barks of most other ducks. They have long necks and legs and usually feed on land by clipping grass. This species lives on grassland and in wetlands in Australia.

BLACK SWAN
The other six species of swan are mainly white, so this one is an exception. It is native to Australia, but is also found in New Zealand and other places worldwide, where it has been introduced as an ornamental bird. In Australia, it forms flocks of up to 30,000 birds.

AFRICAN PYGMY-GOOSE
Only the size of a town pigeon, this is the world's smallest species of wildfowl. It is actually a duck, but is named for its stubby beak that looks more like that of a goose. It lives in Africa, and nests in holes in trees, cliffs, termite nests, or the thatched roofs of huts.

Mallard tips forwards to reach the bottom

◄ DABBLING FOR FOOD

Ducks feed in a variety of ways. Some species dive deep for their food. Others are called dabbling ducks because they patter their bills at the surface to pick up small prey and plant fragments. They filter these out of the water with the sieve-like edges of their bills. Dabbling ducks also up-end to reach food further below with their necks, like this mallard.

MALE MALLARD

BACK FROM THE BRINK ▶
Hawaiian geese are native to the main island of Hawaii. They suffered greatly from hunting and predators introduced by human settlers. By 1949, only 20–30 survived, but captive breeding saved the species from extinction. The geese have been fitted with coded leg rings so that each one can be identified.

▲ FLYING IN FORMATION
This flock of migrating Canada geese is flying in two long lines in a V-shaped pattern, which helps the birds to save energy. Each goose takes advantage of the slipstream produced by the bird in front, in the same way as a group of cyclists racing in a pack. The geese swap positions regularly so that the leader, which has to work hardest, can recover.

Air is trapped between the duck's 12,000 feathers to help it float

Strong bill deals with wide range of food

SNUG NEST ▶
Like other wildfowl, this female emperor goose has lined her nest with a thick layer of soft down feathers plucked from her own breast. This provides a warm layer to insulate the eggs when she goes to find food. Before leaving, she covers the eggs with more down to conceal them from predators, such as foxes.

Heavier body with more flesh than wild birds

Ducklings follow mother as soon as they hatch

Young mature more quickly than wild ducklings

DOMESTICATED DUCK ▶
Wildfowl were first domesticated a long time ago for their meat, warm down feathers (used in clothing and bedding), and eggs. The mallard, which is the world's most widespread duck, was being farmed at least 2,000 years ago. Since then, selective breeding has produced dozens of different varieties. Domesticated mallards are heavier than wild mallards, with more varied feather patterns.

FIND OUT MORE ▶▶ Conservation 22–23 • Migration 30–31 • Mute Swan 204–205 • Polar Regions 70

MUTE SWAN

One of the world's heaviest flying birds, the mute swan has to run over the water's surface and beat its huge wings hard to take off. It lands, as in this image, by skiing across the water on its webbed feet until it finally comes to a halt amid a cloud of spray. The swan lives on fresh water, and uses its long, graceful neck to pull up plants growing on lake or river bottoms. Although it often becomes tame in parks, it will attack intruders who venture too close to its nest.

Scientific name: *Cygnus olor*

Order: Anseriformes (ducks, geese, and swans)

Class: Aves (birds)

Distribution: Native to Europe and central Asia; introduced to North America, southern Africa, Australia, New Zealand, and China

Status: Common

Length: About 1.5 m (5 ft)

Weight: Up to 16 kg (35 lb) – the heaviest example on record was 22.5 kg (49 lb 10 oz)

Food: Mainly aquatic vegetation, grass, and grain; occasionally takes small prey, such as fish

Reproduction: Breeding pair builds large floating nest in shallow water in early spring

Number of young: 5–8

FIND OUT MORE ▸▸ Wildfowl **202–203**

BIRDS OF PREY

With their hooked bills, sharp talons, and excellent vision, birds of prey are formidable hunters. These daytime birds of prey, also known as raptors, are a diverse group of around 300 species. They range from tiny falconets only 15 cm (6 in) long to huge condors, which have a wingspan of up to 2.3 m (7½ ft). Their diets and hunting tactics are equally varied. Some species, especially vultures, depend mainly on carrion (the flesh of dead animals).

Primary flight feathers create lift and turning power

Tail serves as a rudder and brake

Broad wings enable the eagle to soar for hours

◄ TAWNY EAGLE
All birds of prey are superb fliers. Eagles, vultures, large hawks, and buzzards have long, broad wings suited to gliding and soaring for long periods. Their fingered wingtip feathers provide greater control and lift. Falcons and some other smaller birds of prey have narrower, swept-back wings that are suited to high-speed flight and rapid manoeuvres.

Hooked bill for tearing flesh

FEEDING YOUNG ►
Many raptors pair for life and return to the same nest site each year. Most species, such as this North American red-tailed hawk, build bulky stick nests, but they also take over the old nests of crows and other birds. Compared to most birds, raptors raise small families – often of one or two chicks, although falcons and some others may have larger broods.

Feathers cover long legs like trousers

Powerful feet with razor-sharp talons (claws)

Sharp eyes produce a highly detailed image

Prey is taken to a perch to be eaten

◄ **BIRD SNATCHER**
Northern sparrowhawks of Europe and Asia hunt small to medium-sized birds. They rely on stealth and surprise, changing direction or flying behind hedges or other cover, then suddenly darting over the top to strike their prey. This male is plucking its catch. Females are up to 75 per cent heavier than males, and can kill bigger prey.

▲ **DIVING FOR FISH**
The osprey is a fish-hunting raptor. It takes its prey, which can be as large as a salmon, in a spectacular dive, thrusting its legs into the water and sometimes submerging its whole body. Extremely sharp talons and horny spines on the soles of its feet help the osprey to grasp its slippery, powerfully wriggling catch. It also has a special toe that can swivel backwards to provide extra grip.

Bare head ensures feathers don't get dirty when feeding

Wings are spread to dominate the other vulture

◄ **CARRION EATERS**
These white-backed vultures are feeding on the carcass of a goat. They are among several species of vulture found on the African savanna. Each species specializes in eating a different part of the carcass, and there is a strict pecking order in which the biggest species bully the smaller ones. All vultures have hooked bills for cutting skin and flesh, and rough tongues for rasping meat off bones. However, their legs and feet are weaker than those of other raptors as they do not kill and carry off live prey.

Massive wings for effortless soaring

Long neck can reach into the carcass

RANGE OF RAPTORS

MERLIN
A member of the falcon family, the merlin lives in forests and open country in North America, Europe, and Asia. It is fast and agile in the air, with rapid reflex reactions, and swoops low over the ground to catch prey. Small birds such as larks, finches, and sparrows make up most of its diet.

BATELEUR EAGLE
One of the most colourful raptors, the bateleur is a characteristic bird of Africa's savanna. In flight it has a distinctive outline, with very long, pointed wings held in a V-shape and a very short tail. As it sails overhead, it tilts its wings from side to side like a tightrope walker trying to maintain balance.

CRESTED CARACARA
Caracaras are large falcons that are found in the southern USA, and from Mexico to the far south of South America. They mostly live on insects and carrion, and spend a lot of time on the ground. The crested or common caracara is often seen beside roads, feeding on animals killed by traffic.

LONG-LEGGED BUZZARD
This is a bird of semi-deserts, grassy plains, and mountains, which breeds from southeast Europe to North Africa and central Asia. Small rodents, especially gerbils, voles, and mice, are its preferred prey. The buzzard often hovers in mid-air to spot prey below. Its long legs are adapted to seizing victims in long grass.

ANDEAN CONDOR
Condors belong to a group of birds called New World (American) vultures. There are two species: the very rare Californian condor and the Andean condor of South America. The male Andean condor has enormous wings that span over 3 m (10 ft) and is one of the world's heaviest flying birds.

FIND OUT MORE ► Animal Homes 48–49 • Coniferous Forests 65 • Grasslands 56–57 • Owls 220 • Scavengers 41

GAMEBIRDS

These birds are widely hunted for sport, hence their group's name. They include pheasants, partridges, turkeys, and the world's most numerous bird – the domestic chicken. Nearly all gamebirds have plump bodies and strong feet with three thick toes. They scratch at food on the ground, and are strong runners that rarely fly, except to burst from cover to flee danger.

▲ RAPID TAKEOFF

The male Reeves' pheasant of China has one of the longest tails of any bird, measuring up to 2 m (6½ ft). Like most gamebirds, it escapes its enemies by rocketing into the air and powering away to safety, using its broad wings and large flight muscles. The noisy beating of its wings may also startle and confuse predators.

MAGNIFICENT DISPLAY ►

One of the world's most spectacular gamebirds is the peacock. The male's train consists of long, lacy feathers that cover his real tail, which is very short. These plumes are dotted with shiny spots so that the train seems to be covered with staring eyes. The peacock fans out his train to impress watching females, known as peahens.

Train feathers spread out to form a fan

PEACOCK

Long, silky feathers cascade from the bird's neck and back

Flaps of red skin on the neck and head

◄ WILD ANCESTOR

The red junglefowl, a species of pheasant, is the original ancestor of the farmyard chicken. It inhabits forests and scrubland in India and southeast Asia, but has become scarce due to hunting and cross-breeding with domestic fowl. Males use their handsome plumage to display to females. The females lay their eggs on the ground among dense undergrowth.

BRAHMA CHICKENS

DOMESTIC CHICKENS ►

People have bred chickens for meat and eggs for at least 5,000 years. Today, there may be as many as 24 billion chickens worldwide – almost four times the human population. By selecting different features in the offspring used for mating, people have produced many domestic breeds of chicken.

Chicks *are covered in thick insulating layer of down*

▲ INDEPENDENT YOUNG
Gamebird chicks leave their nests within a few hours of hatching. They run about and feed without any help from their parents. These fluffy pheasant chicks, for example, are only two days old and 6 cm (2 in) tall, yet are largely independent. Young gamebirds are vulnerable to predators. This is why gamebirds lay large clutches, often of 8–12 or more eggs.

SNOW CAMOUFLAGE ►
Rock ptarmigans are adapted to survive in bitterly cold, snow-blanketed landscapes in the bare, rocky mountains and Arctic tundra of Europe, Asia, and North America. They have four different plumages each year, varying from mostly grey to all white, so that they blend into the changing scenery through the seasons. They survive severe winter blizzards by tunnelling under the snow.

Grey-brown feathers appear as winter turns to spring

Strong bill is suited to seizing insects as well as cracking seeds

▲ DUAL FOOD
Quails, such as this Japanese quail, are the smallest gamebirds. Some are little bigger than sparrows, but they are much fatter. Like most gamebirds, the adults feed mainly on seeds and other plant material, but the young also catch insects because they provide extra protein needed for growth. Many species of quail make long migrations to their wintering grounds.

COLOURFUL GAMEBIRDS

CHUKAR PARTRIDGE
Partridges are medium-sized gamebirds that live in a variety of places, including fields, deserts, and forests. The chukar partridge is a bird of dry, rocky country from the Middle East as far as China. It has been taken to many other parts of the world, for hunting.

CALIFORNIAN QUAIL
This species is one of several American quails with upright crests. This male has black and white head markings, but females are plainer. Outside the breeding season, the California quail gathers in flocks of hundreds of birds.

TEMMINCK'S TRAGOPAN
The five tragopan species are secretive residents of dense mountain forests in southern Asia. Males have large areas of bare, brightly coloured skin on their heads and necks. On Temminck's tragopan, these are a vivid shade of blue with patches of brilliant scarlet.

WILD TURKEY
The largest of all gamebirds, turkeys live wild in much of the United States, in a mixed landscape of forest, shrubs, and fields or grassland. The males fan out their feathers and make gobbling noises when courting mates. Today, wild turkeys are often shy due to extensive hunting.

SHOWING OFF ▲
As soon as winter snows melt, sage grouse gather together on the flat grasslands of North America. They assemble at the same sites, known as leks, every year. Here, the males act out dramatic courtship displays to huddles of females watching from the sidelines. They strut to and fro, and fan out their spiky tail feathers. At the climax of their display, they suddenly release air with loud pops from yellowish sacs on their breasts.

CRANES

Cranes are tall, elegant, and among the most long-lived of all birds, with some captive individuals being over 80 years old. Perhaps for these reasons, together with their spectacular courtship dances and annual migrations, cranes feature in the beliefs and rituals of many cultures. However, most of the world's 15 crane species are rare or threatened due to hunting and habitat loss.

Spiky crest of strawlike plumes on top of the head

Naked patch of scarlet skin on the throat

Neck is long and slender

▲ ENDANGERED CRANE
The rarest of all the cranes, the whooping crane breeds in the wild only in Canada and migrates to winter in Texas. By the 1940s, it was facing extinction and only 20 birds survived. A major conservation effort using captive breeding boosted its numbers to more than 400, and some birds were taken to Florida to establish a new population.

MIGRATION FLIGHT ▲
Like other cranes, the North American sandhill crane is a long-distance migrant. It breeds in Canada and the northern United States in the summer, and moves south to Mexico in the winter. Most migrating flocks fly at 150–200 m (500–660 ft), but some have reached 3,600 m (11,800 ft). In common with storks and many birds of prey, cranes use aerial highways formed by thermals (rising currents of warm air) to save energy.

Long grey plumes cascade down the bird's neck

Wings are raised and flapped during courtship dances

Long neck amplifies the crane's calls

Head is thrown back to utter loudest sounds

Long legs enable crane to wade through long vegetation

◄ DANCING CRANES
Red-crowned, or Japanese, cranes breed in Siberia, Mongolia, and on Hokkaido, Japan's northernmost island. Pairing for life, mated birds strengthen the bonds between them with bowing, running, strutting, and leaping dances. This pair has adopted a territorial defence posture, which is accompanied by a duet of wild trumpeting calls.

◄ GREY CROWNED CRANE
The cranes are an ancient group of birds, and fossils of this species' ancestors date back 60 million years to the early Tertiary period. The two species of crowned crane live in wetlands, savanna, and farmland in eastern and southern Africa. An inflatable air sac under the chin enables them to produce far-reaching, booming calls.

FIND OUT MORE ►► Birds 192–193 • Conservation 22–23 • Migration 50–51

BUSTARDS

Bustards are bulky, ground-living birds of open and lightly wooded habitats in Europe, Africa, Asia, and Australia. Great and kori bustards compete with the mute swan for the title of heaviest flying bird in the world – males may reach up to 19 kg (42 lb) in weight. However, bustards are reluctant fliers, often spending days or possibly weeks without taking to the air.

◄ GRASSLAND GIANT
The huge Kori bustard lives in dry, flat habitats in Africa. It strides along in search of prey, such as beetles and grasshoppers. The carmine bee-eater often hitches a ride, flying out to seize insects that the bustard disturbs.

Carmine bee-eater

Huge wings are usually kept folded

Long, sturdy legs for a life spent on foot

COURTSHIP RITUAL ►
This boldly patterned male little bustard is performing an extraordinary courtship display. To impress females, it stamps on the ground and repeatedly leaps into the air, its wings producing a hissing sound. At the same time, it snorts as if blowing raspberries, and inflates its neck feathers like a balloon.

FIND OUT MORE ▶▶ Birds 192–193 • Grasslands 56–57 • Mute Swan 204–205

RAILS

Rails are a group of birds that includes moorhens, coots, gallinules, and crakes. Most skulk about in swamps and reedbeds, but moorhens and coots live mainly on open water. Many species found their way to remote oceanic islands, where they evolved to become flightless in the absence of natural predators. Lots of them died out after humans introduced cats and dogs, which hunted them.

◄ PURPLE SWAMPHEN
This big, brilliantly coloured gallinule occurs in southern Europe, Africa, Asia, and Australia. Like most of its relatives, it has very long legs and long, thin toes to creep across mud or grasp swaying reeds. However, coots have unusual fleshy lobes on their toes for swimming.

COOT'S FOOT

RAILS AND RELATIVES

BLACK CRAKE
An adaptable species, this rail lives by tiny creeks in dry country as well as in large wetlands. It is less shy than many of its relatives, feeding away from dense cover and near people. Pairs perform duets: one makes chattering calls while the other makes soft, purring sounds.

BUFF-BANDED RAIL
Although only the size of a thrush, this rail eats a wide range of animal prey, seizing or stabbing at crabs, frogs, small fish, and the eggs and young of other birds. When disturbed, it runs to shelter instead of flying. Its range includes Australia, New Guinea, and Pacific islands.

SUNBITTERN
This unique bird of Central and South America is related to rails. Its mottled plumage makes it almost invisible most of the time. But if it is threatened, the sunbittern suddenly flicks its wings open to flash big, orange, eye-like patches that scare off animal intruders.

SHOREBIRDS

Shorebirds, also known as waders, are a group of birds that inhabit wetlands such as marshes, pools, Arctic tundra, estuaries, beaches, and rivers. They often have long legs and feet for wading in water or mud, and many have long bills for probing the soft ground for food. Several other groups of birds are related to shorebirds, including gulls, terns, and skimmers, most of which live at sea. Auks are a group of totally marine species, including puffins and guillemots, which come to land only to breed.

Bold plumage is black and white

Long, slender bill curves upwards towards the tip

◄ PIED AVOCET
Like all other avocets, the pied avocet from Europe, Africa, and central Asia breeds beside lagoons and other areas of salty water, both on coasts and inland. Avocets feed on shrimps, worms, and other small water animals by pacing forwards slowly with their bills slightly open, just below the surface of the water or mud. They sweep their bills from side to side so that special sensors in the bills can detect floating or swimming prey.

Long legs for wading through water or mud

Webbed feet for walking on mud and swimming

LIFE BY THE SHORE

GOLDEN PLOVER
This species nests on upland moors and bogs throughout northern Europe, where its speckled plumage provides excellent camouflage. In winter it moves downhill to farmland and coasts, often gathering in large flocks.

MASKED LAPWING
The masked lapwing lives in Australia and New Zealand. Unlike other shorebirds, it is often seen in urban areas, although its usual habitats are coasts and grasslands. It has yellow flaps of loose skin at the base of its bill.

INCA TERN
Like all terns, the inca tern from South America is a skilful and graceful flier. It hovers low above the sea and then dips to snatch small fish. Compared to gulls, the wings of terns are longer and more pointed.

BLACK-HEADED GULL
Despite its name, this gull from Europe and Asia has a chocolate-brown, not black, head in summer. This bird is displaying its winter plumage – the dark hood has nearly disappeared, leaving only a smudge.

BLACK-NECKED STILT
Stilts have extremely tall, thin legs, and those of this American species are longer relative to its size than any other bird. They enable it to wade in much deeper water than other shorebirds, where it catches aquatic insects.

DIFFERENT BILLS

Shorebirds have bills of varying lengths and shapes, and use them in different ways. This ensures that many species can live in the same habitat without competing for the same food. Some shorebirds, including plovers and turnstones, have fairly short bills, and snap up their prey on or near to the surface.

Sandpipers, such as knots, use their longer bills to probe further into mud or sand. Other species, including curlews, have very long bills to reach prey hidden far below the surface. Oystercatchers and a few other shorebirds have thick, powerful bills for hammering or prising open the shells of molluscs.

Ruddy turnstone lifts seaweed or stones to find prey

Red knot probes the upper layers of the mud or sand

Ringed plover pecks at prey on or just below the surface

Eurasian oystercatcher hammers open mussels and other shellfish

Eurasian curlew uses long bill to feel for buried prey

Lugworm is typical prey of shorebirds with long bills

Adult plover is hard to see when sitting on its nest

◄ VANISHING ACT
Many shorebirds build their nests on the ground in exposed places, such as shores or grassy areas. These locations are vulnerable to a range of predators, including carnivorous mammals, rodents, and crows, which may attack the adult shorebirds as well as steal their eggs and chicks. For this reason, shorebirds, such as this ringed plover, often have camouflaged plumage in shades of brown, grey, or black.

◄ HERRING GULL
One of the most successful seabirds in the world, this species lives across much of Europe, northern Asia, and North America. In recent times, it has become adapted to feeding on refuse and nesting on the roofs of houses and other buildings, sometimes far inland. These big, bold birds are often unpopular with humans because of their noisy calls, messy droppings, and willingness to dive-bomb people who get too close to their nests. However, many people also love the sight and sound of these seagulls.

Skimmer's bill touches a fish and snaps shut to catch it

▲ SNAPPING UP PREY
The three species of skimmer, including this black skimmer from North and South America, have extraordinary bills adapted for a unique feeding method. The lower, hinged section of a skimmer's bill is longer than the upper one, and as the bird flies over water, it pushes this through the surface like a plough. If the bird feels a fish, it flicks its bill shut and tilts its head back to swallow its prey.

CLIFF-NESTERS ►
Auks, such as puffins, guillemots, and these razorbills, are superb swimmers with webbed feet and streamlined bodies. They hunt fish underwater. Like most auks, razorbills breed on sea cliffs, nesting inside deep crevices in the rock. Guillemots prefer narrow ledges, and puffins dig burrows on clifftops. Auks do not make a nest, but lay their single egg straight onto the rock.

Legs are placed far back on the body

Huge black bill is shaped like a knife

Bird perches upright, like a penguin

ATLANTIC PUFFIN

With its huge, multicoloured bill and clumsy, waddling walk, the Atlantic puffin looks quite comical on land. But at sea it is a different story. This bird is a superb swimmer that spends much of its life far from the coast. It dives to find shoals of small fish, and powers through the water, kicking its orange webbed feet. In summer, both parents carry billfuls of fish to shore to feed their chick. Their rough tongues and tiny spikes inside their bills grip the slippery catches.

Scientific name: *Fratercula arctica*

Order: Charadriiformes (shorebirds)

Class: Aves (birds)

Distribution: North Atlantic and Arctic oceans, from North America, east to Europe and Russia

Status: Common

Length: 26–36 cm (10–14 in)

Weight: About 400–500 g (14–18 oz)

Food: Marine fish, especially herrings and sand eels, plus some crustaceans

Reproduction: In spring puffins gather at breeding colonies on rocky coasts and offshore islands; each pair has its own nesting burrow

Number of young: 1

FIND OUT MORE ▶▶ Birds **192–193** • Coasts **72** • Shorebirds **212–213**

PARROTS

Parrots form a large group of birds, with about 350 species, including cockatoos, parakeets, lorikeets, lovebirds, amazons, and macaws. They are intelligent, social birds with noisy calls, and they usually have colourful plumage. Nearly all parrots live in warm regions, especially in forests in the tropics. But as their forests are cut down and parrots are taken from the wild for the pet trade, many species are becoming endangered.

Crest is raised or lowered to show the bird's mood

Long flight feathers are spread out to increase control

SIGN LANGUAGE ▶
Cockatoos are a group of large parrots found only in Australia, New Guinea, and some Indonesian islands. There are 21 species, including this sulphur-crested cockatoo. They all have tall crests, which they raise to signal that they are alarmed or excited. Almost all have quite plain plumage, unlike most other parrots.

Long, narrow wings are used for acrobatic turns among trees

Powerful bill with hooked tip and sharp edges

Wild budgerigars are always green and yellow

Flock members perch close together

Large feet with flexible toes to grip branches

▲ SIDE BY SIDE
Parrots are very sociable, spending most of their lives in flocks. These budgerigars, for example, are settling down to roost (sleep) on the same branch. By huddling as a group, they are more likely to detect danger than if they perched alone. Budgerigars live in Australia's dry grasslands, and may gather in huge flocks of thousands of individuals.

Female is red and blue with a dark bill

Central tail feathers are green

Male is bright green with a yellow bill

SOLID BOND ▶
Parrots are long-lived birds – some large species have reached over 80 years old in captivity. They mate for life, and their bonds are so strong that in many cases pairs rarely lose sight of one another. In most parrots, the sexes look alike. But a few species, such as the Australian eclectus parrot (right), have different male and female plumages.

AGILE FEET ▶
This yellow-naped amazon from South America is holding a piece of fruit up to its bill so that it can be split open and eaten. Its fat, fleshy toes act like fingers. Parrots are the only birds able to pick up items in their feet and handle them in this way. Their feet also ensure a powerful grip when the birds are climbing through the trees.

Nimble toes can handle food with great care

Two toes face forwards and two backwards

▲ FAST FLIER
Many parrots, such as this eastern rosella, fly long distances each day to find new supplies of food or to reach the trees in which they usually sleep. They can move rapidly due to their streamlined bodies, long wings, and strong wing muscles. They fly with rapid, whirring wingbeats, but often glide for a few seconds between bursts of flapping.

NECTAR-DRINKERS ▶
The diet of many parrots is fruit, seeds, and nuts. However, some species, including lorikeets and these yellow-streaked lories from New Guinea, feed on the pollen and sugary nectar of flowers. The tips of their long tongues have tiny spikes and work like brushes to sweep up pollen grains and soak up nectar.

PARROT PARADE

Long tail for steering in flight

AFRICAN GREY PARROT
This species from West Africa is a familiar cage bird. Many captive parrots learn how to mimic human speech, and the African grey parrot is the best talker of them all. One pet was taught by its owner to count and to identify numerous different objects, shapes, and colours.

GALAH
The galah is 35 cm (14 in) long – about the size of a town pigeon – and is found throughout Australia. This cockatoo was originally a bird of forest and grassland, but it has spread to gardens, parks, and farmland. In some areas, flocks of galahs raid crops and are serious pests.

MASKED LOVEBIRD
Lovebirds are small parrots found in Africa's wooded savanna. They are named for the way in which pairs frequently preen each other. This ritual helps to reinforce the relationship between the birds. Lovebirds feed mainly on grass seeds, although they also eat a few insects.

RED-AND-GREEN MACAW
The world's largest parrots are the macaws of Central and South America. They have massive bills to crack the hardest nuts and seeds. The red-and-green macaw nests in hollow trees or holes in cliffs. It is increasingly rare due to the destruction of its forest habitat.

CUCKOOS

Cuckoos are famous for laying their eggs in the nests of other birds, which then raise the cuckoos' young. But not all cuckoos trick other birds in this way. About 80 of the 135 species of cuckoo, including the roadrunner of North America, build their own nests and care for their own offspring. This is also true of turacos, colourful African relatives of cuckoos. Most members of the cuckoo family are shy, although many have loud calls.

Tall red crest is raised when the bird is excited

Plumage has natural dyes that contain copper

NEST INVADER ►
A baby common cuckoo never sees its real parents. Soon after hatching in its foster parents' nest, it makes sure that it is the only chick there. It heaves the unhatched eggs onto its back one by one and pushes them over the edge. This means that there will be no rival chicks to compete for food.

◄ SHINY FEATHERS
Most species of turaco, including this Fischer's turaco, have glossy green and red plumage. This bright coloration is shown off during the turacos' energetic courtship displays in the treetops. Turacos forage in the canopy and defend their nest and feeding sites from other fruit-eating birds.

BROOD PARASITE ▲
The common cuckoo is the best-known example of a bird that lays its eggs in the nests of other species. Birds that do this are known as brood parasites. After mating, the female common cuckoo explores the area to look for suitable nests to lay her eggs in. She normally chooses several different nests, and nips in to lay one egg in each when the rightful owners are away.

Long tail provides balance while climbing trees to reach fruit

Bill extends into a horny shield on the bird's face

◄ NOISY BIRD
Turacos live in rainforests, where the dense foliage makes even their bold colours hard to spot at a distance. As a result, the birds rely on sound to communicate. This Ross's turaco is calling loudly to contact a partner or other members of its flock. The long choruses of gargling and croaking made by turacos resemble the sounds produced by some monkeys.

FAST MOVER ►
The greater roadrunner inhabits the deserts of Mexico and the southwestern United States. It can fly, but usually runs to catch prey or escape danger. The bird sprints in and out of cover to find prey. It is one of the few animals that can kill rattlesnakes, by seizing them in its strong bill and battering them to death against rocks and hard surfaces.

FIND OUT MORE ►► Behaviour 32–33 • Birds 214–215 • Communication 34–35 • Parenting 46–47

PIGEONS

Pigeons are a large group of birds that includes doves. They have plump bodies, with stubby bills and short legs. Their wings are usually large and are powered by powerful breast muscles, enabling them to be strong, fast fliers. As they walk, they bob their heads backwards and forwards, which probably helps them to balance. Pigeons and doves are most common in wooded, grassland, and agricultural habitats, and in towns.

▲ GLOBAL SUCCESS STORY
The town pigeon is perhaps the most familiar bird to many people living in towns and cities all over the world. Urban areas provide it with everything it needs. It eats all kinds of scraps, nests on buildings and bridges, and seems unconcerned by noise and passing people. The town pigeon's wild ancestor is called the rock dove.

White collar helps wood pigeons to recognize each other

Bulky body is unusually heavy for a bird

PIGEONS AND DOVES

PINK-SPOTTED FRUIT DOVE
Many of the pigeons and doves that live in tropical regions eat fruit. They often have colourful feathers that are totally unlike the dull colours of most town pigeons. The pink-spotted fruit dove lives in rainforests in New Guinea, and searches for ripe fruit in flocks.

PINK PIGEON
This is one of the rarest birds in the world. In the wild, it now survives only in a patch of forest on Mauritius, an island in the Indian Ocean. It declined in numbers due to attacks from rats, monkeys, and mongooses, brought to the island by humans. It was saved by captive breeding.

MOURNING DOVE
The name of this graceful species comes from its soft cooing, which sounds sad to human ears. It is the most common dove or pigeon in North America, and it can be seen in a wide variety of habitats, from grasslands and deserts to farms and suburban backyards.

▲ BIG DRINKER
Unlike almost all other birds, pigeons and doves do not have to take little sips of water and then raise their heads to let it flow down their throats. Instead, like this wood pigeon, they dip their bills into the water and suck it up as if through a straw. Pigeons and doves often have a dry diet containing a lot of seeds, so they are thirsty birds that need to drink frequently. They can drink up to 15 percent of their body weight a day.

PIGEON MILK ▶
Pigeons and doves, including this collared dove, feed their young on a thick liquid that resembles the milk produced by female mammals. Known as pigeon milk, it is rich in essential fats, minerals, and proteins. It enables the nestlings to grow rapidly. Both male and female parents care for the young and supply pigeon milk.

Pigeon nestling looks scrawny until it grows its adult feathers

FIND OUT MORE ▶ Birds 192–193 ▸ Habitats 54–55 ▸ Movement 28–29

OWLS

Most owl species are nocturnal or active mainly in the hours around dawn and dusk. Their large eyes provide superb vision in dim light, but their amazingly acute hearing is more important for finding prey. They hunt by stealth – swooping with their large, soft wings that make barely a sound. Like daytime birds of prey, such as hawks and eagles, owls possess hooked bills and strong claws for seizing victims.

Round facial disc focuses sound towards ears

Eyes are specially adapted to low light levels

Hooked bill for holding and carrying prey

Plumage is covered in fine down for silent flight

Soft, comb-like rear edge dulls the sound of the owl's wingbeats

Shaft provides strength

OWL WING FEATHER

Tail is spread to slow the owl down as it pounces

◄ SWOOPING TO KILL
The barn owl has a heart-shaped face and pure white underparts that appear ghostly when it is glimpsed at night. It lives in open country on every continent except Antarctica, as well as many remote islands. Most of its diet consists of small rodents, such as rats, mice, and voles. To catch them, it flies up and down at a low level and hovers to listen for movements below. When the owl locates its prey, it quickly swoops to attack.

Sharp claws grab prey and stop it escaping

OWLS FROM AROUND THE WORLD

BOOBOOK OWL
This Australian owl is named after the sound of its deep, hooting calls with which it attracts a mate and defends its territory. It often visits roadsides to catch insects attracted to streetlights. It may also hunt mice and small birds.

SNOWY OWL
As its name suggests, the plumage of this owl is mainly white. It breeds in the Arctic, on open expanses of tundra, and its coloration gives very good camouflage among the rocks and snow. In winter, food shortages force the owl to move south.

COLLARED SCOPS OWL
This small owl from southern and eastern Asia weighs just 125 g (4 oz). It is one of about 60 small species of scops owls. During the day, it sleeps in a tree. If the owl perches close to the trunk, it blends in so well with the bark that it seems to vanish.

SPECTACLED OWL
The white circles around this owl's eyes make it look as if it is wearing a large pair of glasses. It lives in forests in Central and South America. Its main hunting technique is to wait on a branch for prey to pass underneath, and then drop down to strike.

BUFFY FISH-OWL
Several species of owl found in Asia and Africa, including this species, catch fish. They have bare toes with extra-sharp claws and spiny soles to help them grip their slippery prey. The buffy fish-owl lives beside forest streams and in swamps.

HUNGRY YOUNG ▶
Tawny owl parents, which stay together as a pair for life, usually nest in holes in tree trunks. The nestlings are of different sizes because the eggs hatch at different times. If food becomes scarce, the younger chicks may starve as their stronger, older siblings snatch most of the meals that the adults bring. This seems cruel, but at least some chicks will survive from each brood.

BONY REMAINS

Owls swallow their prey whole, unlike daytime birds of prey, which first pluck or skin their victims and then tear the meat into pieces. Having digested the flesh of its prey, an owl brings up the feathers, fur, bones, and other inedible parts through its bill in the form of pellets. If a pellet is carefully pulled apart, it reveals what the owl has been eating.

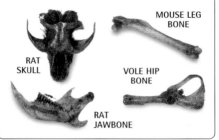

RAT SKULL

MOUSE LEG BONE

VOLE HIP BONE

RAT JAWBONE

NIGHT SENSES ▶
Like other owls, the eagle owl's senses are adapted for a mainly nocturnal life. The owl has large, highly sensitive ears that can detect the slightest rustle of prey in the dark. Its ears are hidden beneath the feathers of its rounded face. The owl also has huge eyes for gathering as much light as possible. The eyes are so big that they cannot move in their bony sockets to look to either side. Instead, the owl can rotate its whole head in an almost complete circle to look all around.

Tufts are not real ears but are for display

Facial disc of stiff feathers surrounds the eyes and ears

Huge eye

Open bill

FIND OUT MORE ▶▶ Animal Homes 48–49 • Birds of Prey 206–207 • Grassland 354–357 • Rodents 306 • Senses 316–317

NIGHTJARS

Nightjars belong to a group of nocturnal birds that includes nighthawks, frogmouths, and potoos. These species all have long wings for acrobatic flight, large eyes for night vision, and dull plumage that camouflages them as they sleep during the day. Although their bills are very short, the birds have huge, gaping mouths. This enables them to scoop up prey, either in flight or by diving to the ground.

TAWNY FROGMOUTH ▶
This bird from Australia and Tasmania uses its enormous gaping mouth to swallow large beetles, cockroaches, and other insects. Sometimes it seizes small frogs, lizards, and birds. The frogmouth's plumage blends in so well with bark and dead leaves that it is virtually impossible to see as it rests by day. If a predator gets too close, often without even noticing that the bird is there, the frogmouth opens its bill wide to startle its enemy.

PERFECT DISGUISE ▶
Frogmouths and potoos live in tropical forests. When not hunting, they perch high in the trees, where they resemble a broken branch or twig. Nightjars, such as this Eurasian nightjar, are found mainly in woodland, scrub, and deserts. They usually sleep on the floor among leaf litter or on bare soil or sand. They remain motionless to avoid detection by predators.

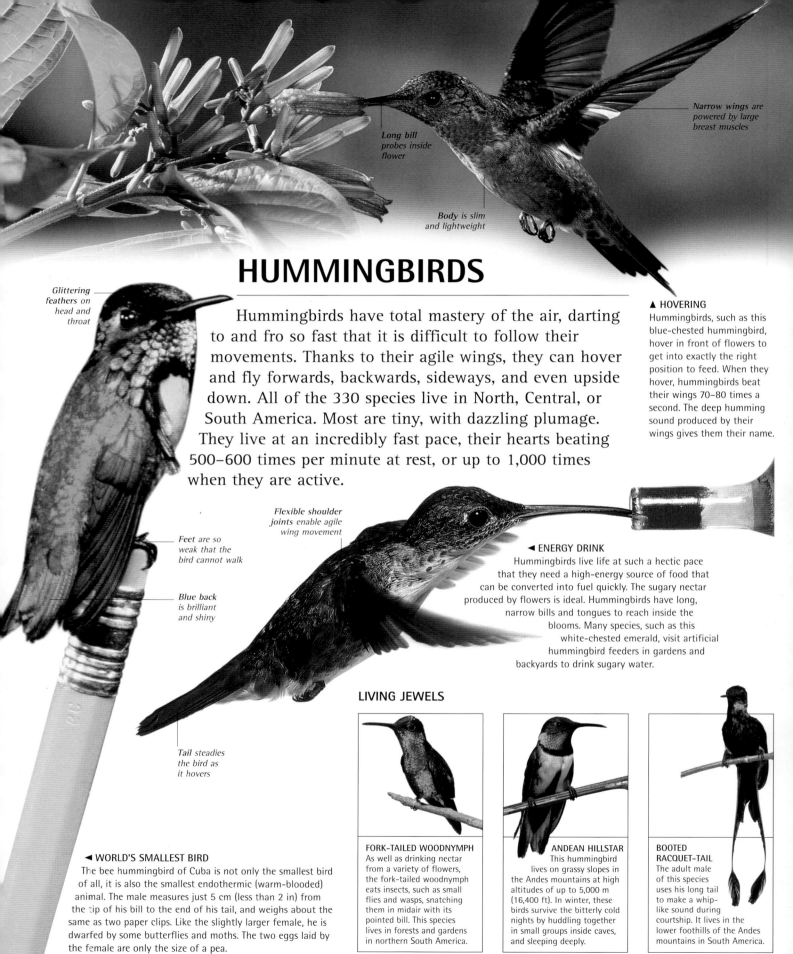

Narrow wings are
powered by large
breast muscles

Long bill
probes inside
flower

Body is slim
and lightweight

HUMMINGBIRDS

Hummingbirds have total mastery of the air, darting
to and fro so fast that it is difficult to follow their
movements. Thanks to their agile wings, they can hover
and fly forwards, backwards, sideways, and even upside
down. All of the 330 species live in North, Central, or
South America. Most are tiny, with dazzling plumage.
They live at an incredibly fast pace, their hearts beating
500–600 times per minute at rest, or up to 1,000 times
when they are active.

Glittering
feathers on
head and
throat

Feet are so
weak that the
bird cannot walk

Blue back
is brilliant
and shiny

Flexible shoulder
joints enable agile
wing movement

Tail steadies
the bird as
it hovers

▲ HOVERING
Hummingbirds, such as this
blue-chested hummingbird,
hover in front of flowers to
get into exactly the right
position to feed. When they
hover, hummingbirds beat
their wings 70–80 times a
second. The deep humming
sound produced by their
wings gives them their name.

◄ ENERGY DRINK
Hummingbirds live life at such a hectic pace
that they need a high-energy source of food that
can be converted into fuel quickly. The sugary nectar
produced by flowers is ideal. Hummingbirds have long,
narrow bills and tongues to reach inside the
blooms. Many species, such as this
white-chested emerald, visit artificial
hummingbird feeders in gardens and
backyards to drink sugary water.

LIVING JEWELS

FORK-TAILED WOODNYMPH
As well as drinking nectar
from a variety of flowers,
the fork-tailed woodnymph
eats insects, such as small
flies and wasps, snatching
them in midair with its
pointed bill. This species
lives in forests and gardens
in northern South America.

ANDEAN HILLSTAR
This hummingbird
lives on grassy slopes in
the Andes mountains at high
altitudes of up to 5,000 m
(16,400 ft). In winter, these
birds survive the bitterly cold
nights by huddling together
in small groups inside caves,
and sleeping deeply.

**BOOTED
RACQUET-TAIL**
The adult male
of this species
uses his long tail
to make a whip-
like sound during
courtship. It lives in the
lower foothills of the Andes
mountains in South America.

◄ WORLD'S SMALLEST BIRD
The bee hummingbird of Cuba is not only the smallest bird
of all, it is also the smallest endothermic (warm-blooded)
animal. The male measures just 5 cm (less than 2 in) from
the tip of his bill to the end of his tail, and weighs about the
same as two paper clips. Like the slightly larger female, he is
dwarfed by some butterflies and moths. The two eggs laid by
the female are only the size of a pea.

Flight feathers are long, thin, and curved

Forked tail is used for steering

Wings are very long for acrobatic flight

SWIFTS

Despite their black or brown plumage, swifts are relatives of brightly coloured hummingbirds. They have a similar wing structure – the wings are very flexible, enabling acrobatic flight with rapid wingbeats and sharp turns. Swifts spend virtually all their lives in the skies, feeding on insects caught in midair. They land only to sit on their nests or sometimes to sleep. Swifts resemble swallows, but have longer, more curved wings.

Nest of tiny twigs is glued to the wall with the bird's sticky saliva

◄ LIFE ON THE WING

A Eurasian swift may fly for up to four years nonstop – from the time it leaves the nest to its first breeding attempt. It feeds, drinks, bathes, mates, and sleeps in the air. To sleep, swifts climb higher and higher, and then fly slowly in spirals.

STICKY NEST ▲

Many swifts nest on cliffs or, like this North American chimney swift, on walls, chimneys, and other man-made structures. The nests are held together with the birds' saliva. In southeast Asia, swift nests are harvested to make birds' nest soup.

FIND OUT MORE ➤ Birds 192–193 • Migration 50–51 • Swallows 234

TROGONS

Trogons are found in forests in warm regions of North, Central, and South America, Africa, and Asia. They have long tails and beautiful plumage in shades of red, pink, orange, yellow, green, blue, or violet. Many species – especially the males – have a circular patch of bare skin around their eyes. Like hummingbirds and swifts, trogons have tiny feet, which are of use only for perching on strong, steady branches. They nest in holes in dead or rotting trees.

Orange ring of skin around the eye indicates that this is a male

Tail streamers are up to 65 cm (26 in) long

◄ SACRED SPECIES

The largest, most spectacular trogon is the male resplendent quetzal from mountain forests in Mexico and Central America. The Aztec civilization of Mexico considered it to be the God of the Air, and it was also sacred to the Mayan people of Guatemala. The quetzal eats mainly wild avocados, small fruits that grow in the canopy.

SITTING STILL ►

Few birds seem more patient than trogons, including this blue-crowned trogon from the Amazon rainforest in South America. They sit motionless for hours on end, half hidden among the foliage. Trogons usually feed in flight, plucking fruit or insects such as cicadas off leaves.

Foot is small and weak relative to the bird's size

FIND OUT MORE ➤ Birds 192–193 • Rainforests 60–61 • True Bugs 105

KINGFISHERS

Kingfishers perch or hover above the surface of the water, diving in to spear fish with their dagger-like bills. Most kingfishers are found in wetlands, but some hunt insects, lizards, snakes, and other prey in habitats such as forests. They often have dazzling plumage, and dig nesting burrows in earth banks, rotten tree trunks, or termite mounds. Several groups of colourful birds are related to kingfishers, including rollers, wood-hoopoes, hornbills, and bee-eaters. All of them nest in holes or burrows.

◀ TAKING THE PLUNGE
The Eurasian kingfisher sits quietly beside streams, rivers, pools, and marshes, watching for the telltale movements of fish below. To attack, it folds its wings and hits the water like a dart. Transparent false eyelids cover its eyes for protection while underwater. When the bird is back on its perch, it eats the fish head first, swallowing it whole.

▲ YELLOW–BILLED HORNBILLS
Hornbills are large birds from Africa and Asia named for their big, banana-shaped bills. The female seals herself inside her nest hole with mud to keep out predators, such as snakes, but leaves a narrow slit for the male to feed her. When the chicks are half grown, the female breaks the seal, escapes, and reseals it. The chicks emerge from the nest chamber when fully grown.

KINGFISHERS AND RELATIVES
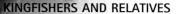

LAUGHING KOOKABURRA
This Australian kingfisher is named for its loud, raucous calls that resemble laughter. It lives in parks, gardens, and woodlands. It catches most of its prey on the ground, battering snakes to stun them before eating them.

WHITE-THROATED BEE-EATER
Bee-eaters hunt bees, wasps, dragonflies, butterflies, and other insects, snapping them up in flight. They occur in Africa, Europe, and Asia. As with some other bee-eaters, this species uses relatives to help raise young. Each pair may have up to five helpers.

GREEN WOOD-HOOPOE
This African bird pokes its curved red bill into holes in tree trunks and branches to find juicy grubs or caterpillars to eat. It also lifts up loose bark to search for prey, and hammers into soft wood.

RACQUET-TAILED ROLLER
The rounded tips to this bird's long tail feathers may help with balance while it perches. However, they are more likely to act as badges that help members of the species to recognize each other. The racquet-tailed roller inhabits bush and woodland in East Africa.

WOODPECKERS

Many types of bird climb trees, but woodpeckers are the real experts. They have strongly built bodies, with specialized feet that have two toes pointing forwards and two backwards. This design gives them a very stable grip on the tree trunk or branch. They use their powerful, chisel-like bills to chip insects and grubs out of the bark, make drumming sounds to communicate, and excavate their nesting holes. Woodpeckers are related to a number of other forest birds, including toucans, honeyguides, and barbets.

Sharp, pointed bill delivers repeated blows to the wood

Huge bill has sharp, saw-like cutting edges

PLUCKING POWER
Toucans are relatives of woodpeckers that live in tropical forests in Mexico, Central America, and the northern half of South America. This colourful species is the chestnut-eared aracari, one of the smallest of the toucans. It lives along rivers and lakes in the Amazon rainforest. As well as for feeding, toucans use their bills during courtship and threat displays.

◄ HAIRY BRISTLES
Barbets are chunky birds named for the beard-like tufts of bristles at the bases of their bills. They have big heads and strong bills, and climb trees in a similar way to woodpeckers. This fire-tufted barbet lives in rainforests in Malaysia and Sumatra, but it is threatened by the illegal felling of trees in its habitat.

MASSIVE BEAK ►
Toucans, including this toco toucan, have spectacular, brightly coloured bills with which they feed on fruit and small animals. The bills are much lighter than they look, and are long enough to reach food on branches that would otherwise be out of reach.

Bill is hollow, with bony struts that provide support

STICKY LICKER ►

Woodpeckers have long tongues with sticky tips to catch grubs hiding under tree bark or ants deep inside their nests. The birds' tongues are so long that they have to be coiled up in the skull when not in use. This European green woodpecker needs to consume about 2,000 ants every day to survive in winter.

▲ HEAD BANGER
Woodpeckers, such as this yellow-fronted woodpecker from South America, may hammer their bills against tree trunks or branches up to 12,000 times a day. Their skulls are thicker than those of other birds, to cushion the impact of the blows. Woodpeckers have strong leg muscles to provide a secure grip while they are hammering, and stiff tails that act as supports.

FIND OUT MORE ➤➤ Animal Homes 48–49 • Birds 192–193 • Deciduous Forests 64 • Rainforests 60–61

PERCHING BIRDS

Nearly 6,000 species – which is equivalent to about 60 per cent of the world's birds – belong to a group called perching birds. They are very varied in appearance, and live worldwide in all habitats except for oceans. Their feet, legs, and toes are adapted for gripping branches, plants, and even swaying grass stems. Another name for most perching birds is songbirds because many of them produce beautiful, complex songs.

Foot has 3 front toes and single rear toe

Shrike is about to impale a bumblebee on a sharp spike

Prey, such as this butterfly, is stuck onto thorns

SPECIALIZED TOES ▲

This Eurasian siskin belongs to a group of birds called finches. Like all perching birds, it has long, slim toes that wrap around whatever it lands on. Its rear toe is particularly long and strong. Tendons in its legs cause the toes to clamp shut automatically, ensuring a firm grip even when the bird is fast asleep.

◄ STORING FOOD

Shrikes, such as this red-backed shrike, are perching birds that resemble miniature birds of prey. They have strong legs and feet for seizing prey, and hooked bills for tearing flesh. Shrikes store their catches by sticking them onto a thorn bush or barbed-wire fence.

Small lizard is stuck down to eat later

BIRD SONG

Loud whistle   WHITE-CROWNED SPARROW'S SONG   *Pause between sounds*

Perching birds are often superb singers, with complicated songs that may vary in tone, volume, and rhythm. The main reason for their singing skill is the structure of an organ called the syrinx, which is located inside their trachea, or windpipe. Compared to that of other birds, the syrinx of perching birds gives much greater control over sound. Each species has its own song. For example, the song of the North American white-crowned sparrow (left) is a long series of many whistles and trills,

with brief pauses between each section. When its song is reproduced as a sonogram (diagram), the separate bursts of noise can be seen clearly. The song sparrow (right) is another common species from North America. Its song has two to six parts. There are several short, loud notes and a longer buzzing trill in the middle. Individual sparrows sing slightly different versions of the species' song.

SONG SPARROW'S SONG   *Long trill*   *Short note*

Large eyes help the bird to spot its prey among foliage

Caterpillars are a major source of food for many different songbirds

Strong feet for perching

INSECT FEAST ▲
Insects are an important food for many perching birds, including warblers, tits, flycatchers, wrens, larks, thrushes, and this eastern bluebird from North America. Insects are available all year in tropical areas. But in cooler regions they become scarce in winter, and so these birds must switch to eating fruit or seeds, or migrate to warmer places.

◄ FOOD FIGHT
This flock of Bohemian waxwings is greedily eating berries - a valuable food in autumn and winter. In their effort to eat as much fruit as possible, the birds squabble for the best positions and feed quickly. In years when the berry crop is poor, flocks of waxwings leave their normal range in northern Europe, Asia, and North America, and fly south to find supplies far from home.

Bright wing and tail markings help flock members stay in touch, especially in flight

PERCHING BIRDS

JACKDAW
Crows, such as this jackdaw, are the largest perching birds. They are famous for their intelligence and great adaptability – for example, they can learn tricks to gain food rewards. Jackdaws nest in holes in trees or buildings, and they eat a wide range of plant and animal food.

BLUE-NECKED TANAGER
The tanagers include many brightly coloured songbirds found in forests in Central and South America, as well as several common garden birds from North America. The species shown here lives in woodland in the Andes mountains and parts of Brazil. It is a fruit-eater.

BLUE TIT
Tits are small, highly acrobatic songbirds, and they include North American species called chickadees or titmice. The blue tit is a much-loved visitor to gardens in Europe, hanging from bird feeders to eat peanuts. Its natural diet is mainly insects, especially caterpillars, and seeds.

RED-CRESTED CARDINAL
The cardinals are a group of boldly plumaged songbirds found in North, Central, and South America, mainly in the tropics. The red-crested species is a lively bird with a spiky crest, which it raises whenever it is excited and during its courtship displays. It eats seeds on the ground.

FIND OUT MORE ➤ Birds of Paradise 231 • Crows 230 • Finches 236 • Migration 50–51 • Sparrows 235 • Thrushes 232

SATIN BOWERBIRD

Male bowerbirds build extraordinary courtship arenas called bowers to attract potential mates. The satin bowerbird weaves twigs into two parallel walls. He decorates this structure with all kinds of blue objects, including feathers, berries, flowers, and items of litter such as drinking straws or clothes pegs. When a green female arrives, the glossy blue male prances around his bower to impress her. He also offers her items from his collection of objects.

Scientific name: *Ptilonorhynchus violaceus*

Order: Passeriformes (perching birds)

Class: Aves (birds)

Distribution: Forests and woodland in east and southeast Australia

Status: Locally common

Length: 28–34 cm (11–13½ in)

Food: Mainly fruit; also insects (especially in the breeding season), leaves, and flowers

Reproduction: Male attracts females to his display ground and mates with several in a single season; females raise their young alone

Number of young: 1–3 per female, usually 2

FIND OUT MORE ▶▶ Perching Birds 226–227 • Reproduction 44–45

CROWS

Crows are a group of large perching birds that includes jays, magpies, ravens, nutcrackers, and choughs. They live everywhere from hot, sandy deserts to rainforests, and are among the world's most intelligent, adaptable, and social birds. Many eat a wide range of foods and can work out new ways of obtaining it. Some crows are black or grey, but jays and magpies may be brightly coloured, sometimes with crests or long tails.

◄ SOCIAL LIFE
Like most crows, the black-billed magpie of Europe, Asia, North Africa, and North America has a complex social life. It lives in pairs or family groups, but these may share their territory with other, non-breeding magpies. Families often join together to roost (sleep) in large treetop gatherings, especially in winter.

Strong bill can deal with a wide variety of food

Plumage has a glossy bluish or greenish tinge

Sturdy legs used to hold down food

◄ CLARK'S NUTCRACKER
Many crows store food to eat later during the winter, and none more so than Clark's nutcracker. It lives in the pine forests of western North America, gathering huge quantities of seeds from coniferous trees in autumn. It carries them in a pouch beneath its tongue, and buries its hoard in up to 2,000 places throughout the forest. The bird can remember exactly where its seeds are hidden up to nine months later, even if they are covered by snowdrifts.

Tail is long, as with all species of magpie

ANYTHING GOES ▲
This hooded crow lives in Scotland, Ireland, mainland Europe, and western Asia. Like many crows, it eats all kinds of prey, from beetles and earthworms to frogs, fish, and rodents. Crows also steal other birds' eggs and nestlings, raid rubbish bins, and scavenge carrion. Most crows feed on plant matter, too.

CROWS OF THE WORLD

RAVEN
This is the largest crow, with a huge bill and a wingspan of 1.2–1.5 m (4–5 ft). It is found in wild, open places, such as moors, mountains, and coastal cliffs. A superbly skilled flyer, the raven can roll over in midair, flying on its back to display to a mate.

PIED CROW
One of the most widespread birds in Africa, this species scavenges waste food at rubbish dumps and feeds on animal carcasses, often beside roads. It shows little fear of humans. Its untidy nest is a common sight on trees and telegraph poles.

CARRION CROW
A great opportunist, this crow likes to perch high up to scan its surroundings. In this way it is often the first bird to spot food, such as an unattended nest of eggs or scraps lying in the street. It learns how to drop shellfish on rocks to smash them.

RED-BILLED BLUE MAGPIE
There are five species of blue magpie, which live in forests in Asia. This handsome, sociable bird feeds in small flocks, often near to villages. The birds follow one another in a line as they fly across valleys and clearings to the next patch of forest.

FIND OUT MORE ►► Animal Kingdom • Bird Behaviour • Birds • Woodland Wildlife • Migration • Wetland Birds • Zoo

Plainer female judges each male's display

BIRDS OF PARADISE

Male birds of paradise are some of the most spectacular birds in the world. They have colourful plumage, often with long wing, tail, or back feathers in the form of flowing plumes or spiralling streamers. Their appearance is shown off to great effect during courtship dances. The females have dull plumage to camouflage them when sitting on nests. Birds of paradise are fruit-eaters found in rainforests, mainly in New Guinea. A few live in eastern Australia or the Molucca islands.

Male shivers his plumes around him in a dazzling cascade of colour

COMPETING FOR MATES ▲
Male raggiana birds of paradise display together, and the area of forest canopy where they gather to dance is called a lek. Up to 20 birds assemble at the lek, including several males and a crowd of females. The females favour males with the brightest plumage and best dancing skills, as this is a sign of their strength. The fittest male usually mates with most of the females.

BALLET DANCER ►
When displaying to a potential mate, this male king bird of paradise puffs up his feathers until he looks like a blood-red ball. At the same time, he expands a glittering green fan on his breast and raises his tail so that the long outer feathers dance above his head. In another display, he hangs upside down from a branch with quivering, outspread wings.

Body is an intense shade of red

Patch of bare blue skin on the back of the head

Outer tail feathers are thin and wiry, and each ends in a shiny green disc

COAT OF MANY COLOURS ►
Several birds of paradise, such as this Wilson's bird of paradise, display to partners in the open on the forest floor. This group of birds evolved (developed) on remote islands with no natural predators, so they could perform such displays without risking attack. Their first serious threat came from humans, who trapped the birds for their exotic feathers. Today, the felling of rainforests is an even greater danger.

FIND OUT MORE ▶ Birds 192–193 • Perching Birds 226–227 • Rainforests 60–61 • Reproduction 44–45

THRUSHES

These perching birds live all over the world in a wide variety of habitats, from town gardens to Arctic tundra, rainforests, and rocky hillsides. They have slender bills and eat both plant matter and small animals, particularly insects. Thrushes are split into several groups, including chats, robins, forktails, and bluebirds. Some of them have bright plumage, but most are duller brown, grey, or black. Many species are famous for their superb songs.

▲ BERRY FEAST

Thrushes are omnivores, which means they have a varied diet. Many species from cooler regions of the world, such as this North American hermit thrush, switch from feeding on earthworms and other invertebrates in spring and summer to eating fruit in autumn and winter. Fruit is a sugary, energy-rich food that helps the birds to survive periods of bad weather.

BEAUTIFUL SINGERS

NIGHTINGALE
The nightingale is a chat that breeds in Europe and spends the winter in Africa. The male is said to have one of the world's finest bird songs. Powerful and far-reaching, it is a long series of fluting, whistling, and trilling notes. It can be heard at night as well as by day.

RED-FLANKED BLUETAIL
This chat inhabits damp, mossy coniferous forests in northern Asia. Like most songbirds, the red and blue male has brighter plumage than the female, which is brown with a blue tail. The male sings his rich, sweet song from the tops of tall trees in spring.

CHESTNUT-CAPPED THRUSH
This species spends most of its life hiding in thick cover on the floor of rainforests in Malaysia, Thailand, and Indonesia. The chestnut-capped thrush has relatively large eyes, which help it to see in the gloomy conditions, and to find food such as berries, insects, and worms.

Wingtip feathers are widely spread for control when in flight

Broad wings for swerving in and out of vegetation

Bill is yellow in adult males, but brown in females and young males

Glossy black plumage of male develops in his second year

Large feet for scratching among fallen leaves for insect food

▲ EUROPEAN BLACKBIRD

In many species of thrush, the sexes look alike, but in others they differ. For example, only the adult male blackbird is black – the female and young birds have brown plumage. Blackbirds use their feet and bills to toss aside leaf litter to hunt for insects, and pull up worms from lawns. They also eat berries and take scraps from bird tables.

TERRITORIAL SONG ▶

In the breeding season, male thrushes sing to attract a mate and to announce ownership of their territory. This Eurasian song thrush can sing up to 100 or so phrases, each repeated several times in a random order. He learned some phrases from his father, but copies the rest from other thrushes or even different species of bird.

STARLINGS

Many starlings have a remarkable ability to imitate the noises they hear, including other birds as well as artificial sounds, such as sirens and ringing telephones. Their normal calls are loud and distinctive, enabling these sociable birds to stay in touch when in flocks. Starlings have stocky bodies, sharp bills, and strong legs and feet. Most of them live in Europe, Africa, and Asia, although several species have been introduced by humans elsewhere.

Loose folds of yellow skin on the neck

Pointed bill is suited to eating a range of foods

COMMON STARLING ►

The natural range of the common starling extends across Europe and Asia. It is an adaptable bird that thrives in city centres, nesting on buildings. On cold winter nights, the starling has learned to sleep in flocks beside the warm vents from air-conditioning units. This species has been introduced to North America, where its numbers have increased hugely, as well as to South Africa, Australia, and New Zealand.

Plumage has a blue, purple, or green sheen

White and buff spots increase in winter

Strong legs with large feet and claws

TALENTED MIMIC

Starlings often mix their own songs with notes copied from other species and with mechanical sounds that they have learned. It is thought that a more complex song makes them more attractive to partners. The best starling mimics of all are the Asian mynahs, such as this hill mynah. Mynahs are popular pets in many countries.

Tear-shaped patch of blue skin around the eye

Body is pure white, apart from black wingtips

Oxpecker snips parasites off the impala's skin

▲ SPECIES IN DANGER

The beautiful Bali starling, or Rothschild's mynah, is one of the world's rarest birds. It is threatened by habitat destruction and illegal trapping for the caged bird market. By 1999, only 12 wild individuals were left, inhabiting a patch of rainforest on the Indonesian island of Bali. To save the species, it is being bred in captivity.

CLEANER BIRD ►

Two African species of starling are known as oxpeckers because of their habit of picking insects off the backs of buffalo, oxen, antelopes, and other hoofed mammals. They grip their host's hide with their strong legs and claws, and use their scissor-shaped bills to snip off ticks, maggots, and other skin parasites. They also peck at wounds to drink the nutritious blood.

FIND OUT MORE ►► Birds 192–193 • Conservation 32–33 • Hoofed Mammals 289 • Perching Birds 225–227

SWALLOWS

Swallows, a group that includes a number of species called martins, are small perching birds that are adapted for catching flying insects. They spend most of their time on the wing, chasing insects with great agility. Their pointed wings and forked tails help them to steer and make sudden turns to snatch their prey. Swallows and martins occur almost worldwide, and some species are long-distance migrants.

Tail streamers are very long feathers

Cup-shaped nest is made of mud, strengthened with woven grass

Forked tail for acrobatic twists and turns

◄ AERIAL FEEDER

The house martin breeds across Europe and Asia, but spends the winter in Africa and southern Asia. It migrates between its summer and winter homes in flocks. House martins usually feed high in the air, sometimes out of sight from the ground. As in other swallows and martins, their bills open wide to act as scoops with which they trap insect prey.

▲ MUD NEST

Some swallows and martins nest in holes in trees, some excavate tunnels in soft earth or sand, and others, such as this barn swallow, build mud nests. Each pair of barn swallows may make as many as 1,000 trips to collect pellets of mud, which dry to form a sturdy structure. Common nest sites include beams in barns or garages, or under the eaves of buildings. The swallows raise two or three broods a year.

FIND OUT MORE IN Birds 192–193 • Migration 58–59 • Perching Birds 226–227 • Swifts 223

NEW WORLD BLACKBIRDS

This varied group of perching birds is not related to the species of blackbird found in Europe. It includes American blackbirds, American orioles, meadowlarks, troupials, oropendolas, cowbirds, and grackles. These species occur from Alaska to the southern tip of South America, although most live in tropical regions. Many are black or brown, but some have brilliant golden, orange, or red areas of plumage.

Plumage is mainly bright orange

◄ RED-WINGED BLACKBIRDS

This is one of the most common songbirds in the world, with a North American population of almost 200 million. Huge flocks of red-winged blackbirds form after the breeding season is over. They roam across farmland, eating large quantities of grain. During courtship, the males deliver a gurgling song and puff out their scarlet wing patches.

Strong feet for grasping tree branches

▲ GOLDEN BIRD

Male American orioles, such as this Bullock's oriole, are much brighter than females. Bullock's oriole breeds in the western United States, migrating south to spend the winter in Mexico. It is a bird of open woodlands, where it uses its pointed bill to feed on insects. In the United States, orioles are used on emblems for sports teams, clubs, and several states.

FIND OUT MORE IN Birds 192–193 • Migration 58–59 • Perching Birds 226–227 • Thrushes 232

SPARROWS

There are about 320 species of bird in this group, including buntings, grassquits, seed-eaters, and juncos as well as sparrows. They are small perching birds with strong, cone-shaped bills for splitting seeds open. Most species feed on the ground in open habitats such as fields, grasslands, shores, or tundra, scratching around for fallen seeds, but several sparrows and buntings live in towns in close association with humans.

Male has a grey cap and black bib

LAPLAND BUNTING ▶
This tough little bird breeds on windswept tundra and on high mountains in the Arctic. It escapes the harsh northern winter by migrating far to the south, where it wanders across coasts, marshes, and grasslands. The rear claw on each of its feet is long and curves downwards, which helps the bird keep its balance as it runs.

Mottled plumage blends in with the tundra vegetation

Bill is short and stout for crushing seeds

▲ GLOBAL SPECIES
The house sparrow's cheeping calls are familiar to millions of people throughout the world. This species is native to Europe and Asia, but it has been introduced to many other countries, and it is equally common in cities or the countryside. It thrives alongside humans, taking advantage of grain stored on farms and food provided at bird feeders in gardens.

FIND OUT MORE ⋙ Birds 192–193 • Perching Birds 226–227

WEAVERS

Weavers are seed-eating birds found mainly in Africa but also in Asia. They are named for the males' skill at weaving together dried grass and leaves to form domed nests, which are often suspended from branches. Many species breed in large, noisy colonies. This group also includes whydahs and widowbirds, which have long tails.

Female is duller than the male, with a much shorter tail

▲ WOVEN HOMES
The intricate nests built by male weavers are among the most complex structures produced by any bird. These village weavers have slung their nests from the tips of slender branches. This makes it very hard for predators, such as mammals, to reach them to steal the eggs or chicks.

▲ AMAZING TAIL
Pin-tailed widowbirds, such as this breeding pair, inhabit grassy plains in Africa. In the breeding season, like all widowbirds and whydahs, the male grows very long central tail feathers. He uses these to impress a potential mate by flying above her in wide circles with his tail dancing behind him.

Nest is shaped like a flask, with the entrance underneath

FIND OUT MORE ⋙ Animal Homes 68–69 • Behaviour 32–33 • Birds 192–193 • Perching Birds 226–227

FINCHES

These small songbirds eat seeds and have strong bills that vary in shape and size according to the species. Some finches have big bills for crushing or splitting food, others have thinner, more pointed bills that act like tweezers. Finches live worldwide, and they include chaffinches, goldfinches, bullfinches, grosbeaks, crossbills, canaries, and waxbills. Most finches live in trees, especially in open woodland, forest edges, gardens, and scrub, but some are ground-dwellers.

Slender bill for delicately pulling seeds out of flowers

Head pattern of red, black, and white feathers

Black wings marked by bold yellow bars

◄ TWEEZER BILL
This Eurasian goldfinch and the three North American species of goldfinch have fairly long, sharply pointed bills. The birds use these carefully to tweak out the small seeds of thistles and other flowering plants. Their small, compact bodies and agile claws enable them to feed while swinging – often upside down – on plant stems.

Spiky seed heads of thistle plant

FEMALE

Female has much duller, grey-brown plumage

MALE

Male has rosy pink underparts

◄ HANDSOME COUPLE
Like many finches, the sexes of the northern bullfinch of Europe and Asia look different, with bright males and plain females. This species has a stout, triangular bill operated by powerful muscles in its broad neck. It uses its bill to strip off and then crush the seeds, flower buds, and berries of trees and wildflowers.

Strong claws can grip swaying plant stems

FINCHES OF THE WORLD

CHAFFINCH
This is one of the most common birds of Europe. It lives in hedgerows and woods, and becomes tame in gardens and parks. Like other finches, the adults feed their nestlings on insects rich in protein, which is needed for growth. Later, the young start eating seeds.

GOULDIAN FINCH
The Gouldian finch was once common throughout the hot, dry grasslands of Australia, but today it is hugely reduced in numbers. Its decline is due to trapping for the caged bird trade and intensive cattle grazing, which reduces the amount of wild seeds available.

JAPANESE GROSBEAK
Grosbeaks are a group of big finches that have massive bills with sharp cutting edges. Like bullfinches, they feed mainly on berries and buds. The Japanese grosbeak inhabits forests and parks, and is shy, hiding among foliage. It forms small flocks outside the breeding season.

ISLAND EVOLUTION ►
The Hawaiian finches are a group of birds that are found only on the remote Pacific islands of Hawaii. They are descended from a single species of finch that arrived there thousands of years ago. With no competition from other birds, it could eat a wide variety of foods. Gradually, it evolved (developed) into about 45 species, each with a different shape of bill suited to its diet. Half of the Hawaiian finches have since become extinct.

Akiapolaau probes bark for insects

Liwi drinks nectar

Apapane eats insects and nectar

HAWAIIAN FINCHES

Maui parrotbill rips bark to find beetles

Nihoa finch uses its heavy bill to crush seeds

Early species, now extinct, ate insects and nectar

Amakihi is a nectar drinker

WARBLERS

Two unrelated groups of birds are called warblers – one in Africa, Europe, and Asia, and the other in North, Central, and South America. All are small perching birds with short, pointed bills adapted for eating insects. True to their name, many have attractive warbling songs. They include many species that make long migrations between their breeding areas in the northern hemisphere and wintering areas in the south.

◄ DEFENDING TERRITORIES
The sedge warbler breeds along riverbanks and in marshes and reedbeds throughout Europe and western Asia, but it spends the winter in Africa. In spring, the males return before the females, to establish territories in which they will nest. They advertise which patch of land is theirs using their song, which is a blend of sweet warbling and chattering notes. Later, when the females have arrived, the males sing to attract a mate.

SEWN NEST ▲
This family of hungry nestlings belongs to a pair of Indian long-tailed tailorbirds. Along with a few other species of warbler, this species constructs an extraordinary nest. It sews two large leaves together using its fine bill as a needle and tough plant fibres or silk from spiders' webs as thread. Alternatively, it folds over a single leaf and does the same with the two halves.

Male has bold black, blue, and white plumage

◄ SHARING NEST DUTIES
Most warblers from North and South America build open, cup-shaped nests from grasses, leaves, bark, and other plant material. They locate them in thick cover on the ground, or hidden among the foliage of shrubs or trees. The female builds the nest, but as with this male black-throated blue warbler, both parents share the task of incubating the eggs and feeding the nestlings. The young are ready to fledge (leave the nest) in 10–14 days, depending on the species.

PRAIRIE WARBLER ▲
This warbler is poorly named, as it does not live in the prairie grasslands of the western United States, but in the eastern half of the country, in open woodland, scrub, and mangrove swamps. It stays low down, often feeding on the ground. In winter, prairie warblers migrate south to Florida, Central America, and the Caribbean, where the warmer temperatures guarantee a good supply of insects.

FIND OUT MORE >> Birds 192–193 • Communication 34–35 • Migration 50–51 • Perching Birds 226–227

MAMMALS

◀ CLOSE RELATIVES
Chimpanzees are like humans in many ways – they are sociable, intelligent, can learn how to use tools, and are great communicators. Both chimps and humans belong to a group of animals called mammals. Mammals come in all shapes and sizes, but have several things in common. They nourish their young with milk; they have hair or fur; and they are able to maintain a constant body temperature, no matter how warm or cold it is.

MAMMALS

Mammals are vertebrates (animals with backbones) that have hair and produce milk to feed their young. They are endothermic (warm-blooded), which means that they generate their own body heat from food. There are 4,700 species of mammal, and they live in almost every habitat, including underwater, in the treetops, in burrows, and in the air. Apart from three egg-laying species, all mammals give birth to live young.

▲ MILK PRODUCER
All female mammals possess mammary glands that secrete milk to nourish their babies. These young domestic rabbits are each suckling (feeding) from a separate teat on their mother's belly. Mammals have different numbers of teats according to how many offspring they usually produce. For example, monkeys and apes have only one pair of teats, but some rats and mice have more than ten pairs.

◄ JAW STRUCTURE
Mammals evolved (developed) from reptiles about 200 million years ago. The jaws of their reptile ancestors were made of several bones and could move only up and down, and their teeth were all the same shape. Gradually, the structure of mammal jaws changed. Mammals alive today have several shapes of teeth, and their jaws, which are made of a single bone, are capable of complex movements. These features enable mammals to chew their food – no other animals can do this.

Wide gape between the upper and lower jaw

Lower jaw is hinged directly to the skull

TEMPERATURE CONTROL

Hair helps mammals to control the temperature of their bodies. Each hair sits in a pocket of skin called a follicle. This is attached to a muscle that raises or lowers the hair. When the hair stands up, a layer of air is trapped against the skin to provide warmth. To help cool down, the hair is lowered so that it lies flat against the body.

SKIN CROSS-SECTION

Hair shaft protrudes above the skin

Muscle raises and lowers hair

Gland that makes an oily substance to waterproof hair

Follicle provides secure fixing for each hair

MAMMAL LIFESTYLES

▲ AQUATIC MAMMAL
Whales and dolphins, such as this bottlenose dolphin, never leave the water. They have streamlined bodies with flippers and a tail. Seals and sea lions are also aquatic, but give birth on land. Other mammals, such as river otters, live equally on land and in water.

Red foxes approach to investigate

Skunk raises its tail to release a smelly defence

TYPES OF MAMMAL

MARSUPIALS
Most mammals in this group have a pouch on the belly in which the young develop. The babies are born at an early stage of development and crawl into their mother's pouch to continue growing. There are more than 300 species of marsupial, such as these red-necked wallabies.

PLACENTAL MAMMALS
Placental mammals, such as this chinchilla, are by far the largest mammal group. Their young develop in the mother's uterus (womb) for a much longer period than other mammals. The unborn young are fed by nutrients and oxygen passing through an organ called the placenta.

EGG-LAYING MAMMALS
The two species of echidna and the platypus are unusual among mammals because they lay eggs. This group of animals, called monotremes, live only in Australia and Tasmania. Echidnas lay their eggs into a pouch on the belly, whereas the platypus lays its eggs in a burrow.

◄ COMMUNICATION BY SMELL

Many mammals have an acute sense of smell and use scent to communicate. They mark their territories with urine and droppings, or with scent from special glands. Smell can reveal the identity of an individual animal, and it may also signal an animal's readiness to mate. A few mammals, such as this North American skunk, use unpleasant smells to deter predators.

▲ AERIAL MAMMAL
Bats, including this Daubenton's bat, are the only mammals capable of true flight. Their forearms have become flapping wings. A few mammals, such as flying squirrels, can glide from tree to tree using flaps of skin that stretch between their arms and legs.

▲ TREE-LIVING MAMMAL
Apes and monkeys, including this proboscis monkey, are at home in the trees. They move by climbing, swinging, and leaping. Their long, strong limbs and grasping hands and feet are adapted for holding branches. Monkeys also have long tails for balance.

▲ GROUND-LIVING MAMMAL
Mammals found at ground level move by walking, running, or burrowing, and the vast majority travel on all fours. Humans are the only mammals to move on two legs as adults, although other great apes, such as orangutans, do so occasionally. One theory is that the first humans started walking upright so their arms remained free for hunting.

FIND OUT MORE ▶▶ Anatomy **26–27** • Classification **308–309** • Egg-laying Mammals **242** • Marsupials **243** • Placental Mammals **247**

EGG-LAYING MAMMALS

Three Australian mammals lay eggs rather than giving birth to live young. The semi-aquatic platypus usually lays two eggs in a burrow. The long- and short-nosed echidnas lay a single egg in a pouch on their belly. Like all mammals, echidnas and platypuses feed their young on milk, but they have no teats. Instead, milk seeps from the mother's mammary glands onto tufts of hair, where the baby licks it up.

Long snout for probing anthills and termite mounds

Spines give protection from predators

ECHIDNA EGG

Strong claws to dig nesting burrows

▲ SPINY BURROWER
The short-nosed echidna lives in Australia, Tasmania, and New Guinea. It measures around 45 cm (18 in) in length and is covered in fur and sharp spines. An echidna uses its flexible snout and sticky tongue to extract ants and termites from their nests. It has no teeth – the insects are crushed between many little spikes on the tongue and the roof of the mouth.

Paddle-shaped tail helps to steer while swimming

Beak-like snout is very sensitive

Webbed feet provide thrust

▲ SWIMMING UNDERWATER
Streams and rivers in eastern Australia and Tasmania are home to the platypus, which grows to 60 cm (24 in) long. Its rounded, rubbery bill is extremely sensitive to touch and to the tiny electromagnetic pulses that all animals produce. The platypus uses its senses to locate its invertebrate prey hidden under rocks or beneath layers of mud on riverbeds.

MARSUPIALS

Most female marsupials have a pouch in whic they carry their babies while they develop. Th majority of marsupials, including kangaroos, wallabies, and koalas, live in the Australian region, but marsupials are found in North and South America, too. In total, there are about 315 species. Some marsupials roam across open plains, deserts, or the forest floor, but many others are excellent climbers more at home in trees or bushes. Their diet may be vegetarian or carnivorous (meat eating).

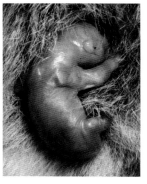

▲ INCREDIBLE JOURNEY
This baby koala is just 2 cm (¾ in) long, yet it has already travelled an amazing distance in its brief life. Marsupial babies are born without fur, sightless, and deaf. Nevertheless, they are strong enough to clamber up through their mother's fur to reach the safety of her pouch. Once there, they attach firmly to a teat to feed.

Baby kangaroo is called a joey

Pouch stretches as the joey grows

HITCHING A RIDE ►
Like most other marsupials, this red kangaroo mother has a pouch below her belly in which she carries her young. Although female kangaroos give birth to just one baby at a time, they can raise two offspring at once. They feed one baby inside the pouch, while a second, older youngster follows them around on foot. At the same time, they may also be pregnant with a third, unborn baby.

FIND OUT MORE ▸▸ Mammals 240–241 • Placental Mammals 247

MEAT EATER ►
Carnivorous marsupials include quolls, which are the size of a domestic cat, and this Tasmanian devil, a fierce animal with massive jaws and pointed teeth. During the day, the devil rests in a den that it makes among rocks or in a cave. It emerges at night to feed on other mammals, lizards, birds, eggs, and carrion. When excited, its pale ears turn red.

Big, upright ears twitch constantly to detect danger

Powerful jaw for grinding grass and leaves

Chocolate-brown fur with pale markings

Stocky body with short, strong legs

Limbs are all of equal size, unlike in ground kangaroos

◄ LEAF EATER
Doria's tree kangaroo lives in tropical rainforests in New Guinea. Tree kangaroos mainly eat leaves, but also feast on ripe fruit. They are slow and clumsy on the ground, but superbly agile in the trees, using their long tails to balance. A diet rich in leaves requires a large gut to help digest the plant matter.

Strong tail helps the animal to balance

FRUIT EATER ►
The mountain brushtail possum has a vegetarian diet that includes lots of fruit. It is nocturnal and has large eyes to help it see in the dark. By day, it rests in holes in tree trunks. In common with several other possums, it has a prehensile (grasping) tail that it can wrap tightly around branches, holding itself steady while feeding.

Powerful back legs for bounding along at speed

EXTINCT MARSUPIAL

Stripes provided camouflage

Muscular tail provides support, almost like a third leg

The Tasmanian wolf or thylacine was a meat eater that hunted wallabies, other small mammals, and birds. The pouch on its belly shows that it was not a real wolf or dog, but a marsupial. In prehistoric times, there were many large carnivorous marsupials, including lion-like species, but the thylacine was the last one to survive. It was hunted to extinction by farmers who accused it of killing their sheep. The thylacine was last seen in the wild in 1933. Today, numerous other marsupials are threatened by habitat loss and the introduction to Australia of new predators.

FIND OUT MORE ▶▶ Extinction **19** • Kangaroos **245** • Koalas **244** • Mammals **240–241** • Possums **246** • Wombats **244**

KOALAS

Koalas live in eucalyptus forests in eastern Australia. There are around 600 species of eucalyptus tree in Australia, but koalas eat the leaves of only 15 or so, probably because the others are too toxic. In the past, koalas were killed for their skins, and their forests were cut down to make way for agriculture. Since receiving strict protection, these bear-like marsupials have gradually increased in number.

Ears are big, round, and furry

Muzzle is black and smooth

Sharp claws grip branches

CLIMBING A TREE ▶
The koala is often mistakenly referred to as the koala bear due to its rounded face and compact body. It has strong limbs, which it uses for climbing, and it spends most of its time in the treetops, descending to the ground occasionally, to travel between trunks. Females have a backward-facing pouch for their young.

◀ LAZY LIFE
Koalas tend to move slowly and sleep for about 20 hours a day. They need this restful time in order to digest their food. Eucalyptus leaves are high in cellulose, a tough, fibrous substance that is impossible for animals to break down. However, koalas have lots of bacteria in their guts, which gradually process all the cellulose and so release useful nutrients.

FIND OUT MORE ▶▶ Herbivores **39** • Marsupials **242–243**

Thick fur for life in cold as well as hot habitats

Broad head

WOMBATS

Wombats are quite closely related to koalas. They have squat, solidly built bodies and can reach 1 m (3⅓ ft) in length. The three different species all live in southern Australia. Two species have hairy noses, but the common wombat's nose is naked. Wombats feed on grasses and they usually graze at night. Each wombat guards its own feeding territory, which it marks using smelly urine and piles of dung. It growls angrily and bares its teeth at intruders.

Short legs act as efficient shovels

Blunt nose is hairless in the common wombat

▲ RAPID BURROWER
Wombats use their strong legs and claws to excavate burrows in the ground. A burrow may have several entrances and connecting tunnels. Female wombats have pouches that open towards the back of their bodies, and this helps to keep dirt out of them as they dig. Wombats give birth to one baby, which stays in its mother's pouch for six months.

FIND OUT MORE ▶▶ Herbivores **39** • Marsupials **242–243**

KANGAROOS

Kangaroos have a distinctive upright posture, and huge back legs for hopping along the ground. Red and grey kangaroos are the world's largest marsupials, but there are many smaller species, known as wallabies. The larger species form herds called mobs, whereas smaller ones may be solitary. All kangaroos are herbivores and live in Australia or Tasmania, often on grassy plains.

▲ EFFICIENT MOVER
Kangaroos and wallabies travel quickly by bounding on their powerful back legs. They hold their long, thick tails out for balance and steering, much like a boat's rudder. Hopping is an energy-efficient method of movement, and it enables kangaroos to top 50 kph (about 30 mph). When feeding, they move slowly on all fours.

RED-NECKED WALLABY ►
Like many of its relatives, the red-necked wallaby feeds mostly in the cool of night, sometimes travelling long distances in search of fresh grazing. It forms groups of up to 30 animals, which scatter in all directions if disturbed.

Heavy tail acts as a prop when at rest

Small front legs are used to feed and groom fur

Powerful back legs are used to propel the wallaby

Rival males attempt to push each other over

KANGAROO SPECIES

QUOKKA
This small wallaby is found in southwestern Australia, particularly on a coastal island called Rottnest Island. It is nocturnal, sheltering under shrubs and bushes during the day, but it often becomes bold enough to beg for scraps from tourists.

FORESTER KANGAROO
The forester kangaroo is a variety of the eastern grey kangaroo, restricted to the island of Tasmania. It usually feeds on grasses, especially in the early morning and evening. Joeys depend on their mothers for milk and protection for 18 months.

WESTERN GREY KANGAROO
Males of this species can reach over 2 m (6⅔ ft) long. They vary in colour from greyish to brown. Females communicate with their joeys using a series of clicks. Western grey kangaroos roam the outback, or bush, in west and south Australia.

◄ BOXING KANGAROOS
Male eastern grey kangaroos fight with one another for control of the mob. They have toughened skin on their bellies to lessen the impact of the blows from their opponents' legs. The largest male usually wins and so will father most offspring. But if food is in short supply, kangaroos may not breed at all – they wait until conditions improve.

FIND OUT MORE ➤➤ Herbivores **39** • Marsupials **242–243**

POSSUMS

Possums are small mammals that live in Australia and on several nearby islands. This group of marsupials, and their relatives, the opossums of North and South America, mainly eat flowers and leaves. Female possums and opossums usually give birth to litters of several young, unlike other marsupials, such as koalas and kangaroos, which have single babies. They have numerous teats to supply the babies with milk.

▲ VEGETARIAN DIET
There are 17 ringtail possum species, all of which have long, prehensile (grasping) tails that curl into a ring shape at the tip. They have greatly enlarged guts to digest leaves, which are their main food. Other types of possum specialize in eating different plant products, including flowers, nectar, buds, fruit, or tree sap.

*Large eyes
for good
night vision*

*Gliding membrane
unfurls like
a parachute*

▲ ALL ABOARD
The opossums of North and South America are the only marsupials found outside Australasia. This female grey four-eyed opossum is carrying her babies on her back until they can move by themselves. Even then, the family may form a train, holding onto each other's tails so that they don't become separated.

*Long tail
allows the
possum to balance*

*Banksia flowers
are a favourite
food*

*Hand is held out
ready to land
on a tree trunk*

◄ FLOWER FEEDER
With a body no larger than a human thumb, the little pygmy possum is one of the smallest marsupials. It emerges after dark to visit flowers to feed on nectar, pollen, and insects hidden in the blooms. The species is an important member of its ecosystem, because it fertilizes flowers by transferring pollen between different plants.

NIGHT GLIDER ▲
Several possums, including this sugar glider, have folds of baggy skin along their sides that can be opened out to form parachute-like membranes. The membranes catch the air, and enable the animals to glide between trees or away from predators. This species inhabits eucalyptus forests, where it drinks the sweet sap produced by the trees.

FIND OUT MORE ▶▶ Defence 42–43 • Ecology 14–15 • Mammals 240–241 • Marsupials 242–243

PLACENTAL MAMMALS

The majority of mammal species are known as placental mammals. In this group, young develop inside the mother's body for a period called pregnancy. During pregnancy, the foetus (unborn young) is nourished with nutrients and oxygen. These cross from the mother's blood to the blood of the foetus through an organ called the placenta. Compared to egg-laying mammals and marsupials, placental mammals have long pregnancies – the longest of all is that of the African elephant, which averages over 20 months.

HITCHING A LIFT ▶
Mammal mothers invest a lot of time in caring for their young. The offspring may rely on them for months or years, first for milk and later for protection and guidance. Most male mammals do not play a large part in raising their young. However, male marmoset and tamarin monkeys, such as this golden lion tamarin, are helpful fathers that often carry their offspring around.

▼ GROUP CARE
Some mammals that live in groups help each other to rear the young. This is especially true of pack-living carnivores, such as these African hunting dogs. Aunts and uncles guard the young while their parents are hunting, and all pack members help to feed the pups. Certain primates also share responsibility for raising younger relatives.

Coat pattern is unique to each dog

Adults watch over all the pack's pups

PREGNANCY IN PLACENTAL MAMMALS

The fertilized egg of a placental mammal divides many times. It eventually becomes a foetus, which grows inside the mother's uterus, or womb. For protection, the foetus is cushioned by membranes and amniotic fluid on all sides. Nutrients and oxygen pass from the placenta to the foetus through the umbilical cord, and waste products pass back the other way.

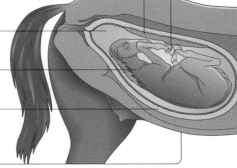

Umbilical cord connects the foetus to the placenta

Placenta lies on the inside of the uterus

Amniotic fluid protects the foetus during pregnancy

Foetus develops in the uterus

Uterus is a muscular sac in which the baby grows

A FOAL IS BORN

GIVING BIRTH
The process of a placental mammal giving birth is called labour. During a horse's labour, the baby's forelegs appear first, followed by the head and the body. Most mammals give birth in secluded places because they are vulnerable to predators at this time.

A NEW LIFE
Horses usually have just one foal at a time. Other mammals may give birth to several young in quick succession. After giving birth, the mother licks the baby clean. She usually eats the afterbirth (the placenta and its membranes) because it contains vital nutrients.

FIRST STEPS
Young mammals born in the open, such as horses and antelopes, have to stand up soon after birth. If not, they will be at risk from predators. Mammals born in nests, tree holes, or burrows underground are much more secure, and so their first few hours are less dangerous.

NUTRITIOUS MEAL
Female mammals produce milk for their babies. This is rich in fat, vitamins, and minerals to help the young grow quickly. It also contains antibodies to protect them against diseases. Newborn mammals have an instinct, or urge, to begin feeding from their mother's teats.

FIND OUT MORE ▶▶ Dogs **272** • Mammals **240–241** • New World Monkeys **259** • Parenting **46–47** • Reproduction **44–45**

THREE-TOED SLOTH

Often mistaken for monkeys, sloths live in the sunlit highest levels of the rainforest. Active for around 10 hours out of 24, they pass the rest of the time hanging virtually motionless, digesting their food. When resting, their body temperature falls to help conserve energy. Sloths live alone, and males find breeding partners by uttering shrill cries. Baby sloths cling to their mothers' chest fur for six months, by which time their diet has switched from milk to leaves.

Scientific name: *Bradypus tridactylus*

Order: Pilosa

Class: Mammalia (mammals)

Distribution: Tropical forests in Central and South America

Status: Common

Length: 56–60 cm (22–24 in)

Weight: 3.5–4.5 kg (7⅔–10 lb)

Food: Leaves. The species is highly selective, feeding from less than 1 per cent of forest trees

Reproduction: Breeding occurs throughout the year; gestation period is 5–6 months

Number of young: 1

FIND OUT MORE ▸▸ Herbivores **39** • Rainforests **60–61** • Sloths **250**

SLOTHS

All six species of sloth live in the lush rainforests of South and Central America. Most of their time is spent hanging upside down high in the forest canopy, feeding on leaves, and resting. Sloths have shaggy coats, which often appear green as a result of algae growing on their fur. This green coloration helps to camouflage them among the foliage. About once a week, sloths descend to the ground to excrete waste.

Thick, hooked claws provide vice-like grip

Long limbs for ease of movement

Algae and a species of moth live on the sloth's fur

Head can rotate through 270° to look for danger

GIANT OF THE PAST

Until 10,000 years ago, enormous ground-living sloths roamed the plains and forests of North and South America. One species, *Megatherium*, was as big as an elephant and evidence suggests that it walked upright on its hind legs. Like other extinct ground sloths and modern tree-dwelling species, it was a leaf eater. It reached food by rearing up and using its huge hooked claws to pull leafy branches within reach. These fearsome claws may also have enabled *Megatherium* to scavenge meat from dead animals.

▲ SLOW MOTION

Sloths have long arms and legs, with three toes on the back feet. There are either two or three toes on the front feet, depending on the species – this is a two-toed sloth. Each toe ends in a curved, hook-like claw for gripping branches. Sloths move extremely slowly, and may stay in the same tree all day. This saves energy, which is vital, as their diet of leaves is low in nutrients. A single meal can take a month to digest.

FIND OUT MORE ▶▶ Mammals 240–241 • Rainforests 60–61 • Three-toed Sloth 248–249

ANTEATERS

All four anteater species live in South and Central America. The giant anteater lives on wide, grassy plains, while the silky anteater and northern and southern tamanduas are forest dwellers. Anteaters are toothless and have pointed snouts with a small mouth at the tip. Their long tongues are covered with spines and sticky saliva to lick up ants and termites.

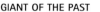

Tail aids balance when walking on branches

▲ HANGING ON

The silky anteater is the smallest of the four species. It never leaves the trees and leads a solitary, nocturnal lifestyle. To help it climb trees, it has a prehensile (grasping) tail that acts like an extra limb. Its feet have claws that can curl under the foot to give an even stronger grip.

SOUTHERN TAMANDUA ▶

Tamanduas may be active at night or during the day, and they can move equally well on the ground or in trees. Like all anteaters, their acute sense of smell helps them to find food. When they have located an anthill or termite mound, they smash the nest open with their powerful front claws.

FIND OUT MORE ▶▶ Grasslands 56–57 • Insectivores 252–253 • Mammals 240–241

AARDVARKS

The aardvark of Africa resembles an anteater, but it is more closely related to elephants and hyraxes. Its name means "earth pig" in the Afrikaans language of South Africa – a reference to its burrowing lifestyle and pig-like snout. The aardvark has fewer teeth than most mammals, with only 20 in total. It is nocturnal, and may roam widely during the night in search of ants and termites to eat. It licks the insects up using its thin, sticky tongue.

Ears stick up to listen for predators

Long snout has hairy nostrils, which stop soil entering it

▲ FAST DIGGER
Aardvarks have large, strong claws for tearing into termite mounds and anthills. They also excavate burrows up to 15 m (49 ft) long in which to raise their young, and dig smaller shelters for sleeping in. Among the fastest burrowers of all mammals, they seem to vanish in a cloud of flying dirt. Their old burrows are used by many other animals, from warthogs to owls.

FIND OUT MORE ▶▶ Adaptation **18–19** • Elephants **288** • Mammals **240–241**

ARMADILLOS

Armadillos possess flexible armour to protect them from predators such as foxes, cats, or birds of prey. There are 21 species of armadillo, which live in a variety of habitats in both North and South America. Their varied diet includes earthworms, ants, insect grubs, spiders, small reptiles, and fruit. Another group of mammals, the pangolins of Africa and Asia, look very similar and behave in much the same way.

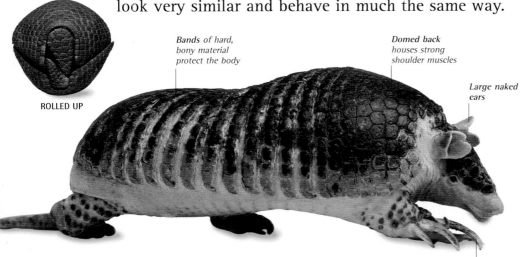

ROLLED UP

Bands of hard, bony material protect the body

Domed back houses strong shoulder muscles

Large naked ears

Strong, curved claws for digging

ARMOUR PLATING ▲
Armadillos, such as this northern naked-tailed armadillo, have protective armour on their backs and the tops of their heads. Each piece of armour, called a scute, is made of a bony plate covered with horny skin. The scutes are hinged so that an armadillo can roll itself into a tight ball that is almost impenetrable to its predators.

▲ TOUGH SCALES
Pangolins resemble armadillos, but evolved (developed) separately on different continents. This Indian pangolin, which is raiding a termite mound, is a typical member of its family. It is covered with overlapping scales, formed from modified hairs stuck together. Like armadillos, pangolins roll into a ball when threatened.

FIND OUT MORE ▶▶ Defence **42–43** • Mammals **240–241**

INSECTIVORES

Of all the mammals alive today, insectivores are perhaps the most similar to the earliest mammals on Earth. They are small and have an incredibly acute sense of smell, although their eyes and ears are usually tiny. Their body shapes vary according to their way of life. Most species are nocturnal and scurry about on the ground, although some burrow and a few swim. Insects form the major part of insectivores' diets, but they also consume a wide variety of plants and small animals.

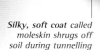

Silky, soft coat called moleskin shrugs off soil during tunnelling

▲ HYPERACTIVE HUNTER
Insectivores usually have fast heartbeats and body processes, which means they must eat a lot of food to get enough energy to survive. Shrews, such as this pygmy shrew, are amazingly active, and must feed every few hours. In addition to insects, most insectivores prey on other invertebrates, such as worms, spiders, and snails.

LIFE UNDERWATER ▶
Three insectivore groups spend much of their lives in fresh water: water shrews, such as this one; otter shrews; and desmans. A species of clean ponds and streams, the water shrew dives underwater to hunt for prey. It mostly eats shrimps and insect larvae, occasionally taking frogs or small fish. It swims by kicking hard with its back feet. Trapped air bubbles form silver streaks in its sleek fur.

▲ SPINY DEFENCE
An adult European hedgehog has about 5,000 spines all over its upper body. Each pale-tipped spike is 2–3 cm (¾–1¼ in) long. When attacked, a hedgehog curls into a tight ball, presenting its enemy with a prickly problem. Baby hedgehogs are born with smooth bodies, but spines soon grow through their stretchy skin. Hedgehogs hunt at night in woodland, and often visit gardens.

Main nesting chamber is lined with vegetation

Molehill is mound of earth above the tunnels

▲ SHIFTING SAND

Golden moles are adapted for life in Africa's hot, sandy deserts. They have soft, dense fur, tiny ears, and are completely sightless. Their chunky bodies are ideal for swimming through loose sand just beneath the surface. As they burrow, they search for termites and other insect prey, such as the locust this mole has captured.

◄ BURROWING MACHINE

The European mole has a range of impressive earth-moving equipment. Its massive hands and long, strong claws are connected to powerful shoulder muscles, so it is excellent at excavating tunnels. The mole digs in with its back feet for support, then uses its front legs to scoop soil to either side of its body.

▲ MOLE BURROW

Moles dig complex burrows that feature a central nest surrounded by a network of connecting tunnels and passages. They throw up mounds of waste soil on the surface, much to the annoyance of gardeners. Moles are very territorial and don't venture above ground unless they have to. They drag grass into the nesting chamber, where they give birth to their young.

Sensitive nose sniffs for prey

Shovel-like hands with huge claws

FIND OUT MORE ▶▶ Animal Homes 48–49 • Senses 30–31

TREE SHREWS

Tree shrews are small mammals with slender bodies and long, bushy tails. They are not true shrews, but share several features with primates, including large braincases. Their habits are similar to tree-dwelling squirrels. Many spend some of their time in trees, but often forage on the ground among the leaf litter. They eat insects, fruit, and seeds.

Thickly furred tail provides balance when climbing

▲ STREAKED TENREC

This extraordinary-looking creature is one of 27 species of tenrec found on the island of Madagascar, off Africa's east coast. Tenrecs look rather like hedgehogs, but have longer snouts and legs. They rub their sharp spines together noisily to communicate, and may bite if cornered. The streaked tenrec, which is active during the day, uses its sensitive snout and fine teeth to catch earthworms.

LESSER TREE SHREW ►

Tree shrews inhabit the tropical forests of southeast Asia and India. These skilful climbers use their superb senses of sight, hearing, and smell to find food. They build a nest among roots or in fallen tree trunks, and mark their territory with urine. Some species also have glands on their chests and stomachs that produce a smelly secretion. To announce their presence in an area, the tree shrews rub these glands onto branches.

FIND OUT MORE ▶▶ Primates 256 • Squirrels 303

Long finger bones support the wing membrane

Large ears pick up returning echoes from prey ahead

BATS

Some mammals can glide through the air, but bats are the only mammals capable of powered flight, using their flapping wings. They are nocturnal and live in many habitats, especially in warm regions. With nearly 1,050 species, bats are the second largest group of mammals after rodents. They are classed in two types: megabats and the smaller microbats. All microbats use echolocation – an extra sense that helps them to dodge obstacles and track down prey in total darkness.

Wing membrane is criss-crossed by tiny blood vessels and elastic fibres

▲ ELASTIC WINGS

A bat's wing is strong but extremely lightweight. Long finger bones provide the strength necessary to hold the wing steady during flight. They are connected by an elastic sheet of skin, or membrane, that forms the surface of the wing. The membrane is tough, despite being so thin that its blood vessels are often clearly visible – as with this long-eared bat. Bats also have a tail membrane, which is used to steer and scoop up prey.

ECHOLOCATION

Echolocation is a navigation system that dolphins and many bats use to build a 3D-image of the world around them. A flying bat produces a stream of high-pitched squeaks from its nose or mouth (shown as red bars on this diagram). These travel through the air and bounce off any objects in the way. The bat listens for the returning echoes to discover what is ahead.

STAGES OF ECHOLOCATION AS A BAT HUNTS AN INSECT

Bat calls more often as it moves nearer to its target

| Seeks prey | Approaches prey | Seizes prey |

FLYING FOX ▶

There are about 170 species of megabat, including the Malayan flying fox, the largest bat in the world. It has a wingspan of up to 1.8 m (6 ft) – wider than that of some eagles. Also known as fruit bats, these animals are named for their fox-like faces. They feed on fruit, flowers, and nectar, which they locate by sight and smell.

Wings fold away neatly when not in use

Small incisor teeth open wound in victim's skin

Large pointed ears used in echolocation

BLOOD-SUCKING BAT ▶

Vampire bats live in Central and South America and are widely feared, although they rarely attack humans. They can fly, but they also move around on the floor, using their forearms like walking sticks. Vampire bats feed on blood by nibbling a wound in the skin of an animal, such as a domestic pig or cow. Their saliva contains a substance that keeps the blood of their victims flowing freely.

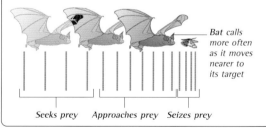

Strong forearm bears long thumb and sharp claw

▲ NIGHT FLIGHT
Bats are highly social animals and often gather in large numbers at suitable roosting (sleeping) places. Mexican free-tailed bats form colonies of up to 20 million individuals in caves in the southern United States and Mexico. At dusk, they swarm out of their roosts to hunt insects. Other bats roost in buildings, mine shafts, and holes in tree trunks.

FACIAL FEATURES

TENT-MAKING BAT
By day, the tent-making bat sleeps in a shelter made by nibbling a large leaf so that its sides curl around it. This species belongs to a group of American bats called leaf-nosed bats due to the flaps of skin, or leaves, on their noses. These direct the calls used in echolocation.

LESSER HORSESHOE BAT
The echolocation used by horseshoe bats is among the most advanced of all bats. Their calls are sent out in long pulses through their modified noses, which have a very broad nose leaf (flap) shaped like a horseshoe. Horseshoe bats live mainly in tropical Africa and Asia.

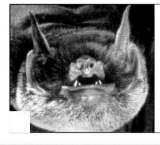

NAKED-BACKED BAT
This species lacks a nose leaf to assist with echolocation. Instead, it purses its lips as if to blow a kiss, to form a disc-shaped hole through which it calls. When the bat closes its wings to roost, they completely cover its furry back so that the bat appears to be naked.

HIBERNATING BAT ▶
This mouse-eared bat is hibernating to survive the winter, when there is little food available in cool, northern parts of the world. Hibernating bats slow down their body functions so that their body temperature is only a few degrees above the surrounding air. They feel cold to the touch and sometimes become covered in frozen dew droplets.

◀ HANGING AROUND
Wahlberg's epauletted bat lives in Africa. Like most fruit bats, it spends the day suspended from the branch of a tree, wrapped up in its wings. The tendons in a bat's ankle have a locking mechanism so that it requires no effort to hang upside down for hours. Hanging upside down means that bats are in the right position to take flight rapidly.

FIND OUT MORE ▸▸ Caves **67** • Animal Characteristics **10–11** • Dolphins **286–287** • Possums **246**

PRIMATES

Primates are intelligent, agile mammals that live mainly in trees in tropical forests. They have the largest brains in relation to their body size of all mammals. They are also among the most nimble, thanks to their grasping hands and feet and flexible limbs. Many species possess a long tail for balancing. Primates are divided into two main groups: lemurs, bushbabies, and lorises; and monkeys, apes, and humans.

Thumb is at a right angle to other fingers

▲ FINGERS AND THUMBS
A primate's thumb is described as opposable. It is very mobile, and together with the other fingers, it can be used to hold objects. Opposable thumbs give primates incredible skill at performing tasks with their hands.

Large forehead and braincase

◄ LIFE IN THE TREETOPS
Primates, including this Bolivian squirrel monkey, are extremely well adapted to life in the trees. They clamber quickly through foliage and spring from tree to tree, using their strong hands and feet to reach for a firm place to hold. Nearly all primates have flat toenails and fingernails.

Dexterous hands comb fur to remove ticks and lice

Long tail grasps branches and aids balance

MUTUAL GROOMING ►
Primates are highly sociable animals. Some species form large groups, while in others male and female couples establish close and lasting bonds. Regular sessions of mutual grooming, such as between these two vervet monkeys, strengthen the animals' relationships. Grooming also helps to keep their fur clean and free from irritating parasites such as fleas.

Monkey sits still to make grooming easier

▲ FACING FORWARD
Primates, such as this night monkey, have forward-facing eyes to give them what is known as binocular vision. The images from both eyes are combined by the brain, for precise depth judgment when jumping.

TYPES OF PRIMATE

APES
Apes are highly intelligent. They lack tails and some can move by swinging through trees using their arms. They are split into the lesser apes, or gibbons, and the great apes – orangutans, bonobos, chimps, gorillas, and humans.

MONKEYS
There are about 280 species of monkey. Most have tails and can run along branches. They are divided into two main groups, found in the New World (Central and South America) and the Old World (Africa and Asia).

BUSHBABIES
Bushbabies, or galagos, are small, nocturnal primates found in Africa. They are related to pottos (also from Africa) and to the lorises of Asia. They are less social than monkeys or apes, and never leave the trees.

LEMURS
Lemurs live only on Madagascar, in the Indian Ocean off the east coast of Africa. They are more closely related to bushbabies than to either apes or monkeys.

FIND OUT MORE ►► Chimpanzees 263 • Gibbons 260 • Gorillas 262 • New World Monkeys 259 • Old World Monkeys 258

BUSHBABIES

Bushbabies, also known as galagos, are named for the baby-like cries they make after dark. All 20 species are strictly nocturnal, with large, light-gathering eyes. These tree-dwelling primates feed on a variety of foods, such as fruit, flowers, insects, and birds' eggs. They regularly urinate on their hands and feet to maintain grip and to leave a smelly trail that marks their territories.

Dense, soft fur provides warmth in cool of night

One toe on the back foot has a grooming claw

Light body for superb agility

Powerful legs kick backwards to enable take off

Long, silky tail helps with balance

Nimble hands have rough palms, which help grip

Enormous eyes function well in low light levels

◄ NIGHT SENSES

Bushbabies have particularly large eyes that gather every last scrap of light to help them see in the dark. Some species also have acute hearing to detect the rustling noises made by insect prey. Insects are snatched from midair by hand, pulled apart, and passed to the mouth. Their keen sense of smell is used to identify the scent signals left by other bushbabies.

ACROBATIC LEAPER ►

This lesser bushbaby of South Africa is launching off a tree with a powerful thrust of its strong back legs. Even in almost total darkness, bushbabies are able to jump from branch to branch with ease. Pottos and lorises are related to bushbabies, but they are slower movers, preferring to climb rather than leap. They also have much shorter tails than bushbabies.

FIND OUT MORE ►► Senses 30–31

LEMURS

Lemurs are a unique group of mammals that live on the island of Madagascar. They vary in size from the pygmy mouse lemur, which weighs only 30 g (1 oz) and is the world's smallest primate, to larger species such as sifakas and the indri. Most lemurs are nocturnal, but a few are active by day. They have glands on their forearms, chests, or rumps, which release scents used to communicate with other lemurs.

Dark mask on otherwise white face

◄ DANCING SIFAKA

Lemurs have long legs for making spring-loaded leaps among trees, but are less well suited to moving on the ground. Ring-tailed lemurs scamper on all fours, whereas Verreaux's sifakas dance awkwardly in an upright position to cross open areas. Baby lemurs cling to their mothers' backs until they are old and strong enough to travel on their own.

Sifaka moves with energetic sideways hops

Ringed tail gives species its name

DOMINANT FEMALES ▲

Ring-tailed lemurs live in territories in bands of 5 to 25 animals. Unlike most mammals, the groups are dominated by adult females rather than males. Females of breeding age bear one or sometimes two young in each litter. These lemurs have a varied diet of flowers, fruit, leaves, bark, and tree sap.

FIND OUT MORE ►► Adaptation 18–19 • Herbivores 39 • Senses 30–31

OLD WORLD MONKEYS

There are 132 monkey species in the Old World (Africa and Asia). Some, such as colobus and leaf monkeys, eat mainly leaves. Others, including macaques, baboons, and mandrills, have a varied diet of fruit, seeds, and insects. Old World monkeys have narrower noses and more downward-pointing nostrils than New World monkeys.

Long, white fur flows down

◄ BLACK-AND-WHITE COLOBUS MONKEY
Colobus and related leaf monkeys are skilful climbers with strong, slender limbs and grasping fingers. This enables them to reach the outer edges of trees where fresh, new leaves grow. Bacteria in their stomachs help them to digest the tough plant material. Even so, their diet is so poor in nutrients that they must spend longer foraging than other monkeys.

BOLD ADVERTISEMENT ►
The mandrill is the largest Old World monkey and spends most of its time on the forest floor, only climbing trees to sleep at night. Males have dramatic red and blue ridges on their noses and long, curved canine teeth. These features present a fearsome display to deter rival males and predators such as leopards.

SEEING RED ►
Old World monkeys, such as this Guinea baboon, sit upright on their bottoms, which are protected by hardened skin pads. In females these pads swell and change colour, often becoming bright red. This signals their readiness to mate. Like humans and other apes, monkeys have full colour vision and are very sensitive to red objects.

Canine teeth protrude outside the mouth

Mature males have goatee beard and white whiskers

◄ STEAM BATH
The vast majority of monkeys live in the tropics, but one species of macaque is found in northern Japan. It copes with cold winters by taking dips in warm volcanic pools. The water is heated by hot rocks beneath the Earth's surface. Like most macaques and baboons, Japanese macaques live in large groups called troops. Troop members spend a lot of time grooming each other to remove blood-sucking parasites. This friendly social contact helps to reinforce the bonds between the monkeys, and to reduce tensions within the troop.

FIND OUT MORE ►► Animal Characteristics **10–11** • Gibbons **260** • Gorillas **262** • Primates **256**

NEW WORLD MONKEYS

The rainforests of Central and South America are home to 125 species of monkey. Known as New World monkeys, this group includes marmosets, tamarins, howlers, capuchins, sakis, and spider and squirrel monkeys. They have flatter faces and more forward-facing nostrils than Old World monkeys, and some species also possess muscular, grasping tails. They may live in compact family groups or in large groups of 100 or more animals.

NEW WORLD VARIETY

WOOLLY MONKEY
The common woolly monkey has a very thick, olive-grey coat and a dark head. It lives in the Amazon rainforest from Colombia south to Brazil. Like other New World monkeys, it marks trees with its scent as a way of communicating.

EMPEROR TAMARIN
Easily identified by its long white moustache, this small monkey feeds mainly on insects, such as stick insects and praying mantises. Like many of the tamarins and marmosets of the Brazilian rainforest, it is threatened by habitat destruction.

BROWN CAPUCHIN
In common with most New World monkeys, brown capuchins are polygamous. This means that they live in groups dominated by one adult male that mates with all the females. He is older and stronger than the other males, which do not breed.

Body is lithe and athletic for graceful movement

Limbs are long and muscular

Prehensile (grasping) tail

Hairless face with big eyes providing superb vision

Nostrils are widely spaced and point forwards

◄ **AGILE CLIMBER**
Howler monkeys and capuchins, such as this weeper capuchin, have specially adapted tails that are prehensile (grasping). These act as an extra limb by curling around branches and holding on to help support the monkey's weight. All New World monkeys are tree dwellers. They are highly active, acrobatic animals that move quickly through the trees, usually in the highest levels of the forest.

Shaggy, red-gold fur

Mouth is wide open in a loud, whooping howl

◄ **HOWLING MONKEY**
At dawn and dusk red howler monkeys make very loud calls that can be heard several kilometres away. This is how a troop (group) defends the trees it feeds from against neighbouring troops, without getting involved in fights. The weird, whooping sounds are amplified (made louder) by the monkeys' baggy throats, where the noise vibrates.

Ear tufts of long, white fur

◄ **MINIATURE MONKEY**
Marmosets and tamarins, such as this common marmoset, are small monkeys – most are under 30 cm (12 in) in length, including their tails. They have bare pink or black faces, and many have tufts or manes of hair. Marmosets and tamarins rush about the trees to find food such as fruit, tree sap, flowers, or insects. This marmoset is holding a grub.

FIND OUT MORE ►► Primates 256 • Rainforests 60–61

Hangs with one arm and swings forwards

Free hand is ready to grab the next branch

Long arms enable greater reach and quick swinging

Grasping feet reach for branch as gibbon comes to a halt

ARM OVER ARM ▲

This action sequence shows a siamang gibbon travelling in the forest. When moving slowly, as this one is, gibbons grasp the next nearest branch before letting go of the previous one. But when moving quickly, they hurtle through the treetops and perform spectacular leaps between branches. This style of movement is called brachiation. The siamang lives in Malaysia and Sumatra. It is the largest gibbon, reaching 90 cm (3 ft) long, and it has an inflatable throat sac to make its calls louder.

GIBBONS

Fourteen species of gibbon inhabit the tropical forests of southeast Asia. These small, slender apes travel through the forest canopy by swinging on their long, strong arms. Male and female gibbons mate for life and pairs sing together daily, usually at dawn. Their strange wails and whoops echo around the treetops. The singing strengthens each pair's bond, and announces their territory to neighbouring groups of gibbons. In some species of gibbon, the sexes are different colours.

Muscular arm supports entire body weight

Forward-facing eyes for judging distance

Dense coat of pale, cream-coloured fur

GIBBON SKELETON

A gibbon's skeleton is adapted for athleticism and speed of movement in the trees. It is lighter than that of other apes such as a chimpanzee or orangutan, with very long arm, leg, finger, and toe bones. Its spine is long and flexible for maximum manoeuvrability. The shoulder and wrist joints are highly mobile, enabling the gibbon to hang from a branch and twist right round without releasing its grip. Like other apes, it has no tail.

Long foot bones hook onto branches

◄ FRUITS OF THE FOREST

Gibbons, such as this Mueller's gibbon, primarily eat ripe fruit. They also feed on young leaves and shoots, as well as insects. During the day, a family group moves throughout its territory to visit trees bearing ripe fruit. When not feeding, the group rests and the animals groom each other.

FIND OUT MORE ►► Anatomy 26–27 • Chimpanzees 263 • Gorillas 262 • Movement 28–29 • Primates 256

ORANGUTANS

These great apes have shaggy, orange-red fur and live in dense rainforests in southeast Asia. One species is found on the island of Borneo, and another occurs on the island of Sumatra. They climb well and move by swinging from branches. Males descend to the forest floor more often than females, which spend nearly all their time in the trees. Orangutans eat mainly fruit and leaves, but catch some small prey such as lizards, and crush and grind their food with their strong teeth.

◄ RED APE

Orangutans, such as this youngster from Borneo, swing with ease from branches and trailing vines. They are heavier than gibbons and so move more slowly, but can travel rapidly if necessary. Apart from mothers with babies, orangutans lead solitary lives and spread out across the forest. Even if feeding in the same tree, they usually ignore each other. As dusk falls, they bend branches together to make a nest to sleep in.

High, domed forehead and bare face

Feet grip branches

Baby has paler, bright orange fur

▲ SLOW BREEDER

Baby orangutans depend on their mothers until they are about ten years old – much longer than chimps or monkeys, for example. A female may have only three or four young in her lifetime. Such a slow rate of reproduction means that orangutan populations take a long time to grow. Logging and poaching are causing a very rapid decline in their numbers, from which they may not recover. Both species of orangutan are now endangered.

Wide cheek flap on each side of head

Long limbs are ideal for swinging

MATURE MALE ►

Orangutan means "man of the forest" in Malay, the language of Malaysia. Male orangutans, such as this Sumatran male, develop broad, flat faces with prominent cheek flaps. They are twice the size of females, with stocky bodies and huge limbs.

FIND OUT MORE ►► Chimpanzees **263** • Conservation **22–23** • Gorillas **262** • Primates **256**

GORILLAS

There are two species of gorilla – eastern and western. These great apes live in dense tropical forests in parts of central and west Africa. They are the world's largest primates, but despite their immense strength, gorillas are peaceful herbivores that feed on leaves, shoots, and fruit. All gorillas are seriously endangered. They are declining rapidly due to habitat loss and illegal poaching.

▲ RESTING TOGETHER
These gorillas belong to the eastern gorilla's rare mountain population, found on forested volcanoes in Rwanda and Uganda. Gorillas live in family groups of 5 to 40 animals. Each group has one, or possibly two, dominant adult males, several adult females, and their offspring. The gorillas rest and doze together in the middle of the day between feeding sessions.

Skull houses large, complex brain

Infants ride piggyback on their mothers

Knuckles in contact with the ground

▲ KNUCKLE WALKING
This female eastern lowland gorilla is knuckle walking – the main method by which gorillas move on the ground. Gorillas walk on all fours with their hands folded into fists so that their knuckles rest on the floor. They can stand upright on their back legs, but this posture requires effort and is rarely used, except as a threat display. Gorillas are mainly ground-living, although they sometimes climb trees in search of fruit.

High forehead due to ridge of bone

Silver fur on the back and rump

Face has strong jaws and broad, flattened nose

◀ SILVERBACK
Mature male gorillas are called silverbacks because their fur turns grey with age. They reach 1.9 m (6¼ ft) in height and weigh up to 200 kg (430 lb) – twice the size of females. Massively built compared to most other primates, they have huge shoulders and arms. Muscles to work their jaws are attached to a bony crest on top of the skull.

FIND OUT MORE ▶▶ Gibbons 260 • Herbivores 39 • Mammals 240–241 • Orangutans 261 • Primates 256 • Reproduction 44–45

CHIMPANZEES

Chimpanzees are the closest relatives of human beings, sharing 98–99 per cent of our genes. There are two species, which look similar. The common chimpanzee lives in forest and savanna across west and central Africa. The rarer, less-well-known bonobo occurs only in rainforest in the Democratic Republic of Congo. Both species sleep and eat in trees, but are also at home on the ground, walking on their knuckles.

CHIMP COMMUNICATION

With more than 30 different calls and a variety of facial expressions and hand gestures, chimps are highly expressive animals. Like humans, they smile when they are relaxed and happy. They bare their teeth when they are frightened, and pucker their lips into a pout when afraid. Some captive chimps have been taught how to communicate with humans and other chimps using sign language.

Flexible lips can create lots of different expressions

USING TOOLS ▼

This party of chimps are fishing for termites. They poke a thin stick or grass stem into the termite mound, then pull it out and lick off the insects clinging to the tool. Chimps also use stones to crack nuts open and use leafy stems to swat flies. It takes several years and lots of practice for youngsters to learn how to use these tools, and some may never get the knack.

◀ PLAYFUL CHIMP
Chimpanzees are exceptionally playful and social animals. Youngsters in particular spend much time rushing and tumbling through the undergrowth. As they chase each other, wrestle, and swing from branches, they rehearse essential survival skills. Chimps are also highly intelligent. They are capable of performing many tricks and tasks if trained.

BONOBO FAMILY ▲
Bonobos, also known as pygmy chimpanzees, are slimmer and lighter in build than common chimpanzees. They have black faces, whereas those of common chimps may be pink, black, or brown. Females are dominant in bonobo society, and young are dependent on their mothers for five years.

Termite mound is home to millions of termites

Adult chimp uses a long stick to fish for termites

Young chimpanzees learn by watching and copying adults

FIND OUT MORE ▶▶ Gibbons 260 • Mammals 240–241 • Orangutans 261 • Primates 256 • Termites 115

◄ AT THE KILL
Meat-eating animals, such as these cheetahs, must either catch and kill living animals or scavenge from the carcasses of dead ones. Different carnivorous mammals usually take different types of prey. Cheetahs are the ultimate speed hunters, so they often target swift antelopes. Having suffocated a victim by biting its throat, they swallow its meat in large chunks.

CARNIVOROUS MAMMALS

Carnivores eat meat or other parts of animals, such as the skin and bones, although they may feed on plant matter as well. About 250 species of mammal are carnivorous, and they occur worldwide. They vary widely in appearance, ranging in size from 30-cm- (12-in-) long weasels to massive bears. Other carnivorous mammals include cats, dogs, hyenas, otters, badgers, raccoons, skunks, weasels, and mongooses.

Coat has shaggy mane, and stripes for camouflage

JAWS AND TEETH

Carnivorous mammals have long canine teeth in the front of the jaw and shearing carnassial teeth at the back. The muscle in the upper part of the skull gives a vice-like bite for holding and killing prey. The muscle at the side of the jaw gives power for cutting flesh.

Canine teeth pierce and grip the prey

Carnassial teeth slice flesh while eating

Strong jaw muscles

Slim, narrow body is ideal for chasing prey down tunnels

Powerful jaws chew meat and crunch up bones

Long legs for speed and agility when chasing prey

OPPORTUNISTIC FEEDER ▲
The South American grison belongs to the same group of mammals as weasels, badgers, and otters. These animals are known as mustelids. They usually have long bodies and tails, and short legs. Mustelids are opportunists – they eat whatever prey comes their way. This might include rodents, snakes, lizards, frogs, birds, and eggs.

Pointed head and elongated, flexible neck

◄ NATURAL ATHLETE
Most carnivorous mammals have a superb sense of smell to sniff out prey. In addition, many are highly athletic, with muscular bodies, which is vital for catching prey. In fast-running species, such as this striped hyena, the foot bones have become lifted to form part of the leg so that the animal walks and runs on the tips of its toes.

FIND OUT MORE ▶▶ Badgers 279 • Bears 274–275 • Big Cats 268 • Carnivores 38 • Dogs 272 • Otters 278 • Weasels 277

SMALL CATS

In all, there are 39 members of the cat family. About 30 of these are considered to be small cats, based not only on their size, but also on the fact that they cannot roar, unlike big cats. Small cats are agile, solitary hunters. They live in many different habitats, including jungles, grasslands, and wetlands. Domestic cats are probably descended from African wild cats, which were kept and worshipped in Ancient Egypt.

SMALL CAT SPECIES

LEOPARD CAT
In common with its much larger namesake, the leopard cat of southeast Asia has a mottled golden and black coat. This provides perfect camouflage in shady forests and thick vegetation. It is an excellent climber.

CANADA LYNX
The Canada lynx is 1.1 m (3½ ft) long, with a short tail and tufted ears. It lives in forests and tundra in Alaska, Canada, and the northern USA. Snowshoe hares are its favourite prey, but it also kills deer and rodents.

SAND CAT
The sand cat of North Africa and the Middle East is one of the world's smallest cats, at just 50 cm (20 in) long. Its pale fur blends in well with its desert home. Hair on the soles of its feet protects it when it walks on hot sand.

OCELOT
Found in forests in Central and South America, the ocelot is an excellent climber and swimmer. The territories of males and females may overlap. Large numbers of ocelots have been killed for their beautiful, spotted fur.

PUMA
Also called the mountain lion or cougar, the puma is the largest of the small cats. It occurs through the Rocky and Andes mountains, from Canada to the southern tip of South America. A few also live in swamps in Florida.

▲ **NIGHT VISION**
Cats often hunt in the dark, so need excellent night vision. A cat's eye has an extra layer behind the retina. This reflects all the light entering the eye so that the retina can produce a much brighter image. It is this layer that glows when a torch or car headlight shines directly into a cat's eyes.

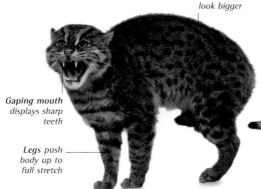

Arched back makes cat look bigger

Gaping mouth displays sharp teeth

Legs push body up to full stretch

▲ **THREAT DISPLAY**
This fishing cat, which lives in swamps in southern Asia, is performing a threat display. If small cats are startled or threatened, they hiss loudly. They arch their backs and make their hair stand on end to make them appear bigger.

Short tail gives bobcat its name

Shoulders are low, as the cat prepares to pounce

Ears locate and then track prey

Forward-facing eyes can judge distances accurately

◄ **STALKING PREY**
Small cats rely on stealth to creep up on their prey, as they lack brute force. This bobcat demonstrates a cat's stalking behaviour. Adopting a very low posture, it is carefully edging towards its victim undetected. When close enough it will suddenly pounce to deliver a lethal bite to the neck of its prey.

FIND OUT MORE ►► Animal Kingdom **12–13** • Big Cats **268** • Conservation **22–23** • Deserts **58–59** • Senses **30–31**

CHEETAH

Famed as the world's fastest land animal, the cheetah may accelerate to over 100 kph (62 mph) when chasing its prey. Such sprints last for only 10–20 seconds, after which the cat tires and must give up the chase. About half of all pursuits end in failure, and to succeed the cheetah has to stalk its target closely before rushing from cover. The cheetah trips its victim up, then delivers a lethal bite to the neck.

Scientific name: *Acinonyx jubatus*

Order: Carnivora (carnivores)

Class: Mammalia (mammals)

Distribution: Savanna, bush, and dry forest in Africa south of the Sahara desert; almost extinct in India

Status: Vulnerable

Length: 1.1–1.5 m (3½–5 ft)

Weight: 21–72 kg (46–160 lb)

Food: Mainly medium-sized grazing animals, such as Thomson's gazelles, impala, and wildebeest calves

Reproduction: Males are sexually mature at 3 years, and females at 2 years. Breeding occurs all year, but especially in the rainy season

Number of young: Up to 6 cubs in each litter; usually 3 or 4

FIND OUT MORE ▸▸ Carnivorous Mammals **264–265** • Big Cats **268**

BIG CATS

The best known big cats are the lion, tiger, cheetah, jaguar, leopard, and snow leopard. Despite their smaller size, the clouded leopard and marbled cat are often also considered to be big cats because they share several features with the other six. The big cats are powerful predators, and each species has specialized hunting skills that suit its habitat and main prey. Most big cats have declined in numbers due to hunting for their beautiful coats.

▲ TREE CLIMBER
Leopards are the only big cats to climb trees regularly. They rest on branches during the day and hunt on the ground at night. Occasionally they drag a kill into a tree to prevent it being stolen by lions or hyenas. Leopards are found throughout most of Africa south of the Sahara desert, and across southern Asia.

Dark spot in centre of each rosette

Strong shoulders for pouncing and leaping

Long tail with black bands

Whiskers help cat to feel its way at night

◄ SPOTTED COAT
Fur patterns break up the outline of big cats, making it hard for prey to see them. Each species has a distinctive coat. This jaguar, for example, has black rosettes on a sand background – ideal for blending in with the light and shade of forests and swamps. There is a spot in the centre of each rosette, which the leopard lacks.

Fur is whitish with pale grey rosettes

LEOPARD'S COAT

Black coloration caused by the pigment melanin in the fur

◄ SNOW CAT
The snow leopard lives in the high mountains of Central Asia. It has long, thick fur to keep it warm and a pale coat for camouflage against rocks and snow when stalking prey such as blue sheep. Like leopards and jaguars, snow leopards are solitary, secretive cats. They are seldom encountered by humans.

Tail held out for balance

Bushy tail may be wrapped around body for warmth

Paw outstretched ready to spring forwards

◄ COLOUR VARIATION
A few leopards have completely black coats rather than the usual pattern of spots and rosettes. This is known as melanism and it is determined by the cats' genes, in much the same way that eye colour is determined in humans. Melanistic leopards, or black panthers, are most numerous in Malaysia. Jaguars also show melanism.

FIND OUT MORE ▶▶ Earthquakes 43 • Rocks and minerals 46–47

LIONS

Lions are the most social big cats and live in groups called prides. They are at the top of the food chain and have become a famous symbol of the African savanna. One subspecies of lion, the Asiatic lion, is found in the Gir Forest of northwest India. It is endangered, with around 300 left in the wild. The African lion is more numerous, but it is also at risk from habitat loss.

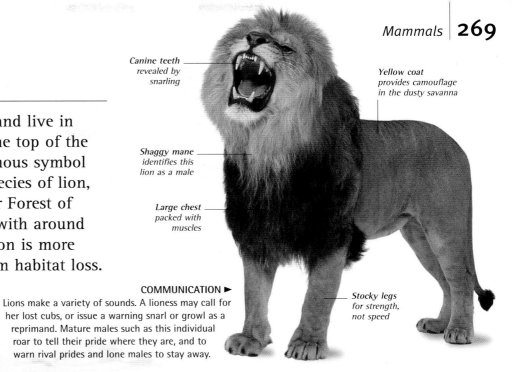

Canine teeth revealed by snarling

Yellow coat provides camouflage in the dusty savanna

Shaggy mane identifies this lion as a male

Large chest packed with muscles

Stocky legs for strength, not speed

COMMUNICATION ▶
Lions make a variety of sounds. A lioness may call for her lost cubs, or issue a warning snarl or growl as a reprimand. Mature males such as this individual roar to tell their pride where they are, and to warn rival prides and lone males to stay away.

TEAM PLAYERS ▶
Each pride has 2 or 3 adult males and up to 10 lionesses, plus their offspring. Lionesses do most of the hunting for a pride, either on their own or cooperatively (working together). Through strength in numbers they can bring down animals much larger than themselves, such as wildebeest (as here), giraffe, or buffalo. Even so, they may suffer serious injuries from the flailing hooves and horns of their prey. Following a successful hunt, the whole pride joins in the feast.

◀ SIZE DIFFERENCE
Male lions grow up to 2.5 m (8¼ ft) long and stand over 1 m (3⅓ ft) tall. Females are smaller and lighter and do not have a mane. They groom the males – and the dominant females – as a display of submission and loyalty. Although the top male rarely hunts, he will fight bachelor males to protect the pride.

PREHISTORIC CAT
Eusmilus was a sabre-toothed cat similar in size to modern-day leopards. It lived 40 million years ago and is known from fossils in North America and southern France. The ferocious curved teeth were probably used to slash open the belly of prey rather than kill it. Sabre-toothed cats may have waited for animals to pass their hiding places before ambushing them.

FIND OUT MORE ▶▶ Earthquakes 43 • Rocks and minerals 46–47

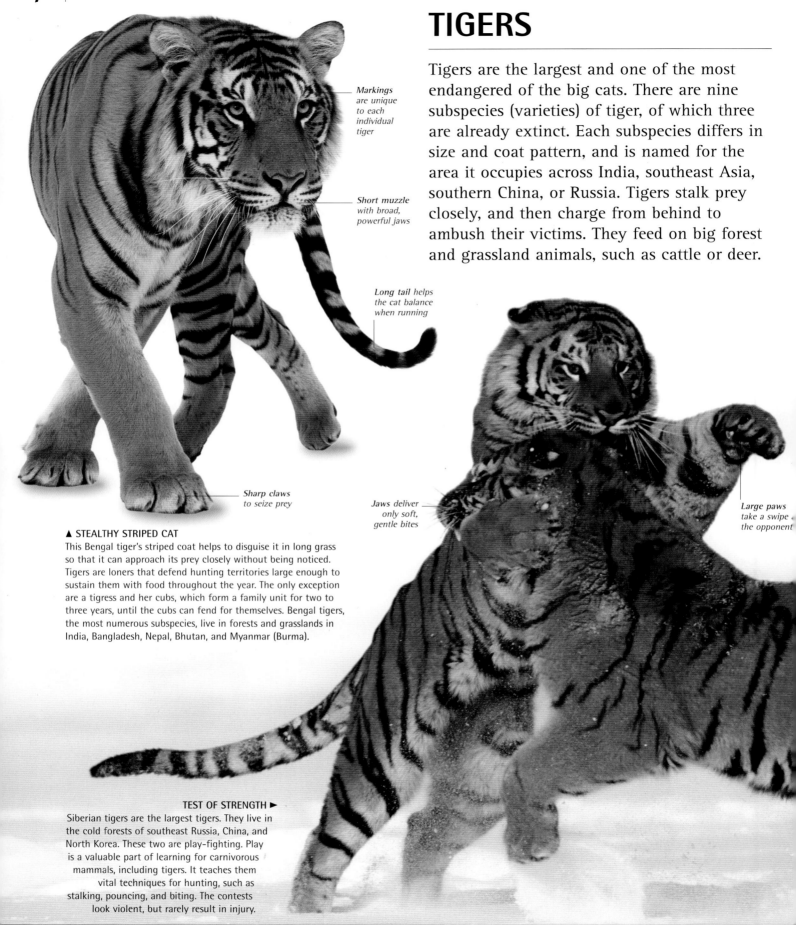

TIGERS

Tigers are the largest and one of the most endangered of the big cats. There are nine subspecies (varieties) of tiger, of which three are already extinct. Each subspecies differs in size and coat pattern, and is named for the area it occupies across India, southeast Asia, southern China, or Russia. Tigers stalk prey closely, and then charge from behind to ambush their victims. They feed on big forest and grassland animals, such as cattle or deer.

Markings are unique to each individual tiger

Short muzzle with broad, powerful jaws

Long tail helps the cat balance when running

Sharp claws to seize prey

Jaws deliver only soft, gentle bites

Large paws take a swipe the opponent

▲ STEALTHY STRIPED CAT
This Bengal tiger's striped coat helps to disguise it in long grass so that it can approach its prey closely without being noticed. Tigers are loners that defend hunting territories large enough to sustain them with food throughout the year. The only exception are a tigress and her cubs, which form a family unit for two to three years, until the cubs can fend for themselves. Bengal tigers, the most numerous subspecies, live in forests and grasslands in India, Bangladesh, Nepal, Bhutan, and Myanmar (Burma).

TEST OF STRENGTH ▶
Siberian tigers are the largest tigers. They live in the cold forests of southeast Russia, China, and North Korea. These two are play-fighting. Play is a valuable part of learning for carnivorous mammals, including tigers. It teaches them vital techniques for hunting, such as stalking, pouncing, and biting. The contests look violent, but rarely result in injury.

FIND OUT MORE ▶▶ Big Cats **268** • Carnivorous Mammals **264** • Conservation **22–23** • Mammals **240–241** • Small Cats **265**

▲ TIGERS UNDER THREAT
There may be as few as 5,000 tigers left in the wild. Some subspecies number only 500 individuals. Even though most tigers now live in protected areas, they are at risk from illegal poaching. Breeding programmes using captive animals, such as this Sumatran tiger, may help to save them from extinction.

YOUNG CUB ▶
Female tigers usually give birth to two or three cubs in each litter. Cubs feed on their mother's milk for the first two months of life, then start to eat meat. Half of all tiger cubs die during their first year. They are vulnerable to attack by other tigers, or they may be orphaned by forest fires and poachers.

MONGOOSES

Mongooses are small, slender carnivores that live throughout much of Africa and southern Asia. They are quick predators, catching insects, scorpions, and small vertebrates. Many of the 38 species are solitary, but some live in large groups called packs. Social species are often active during the day, whereas solitary mongooses are generally nocturnal and larger in size.

Dark bands of fur across the back

Bushy tail

Claws cannot be retracted

Snout is long and pointed

ALERT HUNTER ▲
Lively and inquisitive, the banded mongoose lives in packs of 15–20 animals. Given the opportunity, these mongooses will eat just about anything, including insects, mice, birds' eggs, fruit, and snakes. Like all mongooses, they have scent glands near their tails, which produce a pungent odour to mark territory.

▲ YELLOW MONGOOSE
Mongooses hide and breed in dens called warrens. They may dig these themselves or use a rocky crevice, a termite mound, or the abandoned burrow of another mammal. Yellow mongooses live as a family group consisting of a breeding pair, their young, and several non-breeding adults.

STANDING GUARD ▶
Meerkats (also called suricates) are mongooses that live in large packs on grasslands and in semi-deserts. A communal way of life is useful because at least one meerkat will always be on the lookout while a group is feeding. Sentries bark alarm calls if they see a predator such as an eagle, and all the meerkats dive for cover.

Meerkat stands up on back legs for a better view

Watchful eyes scan horizon and sky for danger

FIND OUT MORE ▶▶ Carnivores 38 • Carnivorous Mammals 264

DOGS

Most people associate the word dog with boisterous, friendly pets or working animals, such as police dogs. However, there are 35 wild species of dog, which are collectively known as canids. This group includes jackals, foxes, wolves, and the dingo. Dogs are long-legged, fast-moving carnivores with acute senses of smell and hearing. They are highly social mammals, often living and hunting together in packs.

Big ears are shaped like funnels to gather sound

Wet nose is excellent for scent detection

Sandy coat provides camouflage in the outback

Powerful paws with fixed claws that cannot retract

WILD AUSTRALIAN DOG ►
All dogs, including this dingo, have long muzzles and sensitive noses. Smell is very important in dog society. Dogs use smell to communicate with one another, for example by urinating to mark their territories. The dingo is the largest carnivorous mammal in Australia. It usually feeds on small mammals, such as rabbits, but also attacks sheep.

DOMESTIC DOGS

Domestic dogs originated about 10,000 years ago through selective breeding from grey wolves. Today, there are as many as 450 different breeds of domestic dog in a multitude of shapes, hair lengths, colours, and sizes. People have bred dogs for different tasks. The dachshund, for example, is ideal for chasing rabbits and badgers down tunnels. Others, such as the whippet, are built for speed. The bergamasco is used to guard sheep.

DACHSHUND

WHIPPET

BERGAMASCO

▲ PLAYING JACKALS
Black-backed jackals live in eastern and southern Africa. They hunt small animals, such as rodents, and also feed on carrion. Like many wild dogs, male and female jackals mate for life. The pair may be accompanied by their previous year's young, which help to raise the next litter of pups. Families of jackals play frequently. Play serves to teach young dogs how to hunt, and also to strengthen bonds between related animals.

◄ HOWLING COYOTE
This coyote of North America has its head thrown back in a howl. Howling is a form of long-range communication to keep pack members in touch and warn other packs to stay away. Individual coyotes and wolves can be told apart by differences in their calls. Dogs also bark, growl, and whine.

FIND OUT MORE ▶▶ Carnivorous Mammals **264** • Evolution **16–17** • Placental Mammals **247**

FOXES

Foxes are solitary hunters that specialize in catching small prey, including rodents, insects, and worms. There are 23 different species, all of which have slender bodies and long, bushy tails. Active mainly at dawn and dusk, foxes usually spend the day in a den, which is often among rocks or roots, but may be another animal's old burrow. Foxes live in a huge range of habitats, including deserts, grasslands, and forests. The Arctic fox inhabits tundra.

Mobile ears can swivel to focus on prey

Whiskers are sensitive to air movements

◄ TREE-CLIMBING FOX
The grey fox lives in woodland, where it often climbs trees to escape danger or to hunt prey, such as roosting birds. For this reason, it is nicknamed the tree fox. It also eats fruit and seeds. Unlike other foxes, its typical den is well above the ground in a tree-hole or the roof space of a building. The grey fox occurs in Central America and the south and west of the United States.

RED FOX ►
Foxes are agile predators, often leaping to pounce on small prey. They are also very adaptable. Many red foxes have moved into urban areas where they eat scraps and scavenge among rubbish. In fact, the red fox has the widest range of any land mammal. It occurs right across North America, Europe, and Asia, and it has been introduced to Australia.

FIND OUT MORE ►► Carnivorous Mammals 264 • Polar Regions 70 • Scavengers 41 • Senses 30–31

WOLVES

Wolves are the largest and most sociable members of the dog family. There are four species – the grey wolf, the Ethiopian wolf, the maned wolf of South America, and the endangered red wolf, which survives only in North Carolina, USA. In many parts of their range, grey wolves have been persecuted for killing livestock. As a result, they now mainly exist in wilderness areas such as tundra and coniferous forests.

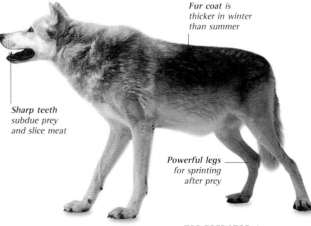

Fur coat is thicker in winter than summer

Sharp teeth subdue prey and slice meat

Powerful legs for sprinting after prey

TOP PREDATOR ▲
When fully grown, the grey wolf stands 1 m (3⅓ ft) high and weighs up to 60 kg (130 lb). However, it can vary in size and also in coat colour, depending on its habitat. For example, in North America tundra wolves are heavier and have whiter fur than the timber wolves found in forests further south.

◄ SHARING FOOD
A pack of grey wolves commonly contains 8–12 animals, and defends a territory covering a very wide area. Each pack is led by a dominant breeding pair, known as the alpha male and female. Members of the pack hunt as a team, which enables them to bring down and kill large animals such as as moose, reindeer (caribou), and bison.

FIND OUT MORE ►► Carnivorous Mammals 264 • Coniferous Forests 65 • Evolution 16–17 • Polar Regions 70

◄ **POWERFUL CARNIVORE**
The grizzly is a variety of brown bear from North America. Every autumn, large numbers of these mammals gather near the mouths of rivers as shoals of salmon return from the sea to spawn. Grizzlies are formidable predators with massive teeth and claws that can reach 15 cm (6 in) long. They are omnivores and will eat both vegetation and animals, including fish, rodents, young bison, and deer.

Long, dark-brown fur keeps the body warm

Muscular legs allow bears to roam long distances

BEARS

Bears are the largest land carnivores. A fully grown polar bear can weigh up to a tonne and stand 3.4 m (11 ft 2 in) tall when it rears up on its hind legs. Bears are powerful predators but they are also adaptable. Most bears eat a wide range of foods, depending on what is available in their habitat. Bears are usually solitary creatures. Apart from mothers with young, they are rarely seen in groups. There are eight species of bear, including the giant panda, and they are found on every continent apart from Australia and Antarctica.

TYPES OF BEAR

SYRIAN BROWN BEAR
This is one of six varieties of brown bear. It lives in the forested hills and mountains of western and central Asia. It has relatively short fur and little body fat, as it is active for most of the year.

AMERICAN BLACK BEAR
By far the most common species of bear, the American black bear has adapted well to human settlement in its habitat and sometimes raids dustbins for food. Although called black bears, some are brown or cinnamon.

SLOTH BEAR
Sloth bears live in India and Sri Lanka. They feed mainly on invertebrates. They use their long, curved claws to rip open termite mounds, then suck up the termites by forming a tube with their lips and tongue.

SPECTACLED BEAR
The spectacled bear is the only bear from South America. It is an extremely good climber and finds much of its food in the trees, clambering out onto branches to reach fruit and bromeliad plants.

SUN BEAR
This is the smallest species of bear, rarely growing to more than 1.2 m (4 ft) long. It inhabits the dense forests of southeast Asia. The sun bear is an excellent climber. It feeds on fruit, insects, small birds, and rodents.

Sensitive ears can hear prey from far off

Sharp teeth to grip prey and tear off chunks of flesh

▲ SPRING WAKE UP
Most bears that live in cool climates spend the winter asleep in dens. Female polar bears dig dens in the snow, where they give birth to their cubs. By the time they emerge in spring, the cubs are already three or four months old. Polar bear cubs stay with their mother for just over two years.

Teeth are displayed to warn opponent

▲ BROWN BEAR
The brown bear is the most widespread of all bears, occurring right across the northern hemisphere, from northwest America to the far east of Russia. During the autumn, these bears feed extensively to build up thick reserves of body fat. In the winter, brown bears retire to dens that they have dug into the ground. They emerge lean and hungry in spring, and look for mates in early summer. Brown bears are now rare across much of their geographical range, particularly in Europe. The largest type, the Kodiak bear, lives in Alaska. Adult males can weigh over three-quarters of a tonne.

Long claws help brown bears dig for roots and tubers

FIERCE CREATURES ▶
Although they try to avoid conflict, bears can be aggressive. Adult males sometimes kill each other during fights over females. Young, male bears, such as these Asian black bears, often play-fight to establish which of them is the strongest. This species has a white crescent of fur on its chest and inhabits forests from Iran, through the Himalayan mountains, and as far east as Japan.

Paws can slash an opponent or prey

White crescent of fur on chest

Standing tall an Asian black bear can exceed 2 m (6½ ft)

FIND OUT MORE ▶▶ Pandas 276 • Parenting 46–47 • Polar Regions 70

Eyes are surrounded by distinctive black, oval-shaped markings

Front teeth are sharp, but the back teeth are flatter for chewing

Thick fur keeps the animal warm in winter

PANDAS

Pandas are unusual carnivores – they hardy ever eat meat. The giant panda feeds almost entirely on bamboo, and the red panda eats a variety of plant matter, including roots, shoots, fruit, and acorns. The rare giant panda is a species of bear and can weigh up to 125 kg (280 lb). The red, or lesser, panda is a much smaller animal, weighing up to 6 kg (13 lb). It is most closely related to raccoons, and is endangered.

▲ GIANT PANDAS

The giant panda lives in the thickly forested hills of southern China. Although it is a large mammal, it is so rare that it was not known to scientists until 1869. When they are not munching on bamboo, giant pandas sleep for much of the time to conserve energy. In the wild they are solitary. Females give birth to one or two cubs that are only 15 cm (6 in) long.

RED PANDA ▶

The red panda lives in the foothills of the Himalayas. It has sharp claws and a rusty coloured coat, with white markings on its face and tail. It is an excellent climber, and spends much of its time high up in the trees. Like the giant panda, the red panda usually lives alone and marks its territory with scent, which it releases from glands under its tail.

Wrist bone is modified for grasping

▲ PANDA PAW

Unlike other bears, giant pandas can grip their food. Their paws have a bony projection covered with a pad of hairless skin, which acts like a thumb. This is helps the panda to hold food and break off bamboo stems. Giant pandas eat huge amounts of bamboo, which is low in nutrients and hard to digest. They occasionally eat other things, including bulbs, grass, rodents, and insects.

Long bushy tail helps with balance when climbing

FIND OUT MORE ▶▶ Bears 274–275 • Carnivores 38 • Conservation 22–23 • Herbivores 39

RACCOONS

Raccoons are small, active mammals with short legs and long tails. They live in North and South America, and feed on a wide range of foods. They are good climbers, but find much of their food on the ground, grasping it with their paws. Other members of the raccoon family include the kinkajou, cacomistle, ringtail, and coati. Most wspecies are solitary, nocturnal hunters.

Fur is thicker than in other raccoon species

Tail has rings of dark fur

Sharp claws give grip and help with climbing

Sensitive nose sniffs out food

▲ FOREST ACROBAT
The kinkajou forages high in the rainforest trees of Central and South America. It has a prehensile (grasping) tail, which it uses to cling onto branches, and it feeds almost entirely on fruit. The kinkajou has a rounder face than most other members of the raccoon family. It also has an unusually long tongue, which it uses to lap up nectar from flowers.

◄ SEARCHING FOR FOOD
Coatis are omnivores and eat fruit, eggs, insects, frogs, lizards, and rodents. They live in the forests of Central and South America. Male coatis spend most of their time on their own, but females live in small bands with their young.

MASKED BANDIT ▲
The common raccoon lives in North America. It has a stocky body, striped tail, and distinctive bandit-mask face markings. Common raccoons will eat almost any animal they can catch, and often supplement their diet with leftovers from rubbish bins.

FIND OUT MORE ▶▶ Omnivores 40 • Scavengers 41

WEASELS

Weasels and their relatives have long, flexible bodies and short legs. They live in a wide range of habitats, and are native to all continents except Australia and Antarctica. Weasels, stoats, and polecats find most of their prey on the ground, but martens are adapted for hunting in the trees. They are active hunters and can kill animals larger than themselves.

▲ PINE MARTEN
This agile animal lives in Europe and western Asia. It hunts squirrels, which it chases through the branches at speed, often making acrobatic jumps to catch its prey. The pine marten is one of eight marten species. The North American fisher is the biggest species, and catches larger prey, including porcupines.

LEAST WEASEL ►
This least weasel is the smallest carnivorous mammal, growing up to 30 cm (12 in) long. It lives in North America and usually hunts rodents, sometimes following them into their burrows. It will also kill rabbits and birds if it can catch them.

WEASEL SKULL

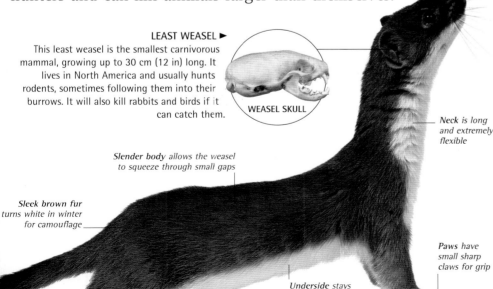

Neck is long and extremely flexible

Slender body allows the weasel to squeeze through small gaps

Sleek brown fur turns white in winter for camouflage

Paws have small sharp claws for grip

Underside stays white in summer

FARMED FOR FUR ►
The American mink has a soft, thick pelt, which has led to it being farmed to make fur coats. Like its cousin, the European mink, this species is more aquatic than most members of the weasel family. As well as rabbits and other burrowing mammals, it hunts fish and water birds, including ducks.

FIND OUT MORE ▶▶ Carnivores 38 • Rabbits 305 • Rodents 302 • Squirrels 303

OTTERS

Otters are mammals that spend time both on land and in water. They hunt fish and other aquatic animals, bringing them to the shore or the surface to feed. Otters are closely related to badgers and weasels. They have short legs with long, flexible bodies that enable them to make tight turns underwater as they chase after prey. Most species of otter have webbed feet, and all have long, sensitive whiskers and thick, water-repellent fur.

RIVER OTTERS

GIANT OTTER
This is the largest of all otter species, reaching 2.4 m (8 ft) long from nose to tail. It lives in the rivers and swamps of tropical South America, forming noisy family groups that often hunt together. Unlike other otters, the giant otter has a flat, paddle-like tail.

EURASIAN RIVER OTTER
This is the most widespread otter, living in Europe, much of Asia, and northern Africa. Although it is called a river otter, it sometimes hunts in the sea. Coastal populations are usually active by day, but those living inland tend to be nocturnal, spending the day in a den called a holt.

AMERICAN RIVER OTTER
There are 13 species of otter altogether. This one is a close relative of the Eurasian river otter and lives in similar habitats. The North American river otter is slightly larger than its Eurasian relative, sometimes growing to over 1.5 m (5 ft) long.

SHELL CRACKER ▼
The sea otter specializes in hunting crabs, sea urchins, and shellfish. Once it has found its prey, it brings it up to the ocean surface and breaks it open by smashing it against a pebble balanced on its belly. The sea otter lives along the Pacific coasts of North America and Russia, and is usually found among forests of giant seaweed, or kelp. Unlike most other otters, it rarely leaves the water, except to give birth. The sea otter has the densest fur of any mammal.

Crab's shell is broken open

Dark nose stands out against light brown fur

Food is balanced on the otter's stomach

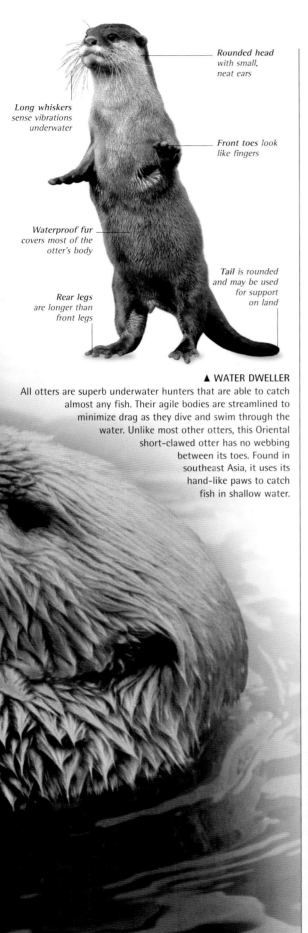

Rounded head with small, neat ears

Long whiskers sense vibrations underwater

Front toes look like fingers

Waterproof fur covers most of the otter's body

Tail is rounded and may be used for support on land

Rear legs are longer than front legs

▲ WATER DWELLER

All otters are superb underwater hunters that are able to catch almost any fish. Their agile bodies are streamlined to minimize drag as they dive and swim through the water. Unlike most other otters, this Oriental short-clawed otter has no webbing between its toes. Found in southeast Asia, it uses its hand-like paws to catch fish in shallow water.

BADGERS

There are ten badger species altogether. Badgers usually have stocky, wedge-shaped bodies and live on the ground, although the four ferret badgers, all from Asia, are more nimble and often climb trees. Most badgers are relatively solitary animals, but the Eurasian species lives in groups known as clans, whose members share a complex of burrows called a sett. Badgers are omnivores, living on a variety of different foods.

Striped face may help badgers to recognize each another at night

Black-and-white hairs cover most of the body

Snout is long and pointed

Stocky legs give the badger a lumbering walking style

Long claws on the front feet are used for digging

STRIPY FACE ►

With its striped, black-and-white face, the Eurasian badger is hard to mistake for any other animal. It lives across Europe and Asia, as far north as the edge of the Arctic Circle. In most of its range it is nocturnal, emerging at dusk to forage for earthworms, other invertebrates, small mammals, and plants.

◄ AMERICAN BADGER

This species is the most carnivorous badger, digging mammals as large as rabbits from their burrows. It wanders widely in search of food, and usually has several dens in its home range. American badgers sometimes form hunting partnerships with coyotes to increase their chances of catching food.

Unguarded bird's nest is an open invitation to this opportunistic animal

FIND OUT MORE ►► Animal Homes 48–49 • Omnivores 40

Tail flippers move from side to side to propel the seal through the water

SEALS

Seals are carnivores that spend most of their life in the water, although they need to come ashore to mate and give birth to their pups. Many species gather in large colonies on secluded beaches to do this. Seals are very graceful in the water, but are clumsy on land and find safety in numbers. Most of the 33 species of seal are coastal animals that live in the ocean, but one, the Baikal seal, lives in fresh water. Its home, Lake Baikal in Russia, is completely landlocked.

ANTARCTIC HUNTER ▶
The leopard seal is a fearsome predator that lurks at the edges of ice floes for prey. It hunts a variety of animals, including krill, fish, and penguins – sometimes, it even kills and eats other seals. The leopard seal is the largest Antarctic seal, growing to 3 m (10 ft) long and weighing as much as 370 kg (816 lb).

Long whiskers help to find food on the seabed

Ear lacks external features

SEALS AROUND THE WORLD

ELEPHANT SEAL
The southern elephant seal is the largest of all seals. Males can reach 5 m (16½ ft) long and weigh 2.5 tonnes. Southern elephant seals gather on Antarctic beaches to breed. Large males fight violent battles for control over areas of beach, with the winners gaining the right to mate with any females on that part of the beach.

GREY SEAL PUP
The grey seal pup's white coat is a throwback to the Ice Age. When this species was evolving, the pups were born on coasts covered with snow and the coat served as camouflage. Today, the ice has retreated farther north and the Atlantic beaches where the pups are born are often snow-free. Adults have grey-brown coats.

Body is smooth and streamlined

STELLER'S SEA LION
This species from the North Pacific is the largest of the sea lions. Adult males can weigh as much as a tonne. As with many seals and sea lions, the males are much bigger than the females. Male Steller's sea lions fight to defend territories on breeding beaches. Only the largest and most powerful males get to mate.

Skin hides a layer of fatty blubber that acts as insulation

COMMON SEAL ▶
Seals are elegant, graceful swimmers. In the water their bodies are extremely flexible, allowing them to make tight turns as they chase after fish. These are common, or harbour, seals, which live around the north of the Atlantic and Pacific Oceans. Common seals are one of the smaller seal species, with adult males reaching 1.7 m (5½ ft) in length.

NEW ZEALAND FUR SEAL
Fur seals are covered with a dense coat of hair. This helps to keep them warm underwater, along with a thick layer of blubber. On land, their fur is so efficient that it often makes the seals overheat. When this happens, fur seals lift up their flippers in the air to catch the wind to help them cool down.

FIND OUT MORE ▶▶ Coasts **72** • Conservation **22–23** • Evolution **16–17** • Otters **278–279** • Polar Regions **70**

WALRUSES

With its huge, rounded body and long tusks, the walrus is unmistakable. These mammals live in the Arctic Ocean and feed on shellfish from the seabed. Both male and female walruses have tusks, although they are longer and thicker on males. They also have thick skin and lots of blubber, which protect them from the stabbing tusks of other walruses. There is just one species of walrus; its closest relatives are fur seals.

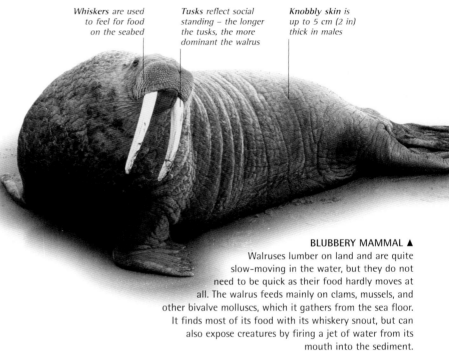

Whiskers are used to feel for food on the seabed

Tusks reflect social standing – the longer the tusks, the more dominant the walrus

Knobbly skin is up to 5 cm (2 in) thick in males

BLUBBERY MAMMAL ▲
Walruses lumber on land and are quite slow-moving in the water, but they do not need to be quick as their food hardly moves at all. The walrus feeds mainly on clams, mussels, and other bivalve molluscs, which it gathers from the sea floor. It finds most of its food with its whiskery snout, but can also expose creatures by firing a jet of water from its mouth into the sediment.

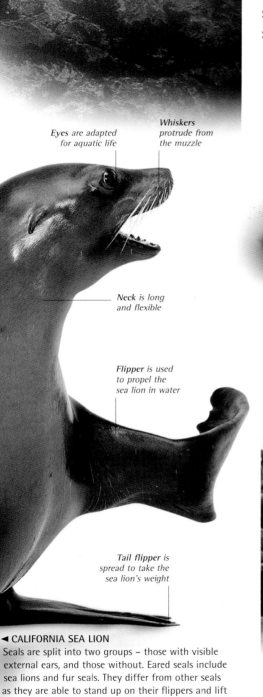

Eyes are adapted for aquatic life

Whiskers protrude from the muzzle

Neck is long and flexible

Flipper is used to propel the sea lion in water

Tail flipper is spread to take the sea lion's weight

◄ CALIFORNIA SEA LION
Seals are split into two groups – those with visible external ears, and those without. Eared seals include sea lions and fur seals. They differ from other seals as they are able to stand up on their flippers and lift their bodies off the ground.

▲ WALRUS COLONY
Walruses are sociable animals that haul themselves onto the shore in groups between bouts of feeding. Large colonies of hundreds of walruses form during the breeding season. Walrus mating usually takes place in the water. Large males hover just offshore, waiting for females to enter the sea. They attract mates and repel rivals with loud, repetitive calls made up of clangs, knocks, and whistles. The sound is amplified by inflatable sacs in their throats.

FIND OUT MORE ▶▶ Mammals **240–241** • Oceans **74–75** • Reproduction **44–45**

WHALES

Whales are the largest creatures on Earth. The biggest of all, the blue whale, can weigh up to 120 tonnes. Whales are marine mammals. They can be divided into two groups: baleen whales, such as the humpback whale, and toothed whales, a group that includes dolphins and porpoises. Some whales hunt large animals, but many eat tiny fish or shrimp-like crustaceans called krill.

SCRIMSHAW CARVINGS

▲ WHALING
Whales have been hunted by humans for centuries. In the past, they were killed in huge numbers for their meat and blubber. To pass the time, the sailors on whaling ships carved designs called scrimshaw on to whales' teeth. Today, whales are hunted on a much smaller scale for food. Whaling has had a huge impact on the numbers of large whales in the oceans. The populations of most species are a tiny fraction of what they once were.

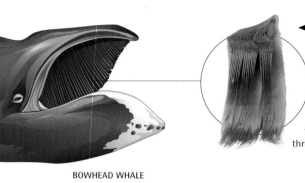

BOWHEAD WHALE

◄ BALEEN WHALE
Baleen whales catch their food by straining it out of the water using brush-like plates made from a horny substance called baleen. A stiff curtain of baleen hangs down from each side of the whale's upper jaw. After taking a gulp of water, the whale closes its mouth and presses its tongue against the baleen, forcing the water through but trapping the prey inside its mouth.

▼ TOOTHED WHALE
Not all whales have baleen, some have teeth for hunting larger prey. Dolphins and porpoises have peg-like teeth and are classified as toothed whales. The largest toothed whale is the sperm whale, which can weigh up to 50 tonnes. It uses its massive teeth to grapple giant squid in the depths of the ocean.

COMMON DOLPHIN

FILTER FEEDER ►
This humpback whale is using its baleen to trap tiny fish. Humpbacks sometimes work together to scoop up fish. Several whales will swim in circles beneath a shoal of fish while releasing air from their blowholes. The resulting bubble net encloses the fish. The whales swim up through this trap with their mouths open and gather up their prey.

Huge jaws give the whale a massive gape

Baleen sieves fish and other food from the water

Barnacles attach themselves to the whale's hard skin

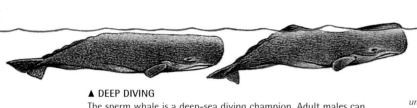

Dive begins
as the whale
dips its head
under the water

Head points
downwards
and tail lifts

▲ DEEP DIVING

The sperm whale is a deep-sea diving champion. Adult males can plunge as far as 3 km (1.9 miles) beneath the surface in their search for food. They can stay underwater for over an hour. Before each dive, the sperm whale loads its body with oxygen. It spends around 10 minutes at the surface, breathing in and out up to 70 times to force as much oxygen into its blood as possible.

WHALES OF THE WORLD

FIN WHALE

Fin whales grow up to 26 m (85 ft) long and can weigh 80 tonnes. They live in seas and oceans around the world, but are most common in temperate waters. Fin whales usually travel in groups of three or more, but can sometimes be seen in gatherings of over 100.

Dive speed reaches
1–3 m (3¹⁄₄–10 ft)
per second

MINKE WHALE

The minke is the smallest and most common of the baleen whales. It lives in all of the world's oceans and is a speedy, agile swimmer. The minke whale grows to 10 m (33 ft) long and can weigh up to 15 tonnes. Like other baleen whales, it feeds on krill and small fish.

NARWHAL

The narwhal is a toothed whale that feeds mainly on fish. It lives in the Arctic Ocean wherever there is pack ice, sometimes gathering in groups several thousand strong. Male narwhals use their long, pointed tusks to fight for dominance in the group.

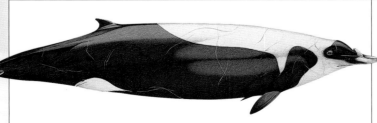

STRAP-TOOTHED WHALE

At over 6 m (20 ft) long, the strap-toothed whale is a beaked whale (a toothed whale with very few teeth). The males have long tusks that are probably used for fighting. Strap-toothed whales are found in cold temperate waters in the southern hemisphere.

COMING UP FOR AIR ▶

All whales have to swim up to the surface to breathe. Air is taken in and expelled through a blowhole. The expelled air is filled with tiny water droplets, creating a towering cloud of vapour above the whale. The shape and size of this cloud is distinctive and can be used to tell different species of whales apart – this is a blue whale.

FIND OUT MORE ▶▶ Communication **34–35** • Dolphins **286–287** • Mammals **240–241** • Orca **284–285**

ORCA

Also known as killer whales, orcas are the largest members of the dolphin family. Highly social and intelligent, they live in groups called pods. Orcas communicate using a range of underwater calls, and with social signals such as flipper slapping or acrobatic leaps.

Scientific name: *Orcina orca*

Order: Cetacea (cetaceans: whales, dolphins, and porpoises)

Class: Mammalia (mammals)

Distribution: Worldwide, from polar to tropical seas, usually in coastal waters

Status: Lower risk

Length: Up to 9 m (30 ft)

Weight: Up to 10 tonnes

Food: Mainly fish and marine mammals, such as dolphins, small whales, and seals; also turtles and seabirds

Reproduction: Adult females breed once every 3 years or so; gestation period is 15–17 months

Number of young: 1

FIND OUT MORE ▸▸ Oceans **74–75** •
Dolphins **286–287**

DOLPHINS

Dolphins are aquatic mammals that spend their lives in the water, coming to the surface to breathe. They are the most abundant and diverse members of the whale family. Dolphins have beak-like snouts and sharp, conical teeth and are predators that hunt fish. Most dolphins are ocean dwellers, although some live in fresh water. Porpoises are smaller than most dolphins and generally live in coastal waters, rather than out in the open sea.

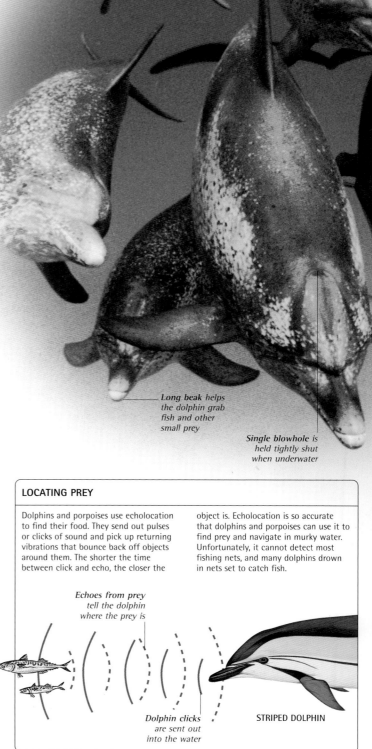

Long beak helps the dolphin grab fish and other small prey

Single blowhole is held tightly shut when underwater

DOLPHINS OF RIVER AND SEA

PANTROPICAL SPOTTED DOLPHIN
This species lives in the Atlantic, Pacific, and Indian Oceans. It is one of the world's most common dolphin species. It is also one of the most active, often leaping right out of the water as it comes up for air.

PACIFIC WHITE-SIDED DOLPHIN
The Pacific white-sided dolphin has a rounded head with a small beak. It inhabits the Pacific Ocean north of the Tropic of Cancer. A fast-moving species, it usually lives in groups of between 10 and 100 dolphins.

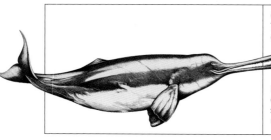

GANGES RIVER DOLPHIN
There are five species of dolphin that live only in rivers. The Ganges river dolphin of South Asia has a long, narrow beak and lives alone or in small groups. Unlike other dolphins, this species lacks a special lens in its eyes, which means it is virtually blind.

HARBOUR PORPOISE
There are six species of porpoise, ranging in size from 1.2 to 2.2 m (4 to 7¼ ft) long. The harbour porpoise is one of the smallest. It lives along the coasts of Europe, Japan, northern Africa, and North America. It swims slowly and is often seen alone.

LOCATING PREY

Dolphins and porpoises use echolocation to find their food. They send out pulses or clicks of sound and pick up returning vibrations that bounce back off objects around them. The shorter the time between click and echo, the closer the object is. Echolocation is so accurate that dolphins and porpoises can use it to find prey and navigate in murky water. Unfortunately, it cannot detect most fishing nets, and many dolphins drown in nets set to catch fish.

Echoes from prey tell the dolphin where the prey is

Dolphin clicks are sent out into the water

STRIPED DOLPHIN

FIND OUT MORE ►► Bats **254–255** • Mammals **240–241** • Oceans **74–75** • Orca **284–285** • Whales **282–283**

SEA COWS

Sea cows are slow-moving mammals that never leave the water. These docile, blubbery animals feed entirely on seaweed and water plants. They live along the coasts of many tropical and subtropical countries. They also inhabit estuaries and large, slow-flowing rivers. Sea cows are closely related to elephants. There are four species: the West Indian manatee, the West African manatee, the Amazonian manatee, and the dugong. A fifth species – the giant Steller's sea cow – became extinct in 1768.

◄ WEST INDIAN MANATEE
This is the largest living species of sea cow, growing up to 4.6 m (15 ft) long. It lives along the coasts of Florida, the West Indies, Central America, and northern South America. Despite its large range, the West Indian manatee is quite rare, as it was once hunted. Like all manatees, it has a flat, rounded tail. The dugong, by contrast, has a sickle-shaped tail.

Skin conceals blubbery fat that helps the manatee conserve heat

Flipper may be used to gather or carry vegetation

Streamlined body helps save energy when swimming

▲ ATLANTIC SPOTTED DOLPHIN SCHOOL
Dolphins are social mammals that live in groups called schools or pods. Most members of the school are closely related, although unrelated dolphins may join from other schools. Dolphins work cooperatively to find and catch prey. When hunting fish, for example, some school members circle the shoal and drive it towards the surface, allowing others to swim through and grab mouthfuls of fish.

OCEAN FORAGER ►
The dugong has the largest range of any sea cow. It can be found from eastern Africa to New Caledonia, in the Pacific Ocean. The dugong feeds almost entirely on sea grasses, pulling them up by the roots from the soft, coastal sediment in which they grow. It differs from manatees, not just in the shape of its tail, but also the position of its nostrils, which are farther back on its head.

SPEEDY SWIMMERS ▲
Dolphins, such as these common dolphins, and porpoises have streamlined bodies, allowing them to cut through the water like fish. They include some of the sea's fastest animals – Dall's porpoise can reach speeds of up to 55 kph (34 mph). By adjusting the angle of their pectoral fins, dolphins and porpoises can turn in tight circles, enabling them to follow shoals of fish.

FIND OUT MORE ►► Elephants **288** • Seals **280–281** • Walruses **281**

ELEPHANTS

Elephants are the world's largest land animals. An adult male African elephant can weigh more than 7 tonnes and stand over 3.6 m (12 ft) tall. All three species are sociable animals that live in extended family groups with strong bonds between individual members. When an elephant dies, the rest of its herd seems to mourn and will often return to visit its bones long after its death. Elephants use a range of body postures and sounds to communicate.

▼ MATRIARCHAL GROUP

Like all elephants, the African savanna elephant lives in herds that are led by the oldest female, known as the matriarch. She uses her years of experience and excellent memory to help the other elephants find food and water. Most members of the elephant herd are related. The adults are all females. Male elephants leave when they are about 15 years old, before they have completed their adolescence. Some join temporary all-male groups. Others live alone.

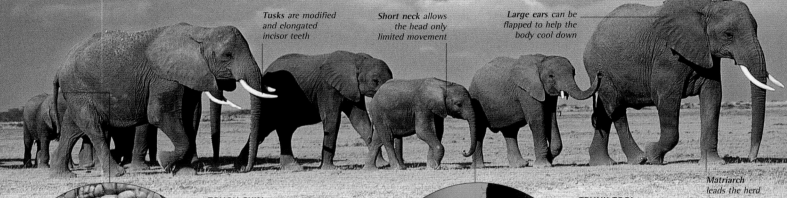

Tusks are modified and elongated incisor teeth

Short neck allows the head only limited movement

Large ears can be flapped to help the body cool down

Matriarch leads the herd

◄ TOUGH SKIN

An elephant's skin is thick and wrinkled to protect it against predators. Adult males are too large for any carnivore to tackle, but females and young elephants are sometimes attacked by lions. When predators threaten a member of the herd, the others rally round in defence – young elephants are surrounded by the adults at the slightest sign of danger.

◄ TRUNK TOOL

An elephant's trunk is formed from its nose and top lip. It is one of the most flexible and powerful limbs in the animal kingdom. An elephant can use its trunk to pick up anything from a twig to a fallen tree. Elephants are herbivores and a trunk can pull up grass or pull down branches for food. The nostrils are at the end of its trunk, which can be used like a snorkel in deep water. The trunk can also be used to suck water up and then spray it into the elephant's mouth.

Smaller ears than those of African elephants

Trunk contains thousands of muscles, but no bones

◄ INDIAN ELEPHANT

The Indian elephant is slightly smaller than its African relative, but it is still a massive animal. Male Indian elephants can weigh up to 4.5 tonnes and measure 3.5 m (11½ ft) at the shoulder. Indian and African elephants are easily distinguished. Indian elephants have smaller ears and a much more dome-shaped head.

▲ YOUNG AFRICAN FOREST ELEPHANT

The African forest elephant inhabits dense jungles. It has many differences from the African savanna elephant, including much straighter tusks, darker skin, and a hairier trunk. The forest elephant's habitat is so dense and unexplored that little is known about how it lives.

FIND OUT MORE ▶▶ Ecology 14–15 • Grasslands 56–57 • Mammals 240–241 • Rhinoceroses 292–293

HOOFED MAMMALS

Most of the world's large land animals are hoofed mammals. This group includes cattle, deer, rhinoceroses, and hippopotamuses. Hoofed mammals are herbivores and have complex digestive systems to break down the plant matter they feed on. They are native to every continent, apart from Australia and Antarctica, and form two groups, each of which is defined by the number of toes on the animal's feet.

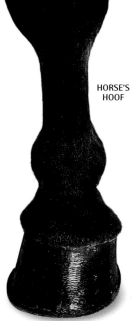

HORSE'S HOOF

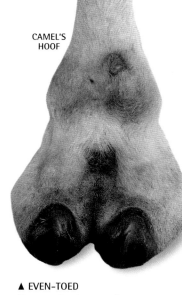

CAMEL'S HOOF

DIGESTIVE SYSTEMS

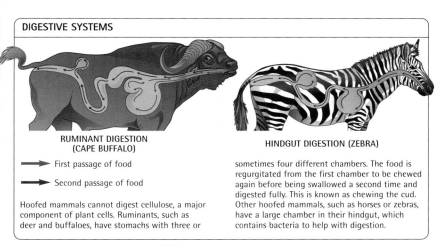

RUMINANT DIGESTION (CAPE BUFFALO)

→ First passage of food

→ Second passage of food

Hoofed mammals cannot digest cellulose, a major component of plant cells. Ruminants, such as deer and buffaloes, have stomachs with three or

HINDGUT DIGESTION (ZEBRA)

sometimes four different chambers. The food is regurgitated from the first chamber to be chewed again before being swallowed a second time and digested fully. This is known as chewing the cud. Other hoofed mammals, such as horses or zebras, have a large chamber in their hindgut, which contains bacteria to help with digestion.

▲ ODD-TOED
Odd-toed hoofed mammals include rhinoceroses and horses. Horses have just one toe on each foot, while rhinos have three. All odd-toed hoofed mammals place their weight on the middle digit, which is covered with a horny sheath, or hoof. Fossils show that the ancestors of horses had several toes.

▲ EVEN-TOED
The even-toed group of hoofed mammals contains 228 species, compared to just 19 in the odd-toed group. Even-toed hoofed mammals put their weight on the third and fourth toe of each foot. In some, such as camels, these are the only toes remaining. Others, such as cattle, have two smaller toes on the heel.

◀ MALAYAN TAPIR
Tapirs are hoofed mammals that have changed little in more than 20 million years. There are four species of tapir alive today. Three are found in South and Central America – this one comes from southeast Asia. Tapirs are forest dwellers. They feed on plants and are mainly nocturnal, solitary animals.

Stocky legs support the barrel-shaped body

Toes spread out on soft ground

HOOFED HERD ▶
Many grassland hoofed mammals live in large groups for protection. Having more pairs of eyes and ears around makes it harder for predators to sneak up. The largest herds are formed by horses, deer, cattle, and antelopes, such as these red lechwe. The herding instinct is strong. If an individual becomes separated from the herd, it quickly rejoins it.

FIND OUT MORE ▶▶ Camels **295** • Cattle **300** • Grasslands **56–57** • Horses **290–291** • Rhinoceroses **292** • Zebras **291**

HORSES

Horses are hardy herbivores built for speed. In the wild, they are herd animals, but domesticated horses are often kept alone. Horses are grazers, feeding on low-growing plants. Their front teeth have sharp, flat edges for cropping grass. Horses have been domesticated for thousands of years. In that time, many different breeds have been developed to do a variety of jobs.

FLEHMEN

This facial expression, which is called flehmen, is something many hoofed mammals have in common. Lifting back the upper lip nearer to the nostrils helps to enhance scent and is used by stallions when checking whether a mare is in oestrous (ready to mate). Horses often perform flehmen around people or new objects – it is simply their way of picking up unfamiliar smells. Although they neigh occasionally, horses are mainly silent animals.

Top lip is curled back showing front teeth

Mane is brush-like and stands upright like that of a zebra

Ears can be turned independently to pick up faint sounds

Neck is long and thick

Belly is rounded and almost white in colour

Hoof has just a single toe

Teeth continue to grow throughout the horse's life

Large ears help the mustang detect predators

Legs are strong and muscular

◄ PRZEWALSKI'S WILD HORSE

This species is the ancestor of the domesticated horse. Until recently it was threatened with extinction, but a captive breeding programme has seen it returned to its native home in the steppes of Mongolia. Przewalski's wild horse lives in small herds of several females and their young, led by a single male. Other males live together in bachelor herds.

WILD ASSES

SOMALI WILD ASS
Only a few small herds of this type of African wild ass survive in remote regions of Somalia and Ethiopia. African wild asses are adapted for life in arid, semidesert habitats – they can lose up to a third of their body weight in water and still survive.

KULAN
This is a variety of Asian wild ass. It lives in Central Asia, and like most wild horses it is highly endangered as a result of hunting and habitat loss. Kulans, and their close relatives, onagers, have buff-coloured bodies, with paler underparts.

FIND OUT MORE ▶▶ Conservation 22–23 • Hoofed Mammals 289 • Mammals 240–241 • Placental Mammals 247

Heavy load of hay is carried on mule's back

Hoof is small and rounded

▲ PACK ANIMAL
Horses and donkeys can carry heavy loads on their broad backs. The two animals can breed together. The resulting offspring is known as a mule if its mother was a horse, and a hinny if its mother was a donkey. Mules and hinnies are unable to produce young of their own but make good pack animals.

DOMESTIC HORSES ▶
Horses have been bred for many jobs. In medieval times, the shire horse was used in battle. Later, it became popular as a farm horse. Small horse breeds are known as ponies. The Shetland pony is one of the smallest – it is never more than 117 cm (46 in) high.

SHETLAND PONY

SHIRE HORSE

▼ AMERICAN MUSTANGS
Mustangs are feral, which means they are domesticated animals that have returned to the wild. They live on the plains of North America and are descended from north African horses brought by Spanish explorers in the 16th century. Although many mustangs were rounded up by cowboys in the 19th century, there are still over 50,000 living wild today.

ZEBRAS

With their black and white stripes, zebras are unmistakable. They are creatures of open grasslands and, like all horses, they feed on low-growing plants. Zebras' stripes make it harder for predators to see them. As they run at speed in a herd, their outlines blur into one another, making it tricky for a hunter, such as a lion, to pick out an individual to attack.

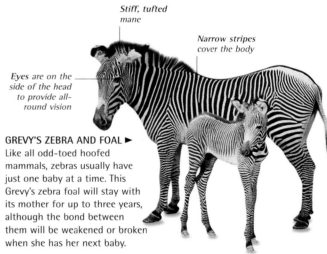

Stiff, tufted mane

Narrow stripes cover the body

Eyes are on the side of the head to provide all-round vision

GREVY'S ZEBRA AND FOAL ▶
Like all odd-toed hoofed mammals, zebras usually have just one baby at a time. This Grevy's zebra foal will stay with its mother for up to three years, although the bond between them will be weakened or broken when she has her next baby.

▼ MOUNTAIN ZEBRA
The mountain zebra is the largest of the three species of zebra. It is found in Angola, Namibia, and a few parts of South Africa. It is more slender than the plains zebra, which is found all over east Africa. The two species form mixed herds where their ranges overlap. The third species, Grevy's zebra, lives mainly in Ethiopia.

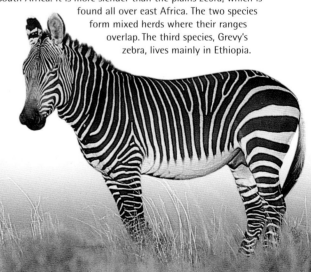

FIND OUT MORE ▶▶ Grasslands 56–57

RHINOCEROSES

There are five species of rhinoceros living in Africa and Asia. Four species are browsers, which means that they feed mainly on leaves plucked from the branches of bushes and trees. The odd one out is the white rhino, which eats mainly grass. Rhinoceroses are large, heavily built animals with thick, armour-like skin. An adult male white rhinos can weigh up to 3.6 tonnes, making it the world's second-largest land mammal.

Tough hide protects the rhino's body

Shoulder hump formed from powerful muscles

Horn used for fighting and defence

Calf never strays far from its mother

RARE RHINOS

SUMATRAN RHINOCEROS
This is the smallest rhino, weighing less than a tonne. It is also the only species to have hair – some individuals are almost completely covered, while others have less. Around 300 Sumatran rhinos are thought to remain in the wild, in the rainforests of Sumatra and Borneo.

INDIAN RHINOCEROS
The Indian rhinoceros is the largest Asian rhino, weighing up to 2.7 tonnes. Its skin is so thick and folded that it looks like armour plating, and protects it from predators, such as tigers. Conservation programmes have helped save the Indian rhinoceros from extinction.

JAVAN RHINOCEROS
This is the rarest of all rhinos. Scientists think that there are fewer than 60 left in the wild. The Javan rhino lives in dense rainforest in the Indonesian island of Java and in Vietnam. It browses for food at night and spends most of its life alone, only seeking others to breed.

▲ RHINO AND CALF
Rhinoceroses are protective mothers. If danger threatens, a female white rhinoceros will stand over her baby and turn to face their attacker. The calf stays with its mother for up to four years, only leaving when she has her next baby. Rhinoceroses usually have just a single calf at a time.

▲ RHINO HORN
Rhino horn is made from tightly packed fibres of keratin, the same substance that forms human hair and fingernails. Male rhinos use their horns to fight one another for mates. Horns are also sometimes used for defence against predators. Most rhinos are endangered because they have been hunted for their horns, which are used in Chinese medicine.

FIND OUT MORE ▶▶ Conservation **22–23** • Rainforest **60–61** • Elephants **288–289** • Hoofed Mammals **289**

PIGS

Pigs are tough, intelligent, and adaptable animals. Unlike most other hoofed mammals, they are omnivores, which means that they eat a wide range of foods. As well as plants, some pigs eat fungi, insects, and even mice. There are nine species of wild pig, ranging in size from the 60-cm (2-ft) long pygmy hog, which lives in India, to the 2.1-m (7-ft) long giant forest hog from Africa. Wild pigs are vastly outnumbered by the world's 900 million domesticated pigs.

▲ CHARGE!
Rhinos have poor eyesight, but good senses of hearing and smell. If they sense a predator, they will often charge to defend themselves. Despite their size, rhinos are surprisingly fast. A charging rhino can reach 56 kph (35 mph). Some rhinos are more likely to charge than others. The black rhino, which is shown here, is a particularly aggressive species.

Pink skin is sensitive and easily burned by the Sun

Large ears can move independently

PERKY PIG ▶
Domesticated pigs share all the features of their wild counterparts. They have large heads, short tails, and robust bodies. They also have very good senses of hearing and smell. Pigs were first domesticated around 5,000 years ago. The ancestor of most domesticated pigs is the wild boar, but in parts of Indonesia and the Philippines some people keep pigs that are descended from the Celebes wild pig.

Trotters have 2 main hooves and 2 smaller ones

Bristly hairs cover the body

▲ FORAGAING FOR FOOD
The wild boar has a larger range than any other species of pig. It is found in Europe and Asia. It also lives in northern Africa and has been introduced to eastern North America. Like most pigs, wild boars have large litters, containing as many as 12 piglets. Wild boar piglets have light and dark brown stripes along their bodies for camouflage. These stripes fade away as they grow older.

Sensitive snout to find and dig up food

FIND OUT MORE ▶▶ Omnivores 40 • Hoofed Mammals **289**

HIPPOPOTAMUSES

Hippopotamuses' large, hairless bodies appear almost weightless as they walk along the bottoms of rivers. Although they spend a lot of time in the water, they feed on land, coming out to graze at night when it is cooler. Wild hippos are found only in Africa. There are two species – the large common hippo and the smaller pygmy hippo, which inhabits dense rainforests in the west of the continent.

WEIGHTY BEAST ►
The common hippo is one of the heaviest land mammals and adult males can weigh over 3 tonnes. Its bulk means that it has few natural predators. Common hippos have just one baby at a time, and the young are able to suckle underwater.

AMPHIBIOUS MAMMALS ▲
When they are not feeding, common hippos gather in water. They do this partly for safety and partly to keep cool. If danger threatens, hippos head for deeper water, where they can lie with just their nostrils, eyes, and ears above the surface. If necessary, they will dive, closing their ears and nostrils to prevent water seeping in.

Snout is covered with bristly hairs

Bulging eyes to see above the water

Stout legs to support the heavy body

Top jaw widens towards the tip

Large mouth is used for grazing on land

Nostrils can be closed by small but strong muscles

Hindquarters slope to short, sturdy legs

◄ MASSIVE GAPE
The hippopotamus has the largest mouth of any land mammal. It opens its jaws like this to threaten other hippos, or to warn predators to stay away. In many places, male hippos maintain mating territories. They will defend long stretches of a river or a lake shore against other males.

Smaller head with less bulging eyes

Tusks may be 50 cm (1 ft 8 in) long in old males

PYGMY HIPPOPOTAMUS ►
The pygmy hippo is about half the size of the common hippo. It rests by day in a mud bath called a wallow or beneath thick vegetation in its rainforest habitat. At night, it enters swamps and rivers to feed on aquatic plants or forages on land.

Layers of fat under thick, flexible skin

FIND OUT MORE ►► Hoofed Mammals 289 • Rhinoceroses 292–293

CAMELS

Camels are hardy hoofed mammals that can go for long periods without food or water, enabling them to survive in the toughest of habitats. The camel family contains seven species. Four of these are wild, but the other three are domesticated, providing people with transport, wool, and food. Unlike other hoofed mammals, camels and their relatives have long, curved necks. They also differ in the way they walk, placing their weight on the padded soles of their feet, rather than the hooves.

▲ BEASTS OF BURDEN
All the world's dromedary camels are either domesticated or feral – descended from individuals that were set loose or escaped from herds kept by humans. Dromedaries have been used for centuries by humans as transport in southwestern Asia and north Africa, earning them the nickname ships of the desert.

MOUNTAIN CAMEL ▲
The vicuña lives in the Andes mountains of South America. The smallest member of the camel family, it lives in groups of a few females and their young dominated by a single, territorial male. The vicuña is one of two wild South American camels. The other, the guanaco, is the ancestor of the domestic llama.

Hump filled with fat acts as an energy store

Front hump is smaller than back one

Flexible neck helps reach leaves high up or down on the ground

Head is covered by a mop of hair

Back legs are long and slender

Feet are broad and flatten out into fleshy pads

Small hoof at the end of each of the two toes

Thick hair for warmth is shed when summer returns

◄ TWO HUMPS
Unlike the dromedary, which has just one hump, the bactrian camel has two. This species still lives in the wild in Mongolia, where it inhabits dry steppe grassland. Like the dromedary, the bactrian camel is often used for riding and to carry goods. Domesticated bactrian camels are found in many parts of central Asia, including China.

DOMESTICATED CAMELS
South America is home to two domesticated camels – the llama and the alpaca. Llamas are used mainly as pack animals to carry heavy loads over rugged terrain. Alpacas are kept for their wool. There are two alpaca breeds – the huacaya, shown here, and the suri.

Eyes are hidden under hair

Mouth is almost hairless

Wool is thick and wavy

FIND OUT MORE ▸▸ Deserts 58–59 • Hoofed Mammals 289

REINDEER

The reindeer, known as the caribou in North America, is a hoofed mammal. Unlike other deer, both male and female reindeer have antlers, which are shed and regrown each year. The reindeer's broad hooves enable it to walk on deep snow during the long Arctic winter, and on springy moss during the short Arctic summer. It also uses its hooves to dig into the snow so it can feed on lichen and fungi. Like other deer, reindeer live in herds for protection from predators.

Scientific name: *Rangifer tarandus*

Order: Artiodactyla (even-toed hoofed mammals)

Class: Mammalia (mammals)

Distribution: North America, Greenland, northern Europe, and Asia

Status: Endangered (in the wild)

Length: 1.2–2.2 m (4–7¼ ft)

Weight: 120–300 kg (260–660 lb)

Food: Grasses, sedges, and herbs in summer; mosses, lichens, and fungi in winter

Breeding activity: Males fight each other during the breeding season in autumn, using their antlers as weapons and to attract a mate

Number of young: One calf born in May-June

FIND OUT MORE ▶▶ Deer **298** • Mammals **240–241** • Polar Regions **70**

Antlers lock with those of rivals

Muscular neck supports the head during battles

DEER

Deer are even-toed hoofed mammals that are found naturally throughout North and South America, Europe, and Asia, and have been introduced to Africa and Australia. They have slender, muscular bodies and long, narrow legs. The males of most species have antlers, which are shed and regrown every year. Deer are ruminants, which means they regurgitate plant matter and chew it for a second time before it digests.

▲ RED DEER RUTTING
During the autumn, mature male deer seek out females for breeding. Once they have found a mate or mates, they do their best to defend them from other males. The dominant males of many deer species call to frighten off rivals. If this does not work, they are forced to fight, locking antlers – rutting – in a test of strength.

▲ RED DEER HIND
Male deer are known as stags or bucks and female deer as hinds or does. The hinds of species that inhabit open ground live in herds to protect them from predators. Other species occupy small areas and live on their own. Red deer hinds usually have just one baby, called a calf or fawn, every year.

Antlers can grow to 1.5 m (5 ft) from tip to tip

Upper lip overhangs mouth

◄ LARGEST DEER
The elk, or moose, as it is called in North America, is the world's largest species of deer. Male elk can weigh more than half a tonne and stand 2 m (7 ft) tall at the shoulder. Elk inhabit the cold, northerly forests of Scandinavia, Russia, and North America. For most of the year, they live solitary lives, wandering the forest in search of food.

ANTLERS

Deer antlers are made of bone, and they are shed and grown anew every year. Growing antlers are covered with a thin layer of blood-rich tissue called velvet. Once they have reached their full size, the velvet is shed, revealing new bone beneath. Male deer lose their antlers after the breeding season is over.

Old velvet dries and hangs in shreds

FIND OUT MORE ▶▶ Antelopes 301 • Herbivores 39 • Hoofed Mammals 289 • Reindeer 296–297

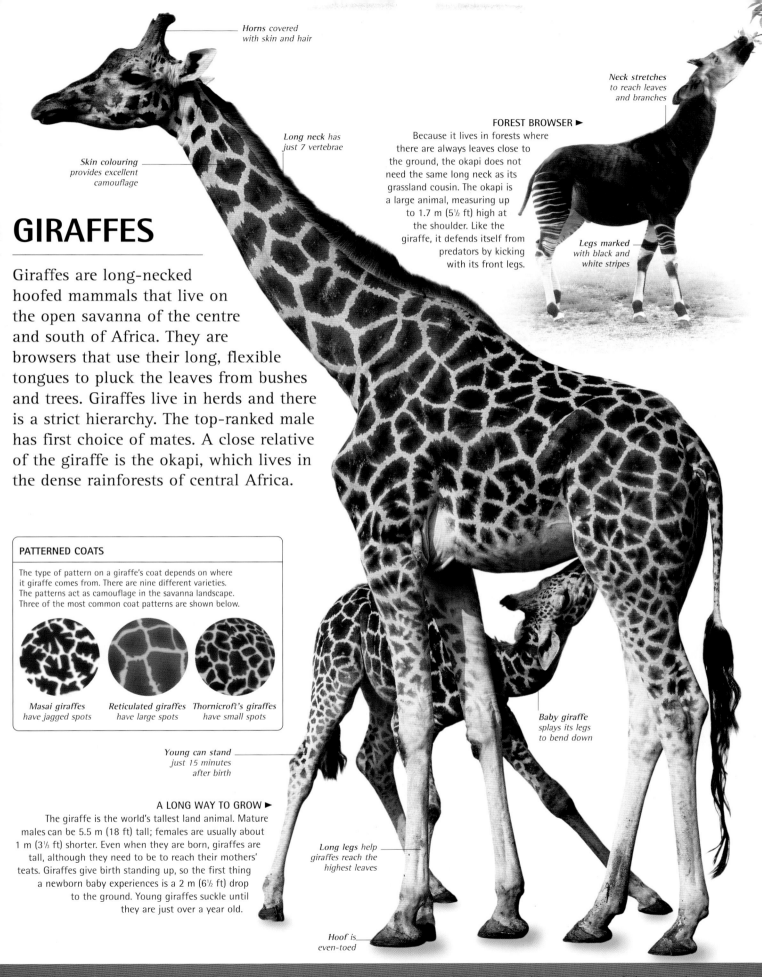

Horns covered
with skin and hair

Long neck has
just 7 vertebrae

Skin colouring
provides excellent
camouflage

GIRAFFES

Giraffes are long-necked
hoofed mammals that live on
the open savanna of the centre
and south of Africa. They are
browsers that use their long, flexible
tongues to pluck the leaves from bushes
and trees. Giraffes live in herds and there
is a strict hierarchy. The top-ranked male
has first choice of mates. A close relative
of the giraffe is the okapi, which lives in
the dense rainforests of central Africa.

Neck stretches
to reach leaves
and branches

FOREST BROWSER ►
Because it lives in forests where
there are always leaves close to
the ground, the okapi does not
need the same long neck as its
grassland cousin. The okapi is
a large animal, measuring up
to 1.7 m (5½ ft) high at
the shoulder. Like the
giraffe, it defends itself from
predators by kicking
with its front legs.

Legs marked
with black and
white stripes

PATTERNED COATS

The type of pattern on a giraffe's coat depends on where
it giraffe comes from. There are nine different varieties.
The patterns act as camouflage in the savanna landscape.
Three of the most common coat patterns are shown below.

Masai giraffes
have jagged spots

Reticulated giraffes
have large spots

Thornicroft's giraffes
have small spots

Young can stand
just 15 minutes
after birth

Baby giraffe
splays its legs
to bend down

A LONG WAY TO GROW ►
The giraffe is the world's tallest land animal. Mature
males can be 5.5 m (18 ft) tall; females are usually about
1 m (3⅓ ft) shorter. Even when they are born, giraffes are
tall, although they need to be to reach their mothers'
teats. Giraffes give birth standing up, so the first thing
a newborn baby experiences is a 2 m (6½ ft) drop
to the ground. Young giraffes suckle until
they are just over a year old.

Long legs help
giraffes reach the
highest leaves

Hoof is
even-toed

FIND OUT MORE ►► Grasslands **56–57** • Herbivores **39** • Hoofed Mammals **289**

CATTLE

Cattle are large, hoofed herbivores – the biggest, the gaur, can reach 2 m (6½ ft) at the shoulder. Although there are just 10 wild species of cattle, they are widespread and occur naturally in North America, Europe, Asia, and Africa. They are also very hardy. One species, the yak, lives at altitudes of up to 6,000 m (19,685 ft) in the Himalayas.

DOMESTICATED CATTLE

WATER BUFFALO
Water buffalo are used as working animals across southern and southeast Asia. They are also reared for milk and meat. Their horns can grow up to 1.8 m (6 ft) long.

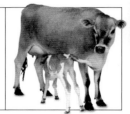

JERSEY COW
Dozens of varieties of the domesticated cow have been bred, some for their ability to produce milk and others for meat. The Jersey cow produces creamy milk.

Rear of the body has much less hair than the front

Large head is covered with a thick mop of hair

Beard of hair hangs down from the jaw

Dewlap of loose skin runs the length of the neck

◄ **AMERICAN BUFFALO**
The buffalo is North America's only native species of cattle. Despite its large build, it can run at speeds of up to 60 kph (37 mph). It once lived in vast herds on the prairies, but was hunted almost to extinction as European settlers moved west across the continent. Today, buffalo numbers have started to recover. The closely related European bison, or wisent, is even rarer. Slightly larger than its American cousin, it lives in forests.

FIND OUT MORE ▶▶ Conservation **22–23** • Grasslands **56–57** • Herbivores **39** • Hoofed Mammals **289**

SHEEP

Female's horns are shorter than male's

Short hair shows this bighorn lives quite far south

Hardy, sure-footed animals, sheep are adapted for life in rocky, mountainous habitats, where they feed on plants few other herbivores can reach. Sheep and their close relatives, goats, form a group of hoofed mammals that contains 34 species. Like their cattle relatives, sheep and goats have permanent horns. The shape and size vary with different species. Sheep and goats are farmed for their wool, meat, and milk.

DOMESTICATED SHEEP AND GOATS

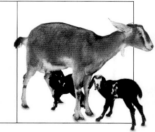

GOAT AND KIDS
Goats were first domesticated in the Middle East. Most modern goats are descended from an animal called the bezoar, which still exists in the wild. Baby goats are called kids.

DOMESTIC SHEEP
Sheep were first domesticated thousands of years ago. Their ancestor was the mouflon, which still lives wild in southern Europe. Sheep have been bred for their wool and meat.

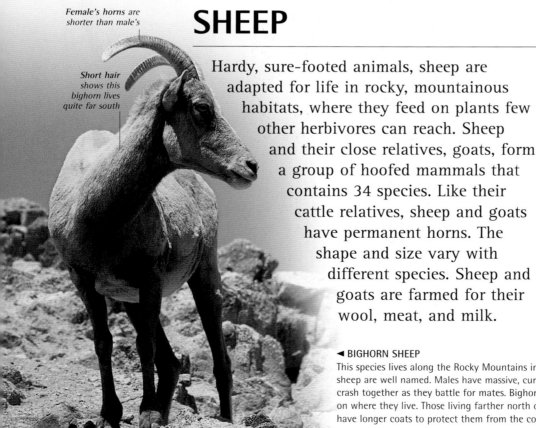

◄ **BIGHORN SHEEP**
This species lives along the Rocky Mountains in North America. Bighorn sheep are well named. Males have massive, curled horns which they crash together as they battle for mates. Bighorn sheep vary, depending on where they live. Those living farther north or at higher altitudes have longer coats to protect them from the cold.

FIND OUT MORE ▶▶ Hoofed Mammals **289** • Mountains **66–67** • Reproduction **44–45**

ANTELOPES

Antelopes live in Africa and Asia. They are even-toed hoofed mammals and are related to cattle and sheep. Antelopes have many similarities to deer, but have horns instead of antlers. Their horns have a bony core that is part of the skull, and they are kept throughout life. In most antelope species, both males and females have horns. The antelope family includes dwarf antelopes, gazelles, and forest-dwelling duikers.

BUILT FOR SPEED ▲
Antelopes include some of the fastest of all land animals. Many species live on open grasslands and have to be quick to escape predators. Some antelopes, such as these springboks from southern Africa, combine their speed with impressive jumps to give them an even better chance of getting away.

◄ GRACEFUL GRAZER
The impala feeds on grasses in the wooded savanna of east and southern Africa, where it is preyed on by carnivores, such as leopards. Females and young form small herds for protection and are joined by males for part of the year. During the breeding season larger males become territorial and chase smaller males from their domain.

Long spiral horns are used for defence and by males to fight for females

Horns are carried only by male impalas

Slender muzzle for plucking leaves from branches

Stripes help to camouflage the kudu among bushes

Brown hair camouflages the impala against dried-out grass

Cloven hoof has two smaller hooves on the heel

Cleft top lip unlike many other hoofed mammals

▲ KUDU
Kudus are among the larger species of antelope. Male greater kudus can be 1.5 m (5 ft) tall at the shoulder. Like many large antelopes, kudus are mainly browsers, feeding on the leaves of bushes and the low branches of trees in the African savannas. The biggest antelope of all is the eland, another African species. It can be 1.8 m (6 ft) tall and weigh almost a tonne.

FIND OUT MORE ▸▸ Big Cats 268 • Deer 298 • Deserts 58–59 • Grasslands 56–57 • Hoofed Mammals 289

RODENTS

The word rodent comes from the Latin "rodere", which means to gnaw. This is because all rodents have long, sharp front teeth. With over 3,000 species, rodents represent nearly half of all mammals. This group includes mice and their relatives; squirrels; and cavy-like rodents, a diverse family that includes guinea pigs, chinchillas, and porcupines. Rodents are extremely adaptable, and are able to live in many different habitats.

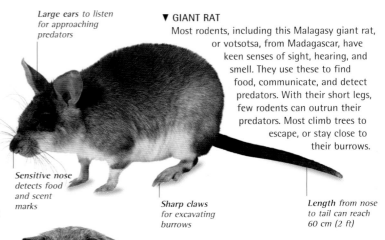

Large ears to listen for approaching predators

▼ GIANT RAT
Most rodents, including this Malagasy giant rat, or votsotsa, from Madagascar, have keen senses of sight, hearing, and smell. They use these to find food, communicate, and detect predators. With their short legs, few rodents can outrun their predators. Most climb trees to escape, or stay close to their burrows.

Sensitive nose detects food and scent marks

Sharp claws for excavating burrows

Length from nose to tail can reach 60 cm (2 ft)

◄ GNAWING JAWS
All rodents have two pairs of front teeth that grow throughout life. In order to keep them worn down and sharp, they have to gnaw things. Rodents put their sharp teeth to good use. Dormice and squirrels, for example, feed on the nutritious kernels of nuts, which they reach by gnawing through the tough, woody shells.

Hamster gnaws at wood to sharpen its teeth

◄ DOMESTIC GUINEA PIG
Guinea pigs are cavy-like rodents that live wild in South America, but in other parts of the world they are popular family pets. Many pet rodents, for example gerbils, look identical to their wild counterparts, but some have been bred to look a little bit different. Pet guinea pigs, for instance, come in a range of colours not found in the wild and some have much longer hair.

Rounded face is typical of cavy-like rodents

Striped face is a distinctive feature of all chipmunks

▲ STRIPY SQUIRREL
Chipmunks are small, bold squirrels that live in North America. They find their food both on the ground and in the branches of trees and bushes, eating everything from nuts and berries to insects. Although they are good climbers, chipmunks make networks of burrows underground. In autumn, they store food in these to last them through the winter.

HEAVYWEIGHT RODENT ▲
The capybara is a cavy-like rodent from South America. It is the largest rodent of all – adult males can reach 1.4 m (4½ ft) long and weigh up to 66 kg (145 lb). Capybaras are superb swimmers, and they spend a lot of their time in water. If they spot a predator, they usually head for the nearest river or pool to escape.

FIND OUT MORE ▸▸ Animal Homes 48–49 • Defence 42–43 • Mammals 240–241 • Mice 304 • Squirrels 303

SQUIRRELS

To most people, the word squirrel conjures up an image of a bushy-tailed, tree-climbing animal that eats nuts. Many squirrels are like this, but many others in this group of rodents live on the ground and in burrows. These squirrels feed on grasses, other low-growing plants, and sometimes invertebrates. Squirrels are found on every continent, apart from Australia and Antarctica.

Front paws clasp food

Standing up provides a better view of the area

Feet have sharp claws to grip tree bark

Long, bushy tail balances the squirrel when running swiftly through trees

▲ TUFTY-TAILED SQUIRREL
The grey squirrel is a typical tree squirrel. Like most tree squirrels, it builds a nest called a drey high up in the branches. Tree squirrels use dreys for giving birth, hiding young, and sheltering during bad weather. Many tree squirrels collect and bury nuts and seeds in the autumn. During winter, they seek out these food stores and dig them up.

Thick fur to keep the body warm

COMMUNAL LIVING ▶
Most ground squirrels are very sociable and live in organized communities. These black-tailed prairie dogs from North America live in large groups called towns. These are made up of numerous smaller groups called coteries, each of which includes a male, several females, and their offspring. Each coterie inhabits and protects its own network of tunnels, and grazes the land above it.

▲ GROUNDHOG
Also known as the woodchuck, the groundhog is a large rodent, growing up to 70 cm (2⅓ ft) long. It lives in North America, preferring grassy areas that are interspersed with trees and bushes. Unlike other ground squirrels, the groundhog spends much of its life alone. It feeds on seeds, plants, grasshoppers, and snails.

Front teeth have very sharp edges

Lower jaw is joined to the rest of the skull by strong muscles

Fur traps air to provide waterproofing and insulation

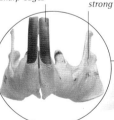

DAM BUILDER ▶
Beavers build larger structures than any animals apart from humans. Using their sharp, gnawing teeth, they cut down trees to dam rivers, and create their own lakes to live in. Beaver dams can be enormous – the longest ever measured was 700 m (2,300 ft). Beavers feed on leafy plants in summer, but survive on tree bark through the winter.

FIND OUT MORE ▶▶ Animal Homes **48–49** • Behaviour **32–33** • Coniferous Forests **65** • Mammals **240–41**

MICE

Mice and their relatives make up more than half of all rodents and a quarter of all mammals. This group includes rats, lemmings, hamsters, voles, jerboas, and gerbils. Most are nocturnal and many feed on seeds. Mice are characterized by their pointed faces and long whiskers. Some species are great travellers and extremely adaptable. The house mouse has even reached Antarctica – it is the only mammal, apart from humans, to live on every continent.

Pointed snout with whiskers to sense surroundings

Light brown fur camouflages the mouse among dry plant stems

HOUSE MOUSE

◄ FAST BREEDER
Like other rodents, mice can produce large numbers of young frequently. Most species have at least three young in every litter, and some can produce as many as 14 litters a year. Rodent babies are born without fur and with their eyes closed, but they grow up quickly. The Norway lemming, for example, can start breeding at just two weeks old.

◄ AGILE CLIMBER
The Eurasian harvest mouse is one of the smallest rodents of all, weighing just 5-7 g ($\frac{3}{16}$-$\frac{1}{4}$ oz). It lives across Europe and Asia, as far east as Taiwan. As its name suggests, the harvest mouse is often found in fields of wheat and other cereal crops. It builds a ball-shaped nest of woven grass far enough off the ground to be out of reach of most predators.

Prehensile (grasping) tail helps the mouse to climb stalk

▲ RATS ON THE RAMPAGE
Rats are larger, heavier-bodied versions of mice. Many rats, including these black rats in India, are opportunists, quickly taking advantage of new sources of food. The fleas that live on black rats can carry human diseases, including bubonic plague, which has killed millions of people throughout history.

▲ LEAPING GERBIL
There are 111 species of gerbil. This is a Mongolian gerbil, which is one of several species that are kept as pets. In the wild, gerbils are usually nocturnal and live in dry habitats in Africa and parts of Asia. They get all the moisture they need from the dew on the seeds that they eat. Unlike many other rodents in this group, gerbils have fur-covered tails.

A MYRIAD OF MICE

SPINY MOUSE
This species takes its name from the short, stiff hairs on its back. The spiny mouse lives in dry habitats, and has adapted for life without regular water.

FIELD VOLE
Voles have rounder faces than other mouse-like rodents, and tails that are usually short and hairy. The field vole lives in Europe and Asia. It feeds on grass and leaves.

HAMSTER
A popular pet, the golden hamster lives in the wild in Syria. It is a burrowing animal with a round body, short legs, and a short tail. It uses its cheek pouches to carry food.

BROWN RAT
This species originated in Central Asia, but is now found almost worldwide. The brown rat has adapted well to city life – it even lives in sewers.

FIND OUT MORE ►► Animal Homes 48–49 • Deciduous Forests 64 • Deserts 58–59 • Fleas 109 • Polar Regions 70

RABBITS

Rabbits and their relatives, hares and pikas, belong to a group of mammals called lagomorphs. They have three sets of front teeth (incisors) that grow continuously. Two pairs, one behind the other, are located at the top of the mouth; the other pair is at the bottom. Although there are just 83 species in this group, these plant-eating mammals are found in a huge range of habitats, from deserts to icy mountain peaks. Rabbits are native to North and South America, Africa, Europe, and Asia.

Long legs for running and hopping

Long, black-tipped ears often detect predators before they attack

Front paws are used to box in the breeding season

Tawny fur provides warmth and camouflage

▲ HAYMAKER
Pikas have shorter legs and more rounded ears than rabbits. These small lagomorphs live in eastern Europe, Asia, and parts of North America. A few species live in deserts, but most, including this North American pika, are mountain dwellers. They spend much time in late summer and autumn collecting grass and other vegetation, which they make into haystacks to feed them through the winter.

Ears can move independently

◄ BIG EARS
Rabbits are often kept as pets. Some have been bred to look very unlike their wild ancestors, with long fur and floppy ears. This species, the European rabbit, has been introduced to many parts of the world. A speedy breeder, it is quick to establish itself in a new environment, so it is regarded as a pest in many countries, including Australia.

▲ HOPPING HARE
Hares are usually larger than rabbits. The brown hare spends its entire life above ground. Baby hares, known as leverets, are born in a flattened area of grass called a form. Leverets are born with their eyes open and are covered with fur. If the form is discovered by a predator, the leverets scatter.

Entrance is one of many

▼ RABBIT WARREN
European rabbits live in groups of up to 30 adult males (bucks), females (does), and young. These groups live in communal burrow networks called warrens, which are excavated by the females. Baby rabbits are called kittens, and are blind and helpless at birth. The position of each rabbit within a group is set by play-fighting when they are young.

FIND OUT MORE ▶▶ Adaptation **18–19** • Animal Homes **48–49** • Mammals **240–241** • Rodents **302**

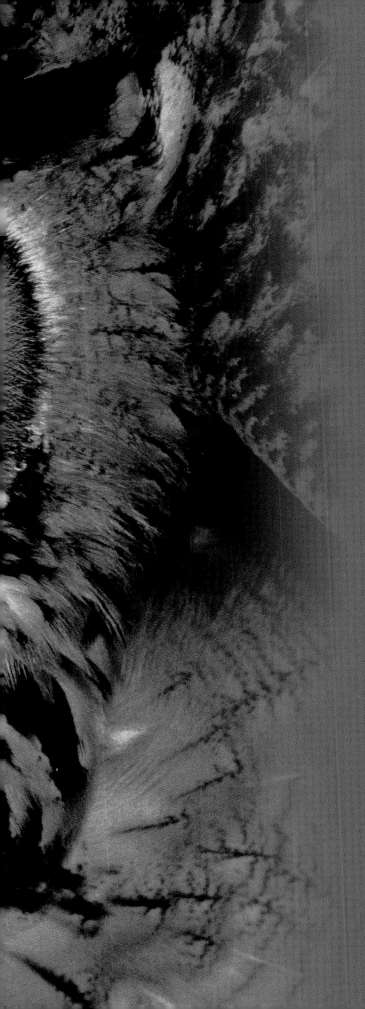

REFERENCE

◄ SILENT PREDATOR
Like most owls, the Cape eagle owl has keen
night vision and excellent hearing. It is a
fierce hunter, silently sweeping down on
outstretched wings, to grab its prey in its
powerful talons. It roosts in rocky outcrops
near grasslands and scrub in southern and
central Africa, where it hunts insects, lizards,
bats, rodents, and rabbits. There are over 200
different owl species around the world.

INVERTEBRATES

More than 95 per cent of all animals are invertebrates. They lack bones of any kind. There are 32 major groups, or phyla, of invertebrates – the main ones are shown below.

SPONGES — Phylum Porifera

Classes 4	Orders 18
Families 80	Species c. 5,000–10,000

CNIDARIANS — Phylum Cnidaria

Classes 4	Orders 27
Families 235	Species c. 9,400

Including: sea anemones, corals, and jellyfish

JELLYFISH   SEA ANEMONE

COMB JELLIES — Phylum Ctenophora

Classes 2	Orders 8
Families 27	Species c. 100

ROTIFERS — Phylum Rotifera

Classes 3	Orders 5
Families 20	Species c. 2,000

FLATWORMS — Phylum Platyhelminthes

Classes 4	Orders 35
Families 360	Species c. 17,500

ROUNDWORMS — Phylum Nematoda

Classes 4	Orders 20
Families 185	Species c. 20,000

HORSEHAIR WORMS — Phylum Nematomorpha

Classes 2	Orders 2
Families 5	Species c. 240

SPINY-HEADED WORMS — Phylum Acanthocephala

Classes 3	Orders 4
Families 18	Species c. 1,000

SEGMENTED WORMS — Phylum Annelida

Classes 3	Orders 31
Families 130	Species c. 15,000

MOLLUSCS — Phylum Mollusca

Classes 8 *(including those listed below)*	Orders 48
Families 232	Species c. 100,000

CUTTLEFISH

GARDEN SNAIL

CEPHALOPODS

Class Cephalopoda   Species c. 660
Including: octopuses, squid, cuttlefish, and nautiluses

BIVALVES

Class Bivalvia   Species c. 15,000
Including: clams, scallops, mussels, and oysters

GASTROPODS

Class Gastropoda   Species c. 75,000
Including: snails, slugs, and cone shells

CLASSIFICATION

All animals on Earth, from tiny worms to human beings, are organized using a system called classification. This groups animals together according to their genetic make up, evolution (how they developed), and behaviour. The largest groups used to arrange animals are called phyla (singular, phylum). Other groups are known as subphyla (singular, subphylum), classes, orders, and families.

WATER BEARS — Phylum Tardigrada

Classes 3	Orders 1
Families 17	Species c. 750

VELVET WORMS — Phylum Onychophora

Classes 1	Orders 1
Families 2	Species c. 100

ARTHROPODS

Phylum Arthropoda   Species c. 1.1 million

CHELICERATES — Subphylum Chelicerata

Classes 3	Orders 14
Families 480	Species c. 77,500

ARACHNIDS

Class Arachnida   Species c. 75,500
Including the following groups: spiders, web-making spiders, scorpions, whip-scorpions, ticks and mites, and harvestmen

SEA SPIDERS

Class Pycnogonida   Species c. 1,000

HORSESHOE CRABS

Class Merostomata   Species 4

CRAB SPIDER

MANDIBULATES — Subphylum Mandibulata

Classes 6 *(including those listed below)*	Orders 85
Families 1,660	Species c. 1 million

INSECTS

Class Insecta   Species c. 1 million
Including the following groups: dragonflies, mayflies, crickets, stick insects, praying mantises, cockroaches, true bugs, beetles, flies, butterflies, fleas, lice, bees, wasps, ants, and termites   FULGORID PLANTHOPPER

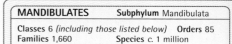

CENTIPEDES

Class Chilopoda   Species c. 3,000

MILLIPEDES

Class Diplopoda   Species c. 10,000

CRUSTACEANS — Subphylum Crustacea

Classes 10	Orders 45
Families 540	Species c. 40,000

CRABS, LOBSTERS, AND PRAWNS

Class Malacostraca   Species c. 20,000

COPEPODS, BARNACLES, AND FISH LICE

Class Cirripedia   Species c. 1,000

MUSSEL SHRIMPS

Class Ostracoda   Species c. 6,000

SQUAT LOBSTER

CHORDATES   Phylum Chordata

A chordate's body has a long rod, or notochord, which provides strength and support. Chordates represent less than five per cent of all animals. They include simple animals, like sea squirts, as well as complex animals, such as mammals, birds, reptiles, fish, and amphibians.

INVERTEBRATE CHORDATES

Around 1,300 species of animal possess a notochord (strengthening rod), but lack a backbone. They all live in the sea, and are fairly small. Some burrow in sand or mud, while others stick to rocks or simply float.

TUNICATES   Subphylum Urochordata

Classes 3	Orders 8
Families 45	Species c. 2,100

LANCELETS   Subphylum Cephalochordata

Classes 1	Orders 1
Families 3	Species c. 24

VERTEBRATES   Subphylum Vertebrata

Classes 7	Orders 129
Families 915	Species c. 51,000

FISH

Fish are an informal collection of aquatic animals, most of which are covered with scales and can breathe underwater using specialized organs called gills. They are split into three main groups.

JAWLESS FISH

Class Agnatha   Species c. 90
hagfish and lampreys

CARTILAGINOUS FISH

Class Chondrichthyes   Species c. 800
sharks, rays, and chimaeras

BONY FISH

Class Osteichthys   Species c. 23,000
Including the following groups:
fleshy-finned fish
sturgeon
bony-tongued fish
eels
herrings
cod
flatfish
carp
catfish
salmon
seahorses
cichlids

CONGER EEL

STRIPED FACE UNICORN FISH

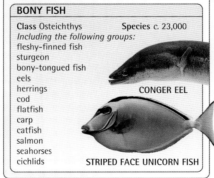

AMPHIBIANS

Class Amphibia   Species c. 5,000
Including the following groups:
frogs and toads
salamanders
caecilians

TREE FROG

REPTILES

Class Reptilia   Species c. 8,000
Including the following groups:
turtles
tuataras
crocodilians
lizards (iguanas, chameleons, agamids, geckos,
    skinks, and monitor lizards)
snakes (boas, pythons, colubrids,
    cobras, and vipers)

SUNBEAM SNAKE

MATAMATA TURTLE

BIRDS

Class Aves   Species c. 10,000
Including the following groups:
flightless birds
penguins
divers
grebes
albatrosses
pelicans
herons and storks
flamingos
wildfowl
birds of prey
gamebirds
cranes
bustards
rails
shorebirds
parrots
cuckoos
pigeons
owls
nightjars
hummingbirds
swifts
trogons
kingfishers
woodpeckers
perching birds (*including:* crows, birds of
    paradise, thrushes, starlings,
    swallows, sparrows, weavers,
    New World blackbirds,
    finches, wrens, larks,
    tits, and warblers)

SCARLET IBIS

TAWNY OWL

RED-BILLED BLUE MAGPIE

MAMMALS

Class Mammalia   Species c. 5,000
Including the following groups:
egg-laying mammals (echidnas and
    duck-billed platypuses)
marsupials (*including:* kangaroos, koalas,
    wombats, possums, and opossums)
anteaters
sloths
armadillos
aardvarks
pangolins
insectivores
tree shrews
bats
primates (bushbabies, lorises, pottos,
    lemurs, monkeys, gibbons,
    orangutans, gorillas, chimps,
    and humans)
cats (*including:* small cats, leopards,
    lions, tigers, and other big cats)
mongooses
dogs (*including:* foxes and wolves)
bears
raccoons
weasels
badgers
otters
seals (*including:* sea lions)
walruses
whales
dolphins
seacows
elephants
hoofed mammals (*including:* horses, zebras,
    rhinoceroses, pigs, hippopotamuses,
    camels, deer, giraffes, antelopes,
    cattle, goats, and sheep)
rodents (*including:* squirrels and mice)
rabbits (*including:* hares and pikas)

FRANQUET'S EPAULETTED BAT

COMMON SQUIRREL MONKEY

EUROPEAN POLECAT

WHITE BENGAL TIGER

▲ ORGANIZING ANIMALS

The position of any animal in the classification system may change as we learn more about them. Recently the African elephant was recognized as two separate species – the one in this image is the African savanna elephant, and the other is the African forest elephant.

BRYOZOANS   Phylum Bryozoa

Classes 2	Orders 5
Families 160	Species c. 4,000

BRACHIOPODS   Phylum Brachiopoda

Classes 2	Orders 5
Families 21	Species c. 350

ECHINODERMS   Phylum Echinodermata

Classes 6 (*including those listed below*)	Orders 36
Families 145	Species c. 6,000

SEA URCHIN

SEA URCHINS

Class Echinoidea   Species c. 975

STARFISH

Class Asteroidea   Species c. 1,500

SEA CUCUMBERS

Class Holothuroidea   Species c. 1,150

BRITTLE STARS

Class Ophiuroidea   Species c. 2,000

MINOR PHYLA

There are also 16 other minor phyla of invertebrates, which contain a total of about 2,000 species.

KEY

◯ Phylum   ◯ Subphylum   ◯ Class

FIND OUT MORE ▸▸ Anatomy **26–27** • Animal Characteristics **10–11** • Animal Kingdom **12–13** • Evolution **16–17**

GLOSSARY

Abdomen The part of an animal's body that contains its digestive and reproductive organs. An insect's abdomen is the last of its three body sections.

Adaptation Any feature that helps a living thing to survive. Adaptations are produced by the process of evolution. They shape an animal's body, and also the way it works.

Alpha male The dominant male in a social group of animals.

Amphibian A vertebrate that lives partly in water and partly on land. Frogs, toads, newts, and salamanders are all amphibians. Most amphibians mate and lay eggs in water, but some make nests on land.

Amplexus A breeding position, used by frogs and toads, in which the male uses its front legs to hold onto the female's body.

Animal A multi-celled organism, usually with muscle and nerve tissues that allow it to react to its environment. Animals make up Animalia, one of the five kingdoms of the living world in scientific classification.

Antenna (plural antennae) Pairs of long sense organs on an arthropod's head. Antennae are commonly known as feelers, but they are often used for taste and smell, as well as for touch.

Arachnid An invertebrate with four pairs of legs. Arachnids include spiders, scorpions, and mites, and most of them live on land.

Arthropod An invertebrate with a jointed body case, or exoskeleton. Arthropods include insects, crustaceans, and arachnids. They are the most numerous animals on Earth.

Backbone A flexible chain of bones running down the body of a vertebrate; also known as the spine.

Bacteria A group of microscopic, single-celled organisms.

Baleen A fibrous substance found in the upper jaw of large whales. Baleen grows in plates that have brush-like edges, and whales use these to filter their food from the water.

Barbel A sensitive filament that is attached to an animal's lips or mouth. Many bottom-dwelling fish use barbels to feel for food.

Binocular vision A type of sight that uses two eyes facing forwards, providing an overlapping view. This kind of vision allows animals to judge depth.

Bioluminescence The production of light by living things. Bioluminescence is common in deepsea animals and insects, such as fireflies and glow-worms.

Bivalve A mollusc with a shell made of two parts, joined together by a hinge. Clams, mussels, and oysters are examples of bivalves.

Blowhole The nostrils of whales and dolphins, which are positioned on top of the head. The blowhole is used for breathing, and it can be closed when the animal dives.

Breed A variety of domestic animal, such as a German shepherd dog or a Siamese cat. Breeds are produced by selecting parents with particular features, such as long legs or soft fur.

Browser A plant-eating animal, such as a deer, that nibbles leaves and twigs, instead of feeding on grass.

Buoyancy The ability of something to float. Many fish can adjust their buoyancy so that they neither rise nor sink.

Camouflage The colours, patterns, shapes, or behaviour that helps an animal to blend in with its surroundings. Some animals, such as stick insects, are camouflaged to resemble inedible objects.

Canine teeth Teeth with a single sharp point, positioned near the front of the jaws of mammals. Canines are used for piercing and gripping prey.

Canopy The layer of interlocking branches high above the ground in a forest.

Captive breeding A way of helping endangered animals by breeding them in captivity. Sometimes their young are released back into the wild.

Carapace A hard shield on the back of an animal's body, or the outermost layer of a turtle's or crab's shell.

Carnivore A mammal with specially shaped teeth that feeds mainly on meat. The word carnivore can also be used in a more general way, to mean any meat-eating animal.

Carrion The remains of dead animals. Scavengers, such as vultures, specialize in eating this kind of food.

Cartilage A tough flexible substance, also known as gristle, which vertebrates have in their skeletons. In most vertebrates, cartilage lines the joints, but some fish, for example, sharks and rays, have cartilaginous skeletons instead of bone.

Caterpillar The wingless larva of a butterfly or a moth.

Cell The basic building block of all living matter. Sponges, the simplest animals, are little more than a loose group of cells, but mammals are made up of millions of cells, organized into different tissues, organs, and body systems.

Cellulose A substance that plants make, and use as a building material. Cellulose is difficult for animals to digest, and most need bacteria in their guts to break it down.

Cephalopod A mollusc with a large head and a ring of tentacles, such as octopus, cuttlefish, and squid.

Cephalothorax In crustaceans and arachnids, the front section of the body, which combines the head and the thorax.

Chordate An animal that has a strong, flexible rod called a notochord running down its body. Chordates include vertebrates and some invertebrates, for example, sea squirts.

Chrysalis The hard and often shiny case that protects the pupa of a butterfly or moth.

Class In scientific classification, a group that is one step up from an order. Mammals, insects, amphibians, and bivalves are examples of classes.

Classification A way of identifying and grouping living things. Classification starts with basic units called species, which are single kinds of living things. Species are arranged in a series of larger groups, called genera, families, orders, classes, and phyla. At the top are kingdoms, which are the largest groups of all. Classification helps to show how different species are related through evolution.

Cnidarian An invertebrate with a hollow body that has a single opening, the mouth, which is ringed by stinging tentacles. Cnidarians include corals, sea anemones, and jellyfish.

Cocoon A silk case that insects and spiders make to protect themselves or their eggs. Many caterpillars spin a cocoon before they turn into a pupa.

Colony A group of animals of the same species that lives together. Some colony-forming animals, such as corals, are physically attached. Others, such as bees and ants, move about on their own, but live together in a complex society.

Compound eye An eye that is divided into lots of separate units, each with their own set of lenses. Compound eyes are found in many arthropods, including insects.

Conifer A tree or shrub that reproduces by forming cones. Male cones release pollen and females produce seeds.

Coral An aquatic animal that catches its food using stinging tentacles. Some corals live on their own, but many hard corals form colonies that help to build coral reefs.

Crop A part of the digestive system, particularly in birds, which stores food after it has been swallowed.

Crustacean An invertebrate with a hard exoskeleton, jointed legs, and two pairs of antennae. Most crustaceans live in water. They include lobsters, crabs, and barnacles.

Deciduous A tree or shrub that loses all its leaves once a year. In parts of the world with cold winters, deciduous trees lose their leaves in autumn, and grow a new set in spring.

Denticles Small, tooth-like projections in the skin of sharks and rays and on the radula (tongue) of molluscs.

Diurnal Active during the day and inactive at night.

DNA (deoxyribonucleic acid) A chemical found in all living things. DNA stores the information needed to build living things, and also to make them work. When living things breed, their DNA is copied and handed on to their young.

Domesticated animal An animal that has been bred and raised under human control. Domesticated animals include those that are raised for food, such as sheep, pigs, and cows, and those that are kept as pets,.

Echinoderm A marine invertebrate with a chalky skeleton and a body that is divided into five similar parts. Echinoderms include starfish, sea urchins, and sea cucumbers.

Echolocation A way of sensing objects by producing high-pitched sounds that bounce off objects and prey. Bats use echolocation to navigate and hunt in the dark, and some whales and dolphins use it in water.

Ecology The study of the relationships between living things, and between living things and their environment.

Ecosystem A collection of living things and their environment. An ecosystem can be as small as a pond, or as big as a forest.

Ectothermic An animal whose body temperature varies with its surroundings. Ectothermic animals include reptiles, amphibians, and fish. They are also known as cold-blooded animals.

Egg A female sex cell. After it has been fertilized by a male cell, it develops into a new animal.

Embryo A young animal at a very early stage of its development.

Endothermic An animal whose body temperature stays warm and steady, instead of varying with the temperature of its surroundings. Endothermic animals include birds and mammals, and are also known as warm-blooded animals.

Environment The physical setting inhabited by a single living thing, or by all the living things in any particular place.

Equator An imaginary line that circles the Earth midway between the North and South Poles. The climate at the Equator is warm all year round.

Evergreen A tree or shrub that has leaves throughout the year.

Evolution A gradual process of change and development that enables a species to adapt to particular circumstances and environments. Evolution takes place over many generations. It shapes the way animals look, and also the way that they behave.

Exoskeleton A hard, outer skeleton that surrounds an animal's body.

Extinction The complete and permanent disappearance of a species.

Family In scientific classification, the next group up from a genus. Rhinoceroses and gibbons are two examples of families.

Fang A long, sharp tooth with a single point. Some poisonous snakes and spiders have hollow fangs that inject venom into their prey. Carnivorous mammals usually have two pairs of fangs called canines.

Feral animal An animal that has escaped or been released from domestication and taken up life in the wild. Feral animals include many different species, including cats and horses.

Fertilization The moment when a male and female sex cell join together to produce a new living thing. In animals, fertilization occurs either inside the mother's body, as in the case of mammals, or outside it, as in the case of most fish.

Filter feeder An animal that eats by sieving its food from water. Filter feeders include many invertebrates, and also flamingos and whales.

Foetus A young mammal that is well developed in its mother's uterus, but that is still not ready to be born.

Food chain A food pathway that connects several different species. On land, most food chains begin with plants. Food passes from plants to animals, and then from one animal to another as predators feed on their prey.

Food web A collection of interconnected food chains in a particular habitat.

Fossil Evidence of past life that has been preserved in rock, amber, or ice.

Fungus (plural fungi) A living thing that absorbs nutrients from its surroundings. Fungi feed on living or dead matter, and they make up one of the kingdoms of the living world. Moulds, mushrooms, and toadstools are fungi.

Gastropod A mollusc with a sucker-like foot, for example, a snail or a slug.

Gene A chemical instruction that helps to build a living thing, or to make it work. Genes are inherited by offspring when living things breed. They are stored within cells.

Genus (plural genera) In scientific classification, the next step up from a species. For example, *Felis* (small cats) and *Panthera* (big cats).

Gills Organs that are used for breathing underwater. Fish and some amphibians have them on the sides of their heads, but insects have them at the end of their abdomen.

Grazer An animal that feeds mainly or entirely on grass.

Grooming Behaviour that animals use to clean themselves or each other and to remove dead skin, dirt, and parasites.

Grub The legless larva of an insect, such as a beetle.

Habitat The natural home of any particular species. A habitat provides animals with somewhere to live and the food that they need to survive.

Halteres In true flies, two knob-like organs that take the place of working hindwings. Halteres help flies to balance during flight.

Herbivore An animal that feeds on plants.

Hermaphrodite An animal that has both male and female reproductive organs. Examples of hermaphrodites include earthworms and garden snails.

Hibernation A winter rest that resembles a long and very deep sleep. Hibernation helps some animals to survive at a time of year when food is hard to find.

Host An animal used by a parasite for food. Some parasites have a single host, while others need more than one kind to complete their life cycle successfully.

Incisor A chisel-shaped tooth with a straight cutting edge, positioned at the front of a mammal's jaw. Mammals use their incisors to bite off food, gnaw, and groom.

Incubate To hatch eggs by sitting on them. When birds incubate their eggs, the parent's body keeps the eggs warm so that they can develop and hatch.

Insect An animal with six legs and often two pairs of wings. Insects are invertebrates that belong to a group of animals called arthropods. They breed rapidly, and are some of the most numerous animals on Earth.

Instinct Any kind of behaviour that animals carry out automatically, without having to learn. Instinct controls simple actions, such as swimming or grooming, and also much more complex ones, such as courtship or migration.

Insulation Any covering that helps to stop an animal's body getting too cold or too warm. Fur, feathers, and blubber are all forms of insulation.

Invertebrate An animal that does not have a backbone or a bony skeleton. Invertebrates are often small, but they outnumber vertebrates many times over. Invertebrates include insects, crustaceans, and molluscs.

Kingdom In classification, the highest grouping of living things. Most biologists recognize five kingdoms: animals, plants, fungi, single-celled organisms, and bacteria.

Larva (plural larvae) The young, immature stage of certain animals, such as amphibians and insects. A larva looks quite different to its parents, and often feeds in a different way. For example, a tadpole is the lava of a frog.

Lens A transparent structure that focuses light inside an animal's eye. Mammals have flexible lenses, which can change shape to focus light from objects that are near or far away.

Mammal An animal with hair or fur that feeds its young on milk. Most mammals give birth to live young, but a few species – called monotremes – lay eggs.

Mammary gland A gland that produces milk in a female mammal.

Marsupial A mammal that develops inside its mother's pouch. Marsupials are found in Australia and North and South America.

Melanism An unusually dark form of an animal, produced by the natural pigment melanin. Melanism is common in butterflies and moths, and it can also be seen in mammals, such as black jaguars (panthers).

Metamorphosis A change in body shape as a young animal develops into an adult. Metamorphosis is common in invertebrates, and also in fish and amphibians. Incomplete metamorphosis happens gradually and the changes are quite small. Complete metamorphosis involves more drastic changes, for example the change from a caterpillar to a butterfly, and happens during a resting stage called a pupa.

Migration The mass movement of animals from one place to another to find food or to breed. Animals migrate in step with the seasons, travelling between their winter and summer homes.

Molar Crushing teeth in the cheeks of mammals.

Mollusc A soft-bodied invertebrate that is often protected by a hard shell. Snails, slugs, oysters, clams, and octopuses are all examples of molluscs.

Monotreme A mammal that lays eggs instead of giving birth to live young, such as the duck-billed platypus and echidnas. Monotremes are found only in Australia and New Guinea.

Moulting Shedding a body covering so that it can be renewed or replaced. Arthropods have to moult their exoskeletons so that they can grow. Mammals often moult their fur seasonally, replacing a summer coat with a winter one. Birds moult and replace their feathers due to wear and tear.

Muscle A body tissue that can contract and relax, making part of an animal move. Muscles are controlled by an animal's nerves.

Mutation A sudden alteration in one or more genes. Mutations can change the way living things look or work. Some of these changes can be harmful, but others provide useful benefits and help living things to evolve.

Mutualism A close relationship between two different living things in which both partners benefit. Sometimes both partners are animals; in other cases, one is an animal and the other a plant.

Natural selection One of the processes that drives evolution. Natural selection takes place because individuals vary and because living things reproduce. Parents better adapted to their environment produce more young that survive and produce offspring of their own. Over the generations, their useful features become more widespread, making their species change.

Nectar A sugary liquid that plants make to attract insects to their flowers.

Nerve A bundle of specialized cells that carry signals around an animal's body. Nerves carry information from sense organs to an animal's brain. They also carry signals from the brain that make muscles move.

Nocturnal Active at night.

Notochord A flexible strengthening rod that runs the length of the body. It is present in vertebrates during development, but is replaced by the backbone.

Nutrient Any substance that a living thing needs to stay alive.

Nymph A young insect that develops by incomplete metamorphosis. Nymphs look similar to their parents, but they do not have working wings or reproductive organs.

Omnivore An animal that eats both plant and animal food.

Operculum A flap of flexible skin that can close to cover a fish's gills. Many fish open and close this flap rhythmically, pumping water through the gills so that they can breathe.

Opposable thumb A thumb that can be pressed against the fingers. Many primates have opposable thumbs, enabling them to grasp objects with precision.

Order In scientific classification, the next step up from a family. Parrots and beetles are two examples of orders.

Pack A group of carnivores, for example wolves, which live and hunt as a team. In a wolf pack, only the dominant (alpha) male and female breed.

Parasite A living thing that lives on or inside another species, known as its host. Parasites often have complicated life cycles, and produce large numbers of eggs or young.

Passerine bird A bird with feet that are adapted for perching on branches and twigs. Passerines make up over half the world's birds, and they include all songbirds.

Pedipalps A pair of leg-like structures on an arachnid's head. A scorpion's pincers are extra-large pedipalps, used for grasping prey.

Pheromone A chemical produced by one animal that has an effect on others of its species. Pheromones are often spread by touch, or through the air.

Phylum (plural phyla) In scientific classification, the first step down from a kingdom. The animal kingdom contains about 30 phyla, such as molluscs, arthropods, and chordates.

Phytoplankton Plant-like microorganisms that live in the oceans and in fresh water.

Placenta An organ in mammals that allows the young to develop inside their mother's body. In the placenta, nutrients and oxygen pass from the mother's blood into the blood of her young, and waste products and carbon dioxide pass out.

Plankton Small or microscopic plants and animals that drift in open water. Plankton is an important source of food for many animals, including fish, seabirds, and whales.

Pollination The transfer from flower to flower of pollen, a dust-like substance that contains a plant's male sex cells, so that plants can make seeds. Pollination is often carried out by animals that visit flowers to feed.

Polyp An animal with a hollow body and a ring of tentacles around its mouth. This body shape is found in cnidarians, such as corals and sea anemones.

Pore A small opening on an animal's surface.

Predator An animal that kills and eats others. Some predators lie in wait for their prey, but most predators actively hunt their food.

Prehensile The ability to grasp an object. Many animals, including monkeys, have prehensile tails.

Prey An animal that is killed and eaten by a predator.

Primate A mammal, such as an ape or a monkey, with forward-facing eyes. Most primates live in trees.

Proboscis The scientific word for a long flexible snout or mouthpart, such as a butterfly's tongue or an elephant's trunk.

Protein A substance made by living things that is essential for life. There are thousands of different proteins, and they work in many different ways. For example, some act as building materials within an animal's body, while others help to speed up chemical reactions.

Pupa (plural pupae) A resting stage in the life cycle of some insects. Inside a pupa, a larva's body is broken down, and an adult is assembled in its place – a change called complete metamorphosis.

Queen In social insects, such as bees and ants, the queen is the founder of a colony. The queen is looked after by her workers, and she produces all the colony's young.

Radula The mouthpart used by molluscs to scrape away at food. The radula is shaped like a narrow belt and is covered with microscopic tooth-like structures called denticles.

Raptor Another word for a bird of prey. Raptors catch other animals with their claws, and often carry them away to feed.

Reproduction The production of offspring. Reproduction is a key feature of animals, and of all other living things.

Reptile A vertebrate, such as a snake or a lizard, with scaly skin. Reptiles are ectothermic, or cold-blooded, and most of them reproduce by laying eggs.

Respiration In cells, the chemical process that releases energy from food, by combining it with oxygen.

Retina The membrane that lines the back of the eye. It is packed with nerve cells that detect light and send signals to the brain to form an image.

Rodent A mammal with sharp, continually growing incisor teeth that are used for gnawing. Rats, mice, chipmunks, and squirrels are all rodents.

Ruminant A plant-eating mammal that has a four-chambered stomach to digest its food. Ruminants include deer, cattle, and sheep, and they often live in herds.

Scales Small overlapping plates that cover and protect an animal's skin.

Scavenger An animal that feeds on the remains of dead animals or plants.

Scent gland A gland that gives off pheromones or other airborne chemicals.

Animals often use scent to attract partners, to mark their territories, or to communicate with other members of their species.

Selective breeding Breeding that is controlled by humans, using parents that have been selected for particular features. Over many generations, selective breeding can produce breeds of animals and plants that are not found in the wild.

Silk An elastic material that can be spun into slender strands. Spiders make their webs out of silk, and some insect larvae use silk to make cocoons.

Simple eye An eye that has a single lens. Simple eyes are found in vertebrates and cephalopods, such as squid. Despite their name, they can be the most complex sense organs in an animal's body.

Snout An elongated part of an animal's head, including the mouth and nose.

Soldier In ant and termite colonies, a soldier is a specialized worker that defends the nest.

Species A group of similar living things that can breed together in the wild, producing young that look like themselves. The species is the basic group used in scientific classification. Each one is identified by its own scientific name, which is used and recognized by scientists all over the world.

Swim bladder A gas-filled bag, positioned below the backbone, which many fish use to adjust their buoyancy.

Symbiosis A close relationship between two different species, particularly the kind where both species benefit.

Tadpole The larva of an amphibian, such as a frog or a toad.

Talons Sharp claws that birds of prey and owls use to catch and kill other animals.

Teat A swelling that baby mammals suck to feed on their mother's milk.

Temperate A region that has a climate that never gets very hot or very cold.

Tentacle A wormlike body part that can wrap itself around solid objects, such as food. Sea anemones and their relatives have a ring of stinging tentacles around their mouth.

Territory An area that an animal claims to protect its food supply or mates, and defends against its rivals.

Thermal A column of warm rising air. Some birds, such as vultures, seek out thermals and use them to soar high in the sky.

Thermoregulation The control of body temperature. Animals control temperature in many ways – mammals, for example, cool down by producing sweat.

Thorax In insects, the thorax is the middle section of the body, which bears the legs and wings. In four-legged vertebrates, the thorax is the chest.

Troop A group of primates, particularly monkeys. The members of a troop work together to find food and defend themselves from attack.

Tropical The regions north and south of the Equator. In some tropical areas, the climate is hot and humid, but in others it can be warm and dry.

Tundra Cold, treeless parts of the world found around the polar regions.

Tusk A specialized tooth in some mammals that sticks out beyond the jaw. Mammals use tusks for defence, and sometimes for digging up food.

Umbilical cord A long rope-like connection between a female mammal and her unborn young. The umbilical cord carries blood to and from the placenta.

Ungulate A hoofed mammal.

Uterus The chamber in the body of a female mammal that contains her developing young before they are born.

Variation Visible and hidden differences between individuals in the same species. Evolution works by favouring helpful variations, and this makes them more successful in a species.

Venom A substance that is made by an animal and delivered in a bite or a sting. Many snakes use venom to kill their prey. It can affect either the nervous or the circulatory system.

Vertebrate An animal with a backbone.

Wallow To bathe in mud or shallow water. Mammals often wallow to keep their skin in good condition.

Worker An insect that lives in a colony and spends its life repairing the nest, foraging for food, and tending the colony's young. Normally, workers do not have young of their own.

INDEX

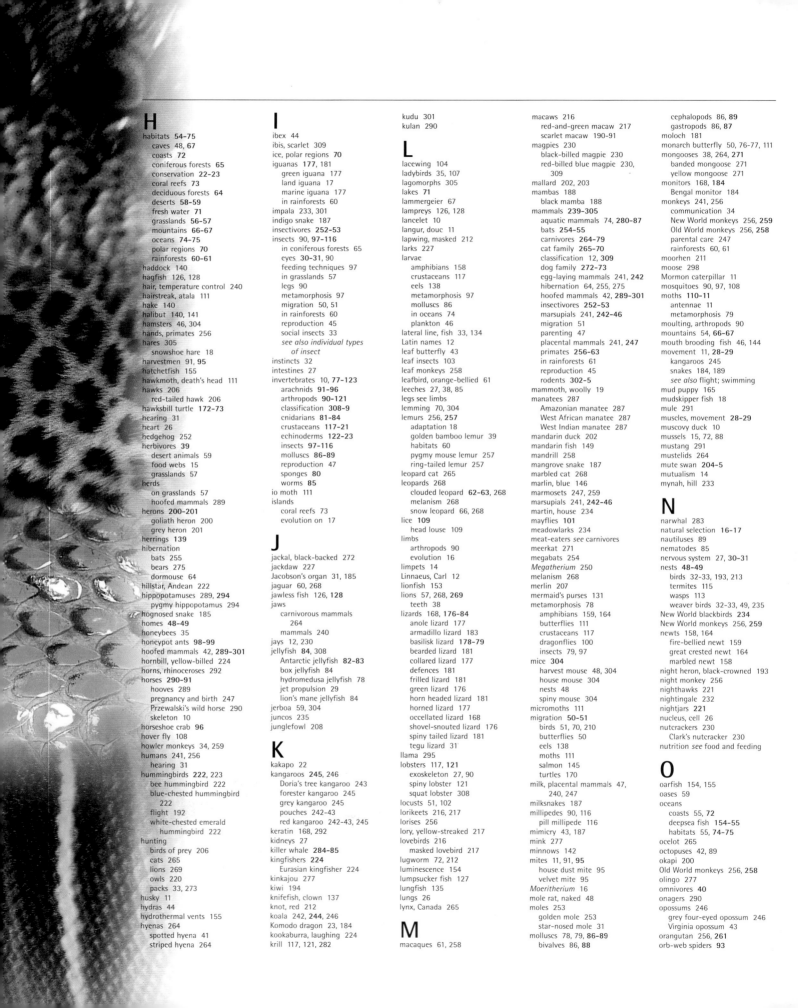

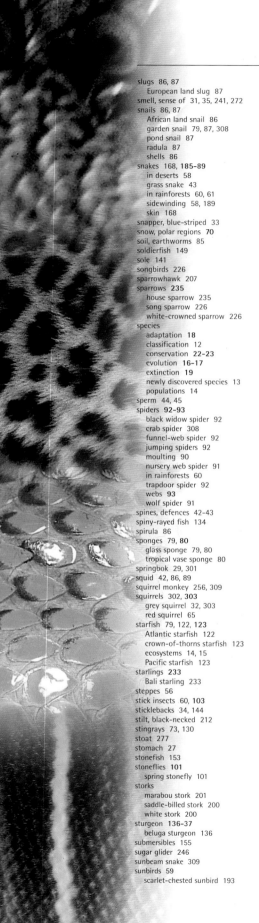

ACKNOWLEDGEMENTS

Dorling Kindersley would like to thank Polly Boyd and Lynn Bresler for proof-reading; Hilary Bird for the index; Christine Heilman for Americanization; Enosh Francis for design assistance; Robin Hunter for illustration; and Aparna Sharma for organizational assistance.

Dorling Kindersley Ltd is not responsible and does not accept liability for the availability or content of any web site other than its own, or for any exposure to offensive, harmful, or inaccurate material that may appear on the Internet. Dorling Kindersley Ltd will have no liability for any damage or loss caused by viruses that may be downloaded as a result of looking at and browsing the web sites that it recommends. Dorling Kindersley downloadable images are the sole copyright of Dorling Kindersley Ltd, and may not be reproduced, stored, or transmitted in any form or by any means for any commercial or profit-related purpose without prior written permission of the copyright owner.

Picture Credits
The publisher would like to thank the following for their kind permission to reproduce their images:

Abbreviations key:
a=above; b=bottom/below; c=centre; f=far; l=left; r=right; t=top.

2 DK Images: Tim Shepard, Oxford Scientific Films (cl). 3 DK Images: Mike Linley (cr); Natural History Museum, London (cfl). 6–7 Getty Images: Kristianbell. 8–9 Alamy Images: Steve Bloom Images. 10 Nature Picture Library: Doug Perrine (ca). 10–11 FLPA – images of nature: Jurgen & Christine Sohns. 11 DK Images: American Museum of Natural History (cr); Craig Lovell (tcl); Jerry Young (tr). N.H.P.A.: B & C Alexander (tcr). Science Photo Library: Volker Steger (br). 12 DK Images: Linnean Society of London (cfl). 13 Ardea.com: Masahiro Iijima (bcl). DK Images: Philip Dowell (cal, cl, tcl). The National Birds of Prey Centre, Gloucestershire (car, tcr); Natural History Museum, London (tr); Jerry Young (car, cbl, cl, cla, cra, tcl, tcr, tr); FLPA – images of nature: Ron Austing (br). N.H.P.A.: Mark Bowler (bc). Science Photo Library: Tek Image (cfr). 14 DK Images: Natural History Museum, London (bl). Science Photo Library: Claude Nuridsany & Marie Perennou (bcl). 14–15 Still Pictures: C & M Denis-Huot (c). 15 Science Photo Library: Jim Zipp (bl). 16–17 DK Images: Natural History Museum, London. 18 DK Images: Oxford University Museum of Natural History (c). Mary Evans Picture Library: (tl). 18–19 The Future is Wild ™: 19 DK Images: Natural History Museum, London (tr); Jerry Young (cra). FLPA – images of nature: Frans Lanting/Minden Pictures (crb). 20 N.H.P.A.: Martin Harvey (tl); Stephen Dalton (tr). 21 DK Images: Royal British Columbia Museum, Victoria, Canada (crb); Dave King/ Graham High and Centaur Studios – modelmakers (cr). N.H.P.A.: Manfred Danegger (l). 22 Nature Picture Library: Anup Shah (cl). Bruce Coleman Ltd: Gerlad Cubitt (r). FLPA – images of nature: Flip Nicklin/Minden Pictures (bl). 23 Corbis: Wendy Stone (tr). Seapics.com: Ronald Seitre (cr). N.H.P.A.: Lady Phillipa Scott (clb). Science Photo Library: Philippe Psaila (br). 24–25 Corbis: Stephen Frink. 26 Science Photo Library: John Walsh (cb). 27 DK Images: Natural History Museum, London (tl). Seapics.com: Michele Hall (tr). 29 Ardea.com: Ken Lucan (r). Corbis: John Conrad (bl); Martin Harvey; Gallo Images (tr). 30–31 Science Photo Library: David Scharf. 31 DK Images: Jerry Young (cb). Science Photo Library: Rod Planck (br). 32 DK Images: The National Birds of Prey Centre, Gloucestershire (cl). 32–33 N.H.P.A.: James Warwick. 34 Corbis: Kevin Schafer (l). Seapics.com: Doug Perrine (bc). 35 Corbis: Ron Sanford (r). Science Photo Library: David Scharf (ca). 36–37 Seapics.com: Doug Parrine. 38 FLPA – images of nature: Alan

Parker (l). N.H.P.A.: Daniel Heuclin (cb). 39 DK Images: Natural History Museum, London (cl). FLPA – images of nature: Frans Lanting/Minden Pictures (cb, tr). 40 Corbis: Joe McDonald (cl). DK Images: Natural History Museum, London (bl). FLPA – images of nature: Steven McCutcheon (cl). Getty Images: Art Wolfe (tl). 41 Alamy Images: Steve Knott (tr). Corbis: Wendy Stone (crb). 42 DK Images: Jerry Young (bl). 42–43 Powerstock: Doug Scott (c). 43 Corbis: George McCarthy (br); Joe McDonald (cra). DK Images: Natural History Museum, London (cr); Jerry Young (tr). 44 Ardea.com: Hans & Judy Beste (cl). DK Images: Geoff Brightling/Gary Stabb – modelmaker (tcr). Still Pictures: John Cancalosi (b). 45 DK Images: Peter Minister – modelmaker (tcl); Stephen Oliver (c); Steve Gorton/John Holmes – modelmaker (bc). Seapics.com: Chris Huss (b). James D. Watt (c). 46 Seapics.com: James D. Watt (c). 46–47 Alamy Images: Nancy Camel (b). 47 Corbis: Brian A. Vikander (t). 48 Corbis: Martin B. Withers; Frank Lane Picture Agency (cr). DK Images: Royal Ontario Museum, Toronto (tl). 49 DK Images: Maslowski Photo (r); Natural History Museum, London (tl – left half), (tl – right half). Jim Chamberlain – U.S. Fish & Wildlife Service: David Cline/Alaska Image Library (tcr). Nature Picture Library: Neil Bromhall (bl). 50 FLPA – images of nature: Frans Lanting/Minden Pictures (l). Nature Picture Library: Sinclair Stammers (br). 51 Alamy Images: Steve Bloom (r). Corbis: Peggy Heard; Frank Lane Picture Agency (cra). FLPA – images of nature: Flip Nicklin/Minden Pictures (crb). 52–53 Corbis: Hans Strand. 54 Alamy Images: Viennaphoto (bla). Corbis: (clb); Yann Arthus-Bertrand (tlb). 55 Alamy Images: Brandon Cole Marine Photography (bra); David Paterson (bl); Fitz Polking/ Peter Arnold Inc. (trb). Corbis: Eye Ubiquitous (crb). Nature Picture Library: Martin Dohrn (tl). 56 Corbis: Tom Brakefield (br). 56–57 Alamy Images: Steve Bloom (t). 57 Ardea.com: Jean Michel Labat (br). 58–59 Corbis: Martin Harvey; Gallo Images (t); Michael & Patricia Fogden (cl). 59 Corbis: Kenneth W. Fink (cra). FLPA – images of nature: Koos Delport (cr). 60 DK Images: Natural History Museum, London (c). 61 Ardea.com: Tom & Pat Leeson (tr). NPA Group: Daniel Heuclin (br). 62–63 FLPA – images of nature: ZSSD/Minden Pictures. 64 DK Images: Tim Shepard, Oxford Scientific Films (bl). FLPA – images of nature: John Hawkins (cl). 65 Alamy Images: Brian Lightfoot/ Nature Picture Library (br). Corbis: W. Perry Conway (tr). 66 N.H.P.A.: Andy Rouse (c). 66–67 FLPA – images of nature: Wendy Dennis (t). Still Pictures: M. Gunther (bl); Manfred Danegger (b). 67 DK Images: Natural History Museum, London (br, cb). N.H.P.A.: A.N.T Photo Library (tl). 68–69 Seapics.com: Bryan & Cherry Alexander. 70 Ardea.com: Andrey Zvoznikov (br); JeanPaul Ferrero (bc). Corbis: Kennan Ward (bl). N.H.P.A.: Bill Coster (t). 71 Corbis: Roy Morsch (b). DK Images: The National Birds of Prey Centre, Gloucestershire (tr). 72 Ardea.com: Chris Knights (tr). 73 Alamy Images: Stephen Frink Collection (br). Corbis: Yann Arthus-Bertrand (cl). Image Quest Marine: Scott Tuason (t). 74 NASA: (tl). N.H.P.A.: Image Quest Marine (cra); Rich Kirchner (cl). 74–75 Ardea.com: Douglas David Seifert (b). 75 Ardea.com: Kev Deacon (r). FLPA – images of nature: Norbert Wu/Minden Pictures (bc). Photolibrary.com: Bush Robin (tl). Still Pictures: Dino Simeonidis (c). 76–77 Corbis: Darrell Gulin. 78 Ardea.com: Ken Lucas (l). DK Images: Sedgwick Museum of Geology, Cambridge (ca); Natural History Museum, London (br). 79 DK Images: Natural History Museum, London (br, cr). 80 Corbis: Amos Nachoum (l). 81 Corbis: Stephen Frink (tr). 82–83 FLPA – images of nature: Norbert Wu. 84 DK Images: Geoff Brightling/Peter Minister – modelmaker (cla, tcl). Seapics.com: Ralf Kiefner (br). 85 DK Images: Geoff Brightling/Gary Stabb – modelmaker (c). Science Photo Library: London School of Hygiene & Tropical Medicine (br). 86 Image Quest Marine: Peter Parks (clb). 87 FLPA – images of nature: Roger Tidman (br).

Science Photo Library: Clouds Hill Imaging Ltd. (cb). 88 Corbis: Stephen Frink (l). DK Images: Natural History Museum, London (bc, car, cr). 89 Corbis: Stephen Frink (crb). DK Images: Geoff Brightling/ Peter Minister – modelmaker (bc). 90 FLPA – images of nature: Norbert Wu/Minden Pictures (crb). 91 Ardea.com: John Clegg (bl). DK Images: Natural History Museum, London (clb). N.H.P.A.: Daniel Heuclin (r). 92 Corbis: Anthony Bannister; Gallo Images (cr). 93 Corbis: Gary W. Carter (b). Science Photo Library: Claude Nuridsany & Marie Perennou (cr). 94 Ardea.com: Ian Beames (bl). DK Images: Jerry Young (tl). 95 Ardea.com: John Daniels (cr). DK Images: Geoff Brightling/Peter Minister – modelmaker (cl). Science Photo Library: Eye of Science (tr). 96 Seapics.com: John C. Lewis (tr). FLPA – images of nature: Fred Bavendam/Minden Pictures (bl). 97 DK Images: Jerry Young (cbr). 98–99 FLPA – images of nature: Mitsuhiko Imamori/Minden Pictures. 101 DK Images: Natural History Museum, London (c). 102 Corbis: Pierre Holtz/Reuters (b). Warren Photographic: Kim Taylor (tl). 103 DK Images: Jerry Young (br, cbl). 104 Corbis: Anthony Bannister; Gallo Images (bl). 105 Corbis: Mannie Garcia/Reuters (tr). 106 DK Images: Jerry Young (bc); Natural History Museum, London (bcl). 106–107 FLPA – images of nature: Mitsuhiko Imamori/ Minden Pictures (t). 107 Corbis: Pat Jerrold; Papilio (tr). DK Images: Natural History Museum, London (br); Geoff Brightling/ Peter Minister – modelmaker (tcl). 108 DK Images: Natural History Museum, London (bl, cfl); Jerry Young (clb); Steve Gorton/ Oxford University Museum of Natural History (cla). 109 DK Images: Andy Crawford/Gary Stabb – modelmaker (c, tl). Science Photo Library: CNRI (cr); Eye of Science (br); Photo Insolite Realite (bl). 110 DK Images: Natural History Museum, London (bc, bcl, bcr, br, cbr, crb, tcr, tr). Science Photo Library: Alfred Pasieka (cfr); Andrew Syred (cla). 111 DK Images: Natural History Museum, London (bl, cr, tl). N.H.P.A.: Stephen Dalton (tr). 112 FLPA – images of nature: S & D & K Maslowski (bl). N.H.P.A.: N. A. Callow (br). 115 DK Images: Natural History Museum, London (bl); Geoff Brightling/Peter Minister – modelmaker (tcr). N.H.P.A.: Daniel Heuclin (bcl). 116 RSPCA Photolibrary: Tim Martin (tr). 117 Brandon D. Cole: (bl). DK Images: Fisons (tr). 118–119 Ardea.com: M. Watson. 121 Corbis: Stuart Westmorland (cl). DK Images: Natural History Museum, London (clb). Seapics.com: Andrew J. Martinez (bc); Mark Conlin (tr). 122 Corbis: Jeffrey L. Rotman (tl). DK Images: Natural History Museum, London (cr). FLPA – images of nature: Fred Bavendam/Minden Pictures (br). 123 Corbis: Jeffrey L. Rotman (c). Seapics.com: Doug Perrine (cla). Science Photo Library: Science Pictures Limited (br). 124–125 Corbis: Bob Abraham. 126 Ardea.com: Pat Morris (cl). DK Images: Geoff Brightling/Peter Minister – modelmaker (tcr). Seapics.com: Doug Perrine (bl). 128 Ardea.com: Pat Morris (cl). Nature Picture Library: Reijo Juurinen/Naturbild (bl). 128–129 Still Pictures: Kelvin Aitken. 129 DK Images: Natural History Museum, London (br). 130 Ardea.com: Wardene Weisser (b). 131 Ardea.com: Valerie Taylor (br). Nature Picture Library: Sue Flood (t). DK Images: Natural History Museum, London (bl). 132–133 Ardea.com: Douglas David Seifert. 134 Photolibrary.com: IFA Bilderteam GMBH (bl). 134–135 DK Images: Natural History Museum, London. 135 Ardea.com: Pat Morris (br). FLPA – images of nature: Gerard Lacz (cr). 136 DK Images: Natural History Museum, London (cr). FLPA – images of nature: Norbert Wu/Minden Pictures (bl). 136–137 FLPA – images of nature: Flip Nicklin/Minden Pictures (t). 137 Nature Picture Library: David Shale (tr). 138 Natural Visions: Heather Angel (tl). DK Images: Weymouth Sea Life Centre (cl). Getty Images: Stephen Frink (cr). Legend Photography-Andy Belcher: (tl). 139 Ardea.com: Ken Lucas (tl). Corbis: Jonathan Blair (br). 140 Ardea.com: Pat Morris (c). DK Images: Natural History Museum,